Design for the Crowd

DESIGN for the Crowd

Patriotism and Protest in Union Square

Joanna Merwood-Salisbury

The University of Chicago Press
Chicago and London

The University of Chicago Press, Chicago 60637
The University of Chicago Press, Ltd., London

Published 2019
Printed in China

28 27 26 25 24 23 22 21 20 19 1 2 3 4 5

ISBN-13: 978-0-226-08082-6 (cloth)
ISBN-13: 978-0-226-60490-9 (e-book)
DOI: https://doi.org/10.7208/chicago/9780226604909.001.0001

This publication is made possible in part with a grant from Furthermore, a program of the J. M. Kaplan Fund.

Furthermore:
a program of the J. M. Kaplan Fund

Library of Congress Cataloging-in-Publication Data

Names: Merwood-Salisbury, Joanna, author.
Title: Design for the crowd : patriotism and protest in Union Square / Joanna Merwood-Salisbury.
Description: Chicago ; London : The University of Chicago Press, 2019. | Includes bibliographical references and index.
Identifiers: LCCN 2018054732 | ISBN 9780226080826 (cloth : alk. paper) | ISBN 9780226604909 (e-book)
Subjects: LCSH: Union Square (New York, N.Y.)—History. | City planning—New York (State)—New York—History—19th century. | City planning—New York (State)—New York—History—20th century. | Plazas—Social aspects—New York (State)—New York. | New York (N.Y.)—History.
Classification: LCC F128.65.U6 M47 2019 NA9127.N5 | DDC 974.7—dc23
LC record available at https://lccn.loc.gov/2018054732

∞ This paper meets the requirements of ANSI/NISO Z39.48-1992 (Permanence of Paper).

Contents

Figures

6.3. Walker Evans, Street Scene in Front of S. Klein-on-the-Square Department Store, Union Square East, New York City, September 1937. © Walker Evans Archive, The Metropolitan Museum of Art/ Artstor.

6.4. Communist Party Headquarters and the *Daily Worker* newspaper, 26–28 Union Square East, ca. 1930. New York Daily News Archive/ Getty Images.

6.5. Unemployed American protestors running through Union Square pursued by tear gas–wielding police, March 6, 1930. Rolls Press/ Popperfoto/ Getty Images.

6.6. Union Square, aerial view, ca. 1944. United States Office of War Information / Museum of the City of New York. 90.28.38.

6.7. Celebration of the 100th anniversary of the founding on Union Square, April 1932. Irma and Paul Milstein Division of United States History, Local History and Genealogy, The New York Public Library, Astor, Lenox and Tilden Foundations.

6.8. Base of Flagstaff looking toward Union Square West. Irma and Paul Milstein Division of United States History, Local History and Genealogy, The New York Public Library, Astor, Lenox and Tilden Foundations.

7.1. Vehicles lined up at the "auto pound" along the edge of Union Square Park, 1949. New York Daily News Archive/ Getty Images.

7.2. Union Square. East Side between 14th and 16th Streets. Samuel H. (Samuel Herman) Gottscho (1875–1971) / Museum of the City of New York. 39.20.8.

7.3. Clown Frankie Saluto races children in Union Square during USA Day celebrations, 1955. New York Daily News Archive/ Getty Images.

7.4. Veterans and reservists on a platform in Union Square, awaiting their turn to burn their military discharge/separation papers. Bettman/ Getty Images.

8.1. Parsons' student project to redesign the facade of S. Klein Department Store on the east side of Union Square, 1973. The New School Archives and Special Collection. The New School. New York, NY.

8.2. Union Square Greenmarket, ca. 1976–78. Edmund Vincent Gillon / Museum of the City of New York. 2013.3.1.528.

Acknowledgments

This book would not exist without the help of many colleagues, friends, and family. At Parsons School of Design my thanks are due to Peter Wheelwright and David J. Lewis, who asked me to teach a graduate seminar on the history of New York City urbanism; and to Kent Kleinman, Bill Morrish, Brian McGrath, Joel Towers, and Nadine Bourgeois, for their ongoing support of my research into Union Square. Brian, in particular, was helpful in conceptualizing the idea of "urban design at the small scale." At Victoria University of Wellington I am grateful to Michael J. Wilson, Robin Skinner, Marc Aurel Schnabel, and Morten Gjerde for allowing me the time to complete this long-gestating project, and to Selena Shaw for helping me balance writing and academic administration.

An early version of some of this material appeared in the *Journal of the Society of Architectural Historians* in 2009. I am grateful to then editor David Brownlee and the anonymous reviewers for their perceptive editorial suggestions. The work of turning a short article into a book was greatly enabled by a Summer Stipend award from the National Endowment for the Humanities. I wish to acknowledge that any views, findings, conclusions, or recommendations expressed in this book do not necessarily reflect those of the National Endowment for the Humanities.

I am indebted to Robert Devens, who helped me develop the book proposal when I first approached the University of Chicago Press. At the press, Susan Bielstein has provided invaluable editorial advice and been generous and patient through the process of writing and revising. I would like to thank the press's external readers for their very helpful feedback; James Toftness, who has ably managed the manuscript; Susan Karani, for her expert editing; and Gerry Van Ravenswaay, who prepared the index. My thanks are also due to the J. M. Kaplan Fund for awarding the press a Furthermore grant to support the production of the book.

Throughout the process of research and writing, Joanie Meharry, Hannah Wolter, and Akari Kidd acted as my research assistants during different periods; I am grateful for their time and talents. My thanks are also due to Carol Willis, to Wendy Scheir of the New School Archives and Special Collections for showing me design projects made by Parsons students, and to Brian Sholis for sharing his unpublished essay on the patriotic monuments erected around New York City during World War I. The final manuscript benefited hugely from a thorough editorial review by Hamish Clayton. Many friends and colleagues have contributed their ideas and expertise; I wish to especially acknowledge Michael Lobel, Gabrielle Esperdy, and David J. Smiley. Special thanks are due to Tom Weaver who, at different times, provided much-needed critique and ably steered me back on course, and to Mary Atwool and Brent Southgate, who made me a reader. Finally I am extremely grateful for the unwavering support of Ned Salisbury, who showed me his New York, and Calum Salisbury, who was born there.

Introduction

Union Square took on a special role following the attacks on the World Trade Center on September 11th, 2001. Thousands gathered in the Square to leave flowers and messages of remembrance and to affirm communal feelings of grief and anger. The violence effected on the Twin Towers and its occupants brought home the privileged significance of public architecture, in this case as a symbol of Western global dominance. In the months and years following the attacks, the Square served as a counterexample. A place of openness and inclusion rather than privilege and exclusion, it affirmed the importance of physical public space in an age where much political discussion and protest had moved into the ephemeral space of the media. For the anthropologist Setha M. Low, the Square served as a positive model of a postindustrial plaza, one to which the designers of the new World Trade Center should pay special attention.[1] For Low, it was an essential referent, countering what she describes as the new defensiveness of public space in the post-9/11 era, a tendency to barricade and guard the common spaces of the city, in doing so denying the civil and political freedoms they represent.

In 2011 the Occupy Wall Street movement seemed to affirm the importance of the mass gathering as a political statement. Even though the movement had no simple, consumable message to convey, images of the encampment at Zuccotti Park in Lower Manhattan were powerful because they made manifest a deeply felt dissatisfaction with the economic and political status quo.[2] At the same time the movement revealed strict limitations on public use of public parks in New York City and other highly regulated urban centers. Zuccotti Park was chosen as the central protest site not only because it is near Wall Street, the site of economic power, but also because, as a privately owned public space (POPS) it is not subject to control by the Police and Parks departments. Ironically Zuccotti Park had fewer restrictions on its use than city-owned public land. In the wake of that protest, the city and private landowners tried to close loopholes in local zoning law, making POPS liable to greater oversight and constraint.

Even as public parks and squares are affirmed as important places of political expression, they are subjected to new tools and methods of control, both visible and invisible. The embedding of digital sensing in urban streetscapes, the sublimation of physical mechanisms of surveillance to more subtle forms of environmental monitoring, and the resultant transformation of urban and architectural form owing to the introduction of digital technologies, has emerged as a major source of anxiety.[3] For the political and social commentator Naomi Wolf, Union Square is notable not as a positive example of the persistence of traditional public space, but as a site subject to sinister new methods of covert observation. In 2012 she noted that "after the Occupy crackdowns . . . odd-looking CCTVs had started to appear, attached to lampposts, in public venues in Manhattan where the small but unbowed remnants of Occupy congregated: there was one in Union Square, right in front of their encampment. . . . These are enabled for facial recognition technology, which allows police to watch a video that is tagged to individuals, in real time. When too many people congregate, they can be dispersed and intimidated simply by the risk of being identified—before dissent can coalesce."[4] For others, such technologies have a positive benefit when they are used, as at Zuccotti Park and in the Black Lives Matter protests, not to separate but to include, not to record but to broadcast. Enhancing traditional forms of protest involving physical encroachment into, and appropriation of, public space, they have the power to escalate protest beyond the limited scale of a particular geographic site, creating a complementary and scaleless public forum within the digital realm.[5]

Debate about the proper form and use of public places is not new: it is as old as the city itself. Created by early nineteenth-century planners who placed little value in such urban devices, Union Square illustrates how abstract ideas of public space are both deformed and reformed by the idiosyncrasies of place and time. The Square occupies a central place in both the geography and the history of New York City. In one sense it is a counterexample to Central Park, both formally and symbolically. While Central Park is an expansive terrain, an American version of the romantic, pseudo-natural landscape popularized in England during the eighteenth century, Union Square is small and formal in its design. Where Central Park was purposefully designed to foster American democracy, Union Square began as an elite enclave on the edge of the city and only later assumed a prominent place as representative of the political life of the nation. But this small area of parkland has assumed an identity far larger than its diminutive size. Unconventional in shape and continually in the process of being reconstructed, it has never been an example of polemical or iconic urban design, and yet it expresses, perhaps more than any other urban landscape in the country, how political ideals are realized, imperfectly, in reality.

Within the enduring framework of the Manhattan grid only a few places are impervious to economically driven cycles of physical transformation. While a few monumental nineteenth-century buildings such as City Hall remain, most others have fallen under the wrecking ball. Legislation aimed at "landmarks preservation" can ensure that the physical fabric of certain neighborhoods, like parts of SoHo, remain intact, but even here the individual buildings are shells filled up with new uses and exhibiting different associations. Within this relatively young city, constants are few. Union Square appears to be one of those rare places. Despite its renovations, its form remains essentially true to its nineteenth-century origins. A green oval defined by trees and statues of American heroes, it has survived in more or less the same composition for nearly two hundred years. Located on Broadway between Fourteenth and Seventeenth Streets, Union Square includes both a major subway interchange and a landscaped park. The Square (which is not a square at all, but an irregular oval) is a glitch uneasily embedded within the pattern of regular blocks. It owes its existence to a moment of incompatibility: it marks the spot where the path of colonial Broadway fails to mesh with the early nineteenth-century republican street plan. As a figure it is a bridge and a node, a link between east and west, between downtown and midtown, as well as the terminus and interchange of several transit lines. In the lexicon of popular association, it is a place for public expression, both collective and individual. This book will show that Union Square, though apparently impervious to change, has borne and continues to bear a social and political meaning that is constantly being enacted, through both daily activity and the slower processes of design and construction.

From the time they were first projected in the early nineteenth century, Manhattan's parks and squares have been considered inadequate for a major urban center in a country founded on the principle of democracy, where the provision of spaces for the public to gather is presumably essential. In this way this book takes as its subject an urban element considered insufficient or negligible. Despite its apparent deficiencies, I argue, Union Square is an important landmark, one that has contributed significantly to the public life of the city and the nation. *Design for the Crowd: Patriotism and Protest in Union Square* traces the history of the Square from its formation as a residential square modeled on European precedents during the 1830s through to the turn of the twenty-first century, with a special focus on the ways in which small changes have impacted its use and meaning. This choice of subject—the historical life of a public park—opens up a range of different ways of writing, from the literal to the metaphorical and allegorical. The intent is to understand Union Square as both a geographical location with real, formal characteristics and also as a stand-in for larger social and cultural concepts. I investigate the history of the Square as both a real public space and the symbol of competing ideas about the operation of democracy in the United States. From the mid-nineteenth-century real estate developer Samuel Ruggles's championing of Union Square as a "theater adequate to the national voice," to the first Labor Day parade of 1882 and Depression-era demonstrations organized by the Communist Party of the United States, the Square has been a physical manifestation of the uniquely American enactment of democratic citizenship and a test case for ongoing debates about the freedoms of speech and assembly guaranteed in the Constitution.[6]

While sited primarily in relation to architectural and urban history, this book is informed by the voluminous scholarship on the subject of public space from diverse fields including history and geography as well as law and political theory. Drawing on historical materials from the New York City Parks Department Library, the New York City Municipal Archives, and the New York Public Library (including official documents, plans, and photographs, as well as reports in mass-market periodicals and newspapers, and descriptions in popular guidebooks and niche-oriented publications such as professional architecture magazines and union newspapers), I examine large-scale proposals made for the Square (both built and unrealized), alongside representations of the events that took place there (lithographs, news photographs, and cartoons, for example), paying attention to the ways in which the Square has been described and depicted at different moments in its history.

The genesis of this project lies in my teaching. Around 2004, I went looking for a history of Union Square to include in the reading list of a course on the history of New York City urbanism. I was teaching graduate architecture students at Parsons School of Design in a converted loft building at 25 East Thirteenth Street, just a block away from the Square. As the public space most immediately available to them, Parsons students were drawn to it for lunchtime and late-night excursions, and it was a frequent site for their speculative design projects. In their analyses they emulated the influential urban sociologist William H. Whyte, observing and documenting the routine pathways of commuters and shoppers, the temporary resting places of office workers, the ritual theatrics of soapbox orators, and the otherwise unstructured forms of contemporary flânerie. Beside these day-to-day activities, the Square also hosted larger and more significant events such as protests associated with the anti-Iraq War and Occupy movements. The form of these events was not left to chance: on these occasions the New York City police department employed a mixture of sophisticated (digital surveillance) and unsophisticated (portable fences known as jersey barriers) methods to control the crowd. The rawness of these actions, and the sense on the part of participants and spectators that the messages being communicated were immediate and urgent ones, seemed to confirm that Union Square's historic identity as a site for political speech and action was still relevant.

Classroom conversations about the design and use of Union Square in the early 2000s were framed by academic literature on the importance of streets and squares as places of urban sociability, on the historic role public spaces have played in the performance of democracy, and on the ways in which capital has reshaped such spaces in the modern era. My students read Don Mitchell on the importance of public space in democratic societies. They read David Harvey and Richard Sennett on the reconstruction of urban form and the turmoil of public life in the nineteenth century. They read Jane Jacobs on the uses of sidewalks and Elizabeth Blackmar, Roy Rosenzweig, and Galen Cranz on the politics of park design. Many contemporary texts presented the current moment as one of crisis: public space was dead or dying, its social and political function was in decline, it had become the realm of the spectacle, an illusion of openness and inclusiveness maintained only in the service of capitalism. Of particular concern to many authors was the "privatization of public space" associated with neoliberal governance practices, when the requirements of the global marketplace came into conflict with desires for openness and accessibility, leading to the segregation of urban populations, accompanied by explicit or implicit restrictions on the provision, design, and use of public space.[7] As a result architects became complicit in the creation of inauthentic enclaves where the imperative of consumption replaced that of citizenship. Proponents of this view warned of an imminent point of no return, one in which true public space, and along with it the opportunity for free speech, for face-to-face political expression and discourse, would be erased once and for all. In these texts the POPS (privately owned public spaces) program instituted by the 1961 revision to the New York City zoning law, where real estate developers are given height variances in exchange for the provision of quasi-public space, was often employed as a defining example. Similarly, commercially driven practices of urban renewal dating to the 1980s and 1990s were subject to particular criticism, with sites such as the South Street Seaport, Battery Park City, and Times Square cited as sinister examples. This view persists in contemporary academic writing where the argument that access to public space is "often in jeopardy and at times threatened by public and private policies" is commonplace.[8] I want to emphasize that I do not refute this statement. Rather my aim is to test a presumption that lies behind the claim of the inevitable extinction of public space as it has been traditionally constituted; this presumption is that public space became especially precarious at the end of the twentieth century. The art critic Rosalyn Deutsch has argued that conflict is a defining characteristic of true public space—conflict about how it should be used and by whom[9]—to which I would add, conflict about how it should be formed or shaped in order to facilitate or represent those uses. In looking at the history of Union Square, I am interested in the changing parameters of this conflict, understanding it as a dynamic process informed by both abstract philosophies and actual events. This is not a relativist argument in which all social and political beliefs and actions are viewed as equivalent; rather it is an attempt to lend historic context to present-day debate.

Situated in a scholarly framework, a study of the history of Union Square could be nostalgic (here is an example of "real" public space), hopeful (see how it persists), or despairing (observe how it is increasingly limited, deployed for ideological purposes). While different sections or chapters of this book might be used to support these various arguments, my aim is to hold none of them absolutely. Rather it is to reveal the complexity of the question at hand beyond the shorthand binaries of public and private, freedom and restriction, authentic and inauthentic. Although the idea that public space has always been a site of conflict is constantly acknowledged in contemporary literature, the argument about its present decline sometimes seems motivated by a sentimental or simplistic view of the history of cities and society. Running through this book is a test of the contention that public spaces are under special threat today, that in the contemporary era they are in the process of eroding completely and permanently away from their earlier, more perfect, incarnations. In fact, as this book shows, despite the rights to free speech and public assembly guaranteed by the Constitution, the distance between the ideal and the real is ever present.

Free access to public space has been constantly precarious throughout the history of the United States. The debate about the true nature and correct use of public places is a long-standing one in this country, beginning with the foundation of the republic. As historians Mary Ryan and Lisa Keller have shown in their essential histories of civic parades and demonstrations, New York City has always been an important archetype in these debates.[10] When it comes to systems of regulation, the mechanisms of control are many; they include not only laws and police practices, but also the material arrangement of a space: its shape, enclosure, access points, and internal components. In other words, its design. As an architectural historian, design is always my primary subject. However, in this book I define the word in the broadest terms, not just through the traditional forms of architecture and sculpture, urban design and planning, but also through patterns of everyday use, and the choreography of special events such as holiday celebrations, parades, and political demonstrations. In relation to Union Square, the creation and deployment of a series of modest fixed and moveable design elements—sculptures, fences, seating, flowerbeds, and bandstands, along with rostrums, banners, flags, and garlands—is meaningful. Taken together, these design elements and the way they are used give us clues to changing ideas about the purpose of public space over the course of time.

Among the writers whose work laid the ground for the academic understanding of public space a generation ago, two continue to be relevant to this study: the sociologist Henri Lefebvre and the literary critic Roland Barthes. Both authors were concerned with everyday urban landscapes and rituals; they understood that a study of what is right in front of you can be as rich or richer than arcane information gleaned from deep in the archive or from analysis of unbuilt design speculations. Both recognized the significance of histories, thematics, and ideologies radiating out of objects and spaces hiding in plain sight. Both recognized that occupying something is a way to begin talking about it. Guided by these thinkers, I have developed a broad understanding of design that recognizes the actions of multiple actors and agents along with many scales and temporalities of engagement. It acknowledges not only grand-scale sculptural monuments created by professional artists, but also ephemeral formations of bodies created by everyday users, both habitually and occasionally. Here my approach is informed by Lefebvre, who understood public space as a social construct, a conjunction of conceptual idea and physical place with particular formal attributes. He argued that "space is permeated with social relations; it is not only supported by social relations but it is also producing and produced by social relations."[11] In other words, the design and use of public space is always ideological, providing tangible evidence of how various social groups see themselves and wish to be seen by others; and how they understand the concept of publicness differently at different times.

This social approach to urban design history inevitably creates a tension between reporting important historical events that took place in the Square and concentrating on efforts to shape it through formal processes of planning and design. While the primary focus is on the physical landscape, it is difficult if not impossible to understand decisions made about shaping that landscape outside of their broader cultural context. Hence I focus the first half of this book on the role of public space within an emerging industrial metropolis, New York City, from the early to the late nineteenth century, recognizing the ways in which the social relations of industrialism and capitalism were played out in public. During these years Union Square was an important site on which conflicts between the working and other classes were spatially enacted. I also touch on, in less detail, the different ways in which the city was experienced according to race and gender. The second half of this book, then, concentrates on the social life of the city in the wake of deindustrialization: as the metropolitan landscape became increasingly decentralized and new sub- and ex-urban hubs appeared to challenge the status of a once-vital urban center, I explore how it was reimagined so as to ensure its enduring importance.

Concerned as it is with the complex relationship between the use and symbolism of public space, the city is not only a form of social product, but also a form of text, a legible object-space whose meaning is constantly being rewritten. In 1967 Roland Barthes proposed the possibility of an "urban semiology," or the application of methods of linguistics to help study the social meaning of cities.[12] For Barthes, figures such as public squares and monuments play a central role in the way we navigate, understand or "read" the city, their images literally impressing themselves in our minds. In this way Barthes understood them as elements of communally constituted language, designed not only for functional purposes but also as signifiers of broader cultural and political ideas. As with texts, he believed, their accepted meanings are fluid, changing over time and sometimes coming into conflict. (Famously, he cited the example of the Eiffel Tower, which began as a symbol of technological progress, and now signifies the city of Paris and France as a nation).[13] Crucially for historians of architecture and urban design, Barthes notes that there is frequent disagreement between the pragmatic use and symbolic association of a particular urban space. In other words, there is often a misalignment between the purpose for which it was designed and the cultural meaning it acquires over time.

Employing Barthes's strategy loosely, I have chosen to focus not only on Union Square itself, an opening in the Manhattan grid that creates its own unique figure, but also on a series of elements built within it. Since it was created, the Square has been occupied by a series of small constructions: first an ornamental fountain erected to commemorate the opening of the Croton Aqueduct, and then a series of statues, the most significant of which depict Presidents Washington and Lincoln. In 1872 the Square's silhouette changed when landscape architects Frederick Law Olmsted and Calvert Vaux reconfigured it, lopping off the northernmost part of the oval to create a supplementary open space adjacent to the landscaped park. This paved rectangular area, known as "the plaza," was specifically intended for public meetings, and was accompanied by a small pavilion that was itself reinvented in the early twentieth century. Throughout this book I give particular attention to the meanings attached to these figures, as well as to the numerous actors engaged in a struggle to control their use and to define their significance. These actors include civic authorities, private citizens' organizations, labor unions, members of various political groups, and self-appointed community representatives. This reading of Union Square supports Barthes's view that the meaning of urban texts is both dynamic and contentious.

Design for the Crowd comprises eight chapters arranged chronologically. Each chapter focuses on a particular moment in the life of Union Square, framing it in the context of historic ideas about public and urban life. The first chapter tells the story of the creation of the Square in the 1830s: its "improvement" or landscaping following lobbying by private citizens, including the lawyer and real estate developer Samuel Ruggles; the capitalist impetus underlying its conception and production; and the challenge it presented to the vision of the gridded city, at a time when that city had barely begun to be constructed. Chapters 2 and 3 describe the way in which Union Square came to represent a different kind of democratic public space in the mid-nineteenth century, a counterpoint to Central Park. Chapter 2 explores the transformation of the Square from the centerpiece of a fashionable residential area into a civic and even national arena during the Civil War. Following the attack on Fort Sumter in April 1861, it was the location of a mass rally; huge crowds gathered in support of the Union cause around a statue of George Washington located in the southeastern corner. The stirring image of this enormous flag-waving crowd was captured using the newly developed process of wood engraving and quickly disseminated around the world through newspaper and magazine articles. Near the end of the war, Ruggles described this rally and others inspired by it as evidence that the Square had realized its potential as a "spacious national opening." The third chapter then addresses the attempted realization of Ruggles's vision for Union Square through Olmsted and Vaux's 1872 redesign, countering the perception of Olmsted as promoting only naturalistic city parks. His work on Union Square shows him to have been acutely attentive to the need for other kinds of city squares and parks—not those associated with individual leisure and respite from urban congestion but with the intensification and orderly expression of public sentiment. As champion of the romantic park movement, his design provided grounds for, and gave aesthetic shape to, a new kind of urban crowd.

In the last two decades of the nineteenth century, Olmsted and Vaux's plaza became a major site for working-class self-representation in New York City, providing a setting for an increasingly formalized tradition of labor meetings. The urban spectacle of these gatherings, their constituent elements, choreography, and ideological intent are the subject of chapters 4 and 5. Adaptations of early artisan parades and labor demonstrations such as the first Labor Day parade, organized by the Central Labor Union on September 5th, 1882, displayed the power of workingmen as a unified political group. As the turn of the twentieth century approached and working people began to organize on an international scale, the issues at hand extended beyond labor justice for American workers: in Union Square socialists and anarchist activists, including the favorite of the tabloid press, Emma Goldman, began to demand radical political reform. Founded in 1890 May Day soon usurped Labor Day as the primary workers' holiday. For some commentators, these mass meetings appeared to prefigure working-class revolt, constituting a threat to democracy rather than its visible exercise. In the lead-up to the American entry into World War I, the nature of protests in Union Square was called into question: were they bona fide political demonstrations, guaranteed by the Constitution, or were they illegal and seditious? Around this time revulsion at the violent police response and suppression of public meetings in the Square created support for an emerging "free speech" movement, led by the newly formed American Civil Liberties Union. Chapter 5 then describes the events that led to the founding of this movement, and argues that action on the ground in this particular place effected cultural and legal changes across the nation.

Chapter 6 describes efforts to reinforce Union Square as a center of civic life in new terms through the first three decades of the twentieth century, reconfiguring it in alignment with Progressive-era political beliefs and City Beautiful planning methods. For early designers such as Charles Lamb of the Municipal Arts Society of New York, efficient and aesthetically pleasing planning could transform the fractious urban crowd into a rational and deliberate public imbued with the power to effect positive social change: all it needed was a suitable venue in which to gather and make decisions. Already recognized as a place of mass gathering, Union Square seemed to fulfill many of the required criteria: it stood close to the geographic center of the city at the nexus of several important streets, and it was already a vibrant place for public gatherings of all kinds. Under the authority of the reformist city administrations of the early twentieth century, it seemed possible to remake the Square according to City Beautiful ideals. The construction of new subway lines and a connecting underground concourse provided the opportunity to remake it in a new image, one designed to quash protest and inspire more benign forms of civic participation.

Much of the literature on mid-twentieth-century New York City focuses on processes of decline and decay, decentralization and depopulation, countered by strategies of urban renewal involving hugely disruptive practices of demolition and reconstruction. Chapters 7 and 8 draw attention to a different form of renewal involving not land clearances and the construction of large-scale buildings and infrastructure projects, but more localized and fine-grained attempts to revive the inner city. Chapter 7 focuses on attempts to neutralize Union Square's reputation as America's own Red Square in the postwar years. These efforts gained traction when the Fourteenth Street Association, a private business group led by restaurateur Jan Mitchell, joined with the Parks Department in an effort to replace the traditional May Day parade with a city-sponsored Loyalty Day. Chapter 8 concentrates on public-private efforts to revitalize Union Square in the last three decades of the twentieth century. These efforts coincided with a new understanding of what the city might be, informed by the financial and environmental crises of the 1970s. Under the influence of new strategies of urban management and a new generation of urban thinkers, including the critic Jane Jacobs who used nearby Greenwich Village as her exemplar, private developers and city authorities joined forces to revive Union Square as the center of a residential neighborhood. This involved typical tactics of gentrification and was piecemeal at first: a playground built at the north end of the Square in 1967; a Greenmarket founded in 1976; and the gradual conversion of surrounding commercial loft buildings to residential use encouraged by changes to the city's building and tax codes. In 1984 this fragmented activity was unified and concretized by the creation of a special zoning district designed to attract mixed-use and residential development, such as the Zeckendorff Towers on the east side of the Square. In 1986 New York City's first Business Improvement District—the Union Square Partnership—began a long-range restoration project, including the reconstruction of the southern end of the park as a large stepped plaza, the landscaping of the southeastern and western corners with new plants and statues, and the reconfiguration of the park according to the principles of "defensible space."

Since 1966 the National Park Service has recognized landscapes as significant, not just for their natural features but also for their historical and cultural value: because of their association with historic events or significant designers, because of their use by specific cultural groups, or because of their very ordinariness, the way they shape and define American vernacular traditions. It is for this historic role that Union Square is now remembered. In 1998 it was named a National Historic Landmark by the National Park Service in honor of the park's role as a focal point in American labor history. The elevation of Union Square in this way says as much about a changing idea of public landscape as it does of the recurring need for preservation and remembrance. As the events I will describe demonstrate, this open ground in the middle of Manhattan that had been formed by a misalignment of the 1811 plan has, historically, been a contested terrain. Based on older forms of European squares, Union Square is not accommodated comfortably within the grid: it is a moment of rupture within it. More than just formally mutable, it has been the site of a contentious debate about the definition and proper use of public space, spanning from the early nineteenth century until today. Accidental, unpremeditated, and irregular, Union Square is a paradox; this one prominent public site fails to conform to the rational perfection of the master plan designed to realize republican ideals. Yet, more than any other place in the city, it has come to define, through its continual reshaping via daily use and regulatory mechanics, how those ideals are enacted in practice.

1

An Ornament to the City, 1811–1850

In 1849 John Bachmann created a picture of the entire city of New York, an aerial view looking south from Union Square to Washington Square and the port beyond. Bachmann was a Swiss-born printmaker who had completed several bird's eye views of American cities in the mid-nineteenth century, views all the more difficult to produce because they were drawn from the imagination: there was as yet no technology in place to raise the illustrator so high.[1] This is the earliest known of his works. As reflected in his mind's eye, Union Square was an urban set piece, the northern terminus of the city and the antithesis of the commercial area around Wall Street and City Hall. This was the home of the "the upper ten thousand," or just "the upper ten"—the elite of New York society, whose members were characterized not by their noble birth but by their possession of money, taste, and good manners.[2] As the astute English visitor Isabella Bird noted a few years later, while in England the word "society" was used to denote the aristocracy and those who moved in their circle, "New York has its charmed circles also; a republic admits of the greatest exclusiveness."[3] Two squares, Washington and Union, were the physical manifestation of that exclusiveness, a spatial realization of the greatly uneven benefits that capitalist speculation had brought to the city. Unsurprisingly, those who lived there did not see their enclave as a sign

1.1 "New-York." Print by John Bachmann, 1849.

of social or economic inequity: to them the squares and the magnificent homes surrounding them were evidence of the supremacy of republican capitalism, under which social and economic advancement was open to all comers. In the mid-nineteenth-century mind-set, the increasingly ostentatious homes built there were ornaments to the city in much the same way the squares were. On display to all who wished to see them, they beautified the city as a whole, providing evidence of its prosperity and an incentive to entrepreneurial newcomers.[4]

The completion of Union Square in 1839 marked the segregation of New York City into two distinct territories. No longer clustered around the site of the colonial settlement at the southern end of Manhattan, the city had grown, its path directed by the ambitious grid plan laid out in 1811. "Downtown," the area around the docks and Wall Street, was the center of the city's business, manufacturing, and political life. Two miles further north, the fashionable "Uptown" district comprised a series of then recently built residential enclaves anchored by landscaped squares. Union Square, where Broadway terminated at Fourteenth Street, was the heart of Uptown. Elliptical in shape, the Square appears antithetical to the 1811 grid plan, whose designers emphatically rejected the inclusion of, "circles, ovals or stars"—typical of public spaces designed after the European model—in favor of a homogenous and orthogonal grid designed to communicate the republican ideal of equality. The creation of Union Square was part of a larger project to improve New York City, a task that encompassed a broad range of activities including planning, drainage, road building, and the construction of transportation systems and a clean water supply, all of which accompanied the rapid growth of the city in the early decades of the nineteenth century. These improvements were grounded in a doctrine of progress that supported the ideals held by the early city planners. Created in the second quarter of the nineteenth century, Washington, Tompkins, Union, Stuyvesant, and Madison Squares were considered "ornaments" to the city, aesthetic counterparts to less visible infrastructural improvements that were transforming the thriving commercial metropolis.

Samuel Bulkley Ruggles, the impresario behind the creation of Union Square, was a practitioner of urban improvement. A lawyer and property speculator, he leased property rather than buying it outright, amassing a large parcel of land holdings between Fourteenth and Twenty-Third Streets, a parcel whose value he sought to increase via the construction of public works. While chiefly remembered as the creator of Gramercy Park, a private square, Ruggles was also a commissioner of the Eerie Canal Company and of the Croton Aqueduct, linked activities that restructured the city and the regional landscape surrounding it. In this way he helped flesh out the cartographic bones laid down by the Commissioners' Plan of 1811, creating elegant public and private parks within it, and linking it productively to its larger geographic terrain. Beginning in the late 1820s he argued for the improvement of the uneven and unkempt parcel of land known as Union Place, one of the few areas designated for public use in the original city plan. Ruggles's efforts to improve Union Place, and the conflicting ways in which his contemporaries viewed those efforts, illustrate the transformation of ideas about the function and value of public space in New York City between the early and mid-nineteenth century.

Private and Public Space in the New York City Grid

Union Place was a product of the expansion of New York City during the prosperous second and third decades of the nineteenth century. Following the end of the War of 1812, which eased trade with Europe, and the completion of the Erie Canal in 1825, which opened up trade with the newly created western states, the city experienced an economic boom, one that financed dramatic growth in business and plentiful new construction.[5] Already a commercial metropolis, New York soon usurped Boston and Philadelphia as the center of global trade on the North American continent. As the population grew and capital accumulated, New Yorkers were anxious to invest their profits in their enlarging city and to improve its appearance befitting its new status. Beyond the colonial-era settlement at the southern end of Manhattan, the rocky and wild island was largely rural, sparsely populated with small farms, country estates, and a few villages such as Harlem to the north. Barely noticeable on the surface of the fields and dirt roads, however, lay a signifier of things to come: a network of survey markers, iron bolts inserted into the ground. These markers were laid out under the direction of a surveyor named John Randel Jr.[6] In 1807 the New York State legislature had appointed a commission to "regulate" the city's streets and to accommodate its growth.[7] The state-appointed "Commissioners of Streets and Roads"—Simeon De Witt, Gouverneur Morris, and John Rutherford—had no doubt that the city would continue to flourish, projecting a fourfold increase in population to four hundred thousand people by the middle of the century. In 1811 they unveiled a plan to cater to this increase, dividing the island of Manhattan north of Houston Street into an enormous matrix of twelve north-south avenues and 155 east-west streets. Once completed, the grid plan would create 2,028 rectangular parcels of land, irrespective of existing geography or settlements. Randel was the surveyor employed to translate the abstract grid into reality. In his hands, Manhattan was about to become a "theater of progress."[8]

The plan that Randel worked for years to implement was one of a series of projects to regulate and improve American towns and cities beginning in the late eighteenth century. Influenced by high-minded if not utopian Enlightenment ideals, they were intended to guide the creation and growth of settlements on the new continent in the most efficient way possible, ensuring those settlements were both socially and economically profitable.[9] Characterized by the subjugation of the environment to human use, they involved the aggressive leveling of natural topography and the application of a rigid urbanizing geometry. As the architectural historian Dell Upton has noted, in the early years of the American republic the simple grid plan with its evenly spaced streets and equally sized city blocks was a popular regulating device, both because it was easy to implement and understand and also because of its egalitarian symbolism. Though it dated back to ancient times, the grid could be seen as the spatial expression of republicanism, a political philosophy that had at its core

> a notion of political sovereignty vested in the people as a whole, understood as a collection of free individuals who were in some fundamental

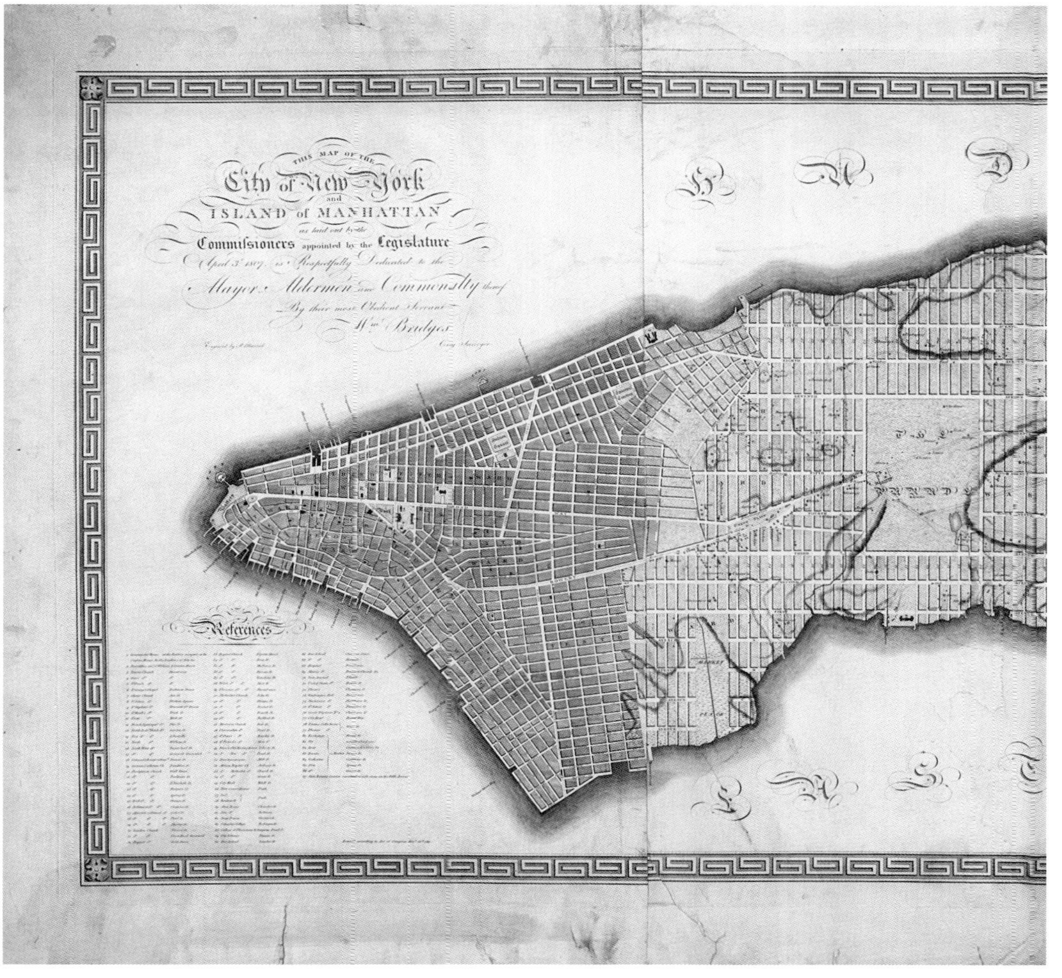

1.2 Southern section of the *Commissioner's Plan for New York City*, 1811.

> way essentially the same, therefore comparable, whatever their contingent differences in status or condition. Order in such a body politic arose from within, from the character of its citizens, rather than being imposed by a higher authority.[10]

In these terms the homogeneity and regularity of the grid plan was a reflection of the democratic ideal: like all citizens, all plots of land were equivalent, and none was valued above another. While Upton credits the gridded towns common to early American city planning with utopian aspirations, other scholars have described them as the outcome of pragmatic thinking rather than applied political philosophy. More specifically, they are sometimes regarded as the spatial embodiment of capitalism, a system under which the process of urbanization is driven solely by the need to ensure the efficient flow of wealth.[11] This interpretation, in which the chief virtue of the grid is that it divides the land available for development into parcels that are easy to measure and trade, is supported by contemporary accounts. The surveyor Randel praised the 1811 plan for Manhattan as an effective mechanism for, "buying, selling, and improving real estate."[12] In these terms it has come to be seen, fairly or not, as a monument to the primacy of real estate speculation, one in which property values outweighed considerations such as the beauty of republican simplicity.[13] There is no doubt that the philosophical and economic justifications underlying the grid plan were inextricably linked: capitalism was the economic and de facto governing system of the new republic. By creating thousands of nearly identical small lots, the Commissioners' Plan greatly increased the amount of land available for sale and settlement and, as a result, greatly augmented the number of land owning (and thus voting) citizens. Over time the expansion of the city was accompanied by the expansion of its polity.

This system of urban organization had a particular and lasting effect on the relationship between private and public space. As the geographer Don Mitchell has noted, emphasizing the interests of private property owners had important consequences for the development of the public realm: "The public sphere of American (and other capitalist) democracies is . . . understood as a voluntary community of private (and usually propertied) citizens."[14] In other words, private landowners acting collectively created public space and determined how it would be used. This was especially true of early nineteenth-century New York City where the municipal government played a relatively small role and attended to a limited range of planning activities. In this context, any public benefit resulting from urban improvements was largely the work of private individuals.

Samuel Ruggles and the Improvement of Union Place

This is the milieu in which Samuel Ruggles began his real estate ventures in the 1820s. While speculative investors were buying up and filling out the grid, few dedicated public spaces existed within it and even fewer were created. Ruggles held no official position when he began his work in what we would today call urban planning. Instead he acted through his connections with the Whig elite who controlled the city government. Born in 1801 to a comfortably well-off Hudson Valley family, he had studied at Yale before establishing a law practice in New York City in 1822.[15] Although a newcomer to New York society, he joined its highest ranks by marrying Mary Rosalie Rathbone, the daughter of a wealthy merchant, John Rathbone. Rathbone began his career in the salt trade, establishing his business, John Rathbone and Co. (later John Rathbone and Son), near the East River docks at Front Street in 1804. Rathbone and his son, John Jr., were so successful that they were regarded as "almost the head of the mercantile body of our greatest commercial city."[16] The family gained considerable political influence when John Jr., Ruggles's brother-in-law, was elected a member of the state legislature in 1823. Before long Ruggles was advising his in-laws and their friends on property management. Soon he began to invest in property on his own accord, using some of his wife's money and a modest inheritance from his father. By the 1830s he was a wealthy man, one of the founders of the Bank of Commerce, with his success enabling him to attain political office: in 1838 he was elected to the New York State Assembly.

While he was only one of many entrepreneurs hoping to benefit from the city's rapid expansion, Ruggles was one of an elite group with the determination and connections to make significant alterations to the fabric of New York City. In this he was particularly well equipped because of his prodigious energy and his skills as a publicist. Until 1830 all decisions about public works were made by the twenty members of the Common Council, the governing body of the city elected by propertied citizens. With the grid plan laid out, this council had little inclination to plan any major urban design initiatives. Instead they responded to the lobbying of an ad hoc "public" made up of propertied citizens who occasionally came together to determine what they saw as a common need. Municipal records from this time consist largely of petitions to the council from private citizens, including requests for the development of particular streets and (in fewer cases) public squares, as well as incidental projects such as the erection of statues. Many of these petitions began with public meetings organized by the urban elite where property owners discussed their own needs and desires, which, they believed, were broadly commensurate with the general public good.

At this time the sparsely populated area north of Fourteenth Street, designated the Twelfth Ward, was undergoing something of a real estate gold rush, and the abstract lines of the 1811 street grid were beginning to assume a physical reality.[17] Enterprising businessmen were buying and leasing land in the area, realizing that the encroachment of commercial premises further and further north along Broadway was making it a desirable investment, despite its current isolation. Ruggles focused his attention on lots between Nineteenth and Twenty-Fourth Streets, the Bloomingdale Road (now Broadway), and Second Avenue. Still rural, the real estate holdings he acquired were part of an old landholding known as the "Gramercy Farm." Because the terrain was irregular, differentiated by hills and swamps, Ruggles began the work of having his properties graded, and in the process he established a contracting business that did similar work for the city.

In the 1830s the social center of New York lay a mile to the south near what is now Cooper Square, around Lafayette Place and Fourth Avenue. Befitting his status as an ambitious and well-connected lawyer, Ruggles lived there, at 36 Bond Street. His neighbors were members of New York's political, social, and business elite, including, as a street manual described it, "the mayor of the city; the town's most popular physician; the pastor of one the largest and wealthiest churches; a Senator of the United States; one of the city's two representatives in Congress; an ex-secretary of the treasury; a major general in the army who became one of our most distinguished soldiers and a candidate for the presidency; and two members of a firm of bankers who in the financial world of their time exercised an influence unequalled on this side of the Atlantic."[18] Situated between Broadway and the Bowery, the two major north-south arteries, Bond Street was lined with trees and grand three-story houses in the Greek revival style, several boasting marble facades. Its residents liked to think of it as "Parisian," a term meant to connote general fashionableness rather than fealty to any specific architectural style. When Ruggles began to develop the properties he had leased, Bond Street was no doubt his model.

While other real estate speculators were content to reap profits from single lots, Ruggles was not. When he had amassed enough parcels of land in the former Gramercy Farm to form a single contiguous site, he approached the Common Council with an ambitious plan to construct the ultimate urban amenity: a landscaped square. This square, which he called Gramercy Park, was to be private, accessible only to those who lived in the houses surrounding it.[19] This request was highly unusual but Ruggles had thought it through carefully: he requested the council's permission to divert the taxes paid on the land comprising the park to the adjacent properties, in this way making his tenants pay for the park while reaping the financial reward a gracious square would bestow. In creating Gramercy Park, he was perhaps influenced by St. John's Park, a privately owned pleasure ground in what is now Tribeca, built on land owned by Trinity Church. In a contemporary city directory this park was described as a "highly ornamented enclosure of about four acres. . . . Surrounded by an iron fence, it contains a most beautiful fountain, and is more abundantly supplied with flowers and shrubs than any other park in the city."[20] In the early years of the century the area around St. John's Park had been considered the most exclusive in the city. With his bold proposal to the Common Council, Ruggles hoped to recreate this exclusivity north of Fourteenth Street.

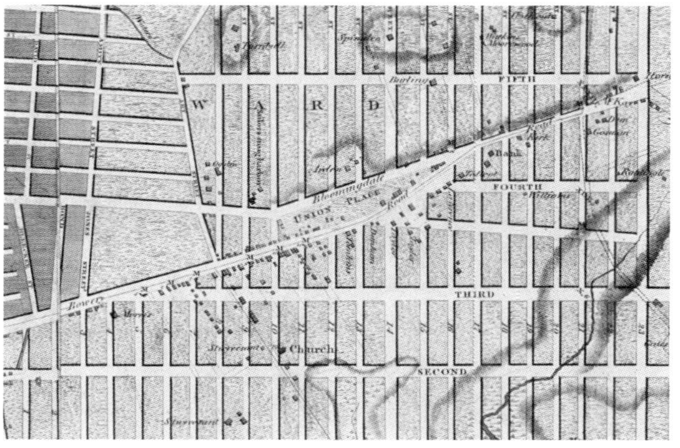

1.3 Commissioner's Plan for New York City, 1811. The area known as "Union Place" is visible as an elongated triangle.

As he worked on founding Gramercy Park, Ruggles also sought to influence the creation of a larger and more public counterpart at the scrappy and undeveloped Union Place, a few blocks to the southwest. Here his motivation was the same, to increase the value of his real estate investments in the area. But in calling for the improvement of Union Place he had a much greater challenge ahead of him: he had no claim on the land except as a public citizen and, though it existed as common land on city maps, Union Place was distinctly unpromising as a site for development. An unkempt commons used for grazing animals, it was a cartographic leftover, the result of an idealized scheme now conflicting with existing topography and historical land use. The ground was uneven and irregular, a parallelogram laid out over the rise of Bowery Hill. Beyond the safety of the Lamp and Watch District, the realm of streetlights and the patrol of "leatherheads," early versions of policemen, it was considered a dangerous and wild area.[21] Occupied by half a dozen wooden framed dwellings, it had been used as a potter's field, or burial ground for indigents. No one in the city government had shown much interest in it at all in those years. In fact, fifteen years earlier the council had successfully petitioned the state legislature to reduce its size by nearly two-thirds, from thirty acres to ten, arguing that the cost of developing a large public square at the site would be "extravagantly great."[22]

Ruggles was unperturbed by these difficulties. In late 1830 he drafted a "memorial," or petition, to have Union Place "improved," and submitted it to the Common Council in the name of local landowners. To "improve" the land in this context had a double meaning: it implied making the land more refined in an aesthetic sense, but also making it useful from an economic point of view.[23] Ruggles's memorial included a diagram of the proposed square (a modified version of the existing one) and a strongly worded rhetorical argument. The city had the legal right and duty, he claimed, to "appropriate and forever maintain Union Place as a public square, for the Common use, benefit and enjoyment of the public."[24] In making this argument, he drew on the status of Union Place as one of the few public spaces designated in the 1811 plan, which he called the "Magna Charta" of the city. But while this founding document gave Ruggles's proposal legitimacy, Union Place was in fact an anomaly within it.

Union Place was created to deal with the awkward conjuncture of existing and projected streets: Broadway, Tenth Street, the Bowery, Bloomingdale Road, Fifteenth Street, Fourth Avenue, and Sixteenth Street.[25] In response to the problem of this complex intersection, the Commissioners enlarged the knot of streets into an asymmetrical opening that they justified in the following way: "This place becomes necessary, from various considerations. Its central position requires an opening for the benefit of fresh air; the union of so many large roads demands space for security and convenience, and the morsels into which it would be cut by continuing across it the several streets and avenues would be of little use or value."[26] No doubt irritating to the rational sensibility of the plan's creators, the result was an irregular trapezium. Though Union Place itself could not be parceled off and sold (or so the Commissioners imagined), Ruggles believed its improvement would encourage development in the area by increasing the value of the properties surrounding it.

In his proposals for Gramercy Park and Union Place, Ruggles was responding to what had come to be seen as a major weakness of the 1811 plan: it did not include enough open space. In fact, as the architectural historian Hilary Ballon has explained in her expansive book on the topic, the Commissioners' Plan contained several public spaces, some already in existence and some as speculative projections.[27] Most were practical in nature: a market, a military parade ground, an observatory, and a reservoir. Others, the so-called uptown squares (none of which were realized) were uniform green rectangles vaguely suggestive of future urban amenities. Anticipating criticism on this point, the Commissioners justified their decision in relation to Manhattan's physical geography:

> It may to many be a matter of surprise, that so few vacant spaces have been left, and those so small, of the benefit of fresh air, and consequent preservation of health. Certainly, if the city of New-York were destined to stand on the side of a small stream, such as the Seine or the Thames, a great number of ample places might be needful; but those large arms of the sea which embrace Manhattan island, render its situation, in regard to health and pleasure, as well as to convenience of commerce, peculiarly felicitous.[28]

As these remarks indicate, the Commissioners were guided by a supreme American pragmatism. They believed that the primary function of open space was to ventilate the city, that is, to provide fresh air for the benefit of public health. As the island was long and narrow with rivers on both sides, the closely set east-west streets would benefit from constant sea breezes, rendering numerous public openings unnecessary. The Commissioners also justified the lack of open space for symbolic reasons. Since "a city is to be composed principally of the habitations of men," they argued (referring specifically to a city in the new American republic), there was no reason to employ European-style urban planning elements such as "circles, ovals and stars."[29] In this way they identified the traditional public square as a symbol of the aristocracy, an unwelcome and unnecessary intrusion in a democratic nation.

By the time Ruggles began his career as a real estate developer there was a general agreement that the open spaces provided in the 1811 plan were insufficient, not only in terms of acreage, but also in terms of the range of activities they allowed. Several, including Union Place, had been reduced in size, and some had been eliminated all together. One historian has estimated that of the 450 acres set aside as open space in the original plan, only 120 had been realized twenty years later.[30] Two of these predated the 1811 plan. Bowling Green, the city's colonial era public space, was a small park enclosed with an iron fence notable for its roughly sawn-off finials where crowns symbolizing the authority of King George III had been triumphantly removed in 1776. Along with the Battery at the southern end of Manhattan, Bowling Green was the favored promenading location for wealthy New Yorkers. Less than a mile to the north, a "common" or open grazing area at the intersection of Broadway and Chambers Street had been improved in conjunction with the construction of City Hall in the first decade of the nineteenth century.[31] Known as City Hall Park, this was the primary public space in the city in the 1820s, the locus of civic celebrations and political gatherings. However, as the city's social elite moved further north, demand grew for more parks. Besides publicly provided squares, the city also housed a number of commercial pleasure grounds featuring musical entertainment and refreshments, including Niblo's on the corner of Broadway and Prince Streets, Vauxhall Gardens at Astor Place and East Fourth Street, and Richmond Hill Garden at Varick and Charlton Streets in Greenwich Village, though these were considered off limits for respectable people.[32]

Adding to concern, New York had begun to acquire a reputation for the noise, confusion, and general hubbub of its busy streets and for the unrelenting nature of the checkerboard grid, unrelieved by great vistas or monuments. As a mid-nineteenth-century guidebook author put it, "The great characteristic of New York is din and excitement,—everything is done in a hurry—all is intense anxiety. It is especially noticeable in the leading thoroughfare of Broadway; where the noise and confusion caused by the incessant passing and repassing of some 18,000 vehicles a day, render it a Babel scene of confusion."[33] This particular criticism recurs in travelers' accounts, in which there seemed no escape from the cacophony of sounds and smells, no place of respite from the grid's straight lines.[34] According to contemporary thinking, the answer was to build more parks: those essential components of nineteenth-century city planning. Just as ornament turned a commonplace building into a piece of architecture, urban parks civilized the city. The Common Council was well aware of the limitations of their city in this respect. In considering Ruggles's proposal to create Gramercy Park, its members lamented, "That the want of a sufficient number of open and public squares in this extensive and densely populated metropolis is the cause of frequent and just complaint, inasmuch as they would greatly tend to embellish and ornament the city, and promote the health and convenience of its inhabitants."[35] The addition of further parks and squares would offer spaces of repose to a city sorely in need of them. The council recommended the adoption of measures to lay out more public squares, and also to "facilitate enterprising individuals in laying out private squares, whenever it can be done without prejudice to the public interest."[36] These squares were best located beyond the existing city, in anticipation of the time when the population would extend as far north as Twenty-First Street.

Although the grid plan has a reputation for rigidity, it was flexible enough to accommodate change. As Ballon has argued, it is best thought of as a framework with no fixed content.[37] Individual private landowners were free to do as they liked with their property, and they held much power in deciding the nature of public improvements in their area. In their plan for the expansion of New York City, the Commissioners had included a number of "uptown squares" designed for leisure and sociability, but these were located far to the north of the existing settlement. By the 1820s New Yorkers with influence sought to insert into the grid plan just this type of public space, but much closer to the built-up part of the city. Prompted by active lobbying on the part of private citizens, half a dozen landscaped squares were created or improved between 1826 and 1847; these squares were thought of as "ornaments" or "embellishments" and were intended to make New York the equal of the great cities of Europe. Washington Square, developed at the urging of Mayor Philip Hone was the model for those that came after. Purchased by the city in 1789, the open land had been used as a place of execution and as a burial ground for criminals and the indigent. In 1826 it was transformed into a military parade ground, replacing the much larger one proposed in the 1811 plan. Graded and surrounded by a wooden fence, Washington Square was soon surrounded by fashionable houses and upscale institutions including two churches and the buildings of New York University. Soon afterward, in 1834, the city purchased a portion of the land on the east side of Manhattan in order to create Tompkins Square. Originally known as the "Salt Meadow," this swampy, low-lying land had little value for property speculators and was set aside as a public market in the original grid plan. In 1836 a wealthy New Yorker, Peter Stuyvesant, donated a portion of his family estate to the city on the condition that it be kept open for public use. In 1847 this was opened under the name "Stuyvesant Square." Further north the city eliminated Harlem Square, one of the uptown squares in the 1811 plan, and created instead Mount Morris Square (now known as Marcus Garvey Park). Though the development of these squares was subsidized by the city, of the hundreds of thousands of dollars spent to make them, the vast majority of the cost was born by local property owners via tax assessments.[38]

Although the creation of these squares appears to counter the principles of the 1811 grid plan, which disallowed such extravagant urban set pieces such as "circles, ovals and stars," their establishment was motivated by the same republican and capitalist principles that had guided the grid plan. These principles were established partly for pragmatic reasons. In response to outbreaks of infectious diseases like cholera, they provided the fresh air thought necessary to maintain public health before the germ theory of disease was understood.[39] And they were also instruments for urban growth, advancing the interests of real estate speculation and benefiting the city as a whole by increasing tax revenues. In considering the project to improve Union Place, the Board of Assistants, which has succeeded to the Common Council, noted that "the pecuniary interest of the public will be promoted by the liberal embellishment of Union Place. The real estate of the inhabitants of this city pays upwards of two-thirds of the public taxes. By fostering its growth and encouraging the efforts of enterprising individuals to enhance its value, the public resources will be correspondingly increased."[40] In other words, private fortune would subsidize public benefit.

In aesthetic terms the new squares were regarded as ornaments to the city, "desirable for public convenience," but they were not necessarily shared spaces in the way we understand public parks today.[41] Far from democratic in a practical sense, they were built in emulation of European precedents—residential squares built by and for a privileged few. In its report considering Ruggles's proposal for Gramercy Park, the Common Council compared it in size to Grosvenor, Portman, Berkley, Cavendish, and Manchester Squares in London.[42] Created in the seventeenth and eighteenth centuries, and sited on the outskirts of London with open views to the countryside to the north and west, they were built as centerpieces for new residential neighborhoods intended for courtiers, the gentry, and the wealthy professional classes who were moving away from the governmental and financial center to the east.[43] While some were established on common land, many were carved out of private aristocratic estates or land belonging to the Crown. Initially they were rough, dirty, and unpaved. In 1725 those living around St. James's Square petitioned the British parliament for the right to improve, maintain, and enclose it. The private act authorizing this request granted residents the right to levy a fee in order to carry out these improvements, a law which set a precedent, providing a legal framework for the management of London squares for centuries to come. Soon after St. James's Square was improved by the planting of trees and shrubs and enclosed by a fence, residents of other squares followed suit. Berkeley Square was improved in 1766 and Grosvenor Square in 1774. In formal terms these squares followed the same pattern: a large grassed plat with a gravel walk around it and a palisaded iron fence surrounding that. As the historian of landscape architecture Todd Longstaffe-Gowan has observed, the building of a fence, an act of exclusion, was vital to their success. These were protected realms, guarded by locked gates and by night watchmen and private constables employed to prevent the entry of "disorderly" persons.[44]

Although early nineteenth-century America was governed in a wholly different way, the wealthy inhabitants of New York City had a similar understanding of the value and function of the squares they created in the 1830s and 1840s. Enclosed with high fences, their use was limited to a particular segment of the population: those who could afford to live nearby. While their creation was supported by the Common Council and they were generally understood to benefit the city as a whole, they were initiated and largely paid for by private citizens who continued to think of them as private parks dedicated for their own use into the middle of the nineteenth century. As the controversy that accompanied the creation of Union Place demonstrates, the contradictions embedded in this attitude were subject to debate even at this early date.

In histories of New York City the physical expansion of the city northward during the nineteenth century is often presented as a frictionless progression, almost as if it were a mechanical process, meeting no resistance either natural or man-made. In fact it was slow, grinding, disruptive, and contentious. As an exercise in large-scale urban planning, the development of the uptown district north of Fourteenth Street may be compared to the transformation of Paris under Baron Haussmann twenty years later. However, in this case it was not the urban poor who were displaced, but rather New Yorkers of means who were trying to escape them. In the process of this urban development the topography of the island of Manhattan was remade; buildings and trees were uprooted, the course of existing roads was diverted, and new infrastructural systems including drains and streetcar lines were embedded throughout. As in Paris, this activity was accompanied by controversy. While the city government and powerful private lobbyists argued that the spectacular reconfiguration of the landscape was an act of civic foresight essential to the continued growth of the city, others accused the Common Council of wasteful spending, of engaging in financial speculation for the benefit of its members and their social connections rather than for the good of all citizens.

While Gramercy Park was completed relatively quickly, Union Place was not. Cleared and leveled in December of 1831, the private square Ruggles initiated was planted with trees and shrubs, paved with walks, and surrounded by an iron fence over the course of the following year, after which houses were constructed on the surrounding lots. The improvement of its public counterpart was much slower and much more controversial, subject to debate at every stage. Every step involved in the process of improving Union Place, from collecting assessments, to demolishing existing buildings, grading the site, and paving, planting, and enclosing it, was accompanied by public objection. The work began in 1832 when the Board of Aldermen, a newly created body that worked alongside the members of the Common Council, ordered that

> all the lands lying within the limits of Union Place . . . be enclosed with an iron fence and stone coping, with convenient and appropriate gates;—that the surface of the enclosure be reduced to proper and sufficient levels, and prepared to receive grass or shrubbery with convenient foot walks;—that a flagged side walk be laid around the exterior of the enclosure not exceeding 15' in width;—that in the meantime, and until further order of the Common Council in respect to the permanent paving of the carriageways around the exterior, such portion thereof, as may be necessary, be rendered passable for carriages and vehicles.[45]

The practice of enclosing urban parks with iron railings to control what happened inside them began in Europe in the eighteenth century. Such fences defined a space set aside for activities outside the realm of the commercial, and protected it from incursions by the vulgar populace. In times of unrest, the gates could be securely locked. Supplementing the fence and gates, such squares often employed a resident "keeper," a sort of private security guard charged with maintaining order.[46]

In April of 1832 a bill authorizing this work was passed in the State Senate, and an assessment of $110,000 was imposed on 1,009 lots in the surrounding area to pay for it.[47] One thousand dollars per lot was assessed on each of the seventy-six lots fronting the square, with proportionate amounts assessed on adjacent ones. The city aldermen (whose authority was derived from elections) were anxious to remind their constituents that the improvement of the square was undertaken without expenditure of public money:

> Union Place, embracing an area as large as the Battery, comprehending ten acres of land in a central and very valuable portion of the city, and destined to remain forever open, for the embellishment of the metropolis and the health and recreation of its inhabitants, literally cost the public nothing. The owners of the adjacent lands virtually bought the square and bestowed it gratuitously on the public.[48]

Despite these apparent advantages, not everyone was convinced that the project was worthwhile. From the first some were skeptical about the benefits the square might bring. A group of local landowners filed a formal protest on the grounds that they were not being offered a fair price for their land. They also believed the construction of the square would impede the flow of traffic along Broadway. In response to these concerns Ruggles's original proposal for a rectangular square was abandoned in favor of an ellipse, 677 feet long and 302 feet, 9 inches wide, allowing traffic to flow smoothly around it via a generous 100-foot-wide carriageway.[49]

Besides its practical advantages, the elliptical shape lent Union Place an association with gentility: Bowling Green, the fashionable park at the southern end of Broadway was an ellipse, as were several of the English prototypes, including Grosvenor, Portman, and Bedford Squares. With its new shape established and the necessary private land purchased, work began on grading the uneven site using explosive charges. In 1833 a Mr. William Bear petitioned the Board of Aldermen for payment for his work "blowing rocks" at Union Place.[50] Despite claims that the project would cost the public nothing, the city appropriated an initial five thousand dollars to begin the work and a further fifteen thousand dollars in 1834 to "embellish" the park.[51] Public funding did not ensure rapid completion, however. Infuriating those who had begun to build houses in the area, the enclosure and landscaping

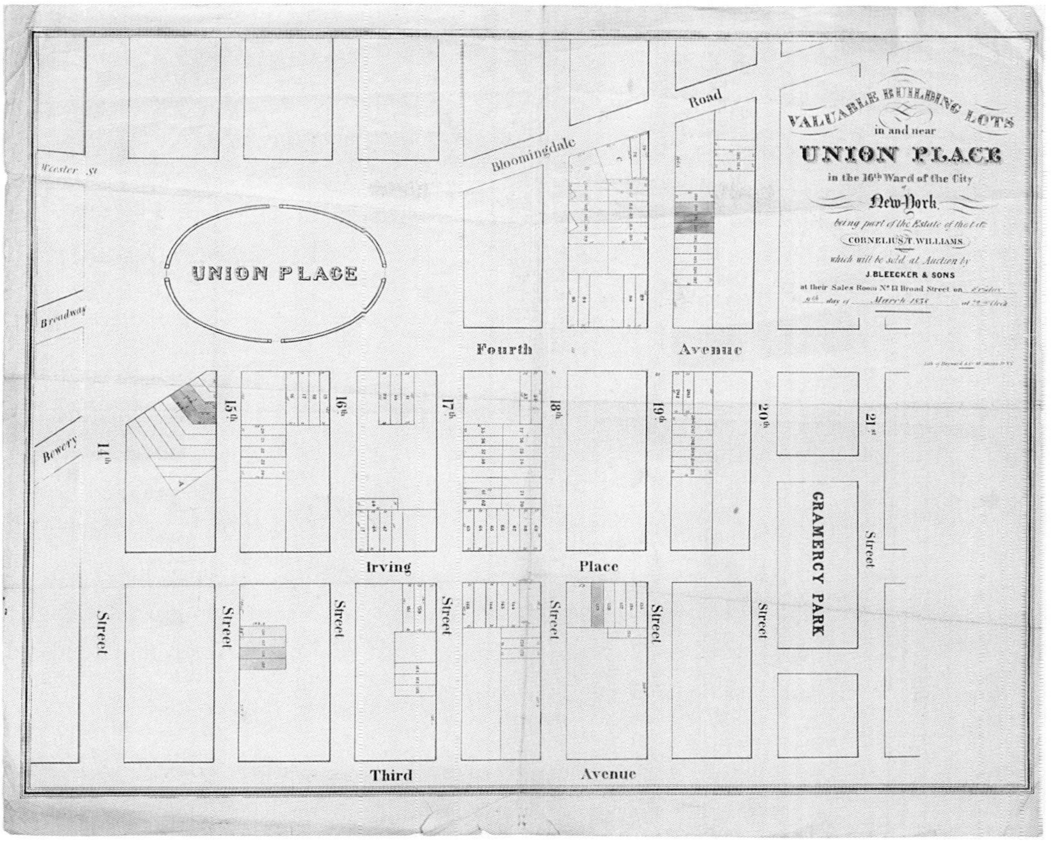

1.4 Valuable building lots in and near Union Place in the 16th Ward of the City of New York, ca. 1838.

were delayed again and again. Following the financial panic of 1837, when the rapid economic expansion of the 1820s and 1830s suddenly collapsed, members of the Common Council refused to authorize payment for placing stone flags on the sidewalks of Washington Square and Union Place, arguing that "these public places, although they are an ornament to the city, and conducive to the health and pleasure of the citizens, are nevertheless of local benefit, not general."[52] After six years of work, Union Place was desolate, unpaved, and unfenced, planted with only a few scrawny trees described by a journalist of the time as "spindling-bushes."[53]

In its unfinished state, Union Place was a source of contention, a political football kicked between those who saw it as a farsighted and benevolent project benefiting the city as a whole and those who saw it as a dubious scheme for the enrichment of a few already wealthy members of the Whig-dominated Common Council and their business associates. During the early 1830s, newspaper editorialists and politicians associated with the

Democratic Party criticized Union Place as a corruption of the republican ideals exemplified by the grid plan: it was a form of economic favoritism, they argued, a waste of public funds benefiting the few, privileged citizens who lived or owned property in the immediate area.[54] The *Evening Post* was especially critical. The paper published a letter from a writer signing himself "Moonshine," accusing the Council of favoritism to the Twelfth Ward, and including a satirical description of a journey there in the not too distant future:

> What splendid sight bursts upon my delighted vision—I see towering mansions adorning the four sides of Union Place, while wherever I turn my wondering eyes, a long perspective of closely built streets meets my gaze; ever and anon, a well laden car glides along, and here and there it pauses, passengers descend, and after a short walk enter lordly mansions. Methinks I may address one—a portly, rubicund individual—an Alderman. . . . He tells me how his property has increased—how it has doubled in value within five years, and departs muttering, "Oh! Happy speculation! Oh! The pleasures and delights of office!"[55]

Debates about this and other improvements centered on an emerging divide between uptown and downtown interests. Though the new squares (with the exception of Gramercy Park) were intended to be public, many New Yorkers could not imagine traveling to parks so far away from where they lived. On the other side, those who supported their creation argued that the rapid pace of population growth made such urban planning necessary. Prompted by Ruggles, the Common Council even considered the possibility that Union Place might, at some time in the future, become the new civic center of New York City. Early in 1833 the Board of Aldermen debated buying land north of the not yet realized square, bounded by Seventeenth and Nineteenth Streets, Fourth Avenue and the Bloomingdale Road, as a site for future municipal buildings.[56] Those arguing in favor of the proposal claimed that the city needed to be ambitious in its thinking, but most aldermen were against the idea, arguing that the expensive purchase was unnecessary.

In 1833, journalistic ire, already raised by the city's apparent wastefulness when it came to public spending in the distant Twelfth Ward, was inflamed all the more by a whispering campaign that the city was considering relocating the seat of city government to Union Place.[57] According to gossip, the city would sell the present City Hall building and grounds to the federal government for use as a Customs House and Post Office. This rumor created an uproar: the Chamber of Commerce, a private businessmen's organization, called a public meeting to oppose the plan and even sent a delegation of its members to Washington, DC, to lobby against the idea. The basis of their complaint was that, if relocated to Union Place, City Hall would be too far removed from the city's commercial center at Wall Street. A doggerel poem about the issue began, "For sale—the Hall—the City Hall—The Park—the Jail—the Alms-House and all,"[57] and concluded by conjuring up a chimerical image of a future city center at distant Fourteenth Street:

> A city found at Union Place,
> For benefit of the human race;
> A new Hall built for the use of those,
> A century hence—as the city grows![58]

Although this particular plan never came to anything (the Federal Post Office was built instead at the southern end of City Hall Park and City Hall remained where it was), speculation about Union Place as a future site for civic buildings lasted well into the 1850s. As we will see, in the early twentieth-century proponents of the City Beautiful movement raised this idea again, seeing Union Square (as it had then become known) as a monumental urban center linking the disparate parts of the city together.

While debate continued over the wisdom of public spending on Union Place, and on the erection of civic buildings there, work went ahead regardless: the landscape was subjected to dramatic upheaval with the Square positioned as a showcase and staging area for future urban development. In 1833 the New York and Harlem Railroad Company began to lay tracks on granite sleepers around the square, extending its existing line from Prince Street in SoHo along Fourth Avenue as far as Twenty-Third Street via deep cuttings made through solid rock and on newly constructed embankments.[59] In June of that year horses began pulling carriage loads of passengers up and down this line. Though the company was private, it played a large part in promoting the growth of the city and its economy. As its name suggested, this railroad line was intended to eventually connect the existing city to Harlem, improving the value of properties along the way, and creating a new industrial center for New York at the northern end of the island. At the same time other changes were made to the street grid, many intended to facilitate north-south travel. In 1833, the same year that the streetcar company began operation, Ruggles petitioned to have Wooster Street extended northward from Eighth Street, connecting Washington Square and Union Place together (this street was later renamed "University Place" in honor of New York University).[60] He also created Irving Place, between Fourteenth

1.5 "Union Park New York [East side]." From Mary Louise Booth, *History of the City of New York* (1867).

Street and Gramercy Park, and what would become Lexington Ave on land he owned between Third and Fourth Avenues. Not content to stop at the boundaries of his own property, he urged the city to establish Madison Avenue between Fourth and Fifth Avenues.[61] With these new streets in place, Union Place was being sculpted into an elaborate urban set piece, an important civic center built on what had been waste ground on the periphery of the city.

While ultimately invisible, perhaps the most dramatic change to the urban landscape was the construction of drain and sewer lines accompanying a new citywide water supply system. The creation of Union Place coincided with, and was enabled by, an urban improvement project of a different sort, the inauguration of the first municipally owned waterworks supplied via aqueduct from the Croton River, a project in which Ruggles was also closely involved.[62] Up until the 1830s New Yorkers collected rainwater in cisterns for general washing purposes. For drinking, they used groundwater drawn from a series of wells by pumps, but this water was generally considered "bad and deleterious in its character," as a 1834 guidebook put it.[63] Following the 1832 cholera epidemic in which three thousand people died, political and business leaders began to investigate the construction of a public water supply system, leading to a proposal to divert water from the Croton River in upstate New York. Despite reluctance to approve a project that would increase taxes, voters approved the construction of the Croton Aqueduct in 1835 and work began that summer. The aqueduct supplied a large receiving reservoir, a massive stone structure on the site of the present New York Public Library at Forty-Second Street and Fifth Avenue. From there water was piped two miles south to a smaller distributing reservoir in Murray Hill.[64] This reservoir serviced more than one hundred miles of subterranean pipes feeding the houses and businesses of the city, as well as fountains and public hydrants which "street inspectors" turned on for an hour or two every day for the benefit of those without indoor plumbing. The opening of the Croton Aqueduct was so important to the city that it was celebrated with an enormous five-mile long parade on July 4th, 1842, in which representatives of all classes, societies, and trades in New York City marched in rank in celebration of the initiative. The Croton Parade built on a model established by a parade held in 1825 to celebrate the opening of the Erie Canal, and followed the same path from the Battery up Broadway to Union Place and back down the Bowery.[65] As labor historian Sean Wilentz has explained, these parades had ties to British craft festivals dating back to the seventeenth century, such as the Lord Mayor's Show in London.[66] In New York these parades marked the length and breadth of the city, with Union Square formally acknowledged as its northernmost boundary.

The Croton Aqueduct project exactly coincided with the improvement of Union Place and the other uptown squares. Although the aqueduct was of undoubted benefit to public health, its primary motive was economic. As the geographer Matthew Gandy has argued, the provision of fresh water was part of a wider effort to increase the investment of capital in the growing city: "The construction of the Croton Aqueduct marked a new era in North American urbanization. Had it not been built it would have been impossible for New York City to retain its position as the largest and fastest-growing city in America."[67] The completion of the aqueduct ensured a safe and consistent water supply for the growing population, and reduced insurance and manufacturing costs for businesses. It was fitting, then, that when the Croton system was launched in 1842, Ruggles (who later became head of the Croton Aqueduct Department) and others who lived in Union Place chose to commemorate the occasion by erecting a magnificent fountain right in the middle of the square, now landscaped and surrounded by an iron fence and stone gates. Sixty feet in diameter and three feet deep, this fountain was grand enough to draw comparisons with famous European precedents. A contemporary newspaper reported that, once operational, it featured "jets 60' high, the most imposing of which presents the form of a wheat sheaf, resembling one in the Palais Royale in Paris."[68] Besides offering a splendid spectacle and cooling breezes during the hot and humid New York summers, the fountain expressed in aesthetic form the transformation of everyday life that was taking place inside private homes around the square. As Gandy notes, "Croton water" was a luxury. Access to fresh water changed domestic life profoundly, making possible the ritual of daily bathing in rooms set aside for this practice equipped with associated accouterments such as bathtubs, soaps, and other cosmetics. These practices, rooms, and objects were understood as signifiers of social standing and of modernity. The partner of another fountain installed in City Hall Park at the same time, the Croton Fountain illustrated the close connection between the privileged life lived in the new neighborhoods being created to the north of the city and the infrastructure that made it possible.

When the Croton Fountain was activated in 1842, Ruggles's vision of Union Place was complete. The city was rousing itself out of economic depression and ready to build again, while the square was positioned as the centerpiece of an elegant uptown district. The elliptical garden, with the fountain at its center, was planted with privet hedges and beds of roses, and surrounded by an ornamental iron fence set in large stone blocks erected two stages between 1838 and 1839.[69] Facing Broadway at the southern entrance, impressive stone gates were surmounted with two cannon balls (according to neighborhood lore, these were brought to New York from Constantinople by Commodore David Porter, United States Ambassador to Turkey).[70] For a time the residents of Union Place employed a keeper to lock and unlock the park gates, though this position was disestablished in 1844.[71] In half a century, Union Place had been transformed from a semirural outpost at the edge of the city to the centerpiece of an elite residential enclave, and a model for urban development further north. Modeled closely on the great London squares, it was the creation and expression of a particular social group, wealthy Americans who had made their fortunes through commerce.

The Home of the "Upper Ten"

The architecture around Union Square reflected the wealth and cultural values of its residents. As the *New York Herald* noted in 1845, "This part of the city is rapidly becoming one of the most splendid and becoming of all our environs, and those streets that but a few short years ago were looked on as the acme of all architectural beauty in New York must make way and be content to rank second."[72] John Bachmann's 1849 print depicts an idealized view of the scene. In the center, lush trees and plants surround the magnificent Croton fountain, providing shade and cooling breezes. To the left, on the eastern side of the square, the horse-drawn cars of the New York and Harlem Railroad (of which Ruggles was naturally a director) work their way up Fourth Avenue connecting the two worlds of uptown and downtown. In the foreground they pass in front of the eight bow-fronted, Greek revival–style row houses that Ruggles had erected in 1838–39 at Union Square East, between Fifteenth and Sixteenth Streets. Built of brick, these houses were set back from the street to allow for a small garden in front. Ruggles himself lived in one of them, at 24 Union Place, for the next forty years.[73] As with his former home in Bond Street, his neighbors were of the highest rank, including at 32, Sir Richard Tighe, a director of the Manhattan Fire Insurance Company, and at 36, Elihu Townsend, a director of the Boston and New York Transportation Company and the New Jersey Railroad. John Griswold, a shipping magnate whose Black X line was one of the first to carry mail between New York and London on a regularly scheduled service, was also a neighbor.[74]

Although large, comfortable, and well appointed, Ruggles's townhouses were not ostentatious. Similar to those that lined Bond Street, their simple style, with flat fronts and unornamented windows, reflected his social and business ties to the "Knickerbocker aristocracy," families with roots extending back to the Dutch colonial era. Though wealthy, these families favored discrete and unpretentious architecture. It was not long, however, before Union Square became a favored home for newly prosperous merchants, self-made men who had made their fortunes during the economic boom of the 1820s and 1830s. Of these houses, Miss Bird commented, "Such mansions were rather at variance with my ideas of Republican simplicity; they contained apartments which would have thrown into the shade the finest apartments in Windsor Castle or Buckingham Palace."[75] In 1844 Courtland Palmer built a row of houses along the south side of the square between Broadway and University Place, one of which was bought by Cornelius von Schaik Roosevelt (grandfather of the future president, Theodore). Though he was a descendant of Dutch colonial families, Roosevelt had made his fortune with a hardware and plate glass importing company. The financial broker James Phalen and James F. Penniman, who expanded the sperm and whale oil trade of his father-in-law into a large fortune, occupied other houses in this row.[76] Anson Green Phelps, owner of a large metal works that supplied copper for the United States navy, built a house at Fifteenth Street and Union Square West.[77] Dry goods merchant Henry Parish and his brother Daniel purchased adjacent properties on the northwest corner of

Union Place in 1843, building houses there in 1848.[78] What became known as the "Parish mansion" was described in contemporary accounts as one of the largest and most handsomely appointed in the city, introducing elements of the newly fashionable "Italianate" style modeled on the city palaces built by the merchant princes of Renaissance Italy.[79] In the first week of January 1849, Mrs. Parish "threw open her home to the *beau monde* of New York."[80] As she quickly discovered, the race to build the finest house in the neighborhood was a highly competitive one.

Next to the Parish mansion at 32 Seventeenth Street, William B. Moffat built an equally luxurious home. Moffatt was a wealthy dealer in patent medicines whose wares included "Moffat's Vegetable Life Pills."[81] His business was located in a large commercial building on lower Broadway; uptown he commissioned a five-story brownstone complete with portico and cupola. Noted as "one of the most splendid family establishments in the United States," his house was lavishly decorated inside:

> There are frescoes, carvings, statues and paintings, shields of heraldry, coats of arms, poets, patriarchs, gods and goddesses in bas relief, angels and all sorts of ethereals in hazy splendor. Four seasons smile through the stained skylight, and myriads of unnamable creatures and combinations glitter from stained doors and windows.[82]

An 1847 newspaper article described the luxurious interiors of the homes around the square, including plentiful supplies of "Croton water":

> Turning up Fifteenth Street [from Irving Place] we enter Union Place, where a fountain like that of the City Hall sends up its jet some sixty feet from the oval enclosure; and where we are again surrounded with these lordly mansions, two of which have cost between fifty and one hundred thousand dollars each! Enter any one of all we have passed, and you will find perhaps marble floors or staircases. In every room the gas flies out from gilded or glittering burners; the Croton is found on every floor and in almost every room, hot and cold, and dispensing with the necessity of any outdoor buildings. Do you wish to speak to a servant? A trumpet communicates from every floor directly to the kitchen. Do you wish for heat? In every room you have but to turn the regulator, and in rushes heated air. Between all the chambers are extensive clothes presses, drawers and permanent marble wash bowls, dispensing with the necessity of purchasing wardrobes or washstands. In the dining room a dumbwaiter brings up the dishes. The very basement rooms are equal to many parlors, and in the under cellars

your coal is slid down through an opening in the front pavement, where there are front court yards; a little fountain cools the air in summer and waters the flowers. Is not this luxury?[83]

The fountain mentioned here is probably that of Moffat, whose large mansion was notable for a street front garden complete with "a gigantic bust of Galen or Hippocrates, from the top of whose forehead shoots up a silvery jet of water."[84] These fine houses were not destined to be permanent monuments, however. Wealthy New Yorkers regarded their Union Square homes not as repositories of domestic comfort and memory, but as objects of social display, speculative investments like any other. Henry Parish was never happy in his new house. A businessman above all, he intended from the first to rent his house out "as soon as the rapid growth of the city . . . should render his residence undesirable."[85] He was never sentimental about it; indeed he was seldom there, spending "all day downtown at his office; after dinner [going] to the Club, where he remained until one or two o'clock."[86] By the mid-1860s neither the Parish nor the Moffat mansion were used as private homes.

In addition to their houses, members of the upper ten commissioned institutional buildings to embellish the Square, buildings that advertised the wealth and taste of their patrons. Employing the newly fashionable Gothic Revival style, the young society architect James Renwick designed several churches in the area. In 1843 he secured the commission to build the Episcopal Grace Church just south of the square on Broadway between Tenth and Eleventh Streets, which may be seen in the middle distance of Bachmann's print. Denigrated by some critics for the frivolous lath and plaster work in place of stone, and for the lack of attention to the principles of structural design, this church was nevertheless one of the most important institutions in New York society.[87] Renwick became the architect of choice for other nearby churches, including the Congregationalist Church of the Puritans on the west side of the Square at Fifteenth Street (1843–46), which may be seen on the right hand side of the Bachmann print. While Grace Church was the choice of the socially ambitious (Mrs. Henry Parish and many of her neighbors had pews there), the Church of the Puritans attracted progressive thinkers, and was famous for the fiery sermons of its minister, the Rev. George B. Cheever, a notorious and divisive figure who advocated women's rights and the abolition of slavery. Next door to the Church of the Puritans, another progressive, the Rev. Gorham D. Abbott, opened the Spingler Institute in 1847. This school for young ladies provided "a first-rate English education, including French, dancing and drawing."[88] Attended by girls from well-off families from New York and abroad, Abbott intended his institute to be the female equivalent of Yale, Princeton, and Harvard.[89] Its high-minded prospectus assured parents that the curriculum was intended "by a systematic and progressive course of higher instruction, and suitable attention to physical education, to give the varied mental and moral powers appropriate and symmetrical culture."[90] The annual fee was a steep five hundred dollars which included "Board, Washing and Seat at Church."

Not everyone was impressed by the extravagant display, however. In 1852 a visitor from Charleston wrote a lively account of his trip to New York City for the edification and amusement of his friends in South Carolina. This report included a satirical assessment of Union Square as the place "where many of the nabobs reside . . . the center of the fashionable portion of New-York. Here at high tide you can see the glory of snobdom, the quintessence of codfish-ocracy, and the beauties of japonicadom."[91] "Codfish-ocracy" is a derogatory term referring to those who earned their fortunes from trade, and "Japonicadom" refers to the contemporary craze for Japanese design. In other words, the Square was the place where new money demonstrated its taste through the display of the latest fashions. This tourist's reference to snobbery indicates that, as with any newly established class, the inhabitants of Union Square thought a great deal about display and differentiation: the park around which they lived was a prime site for the creation of this self-image.

Although ostensibly open to all, the park at Union Square served as an extension of the private activities taking place inside the grand houses surrounding it. Access was tightly controlled and, once inside, behavior was closely monitored. Within the fenced enclosure, members of the upper ten undertook the ceremony of the promenade, the ritual stroll during which society members would slowly walk up and down, greeting each other and showing off their fashionable attire and refined manners. In the early years of the nineteenth century, the Battery, Bowling Green, and the shady west side of Broadway had been the primary sites for promenading in New York City. By the 1840s the new uptown squares had begun to compete as sites for the daily ceremony. The event was finely choreographed: a man would acknowledge a woman of his acquaintance by raising his hat and the woman would respond with a modest nod of the head. If words were exchanged, they were apparently of the most inconsequential nature; looks and attitude held a deeper meaning. In a city regarded as the capital of social mobility, where new immigrants arrived every day and new fortunes were made almost overnight, the promenade provided a vital means by which to learn and display the fine delineations of social distinction. The daily stroll around Union Square was a custom by which the wealthy and newly wealthy created a shared culture, demonstrating their manners and "politesse."

An enclosed and protected realm, in its early years Union Square was essentially "gentrified" in that it was created by and for the gentry, members of the highest ranks of New York society.[92] More closely aligned to the private world of the home than with the public world of the street, it was used not only for promenading but also as a place where the children of local families played, supervised at all times by their nursery maids, an extension of the upper-class domestic world. Contemporaneous with the creation of the earliest American suburb, residential squares such as Washington Square, Gramercy Park, and Union Square shared many of the suburb's essential qualities. The realm of women and children, it was a feminized periphery located on the edge of the masculine city, a geographical separation that protected private life. As historian Kenneth T. Jackson has shown, the nineteenth-century cult of domesticity raised the private house to a new status as a place of retreat from the world of business.[93] Like the suburb, the residential square provided a safe place for society women and their children to venture out of doors. The essentially private and feminine nature of the park in Union Square is evident in the ways in which it was described in the press. In 1848 the *New York Herald* reported that "this delightful spot has become one of the most popular places of resort for the ladies among the city." On pleasant afternoons one can see "from three to five hundred children assembling, where they can all take necessary exercise without the slightest danger. It is kept in perfect order and the ladies of the vicinity are blessed with all that makes a sultry evening agreeable—a walk in its bough-covered avenues."[94] However, the square was not destined to be defined by its quiet and seclusion for long, something even its founders realized. Almost as soon as it achieved its status as the center of the most fashionable residential district in New York City, that status was under threat. As the process of urbanization ground on, Union Square lay directly in its path, and entrepreneurs soon turned their minds to commercializing its prestige. In 1850 Bloomingdale Road was officially renamed the northern extension of Broadway, soon replacing the Bowery as the main route between the city and points further north.[95] Located right in the path of this busy thoroughfare, the Square could not remain a quiet suburban enclave.

As we have seen, urban expansion was the result of much-debated legislation, noisy and dirty earthworks, and expensive real estate speculation; it was, then, no less than an entwined social, economic, and political phenomenon. At the time observers preferred to overlook human agency, describing it instead in terms of natural processes. In 1853, a writer for *Putnam's Magazine* compared the city to a natural organism:

> New-York City is just like a sponge; and the water, that is, the business, is creeping gradually up into all the hitherto dry and contracted pores. . . . No magnetic attraction, which draws the iron particles to itself from every adjacent quarter, and makes itself felt by those it cannot move, is surer than the spell that has drawn the business of New-York within the last few years, away from the old channels and time-hallowed abodes.[96]

In the case of Union Square, two metaphors of nature were operational. The green oval with the fountain in the center was a carefully manicured replica of nature, a genteel retreat from the rough world of business downtown. However, within a few years of its completion, it was also appeared as an attractive void, an area where the absence of commercial activity was unnatural and unsustainable.

Soon luxury hotels, scaled-up approximations of private mansions intended for well-off travelers, began to appear in the area. As the American hub for transatlantic shipping and a major tourist site, New York catered to thousands of visitors every day. Europeans commented on the peculiarly American features of New York's hotels: their impressive size, the large number of guests they accommodated, the sumptuousness of the furnishings, and their splendid amenities, including barbershops, bars, and bridal suites.[97] (As they would continue to be for the next one hundred and fifty years, English guests were particularly entranced by the apparently never-ending supply of ice water.) The Astor House Hotel at Broadway between Vesey and Barclay Streets was an early model of magnificence, but, as early as 1852 some considered it, "too far downtown to be fashionable."[98] By the middle of the century several grand hotels were open for business in the vicinity of Union Square.

Considerably more exclusive than the commercial hotels lining Broadway further south, these hotels catered to aristocrats, celebrities, and the very well off. The Clarendon Hotel, built in 1847 at Eighteenth Street and Fourth Avenue between Union Square and Gramercy Park, was an early venture. Designed by James Renwick, the architect of several churches in the area, it had a precarious beginning, with its owners going into bankruptcy soon after it opened. More immediately successful was the Union Square Hotel at Fourth Avenue and Fourteenth Street. Opened in 1848, it had fifty suites, each appointed with the luxurious amenities found in nearby private houses, including "an ample bath, marble washstand and closets of the best material, and all lighted with gas," and, of course, "free use of Croton water, for warm, cold and shower baths, water closets and etc."[99] The Everett House Hotel, which opened in 1853 on the northeastern corner of the Square at Seventeenth Street, was even more magnificent. In 1857 a German guidebook commented on the hotel's splendid situation fronting the Square:

> We saw nothing in the United States, and we know of nothing in Europe, to compare for a moment with the Everett House in New York. The edifice is of vast extent, admirably proportioned and tastefully constructed. Its main front is on Union Square, one of the most spacious and elegant promenades of the city. The center is enclosed with iron palisades and laid out as a garden, which is adorned with umbrageous trees, flower beds and *jets d'eux*. On all sides of the square are constructed mansions of unusual dimensions and imposing appearance.[100]

The Everett House was host to a series of notable visitors and grand social events. It also played a role in national politics: President Franklin Pierce addressed a crowd from the balcony of this hotel on his return from a trip to England in 1856.

Public events such as this suggest that Union Square was taking on a new identity, one more entwined with public life. Though he continued to live in Union Square, Ruggles himself was moving his attention elsewhere. In the early 1840s he was one of the chief promoters of the improvement of Madison Square just to the north at Broadway and Twenty-Third Street, again financed by assessments on local landowners. While the legal proceedings for the opening of Madison Square were delayed several times, they were finally completed in June of 1847. For Ruggles, this marked the end of a remarkable period in which he, a private citizen, exerted considerable influence on the shaping of New York City; it is fair to say that the group of squares built in the Twelfth Ward in the 1830s and 1840s owed their existence largely to him. In 1851 he suffered professional embarrassment when one of his investments, the Atlantic Docks in Brooklyn, failed and he was forced to return to his legal practice.[101] However, he remained a respected member of New York society, a consultant on various public works projects and an active promoter of public parks—elements of urban design that he described in increasingly metaphysical terms as the years went on. While Ruggles at first argued for the creation of public parks on economic grounds (they would raise the value of surrounding property and increase the tax revenue collected by the city), later in his life he placed greater emphasis on their benefits from a social point of view, elevating them to the status of quasi-sacred urban entities. During the next two decades, and particularly during the time of the Civil War, he witnessed from the balcony of his home the dramatic transformation of Union Square from the centerpiece of a quiet residential neighborhood to a vibrant center of political activism. These events would lead him to boast that the Square was not so much an economic machine, but rather a "theater adequate to the utterance of the national voice."[102]

2

The Altar of Patriotism, 1856–1865

Despite the ambitious plan for northward expansion set out in the 1811 Commissioners' Plan, fifty years later the city's leaders were still unsure about the direction of urban growth. An 1853 report to the Board of Aldermen speculated about the location of the future city center. Should Brooklyn and Williamsburg join together with New York, the author wrote, then City Hall Park would continue to serve as the center of the whole. On the other hand, "if the cupidity of commerce and the mania for Mammoth stores should over stride their own true interests and force the great hotels to abandon the southern wards and climb towards the Highlands and Harlem River, then would Union or Madison Square or both united as a double center form the future focus of the Metropolis."[1] Though amalgamation with Brooklyn would not happen for another four decades and the city expanded rapidly to the north, City Hall in lower Manhattan remained the official center. But within a dozen years an alternate civic center emerged, associated not with the city government but with a different kind of social and political power.

Union Square was designed in the 1830s as an ornament to the city by and for the upper ten thousand, New York's social elite, during a period of rapid urban expansion. Its creation was socially divisive: was it a true public space, of benefit to the city as a whole, or an exclusive amenity designed to be enjoyed by only a few? Although the Square was modeled after the quiet residential squares built in fashionable areas west of London, and was used as such during the 1840s and early 1850s, during the Civil War it was remade as a symbol of patriotism, a public space strongly associated with support for the war effort. While its physical form changed hardly at all between 1839 and 1865, the identity of the Square was fundamentally altered by the events that took place in the streets surrounding it. From the center of a residential area on the northern edge of the city designed by and for the urban elite, it became a stage on which New Yorkers enacted their support for President Lincoln and the Republican idea of American democracy.

The association between Union Square and the ideals of the united republic began in an almost accidental way, with the erection of a statue of George Washington in 1856. Originally planned as a monumental building, the memorial to the first president was a relatively modest equestrian statue situated outside the fenced-off green park, on a traffic island at the intersection of Broadway and Fourth Avenue at the southeast corner of the Square. This statue made a fitting backdrop for a series of patriotic demonstrations held between 1861 and the end of the war, concluding with the grand Metropolitan Fair held in support of the United States Sanitary Commission in 1864. In their efforts to unite New Yorkers in support of the Union during the Civil War, municipal authorities and members of the propertied middle class employed Union Square as a form of spatial propaganda. The wartime rallies staged there by the Common Council, the Chamber of Commerce, and private organizations, such as the Union League Club, turned it into a form of urban spectacle complete with flags, decorations, music, military parades, and stirring speeches. These rallies forever altered its identity, transforming it from the quiet centerpiece of a fashionable residential enclave into the primary location for civic celebrations, demonstrations, and political rallies into the twentieth century. Far from spontaneous, these spectacles were carefully choreographed displays intended to project the image of a unified citizenry dedicated to defending the city and the united republic at any cost, a message that masked an essential division between New Yorkers, one drawn along class and ethnic lines. Widely reported in the popular press, these meetings were highly effective in creating a new image for Union Square: by the end of the war it had come to be seen as a memorial to American democracy, described by Mayor George Opdyke as an "altar of patriotism." In the process its history was rewritten. No longer remembered as the unplanned result of cartography meeting topography, or as a spur to real estate development, it was reimagined as an open space purposely set aside to function as a public forum. During these wartime years the association between the Square and the ideals of the republic became ingrained in the popular imagination.

The Washington Monument

Today the statues of Washington, Lincoln, and Lafayette in Union Square are so familiar and unremarkable that we almost fail to notice them. As design elements within the wider public space they have little impact. But that was not the case when they were first completed. The statue of George Washington erected just outside the Square in 1856 was the highly potent symbolic centerpiece of a series of Civil War–era rallies. While later histories assumed the association between Union Square and this figurative embodiment of American democracy to be almost preordained, the choice of the Square as a site for a memorial to the first president was in fact somewhat arbitrary: it had no special significance in Washington's biography; rather it was a convenient open location, one frequented by the kind of affluent New Yorker that the organizing committee hoped would contribute money toward his memorial. Originally proposed in 1833, the statue was a part of a wave of civic memorials coinciding with the 1832 centennial of Washington's birth, including the magnificent column designed by Robert Mills erected in Baltimore in 1829.[2] Like most public statuary of this period, these memorials were not state-controlled projects but the work of small associations made up of citizens of a certain class and political perspective. As the art historian Kirk Savage has noted, these associations "achieved legitimacy only by manufacturing public enthusiasm (and money) for the project. Sponsors usually worked hard to sustain the fiction that they were merely agents of a more universal collective whose shared memory the project embodied."[3] In New York, local efforts began in 1833 but it was not until 1843 that the "New York Washington Monument Association of the City of New York," or Washington Monument Association (WMA), was incorporated. As with other organizations of the urban elite in this time period, "these patrician leaders assumed . . . that they were the natural custodians of the common good rather than the representative of a single social group or 'special interest.'"[4] The WMA raised funds via popular subscription—that is, private donations. In this way the group could claim that its offering was a spontaneous gift from the people to the city in which they lived.

When it was formed, the WMA acted on the understanding that the people of New York wished Washington to be memorialized in their city, but it had no clear picture of where that memorial would be placed, or what form it would take. It quickly became apparent that New Yorkers were far from united in agreement about these important details. The project received a burst of publicity in 1843 when the architect Calvin Pollard published a scheme for a 425-foot-high neo-Gothic tower commemorating the first president and the war of Independence, a scheme he sited right in the middle of Union Square, replacing the recently constructed and much celebrated Croton Fountain.[5] With a centralized pentagonal plan and ecclesiastical spires, Pollard's tower was a substantial building incorporating a large hall opening onto five projecting wings housing among them a library, memorabilia of the American Revolution, and an art gallery. The second story was to house a 100-foot-high monumental rotunda with a statue of George Washington at the center.[6] The third floor was to be used as a studio by students of the fine arts, and the spire was to be an observatory.

Pollard's audacious proposal quickly came under attack for both its architecture and its suggested location. Critics considered the choice of neo-Gothic style absurdly inappropriate for the hero of the revolution since Gothicism represented a medieval social world very much removed from the ideals of American democracy. Surely the neoclassical style was more suitable, linking as it did the modern republic with its ancient precedents? An essay in *Scientific American* argued that "Washington's monument should have been in pure Grecian, the republican style."[7] At the same time those who lived around Union Square were greatly alarmed that their newly completed park might be obliterated by the construction of such a large building. Pollard's tower was enormous, nearly twice as high as the magnificent spire then being constructed for Trinity Church on lower Broadway (then the tallest structure in the city), and its huge base would occupy almost the entire Square. While this project had little support, it clearly had some influence on the WMA: a year after an image was published in the *New York Daily Tribune*, the WMA formally solicited from the Board of Aldermen "a site on Union Place, whereupon to erect a monument to the memory of Washington, the father of his country."[8] Much to the dismay of local residents, the board granted this request. In response Samuel Ruggles, the Square's founder and a prominent local resident, and others argued that as they had paid for the improvement of the Square themselves, and gifted the resulting green space to the city, the city had no right to erect a building on it: it was to be kept as it was, forever open for use as a public space.[9] Happily for Ruggles, the mayor sided with the objectors and vetoed the resolution. This challenge to the Board of Aldermen's decision was to have important consequences, rehearsing as it did a narrative in which the public squares created in New York city between 1811 and the 1840s were transformed from spaces set aside for public use by state and city authorities for pragmatic reasons of

2.1 Calvin Pollard, Proposal for a Washington Monument in Union Square, 1843.

health and economic development, into quasi-sacred openings in the urban fabric, created by a higher power and inviolate. Ruggles was one of the chief promoters of this idea, which he summarized in the following terms: "Come what will, our open squares will remain forever imperishable. Buildings, towers, palaces may molder and crumble beneath the touch of time; but space—free, glorious, open space—will remain to bless the city forever!"[10]

Undeterred, the WMA continued to pursue the construction of a large memorial building framed within a suitably spacious urban setting. In 1847 the association announced a design competition, and Pollard was announced the winner with a scheme substantially similar to the one he had previously offered, except that it sat on a different site. The cornerstone for this building was laid with great ceremony later that year in Hamilton Square, which the city offered to the WMA as a consolation prize.[11] Located at far distant Sixty-Sixth and Sixty-Eighth Streets between Third and Fifth Avenues, Hamilton Square was one of the uptown squares laid out in the 1811 plan. Then safely undeveloped, the possibility of a memorial to Washington there stirred up far less controversy than in Union Square. Unfortunately for the association, this new site also stirred up little enthusiasm: following the cornerstone-laying ceremony, Pollard's grandly scaled proposal did not progress further. After the construction of the national Washington Monument began in Washington, DC, in 1848, support for a similar one in New York City dwindled.[12] However, the WMA was unwilling to give up on Union Square altogether. Starting over under the direction of James Lee, a shipping merchant, the group agreed to commission a more modest and less expensive memorial, an equestrian statue of Washington in bronze, to be sited in the middle of a traffic island at the southeast corner of Union Square, where Fourth Avenue meets Fourteenth Street. (Because of the Croton Fountain, it could not be sited in the middle of the Square, as at Grosvenor and Berkeley Squares in London, where equestrian statues of the king held central positions.)

Unlike Pollard's colossus, this revised version of the Washington Monument project had the support of local residents: situated outside the park, it would complement Union Square rather than subsuming it in the shadow of an enormous tower. In 1851 the sculptor Horatio Greenough was offered the commission, and Henry Kirke Brown, a young American sculptor just returned from Italy, was also asked to submit a study.[13] When Greenough died in December that year, Brown was offered a contract to complete the work alone. This contract specified that the statue should be at least fourteen feet tall, including the base, and that Washington should be depicted in military uniform. The total budget was twenty-five thousand dollars, raised by subscription in units of five hundred dollars each. (The generosity of the ninety-seven eventual donors was recognized publicly on a bronze plate affixed to the granite base of the statue.) Beginning work in his Brooklyn studio, Brown modeled his sculpture using the French sculptor Jean-Antoine Houdon's 1786 portrait bust of Washington as a reference point, along with one of the great general's actual uniforms loaned from the Capitol. The statue was cast in a Massachusetts foundry and finished in Brooklyn in June 1856, then transported in pieces via the Fulton Ferry to Union Square where it was assembled and unveiled, appropriately, on July 4th.[14] As seen in a 1903 engraving, Washington sits astride his horse with his head bare, his hat under his left arm, and his sword sheathed.[15] His right arm is raised as if to quiet his troops. Sitting atop his horse, twenty-nine feet above the ground, and pointing to the southwest, Washington was an imposing sight, one that immediately provided a new focus for the Square, drawing attention away from the fountain at the center.

Depicting Washington as a heroic emancipator, Brown's equestrian statue evoked imperial precedent. By contrast, those responsible for commissioning the Washington Monument in Washington, DC, were careful to avoid such connotations. In his 1791 design for the layout of the new national capital, the French engineer Pierre L'Enfant had included a giant equestrian statue of Washington at the point where the two axes of his plan converged at the edge of the Potomac River. In this way, Washington was the generator and point of origin for the whole city. However, L'Enfant's use of such Baroque symbolism, with a single imperial figure at the center, was rejected as inappropriate for a nation built on the republican principle that men should govern themselves, that no one citizen should be raised up above the rest. When Washington died in 1799, Congress agreed to erect a tomb, an outdoor mausoleum in the form of a 100-foot-high stepped pyramid designed by architect Benjamin Latrobe, clearly indebted to the work of French revolutionary architect Étienne -Louis Boullée, who employed simple geometric forms and enormous interior spaces to evoke a sense of the sublime. While Latrobe's scheme was never realized, and various other proposals for a national Washington Monument were debated until Robert Mills's simple obelisk was finally completed in 1884, the monarchical associations of the equestrian statue were always emphatically rejected in the capital.[16]

New Yorkers did not share those reservations, however. Though he had returned from Italy in search of a naturalistic form of American sculpture, Brown remained indebted to the classical tradition in which the pose of the equestrian rider is typical for a military commander. His model for Washington was probably the classical statue of Emperor Marcus Aurelius on the

2.2 Henry Kirke Brown, Statue of Washington, 1856. George R. Hall, engraver, 1903.

Palatine Hill in Rome.[17] Brown's statue was intended to depict the General on "Evacuation Day," November 25, 1783, the date of the retreat of British troops from New York City following the end of the Revolutionary War. On that day Generals Washington and George Clinton led their troops down Broadway to reclaim the city, and the Stars and Stripes replaced the British flag at the Battery.[18] The erection of Brown's statue cemented a popular story that crowds of rejoicing citizenry met Washington on his journey into the city at the future site of Union Square.[19] Over time the original reason for locating New York's Washington Monument there was forgotten, and the site came to be seen as the natural and only possible one.

If realized, Pollard's neo-Gothic Washington Monument would have offered the residents of New York City a very different kind of public memorial than Brown's statue, both a monument and also a functional public building. Pollard's tower was not only a repository of relics of the revolution; it also contained within it a number of educational resources: a library, a museum, and an art gallery. It was, in effect, a building of "living memory," dedicated to the president's life and achievements and also to the continuation of his political ideals via a program of public education. Brown's Washington Monument was quite a different, not an autonomous building but the figurative center of a larger public space. This space had no designated function such as that of a library or museum; rather, the activities that took place there came to symbolize in a more direct way the democratic ideals upon which the nation was founded.

In a city lacking many public monuments, Brown's statue quickly assumed an important role. Erected as a permanent memorial to Washington and the Revolutionary War, it became the focal point for public celebrations and meetings over the next two decades, events that would fundamentally reshape the meaning and use of Union Square as a public space. On regular days the statue served as the center of a traffic intersection, bypassed by horse-drawn carts and railcars. On days of celebration and demonstration, however, it became the center of attention, saluted by military parades, strewn with flags and illuminated by gas lamps and fireworks. Soon after it was completed the statue was incorporated into major civic rituals including a parade celebrating the completion of the Atlantic Cable connecting the United States and Ireland via telegraph on September 1st, 1858. Though Union Square did not serve as a terminus for this parade (it extended from the Battery to the Crystal Palace on the site of what is now Bryant Park), the route took a detour in order to march around Washington's statue.[20] In an unintentionally incongruous act of civic pageantry, the Revolutionary army general responsible for cutting ties with Great Britain was incorporated into an event celebrating renewed ones. During the Civil War, lithographed images of huge crowds gathered around the statue would be circulated across the country and the world, intended as illustrations of New York's apparently unanimous and unequivocal support for the continuation of the American republic.

The Sumter Rally

While City Hall Park and the Battery were given over to military barracks and a hospital during the Civil War, the elliptical green park at Fourteenth Street and Broadway served a different function.[21] Adjacent to the homes of the city's monied elite, it became a public extension of their political views, a space of spectacle and rhetoric that they manipulated in order to collect support for their own agenda. Organized with great haste, the first and largest rally held in Union Square was convened a little over a week after Confederate troops fired on the besieged Fort Sumter in Charleston, South Carolina, on April 12th, 1861. This attack, made on behalf of the seven Southern States that had declared their secession from the Union between December 1860 and the spring of 1861, effectively started the Civil War. Though New Yorkers were deeply ambivalent about the coming war, news of the attack generated a brief period of unity.[22] The event produced a rare and temporary unanimity between the Democrats who controlled city politics, businessmen with strong economic ties to the Southern States, and the wealthy Republican minority with social links to the abolitionist movement. Beginning with a meeting of the city's elite at one of the grand houses on the periphery of Union Square, leading figures of these factions came together to plan a mass gathering that would demonstrate to the city, the nation, and the world, that New York supported the Union and the authority of the Constitution.

When a group of self-described leading merchants of the city met at 10 East Fourteenth Street, the home of the merchant Robert McCurdy, on April 15th to plan an immediate response to the Southern hostilities, theirs was one of several planned public demonstrations. In another location a group affiliated with the Democratic Party was organizing a meeting for the steps of City Hall, the traditional location for civic meetings. In order to coordinate these efforts into a single event with greater impact, a meeting was arranged of two hundred representatives of various groups at the Chamber of Commerce at William and Cedar Streets on April 17th.[23] This meeting brought together representatives of various political factions in order to plan what the *New York Times* described as a "Mass Meeting of the citizens of New-York to sustain the Government in the approaching contest with treason and rebellion."[24] At first the organizers planned to hold the rally in the Great Hall at the Cooper Institute in Astor Place, the site of President Lincoln's famous election oration a few months earlier. However, it soon became apparent that this auditorium was insufficient for the size of the planned event; it would hold three thousand men at the most, and at least twenty-five thousand were expected at the rally. Dry-goods merchant

Simeon B. Chittenden proposed Union Square instead (the seconder was Samuel Ruggles), with the Washington Monument as the site of the main speaker's stand, an idea that was enthusiastically adopted.[25]

Union Square had been used for political rallies before, particularly during the 1856 and 1860 presidential elections, and various strategies had been established for choreography and decoration, including the placing of stands and the arrangement of flags, lighting, and music.[26] The new publicness of these events reflected the expansion of the electorate. Between the 1820s and the 1850s the ranks of voters had augmented significantly from an increase in urban population and the extension of the franchise to white men who did not own property. (Black male property owners could also vote in New York State after 1821, although this restriction meant that less than 1 percent of the black population were entitled to do so.)[27] Consequently the spaces associated with the political process grew beyond meetings in private homes and public halls to include outdoor rallies in city parks. Once candidates had been selected through the mechanism of sometimes raucous public meetings, campaigns adopted the theatrical dressing and choreography of earlier civic celebrations in their outdoor rallies, rallies that proliferated during the fall electoral season. In September of 1856, for example, the *New York Herald* reported that Republicans held a nighttime rally at which Massachusetts Senator Anson Burlingame gave a rousing speech denouncing slavery. Describing the scene, the *Herald* noted that "there was music on the platform, a large torch light kept blazing at the base of the Washington Monument, and two electric lights stationed at either side in front. . . . There was the usual display of flags and banners."[28] A month later the anti-immigrant "American" or "Know Nothing" party held a demonstration on the same site in support of their presidential candidate, Millard Fillmore, at which "three large platforms were erected at as many angles on the Square. An electric light was stationed in front of the Union Square Hotel . . . and large bonfires at various points were kept blazing."[29] In May of 1860 a rally was held in the same location in support of Texas Senator Samuel Houston's bid for the Democratic presidential nomination. This included "a band of music, a bevy of boys with flaming torches, a number of lanterns, a display of fireworks, calcium light, bonfires, and the firing of cannon."[30] These events were lively affairs with much heckling, and the wittiest interjections were duly reported in the newspapers the next day along with the text of the speeches.

Following the attack on Fort Sumter, the 1861 rally was to be entirely serious, befitting the gravity of the situation. This was a highly unusual gathering of civic groups of opposing political views—a rare display of unanimity. The organizing committee had eighty-seven vice presidents chosen from among the leading men of the community, including the millionaire industrialist Peter Cooper and the financier John J. Astor. The Republican-supporting *New York Times* had no doubt it would be a momentous event: "This will doubtless be the largest public meeting ever held in this City, or indeed on this continent. For once the people of New-York are entirely united, and in promoting the objects for which this meeting is held, they will speak with one voice."[31] The *New York Herald*, which backed the Democratic Party, also voiced its support. The meeting was scheduled for Saturday, April 20th, beginning at three o'clock in the afternoon. Most businesses (which would normally be open) obeyed the request of the organizing committee to shutter their doors for the day. From the early morning, people began to surge northward along Broadway and Fourth Avenue from the heavily populated downtown district. Soon after midday crowds began to gather. As the organizing committee later reported,

> The streets were thronged with a surging mass of people, and the national colors waved from every building. The inhabitants, with scarcely an exception, wore the national colors in some form—rosettes, badges, or improvised cockades. Union Square was a red, white and blue wonder; not only the adjacent hotels, the Clarendon, the Everett, the Union Place, and the Monument House, displayed national colors in profusion, but from nearly every private house, the Spingler Institute, and from the Church of the Puritans, the flag of our Union waved proudly.[32]

Estimating the crowd at between 100,000 to 250,000 people, newspaper reports placed great emphasis on its inclusiveness. "It was a gathering of all classes of our citizens," reported the *New York Post*, "old and young, merchants and mechanics, professional men and laborers, who gathered to express their determination to uphold the union and the Constitution."[33]

Since the theme of the rally was the defense of the nation, the Washington Monument was an appropriate focal point, one that provided a suitably stirring backdrop for patriotic speeches. The organizers played this to full advantage: the tattered flag that had hung over Fort Sumter was hoisted over Washington's head as a poignant talisman of the cause. The meeting was presided over by former United States Senator and Secretary of the Treasury, John A. Dix, who addressed the crowd from the main speakers' stand constructed at the base of the monument. According to popular lore, Dix, a Democrat, had sent a particularly direct telegram to Treasury agents in the south early in the hostilities: "If any one attempts to haul down the American flag, shoot him on the spot."[34] Linking the rally directly to the attack on Fort Sumter, Major Robert Anderson, the commanding officer of the Fort, was the guest of honor. In the age before mechanical sound amplification, no single voice could reach a crowd of this size, so in addition to the main stand three additional ones were erected next to the iron fence surrounding the Square; one opposite the Everett House Hotel on the north side at Seventeenth Street and Fourth Avenue; one opposite the Parish House at the corner of Seventeenth Street and Broadway; and one to the south opposite University Place and Fourteenth Street.

After Major Anderson and his officers were introduced and the benediction was given, the speeches began. They were blunt in their message: the time for diplomacy and political debate was over; the South must understand that New York was unified in its support of the Union; and finally, New Yorkers were ready to take up arms.[35] The speech of Senator Edward Baker of Oregon, who had led a New York regiment in the Mexican-American War, summarizes the tone: "The hour for conciliation is past," he said. "The gathering for battle is at hand and the country requires that every man shall do his duty. . . . If Providence shall will it, this feeble hand shall draw a sword, never yet dishonored, not to fight for honor on a foreign field, but for country, for home, for law, for government, for Constitution, for right, for freedom, for humanity."[36] The speakers included not only Republicans like Baker, a close friend of the President, but also those who had adamantly opposed the coming war, including the Democratic mayor of New York City, Fernando Wood. Acting to protect the economy of the city, which he believed would be devastated by war, Wood had at one time advocated that New York City secede from the state, forming a neutral city he called the "Free City of Tri-Insula," made up of Manhattan, Long Island, and Staten Island. This city would continue to trade with the southern states.[37] On the rostrum at the mass rally, however, Wood was unambiguous in his support for the war, saying,

> The Chairman has announced that Col. Baker, the gentleman who has so eloquently addressed you today, proposes to raise a brigade of New-Yorkers if New-York will bear the expense. I here, as Mayor of this City, so far as I have the power to speak, pledge for the Corporation that same. . . . I am willing to give up all sympathies, and, if you please, all errors of judgment upon all national questions. . . . I am with you in this contest. We know no party now. We are for maintaining the integrity of the National Union intact.[38]

2.3 "The 'Union' Mass Meeting Held in Union Square, New York on the 20th of April 1861," *Illustrated London News* (May 18, 1861).

The practical outcome of this meeting was the creation of the bipartisan Union Defense Committee (UDC), made up of the mayor, other city officials, and prominent citizens, comprising thirteen Democrats and twelve Republicans in all.[39] With the support of Congress, the UDC immediately began to mobilize, raising money to purchase supplies including weapons for the Union army, and arranging for the enlistment of troops. Beyond this the UDC kept up the publicity machine for the Union cause in New York, capitalizing on the success of the Sumter rally by organizing others of a similar nature.

Deliberately staged as a media event, the April 1861 rally was widely reported in newspapers in the United States and abroad. The meeting resulted in some of the earliest photographic depictions of large urban crowds, including stereoscopic views. These images were turned into engravings reproduced in popular magazines including the American *Harper's Weekly* and *The Illustrated London News* in the month following the event. In these two journals, images placed the viewer at the southern end of Union Square, looking north toward the Washington Monument, with the Everett House Hotel in the distance, and the park surrounded by its iron fence to the left.[40]

In both cases the huge crowd, vigorously waving American flags, takes up the foreground and stretches as far as the eye can see; George Washington has been given an enormous flag almost as big as he is. While the American publication clearly shows orators atop the speaker's stands (one under the Washington Monument and one next to the park fence), the English journal eliminates the stands, giving the impression that this meeting was a spontaneous gathering comprised only of the surging crowd and Washington himself. This reading of the meeting is no doubt one that its organizers hoped to encourage; in this way support for the Union would be seen as the will of the people of New York.

The Sumter rally in Union Square initiated a huge mobilization of people and matériel, an effort that lasted four years. The unanimity of that rally was short-lived, however. As the wealthiest city in the nation, the center of trade and industrial production, New York was the major financial backer of Lincoln's army, supplying uniforms and equipment for soldiers and their horses, ships for the navy, and medical care for the wounded. Its publishing industry also generated support for the Union cause through the Republican newspapers, led by the *New York Times*. Additionally, the city was a great source of manpower because of its large population. In the early months of the war, dozens of volunteer militias formed, comprising men of all occupations and classes. But despite this heavy investment, the city soon retreated into its established political cliques; support for Lincoln's government began to disintegrate during the summer, particularly following the disastrous Battle of Bull Run. Democrats were split between those who supported the war but not what they saw as Lincoln's unwarranted expansion of federal powers (so-called War Democrats), and those who sought peace with the South and the continuation of a national economy based on slavery (known as "Peace Democrats"). Subsequent rallies were organized in order to revive the patriotic fervor of the first mass meeting, but none matched it in size or bipartisan support.

Union Square continued to play a symbolic role as the center of support for the war effort. It was the site of major rallies in July 1862 and April 1863, and in April 1864 it hosted the great Metropolitan Fair organized to raise funds for the United States Sanitary Commission. The 1862 and 1863 meetings were designed to recall the Sumter rally, with the same placing of speaker's stands, including a principal one under the Washington Monument. The theme, as before, was the need to put aside party differences in order to support the government and answer its practical needs. Organized by the Chamber of Commerce and the Union Defense Committee, the 1862 rally came at a difficult time: the president had called on New York State to deliver three hundred thousand volunteer troops, an unpopular request. As the Union Army faced a grueling campaign, the patriotic fervor of 1861 had declined significantly, and opinions about the war were increasingly divided along class lines. New York's role as a major supplier to the military had led to a boom in business and the creation of many jobs, making it difficult to persuade men to enlist. Working-class families were wary about the loss of income should a male family member, often the only breadwinner, enter the army.[41]

At the 1862 rally speakers hammered on the theme that the men of New York had a duty to enlist, and offered up Union Square as the fitting place to pledge support for the army. Mayor George Opdyke conjured up a religious atmosphere, saying, "We have come to renew our vows on the altar of patriotism; and at what place so fitting as in the presence of a monument erected to the memory of Washington?"[42] The rally was a somber affair: the flags, bunting, and cheering crowds of earlier meetings were now augmented by the presence of soldiers who had seen battle. The *New York Times* reported: "Two immense wagons, drawn by superb six-horse teams, with fancy trappings, and wreathed with streamers, indicating that they belonged to 'the New-England Soldiers' Relief Association,' contributed greatly to the emotions of the scene with their pallid loads of wounded men, whose sufferings are identified with nearly every struggle of the war."[43] Facing these men, the businessman and financier Abiel Abbott Low claimed Union Square as a sacred site, "consecrated to the Union by the great pledges recorded here a year ago in April," its "vast concourse" representing the nation itself. The same rhetoric was employed the following year on the second anniversary of the fall of Fort Sumter, April 11th, 1863. Decorated with American flags and evergreens, the number one stand erected under the Washington Monument was now supplemented by a "contrivance got up by Prof. Grant to render the speaker's voices audible at a greater distance." Here Mayor Opdyke reinforced the sacred imagery of the Square: "For the third time since the outbreak of this wicked rebellion we have assembled at this spot, consecrated to civil liberty by the statue of Washington, to renew our pledges of patriotic devotion to our country."[44] And once again the monument was invoked as a repository of patriotic fealty: with soldierly directness, General John Fremont asked the crowd to renew the pledge they had made two years earlier to return the flag that hung from Washington's hand to fly over Fort Sumter once again.[45] Despite the soaring rhetoric and the claims that party politics had been put aside, the 1863 rally did not represent all New Yorkers. This meeting was the work of a new organization, the Loyal National League, which had close ties to Lincoln and the Republican Party. At the same time

War Democrats were planning their own gathering under the auspices of their own organization, the Loyal League of Union Citizens, to be held in Madison Square a few days later.[46] Though the two meetings had the same aim, it was clear that the Union Square rallies were now overtly political, associated with the agenda of a minority, the city's wealthiest and most socially connected citizens.

The war was not going well for the North, and New Yorkers were voicing their doubts even more loudly than before. The city was a major conduit for trade with the South and many local businessmen believed the abolition of slavery would lead to economic disaster. In the fall of 1862 Democrat Horatio Seymour was reelected as governor of New York on a platform deeply critical of the president. Democratic politicians were also in power at City Hall and some spoke openly of making peace with the Confederacy. In response, a group of the self-described "intellectual aristocracy" created a social organization designed to change the tide of popular opinion.[47] In February 1863, the Rev. Henry Bellows, minister of All Souls Unitarian Church at Twentieth Street and Fourth Avenue, and a group of like-minded associates including Samuel Ruggles and Frederick Law Olmsted, then the Superintendent of Central Park, founded the Union League Club. This was to be a gentlemen's club with its own quarters, including a wine room, restaurant, and billiard room. A prospectus solicited members from socially prominent families, the future leaders of the city and of the country. In May of 1863 the club opened its doors at the former Parish mansion at 26 East Seventeenth Street.

Union Square was an attractive location for the Union League Club. As the city expanded northward wealthy families like the Parishes vacated their homes for newer and grander ones near Gramercy Park and Madison Square. Though increasingly commercial, the area was still highly respectable, well regarded for its fashionable restaurants including the French-style Maison Dorée, which had opened in the former Penniman House at Fourteenth Street between Broadway and University Place, and the uptown branch of Delmonico's a block further west at Fourteenth Street and Fifth Avenue.[48] An imposing four-story building with a balcony over the entrance, the Parish mansion was ideally situated for the Club's purposes. As Bellows wrote, "It was a fortunate site for the opening labors of the club—in full view of one of the chief places of public gatherings, military reviews and popular demonstrations; easy of access, and an advertisement in itself of the existence and activity of the association."[49]

If the Republican-dominated Union League Club was small and private, open to only a few male members drawn from the city's most elite strata, Union Square was its large and public extension. Over the course of the war, the club commandeered it as a site on which to manifest its political ideals and demonstrate its power. When Bellows wrote the early history of the organization, he claimed the spectacular Sumter rally of April 1861 as its first success.[50] Though the meeting was staged a full two years before the club was established, many of those involved in planning it lived around Union Square and would go on to be its founding members. As historian Michael Shapiro has noted, "The Republicans considered themselves the national party and Union Square had become their national stage."[51] No event proved this more than the trooping of the colors of the Twentieth United States Colored Regiment in front of the Union League Club on March 5th 1864. This was an elaborately staged spectacle designed to reassert Republican control over the urban landscape and to counter the anarchic political violence of the previous summer's draft riots. Infamous in the history of New York City for their wide geographic extent and brutality, the riots were sparked by the threat of conscription.[52] On March 1st, 1863, the Federal Enrollment Act was passed; this was a form of conscription requiring male citizens between twenty and forty-five years of age to make themselves available for military service. The act enflamed the city's Irish immigrant population, an ethnic group hostile to abolitionism and resentful of being made to fight what they saw as a "rich man's war." On the morning of July 13th a draft lottery taking place at Third Avenue and Forty-Seventh Street was attacked by members of a local fire company. After setting fire to the draft office, the anti-conscription mob marched south, increasing in size. Rioters ransacked and tried to burn the homes of draft officers and wealthy New Yorkers believed to be Unionist supporters, including the Fifth Avenue mansion of Mayor Opdyke. Black men and women and the institutions associated with them such as the Colored Orphan Asylum at Forty-Third Street and Fifth Avenue also became targets.[53] Heavily outnumbered, the police at first concentrated on protecting downtown commercial properties near the docks, as well as armories and government storehouses.

Though New York had seen politically motivated riots before, including the Astor Place Riot of 1849 and the Dead Rabbit Riot of 1857, the draft riots were unprecedented in their scale and scope, and horrifying to those who witnessed individuals beaten and lynched. They underscored not only the conservative beliefs of many working-class New Yorkers, including acceptance of the continuation of slavery, but also a deep-seated anti-authoritarianism. As historian David Scobey has written, "The draft riot was the signal event in translating [a] geography of working-class violence into a cartography of bourgeois fear. The riot offered propertied New Yorkers a nightmare vision of insurrectionary violence, obscure and subterranean in its origins, but contagious and ubiquitous in its effects."[54] In response property owners formed militias such as the Stuyvesant Square Home Guard in order to defend their homes and businesses.[55] Members of the Union League Club armed themselves and barricaded their clubrooms in the belief that they too were in danger. Olmsted in particular was furious. Claiming that "the most dangerous foes of the Republic are in New York City," he proposed that "the metropolis be treated like New Orleans or any other city in the occupied South."[56] In the weeks following the riots, the club vowed to come to the aid of black New Yorkers, both to help individuals in need and to publicly express abhorrence at the results of the riot. Besides supporting charities that gave food, clothing, and shelter to the wounded and destitute, it lobbied the government to allow black men to join the Union army and financed the formation of the Twentieth United States Colored Regiment, the first of its kind in New York.

Given the circumstances of its formation, the Twentieth attracted a great deal of media attention. When the thousand-strong regiment was sent to New Orleans in the spring of 1864, the Union League capitalized on this interest with an elaborate sending-off ceremony they knew would be covered in all the newspapers. On March 5th the soldiers were ferried from their training camp on Riker's Island to a dock at East Twenty-Sixth Street; from there they marched in formation with muskets and fixed bayonets to Union Square. *Harper's Weekly* noted the emotion accompanying the event: "The regiment advanced into the open space amidst the cheers and tears of those who felt the significance of the spectacle. The soldiers had handled their muskets but five days; but when they obeyed the 'order arms' there was a solid, simultaneous ring upon the pavement, which enforced the heartiest applause."[57] Standing to attention in front of the Union League Club, the regiment was presented with its regimental flag by Mrs. John Jacob Astor on behalf of the "Mothers, Wives, and Sisters of Members of the New York Union League." Afterward, a segregated luncheon was served: "On the Square the regiment regaled itself on sandwiches, coffee and cake furnished by the club, while the members, their ladies and the officers had luncheon at Jauch's or Delmonico's or the Maison Dorée."[58] League members wore formal daytime dress of black frock coats, light trousers, cravats, and top hats, while the soldiers were clad in crisp blue Union army uniforms. The whole event was a carefully crafted display of Republican propaganda intended as a message to those who had supported the assault and murder of black New Yorkers during the draft riots: Union Square was a place of order and Christian brotherhood where white New Yorkers associated with, protected, and were willing to be protected by black men. The symbolism of

2.4 "The Twentieth United States Colored Troops Receiving Their Colors on Union Square, March 5, 1864," *Harper's Weekly: A Journal of Civilization* (March 19, 1864).

the ceremony was clear to journalists. Both the *New York Times* and the *New York Tribune* wrote in enthusiastic support, with the *Tribune*'s editor Horace Greeley describing the event as a historic one that should make all New Yorkers proud. The vehemently anti-abolitionist *Herald*, however, warned that the ceremony, in which upper-class white women mixed with black soldiers, was a trigger to "miscegenation."[59]

As politically potent as it was, the trooping of the colors of the Twentieth Regiment was an ephemeral event. Less than a month later, on April 4th, 1864, a different and more ambitious undertaking confirmed the identification between Union Square and the war effort.[60] While the trooping of the color was intended to display New York's social progressiveness through its commitment to abolition, the Metropolitan Fair was intended to showcase the formidable economic and industrial power the city had marshaled in support of the war effort, and to raise funds for the United States Sanitary Commission, a privately funded organization dedicated to overseeing and improving sanitation in military camps and hospitals. The same men who had started the Union League Club founded the commission: Henry

Bellows was its first president and Frederick Law Olmsted acted as its executive secretary. The fair itself marks one of the earliest times that women had a significant say in designing the public space of the city.[61] A twenty-five-member committee of Union League Club wives secured the site from the city, advised on contracts for the temporary buildings, and arranged the exhibitions displayed inside. The effort involved was considerable: the ladies persuaded businessmen and manufacturers to lend or donate a huge variety of objects from clothing and musical instruments to fine art and agricultural equipment, all intended to represent "the material resources of the great city of New York, and of the regions directly tributary to it."[62] The fair opened with a parade of military bands and ten thousand troops which marched from Union Square to City Hall Park, where it was reviewed by Major Robert Anderson, the hero of Fort Sumter.[63]

Occupying half a dozen existing buildings and three purpose-built ones, the scale of the fair was impressive, especially during wartime. The focus was a wooden exhibition hall three hundred feet long and ninety feet wide erected immediately in front of the Union League Club rooms. The architect was Peter B. Wight, better known for his Venetian Gothic–style National Academy of Design then nearing completion close by at Twenty-Third Street and Fourth Avenue. The National Academy was a monument to the antislavery cause and to the cultural aspirations of the city's elite after the war was over. For the purposes of the Metropolitan Fair, Wight designed a temporary and much simpler building. This housed a display of technological innovations from countries around the world, a music hall for concerts, and a children's area complete with ice skating rink and ice cream parlor. One of the most popular features was the "Knickerbocker Kitchen," a replica of a colonial-era New Amsterdam kitchen where black servants dressed in eighteenth-century clothes served coffee, doughnuts, and waffles to visitors.[64] Outside the main exhibition building, the park was temporarily renamed the "Ladies Garden," featuring a specially created floral display and an observatory tower from which the spectacle could be viewed. As with the earlier patriotic rallies, images of the Metropolitan Fair were published in all the major national newspapers and popular magazines, including a newspaper produced by the fair organizers. Thirty thousand visitors attended, raising over one million dollars for the Sanitary Commission.

In the early months of 1865, the war drew to a close following a series of debilitating losses by the Confederate army. New Yorkers once again came together to plan a monster rally, this time to celebrate peace, and Union Square was the logical place to hold it. This event, which took place on March 6th, served as a bookend to the great rally of 1861, reintroducing

2.5 The Metropolitan Fair Building, Union Square, 1864.

the various themes rehearsed there over the previous four years: the political unity of the initial Sumter rally; the consecration of Union Square as an "altar of patriotism"; and the display of New York's industrial might exhibited at the Metropolitan Fair. It was at this concluding rally that a new narrative about the role of New York City in relation to the nation, and the role of Union Square in relation to the city, emerged. Organized by a Citizens Committee made up of both Republicans and Democrats, the celebration began with a victory parade around the city in the old style, traveling south from Union Square down Broadway to City Hall Park and back again via the Bowery, Fourth Avenue, and Madison Square Park. Extending seven miles and lasting six hours, it followed the formula set by earlier parades dating back to the eighteenth century, including three divisions: military, civic and industrial, and the fire department. Mounted on horse-drawn carts, the industrial displays included the representation of the manufacture of a Steinway piano, working displays of Singer sewing machines, and four horse trucks distributing packaged coffee. Two elephants and two camels brought up the rear.

Again, speakers addressed the crowds from stands erected around the east, west, and north edges of the Square. The 1861 Sumter rally had assumed the character of a mass civic vow made by the people of New York to the president to help defend the nation, and this was a recognition that the vow had been kept. The Citizens Committee resolved that the "solemn pledges given to the Government by the people of the City of New York, assembled in Union Square on the 20th of April 1861 have been redeemed with fidelity and with honor, and . . . it is fitting and just that upon the same spot the tidings of victory should be mingled with the acclamations of a grateful people."[65] The speakers emphasized New York's unique contribution to the war both practically and symbolically, referring to the city's role as the economic engine of the country, and to its historic significance as the first capital of the republic: "Commercial and manufacturing New York comes here to take an account of stock and war of victory. . . . Her merchants of all parties and her mechanics of all creeds have poured forth their wealth or sacrificed their hard earnings to maintain inviolate the Republic of Washington."[66] The incredible growth and great economic success of New York City in the first half of the nineteenth century had seen it emerge as the most powerful city in the nation, and now it was being invoked as the preserver of the republic, with Union Square, and the Washington Monument as the physical embodiments of that heroic role.

The celebration of 1865 was tempered by news of the fatal assassination attempt on President Lincoln a month later. Lincoln's death was the occasion of yet another massive parade up Broadway, a somber one this time, and one of the last to include representatives from all sections of New York City society, from wealthy merchants to common laborers. As part of its final journey from Washington, DC, to his home state of Illinois, the president's coffin lay in state in City Hall before being ceremoniously paraded to Union Square where he was eulogized.[67] In the following months, the Union League Club commissioned Henry K. Brown to sculpt a bronze statue of Lincoln to stand at the southwest corner of the Square as a complement to the Washington Monument.[68] As with the earlier sculpture, it was paid for by popular subscription, at a total cost of fifteen thousand dollars. However, the political power structure of the city had changed since the 1850s. When the League petitioned the city for an area of land equivalent in size to the one on which Washington stood, the Democratic-controlled council refused. When Brown's statue was dedicated in a modest ceremony in the fall of 1870, it stood on small granite plinth, inscribed with words from Lincoln's Second Inaugural address: "With malice toward none, with charity for all."[69] Though denied a monument as large as Washington's, the erection of the statue was a major victory for the elite New Yorkers associated with the Union League Club. Throughout the war they had battled the majority of citizens who remained highly ambivalent about the war. Now Union Square had gained a second memorial, one that publicly commemorated Lincoln as a counterpart to Washington.

Depicted wearing contemporary dress, the statue was an affront to the conventions of art that many critics saw as an assault on the dignity of the great man. The *Tribune* summarized the general view of the popular press;

2.6 Lincoln Statue, Union Square, ca. 1917.

the statue was, "ugly, ungracious, undignified. The pantaloons are hideous, the cloak is an anachronism, wholly misplaced on his shoulders."[70] Lincoln's face was rendered vacant, inexpressive, others thought. Even the siting of the statue was subject to derision; facing south, Lincoln turned his back on the Square, looking instead toward a less lofty focal point, the stores strung along Fourteenth Street. These criticisms perhaps masked enmity for Brown's larger goal: to salute Lincoln not as a military hero, but as a civilian one. An adamant believer in the cause of abolitionism, Brown had initially planned to depict Lincoln pointing heavenward with one hand and gesturing with the other toward a partially clad black male figure kneeling at his feet, representing a freed slave. As the art historian Kirk Savage has noted, this would have been exceptional since the figure of a contemporary slave did not otherwise appear in American statuary until the 1870s. According to Brown's biographer, the commissioning committee rejected this proposal "because of fear that the figure of a negro in a public monument would arouse the resentment of Irish citizens."[71] Brown instead depicted the president clutching a scroll on which the Emancipation Proclamation was inscribed. Though the Union League was happy to support the ceremonial presence of the Twentieth Regiment in "their" Square, they shied away from including a black man as part of a permanent memorial.

While the final result was generally regarded as artistically poor, the dedication of the Lincoln statue continued the precedent set by Brown's earlier statue: Union Square would be a place to commemorate American heroes. In 1870 *Appleton's Journal* voiced the opinion: "We could wish now to see other angles of Union Square filled with similar memorials to some of our great men."[72] Their suggestion of Admiral David Farragut, the Civil War hero of "Damn the torpedoes!" fame, as a suitable subject was not acted on, but in 1876 a third statue was erected, a depiction of the Marquis de Lafayette, the French-born general who had fought on behalf of the Americans during the Revolution. Sculpted by Frédéric-Auguste Bartholdi, who later designed the Statue of Liberty, it was commissioned by the French government in appreciation for aid that New York had sent to Paris after it was besieged by Germany in the winter of 1870–71. Lafayette is presented "stepping from a boat onto the American shore, his left hand extended, his right held against his breast, clasping his sword."[73] After the French consul presented the statue to the city and Bartholdi pulled a cord to unveil it, a military band played the "Marseillaise," the revolutionary anthem of the French Republic. Twenty years later, the Square would often echo with that stirring tune, played at public gatherings where orators demanded a new American Revolution. However, at this time the music signified only a memorial to the revolutionary wars of the previous century.

A Theater for the National Voice

After the Civil War, Union Square took on the form of a public memorial to patriotism, a civic expression of national unity all but erasing the deep divisions that existed over the validity of the war at the time it was fought. As Savage has noted, though nineteenth-century public monuments such as this were designed and commissioned by particular people with their own agendas, they often "exercised a curious power to erase their own political origins and become sacrosanct."[74] Following the Civil War the Square became the site of annual Memorial Day celebrations organized by the Grand Army of the Republic, a veterans organization, at which the statues of Washington and Lincoln were decorated with floral bouquets and wreaths in memoriam to the war dead.[75] Memorial Day attracted crowds made up of all classes and ethnic backgrounds, together with many African Americans, including the journalist Frederick Douglass, who gave the oration speech in 1878. Douglass accepted the invitation to speak "in generous recognition of that class of our fellow-citizens to which I belong; a class hitherto excluded by popular prejudice from prominent participation in the memorial glories of our common country."[76]

Though the symbolic power of these statues remained strong (ceremonies decorating them with wreaths were held every Memorial Day well into the mid-twentieth century, when they became symbols of patriotism designed to counter the "red" identity of Union Square), it was the open space itself that was increasingly revered. Even at the time of the Metropolitan Fair, Samuel Ruggles, the Square's founder, regarded the park and not the statue of Washington as its most sacred component. In a speech given at the opening of the fair, he claimed important roles for Broadway and Union Square in the founding of the nation, telling his audience that Washington rode down that street on his way to take New York City from the British in 1783, pausing at the present-day Fourteenth Street to receive the adulation of grateful citizens. Ruggles also asserted that the Square had a link to the Constitution through another historical figure, Gouverneur Morris.

> The self-same Gouverneur Morris who gave the finishing touch to the draft of the Constitution, as Commissioner of the State of New York, under the act of 1807, stamped indelibly upon the map of this our Island of Manhattan the large public square known as "Union Place." With eagle eye piercing the future, Mr. Morris selected the very spot on which we are now standing, then far away from the dust and din of the city, to become the very center and heart of the great metropolis—discerned by his prophetic vision, to bear the name, and to be forever consecrated to the memory of that glorious and immortal Union which he had labored so successfully to call into being.[77]

With these stirring words, Ruggles laid claim to Union Square not only as the geographic center of the city, but also as a national monument to the political ideals on which the nation was founded. Despite the iconographic power of the statue of Washington, Ruggles located its symbolic value in its emptiness:

> Enclosing nothing but open space, the very creation of God himself, subject to no decay, and impervious to the "tooth of time," it is destined, like the square of imperial Trajan in the Eternal City, to remain for all coming time the type of our continental Union, and the bright and imperishable jewel of the city.[78]

In other words, he assigned the Square a quasi-sacred identity as the symbol of American democracy and in the process rewrote its history as a space expressly designed for this purpose.

The Metropolitan Fair had propagated a considerable amount of mythologizing about "old" New York, including the Knickerbocker Kitchen, and Ruggles's speech extended that mythologizing to include Union Square itself. In his speech he claimed it was deliberately designed to support participatory democracy. The triangular parcels of land left over by the imposition of the ellipse on the grid were expressly made for "the assemblage of large masses of our citizens in public meetings," he claimed, ignoring the more practical function of the ellipse as a way to ensure a smooth flow of traffic.[79] The use of the Square for huge rallies in support of the Union demonstrated the correctness and utility of that original design, he believed. These meetings illustrated the particular role it played as a site for expressions of public will, a "spacious national opening," "a theater adequate to the utterance of the national voice."[80] At the time of Ruggles's 1864 speech, the city was invested in a significant public works program to create a large new park in the northern section of Manhattan, a park intended by its creators and supporters to be a model democratic landscape notable for its naturalism. In his description of Union Square, Ruggles's conjured up an image of a different kind of democratic public space: a large, empty plaza where the crowd rather than commemorative statuary or natural terrain was the aesthetic focus. The coexistence of these two models of public park—one dedicated to passive recreation and the other to active political action—was to become even sharper in the next decade, when Frederick Law Olmsted and Calvert Vaux were called upon to undertake major renovations.

3

Olmsted and Vaux's Plaza, 1865–1872

In 1867 the *New York Times* took stock of the businesses that had moved into the south and west sides of Union Square during the past year. While some private dwellings remained on the northern and eastern sides, a post–Civil War economic boom had led to "numerous and striking" changes.[1] On the southwestern corner a dry goods store, W. F. Sherwin, had replaced the elegant society restaurant, the Maison Dorée. Nearby, Henry Maillard, a confectioner, opened an iron-and-brick store with plate glass windows and elegant and costly decorations, where he created his "Chocolat de L'Union Franco-Americane."[2] On the west side of the Square shoppers could find Messrs. Miller and Co., a ladies boot and shoe emporium; John T. Terry, a hatter and furrier; Mme. Deiden, a fashionable dressmaker (an English tourist commenting on the American deference to French fashion noted that "no dressmaker is now considered orthodox who cannot show a prefix of Madame")[3]; Mrs. G. Brodie, who sold "mantillas and cloaks exclusively"; and, prefiguring what was to become a major source of trade in the district, Phillip Phillips and Co., a piano and organ manufacturers.[4] Borrowing freely from architectural stylebooks, the new commercial palaces arrayed around the Square also followed French fashion, and were designed to encourage consumption on a grand scale. Foreign visitors frequently described these as among the most important public buildings in the city.[5] Given the steady encroachment of trade, the *Times* argued, it was possible the entire neighborhood would be given over to mercantile use, perhaps rendering the quiet Square obsolete in the new age of business.

While Washington Square preserved its genteel reputation as a place of "established repose," in the words of the novelist Henry James, Union Square did not.[6] By 1870 it was no longer a quiet urban retreat, an amenity only the wealthiest New Yorkers could afford to enjoy, but a vibrant shopping and entertainment center where members of all classes congregated both day and night. The elliptical green park was now not the terminus of Broadway but a local node along it. Following their customers uptown, furniture and clothing stores, theaters and restaurants breached the barrier of Fourteenth Street and opened new premises around the Square. Flooded with shoppers and theatergoers, it became the new commercial and entertainment center of the city. Replacing private mansions, purpose-built buildings catered to popular and commercial functions and offered new forms of urban sociability. At the center, the landscaped park became an increasingly crowded pleasure ground for a newly powerful class of consumers.

In order to accommodate these new users, the increasingly overburdened park needed to change. This opportunity came in 1870 when the Tammany Hall–led Department of Public Parks embarked on a project to renovate and popularize the downtown parks, remaking them for a diverse urban populace, with working-class New Yorkers catered to rather than the urban elite. When this era came to an abrupt end after only eighteen months, these park projects were left partially completed. Called in to advise the Parks Department on what to do with the half-renovated Union Square, the landscape designer Frederick Law Olmsted and his architect partner, Calvert Vaux, made perhaps the single most significant modification in the Square's history. Building on the Tammany efforts, they created a paved plaza at the northern end, along Seventeenth Street. Situated between the busy street and the landscaped park, this plaza was expressly intended for public gatherings. Seemingly a pragmatic response to the problem of crowding, Olmsted and Vaux's solution resonated with larger questions related to the control of the city and its public spaces at a time of tremendous ethnic and class tension. While the two designers are best known for their work on Central Park, their renovation of Union Square is a remarkable alternative vision of a public park as democratic landscape. Following their redesign, the Square acquired a permanent open space whose presence would come to challenge the iconic and symbolic power of the statues of Washington and Lincoln.

A kind of third space, between the park and the street proper, the plaza was designed to give public utility to the association between Union Square and democracy. Its completion fundamentally altered the temporal orientation of the Square: while the statues commemorated the military and political triumphs of the past, the plaza was designed to facilitate democracy as an ongoing and active process.

Ladies' Mile and the Rialto

The class of wealthy New Yorkers who built their homes in Union Square in the 1840s and 1850s was defined by its social mobility, a trait that included geographic transience and a desire to build ever more luxurious homes in ever more fashionable neighborhoods. Insecure in their own status, they followed the lead of the topmost strata of the upper ten. In the 1850s, the Astor brothers, John Jacob II and William B. II, scions of the undisputed first family of New York and lords of the Knickerbocker aristocracy, established a new beachhead for the social elite north of Fourteenth Street. Fleeing the family seat at Astor Place, they built new houses at Fifth Avenue and Thirty-Third and Thirty-Fourth Streets, respectively, vaulting over Union Square completely. The new money quickly followed them, including Alexander T. Stewart, the Scotch-Irish immigrant turned dry goods king. In 1846 Stewart had pioneered the department store when he built a magnificent Italianate style commercial palace in white marble just north of City Hall at Broadway and Chambers Street. In the 1860s he extended his empire, beginning construction of a magnificent new store on the southeast corner of Broadway and Tenth Street, just below Union Square near the fashionable Grace Church. Seeking to cement his place in New York society, he built his own showy mansion directly opposite the Astor brothers in 1864. With the social elite moving uptown and department stores creeping up Broadway, Union Square was caught in the middle. Excepting those belonging to Ruggles and a few others, commercial landlords claimed the grand houses surrounding it. As early as 1852 a guide to New York society noted this change to the character of the neighborhood:

> Scarcely a private residence remains [on Broadway], except in the most northerly half mile [near Union Square], which still partly sustains its claim to be in the fashionable quarter of the town. Even here the dwelling houses are interspersed with shops; elegant mansions are beginning to be elbowed by dentists and boarding houses, and to assume an appearance of having been in the aristocratic precincts.[7]

If local mansions were not being converted into stores, they were being monetized in other ways, as restaurants and boarding houses. As the wealthy left their large homes, many were converted into rental rooms for professional men and their families, who paid from twelve to fifteen dollars per week to live at the still prestigious address.[8] In 1866 the *New York Times* noted the growing number of boarding houses lining nearby Irving Place. In his guide to the city, Junius Henri Brown noted that the boarding houses around Union Square were exclusive enough that guests had to be recommended to their proprietors. Although they were considered quite respectable, however, they were a definite step down from a private home. As Brown noted archly, the interiors of these boarding houses seldom lived up to expectations:

> When you enter a tall, handsome brown stone front, exactly like its next door neighbor where the Wall Street banker or beaver merchant resides in the midst of velvet curtains, ormolu clocks and classic bronzes, you cannot help but be surprised. The drawing rooms look dismal, the furniture worn and scanty; the stairways treacherous and untidy; the walls soiled and of marvelous acoustic property. Nothing like comfort or content anywhere and the opposite of what you mean when you talk of home . . . everything that meets your eye is thin and unreal, save the landlady who weighs two hundred [pounds]."[9]

Fleeing the influx of striving professionals, the institutions associated with the social elite also moved uptown and new ones dedicated to middle-class interests took their place. In 1860 the Spingler Institute, the exclusive school for young ladies, closed and was converted into a hotel. The former Union League Club in the old Parish mansion was now the showroom of a fashionable upholsterer. Around the same time the Athenaeum, Travelers, and New York clubs moved to new premises, and "club men" were no longer to be found smoking their pipes near the soothing murmur of the fountain on mild evenings.[10]

Along Seventeenth Street, political assemblies of a different kind replaced the rousing political meetings of the wartime era when the Irish nationalist "Fenian Brotherhood" relocated from its downtown headquarters to the Moffat mansion. Moffat's stained-glass cupola was ornamented with both the Stars and Stripes and a green flag bearing a gold harp as William B. Roberts, a dry goods merchant and leader of the Brotherhood, declared it the seat of the free Irish government in exile. The *New York Herald* noted that this building, much grander than that formerly occupied by the Brotherhood on

Duane Street near City Hall, was only fitting for this political organization, standing as it did adjacent to the nearby statue of Washington, "the world's greatest revolutionist."[11] The grand reception room was ideally suited for political meetings and, the newspaper speculated, the outbuildings in the rear might be used for an arsenal. Growing in influence, the Fenian Brotherhood gained support from local Democrats, who tied their own republicanism to the goal of Irish emancipation. The link between the Irish cause and the American Revolution was made explicit at a mass outdoor meeting held in Union Square on June 26, 1866: the dominant message of the speeches was that interests of republicanism were the same the world over. The meeting concluded with the resolution: "It is a moral and political duty of the citizens of this republic to sympathize with every people struggling for the attainment of freedom."[12] These words were not just empty rhetoric: efforts toward Irish independence were soon put into action. That same year the Fenian Brotherhood launched an unlikely plot to invade Canada and hold its government hostage in exchange for the British return of Ireland to the Irish.[13] Though this audacious plan was well supported with American money and weapons, it was perhaps not surprisingly unsuccessful. Canadian militiamen repelled the Fenian invaders north of Buffalo, and some were subsequently captured by the American navy. However, this ignominious failure did not stop the Brotherhood from organizing a grand rally on the south side of Union Square to welcome back the released prisoners, attended by forty thousand people.[14] This rally was widely taken as a sign of the strength and legitimacy of the Irish nationalist cause in the United States.

Following the lead of the Fenian Brotherhood, other political groups began to move into the area, claiming the prestige of the fashionable address. In 1868 the Tammany Society, a powerful Democratic Party social club, opened a grand new building just around the corner on Fourteenth Street between Irving Place and Third Avenue. Tammany Hall, as this building was known, was a venue for political meetings as well as social events and the name "Tammany Hall" came to signify the Democratic Party organization or "machine" that controlled New York city politics for many years. Designed by the architect Thomas R. Jackson, the red brick building contained a theater used for political conventions as well as popular entertainments. Soon after it opened it hosted the National Democratic Party Convention at which Governor Horatio Seymour was nominated as the party's presidential candidate after twenty-two exhausting ballots. When not used for political meetings, it housed popular attractions such as Dan Bryant's minstrel show, which, according to a contemporary city guide, "raised negro minstrelsy

3.1 "Headquarters of the Fenian Brotherhood, Union Square, New York," 1865.

to the dignity of a fashionable amusement, and banished from it all that is coarse and offensive."[15] As historian Michael Shapiro has noted, along with the Fenian Brotherhood's occupation of the Moffat mansion, the construction of Tammany Hall illustrates the transfer of power over Union Square from the Republican elite who organized mass rallies there during the Civil War to a new generation of political agents associated with the Democratic Party and, increasingly, with working-class New Yorkers.[16]

Beyond these political organizations and their associated theatrical displays, Union Square was increasingly known as a center for luxury shopping: the homes of the social elite were replaced by stores selling fashionable domestic goods. As with the civic and political gatherings, the key aspect of this new landscape was spectacle, this time in the service of profit. Goods were not only sold, they were exhibited like works of art in awe-inspiring new surroundings, bigger, brighter, and more lavishly decorated than ever before. Patrons did not just shop; they themselves were part of the tableaux. The stretch of Broadway from Ninth to Nineteenth Streets became known as "Ladies' Mile," a showcase for new kinds of retailing and the most up-to-date architecture styles.[17] Two department stores erected just south of Union Square set the precedent: A. T. Stewart and Company (1862–70) and James McCreery and Company (1869). The industrialization of manufacturing and New York's position as a center of global trade made it possible for these companies to buy and distribute relatively inexpensive goods from all over the world for consumption by New Yorkers.[18] Alexander T. Stewart, in particular, developed an innovative retailing strategy of high-volume sales that required a different kind of store architecture. Prior to the mid-nineteenth century, because of the enormous expense of real estate along Broadway, stores generally occupied narrow buildings with small street frontages, keeping the majority of the goods "out the back." Stewart broke with that custom. With stock organized in "departments" because there was so much of it, his downtown store was of unprecedented size, occupying the full frontage of Broadway between Chambers and Reade Streets. With its gleaming white facades and Corinthian columns framing expansive display windows, Stewart's overshadowed the small brick stores surrounding it, radiating the modern glamour of mass market luxury. Although Stewart sold relatively inexpensive goods and catered largely to middle-class customers, his business thrived because of its association with high fashion. When wealthy New Yorkers began to move northward, he followed them. In 1862 he engaged architect John Kellum to design a new store at Broadway and Tenth Street. Completed in stages over the next eight years, Stewart's new store set an even higher bar for his competition.

Strategically located at a bend in Broadway, the new A. T. Stewart store was a monument to commerce; five stories high, it occupied the entire 328 feet by 200 feet block between Ninth and Tenth Streets, Broadway, and Fourth Avenue. Like the company's previous premises (now converted into a wholesale store), it was gleaming white, easily mistaken for one of the most important public buildings in the city. Inside a grand light well encircled by balconies pierced the building, creating a sort of stage on which female shoppers could perform and be observed. Such a large building with huge plate-glass windows in every level required structural expertise and Stewart had engaged Kellum because of his knowledge of cast-iron commercial

3.2 A. T. Stewart Department Store, Broadway (West 9th–West 10th Streets).

construction. The facade of the new building was made up of repeated cast-iron panel bays stamped with a repeated neoclassical ornamental motif.[19] Though journalists praised the sublime effect of the building's size, porosity, and lightness, it failed to please many architecture critics. Typically for this time, Kellum had worked his way up from builder to architect. Both the influential critic Montgomery Schuyler and the architect Peter B. Wight decried the enormous and undifferentiated expanse of the building's street walls. Comparing them to an iron railing with its "oft-repeated balusters," they called these facades "monotonous," "overpowering" to the eye, a "huge wilderness of cast-iron ellipses."[20] For these aesthetes, the Stewart store seemed to reduce architecture to the same status as the goods being sold inside: like the shiny baubles made possible by mass production, it was a cheap luxury made possible by machine manufacture.

While unloved by critics, the airy cast-iron palace became the new commercial vernacular. Kellum went on to design several other buildings in the area, including the McCreery Store across the street from Stewart's at the northwest corner of Broadway and Eleventh Street. Though it was substantially similar to Stewart's, Kellum softened the building's sizable bulk by adopting the newly fashionable Second Empire style.[21] With its ornate mansard roofs, this was a translation of contemporary Parisian architecture, still seen as the ultimate reference point in matters of style and good taste. At the street level, Kellum pioneered what would become a storefront staple, the bay-fronted display window, which allowed the goods inside to be seen from a variety of angles. Alarming critics used to more substantial masonry buildings, the bay window was hugely advantageous to the retailer: the attractive goods inside were now visible not only to patrons inside the store but also to the crowds of people passing by on the street.[22]

Kellum's building for the jewelry company Tiffany and Co. at Broadway and Fifteenth Street was the first purpose-built commercial structure in Union Square. Formerly located on lower Broadway between Prince and Spring Streets, in 1867 the company purchased the Church of the Puritans and demolished it two years later. Like the Stewart and McCreery stores, Kellum's Tiffany and Co. was a cast-iron structure with expansive storefront windows. It contained a magnificent showroom on the ground floor, with offices and manufacturing rooms in the four stories above. According to an admiring appraisal in the *Herald*, the interior was daringly modern, "devoid of flashy ornament . . . uncarpeted [with] the ceiling of iron beams painted white."[23] Designed in the neoclassical "Roman composite style," the building featured fireproof ironwork (necessary in any building, but especially so here because of the valuable goods it contained) and over two hundred single-pane windows filled with imported French glass. Perhaps stung by criticism of his earlier work, Kellum tried to break up the monotony of the two street facades by offering a greater variety of ornament. This was not enough to mollify his critics, however, who were particularly enraged at the cast-iron "rustication," or faux stonework, separating the bays.[24] Nevertheless, the company must have been quite happy with Kellum's work because it continued to operate in these premises until 1936, long after most other purveyors of luxury goods had deserted the area.[25]

Besides domestic goods and fine jewelry, Union Square also became known for other, more modern luxuries such as pianos.[26] In 1866 the Steinway and Sons piano company opened at 71–73 East Fourteenth Street between Union Square and Irving Place. Housed in another white marble commercial palace, this building served as a retail partner to the company's enormous factory uptown.[27] In 1870 the Decker Brothers piano company erected its own narrow building at 33 Union Square West, with display floors on the first and second floors and the upper levels rented out to Masonic lodges. Designed in the fashionable Venetian Gothic style by the architect

3.3 Tiffany and Co., Union Square and 15th St., ca. 1903.

Leopold Eidlitz, this polychromic masonry building was received far more favorably by critics than its cast-iron neighbors.[28] The northwestern corner of the Square, where the Decker Building stood, soon became a popular gathering spot for those with artistic and literary pretentions, prefiguring the area's later Bohemian reputation. Several artists had their studios in buildings on this row, as did the theatrical photographer, Napoleon Sarony, famous for his portraits of actors and actresses in theatrical costume. The Square's reputation as a literary center began when Agosto Brentano, an immigrant from Sicily, established a newsstand in the basement of the Decker Building before moving into larger premises a few yards to the south in 1876, where he expanded his stock to include books and plays. Known as "Brentano's Literary Emporium," this store soon became known as "the 'great literary headquarters' of New York."[29] Fashionably dressed crowds gathered daily outside its doors, reading playbills and broadsheets advertising the latest publications.

Union Square's reputation as a fashionable retail center attracted another sort of company, the manufacturers of sewing machines. A mid-nineteenth-century invention, the sewing machine democratized ladies' fashion, significantly reducing the hours of painstaking labor necessary to construct the voluminous gowns worn during this period.[30] One of the most imposing new buildings on Union Square was the Domestic Sewing Machine Company Building at the prominent southwestern corner of Broadway and Fourteenth Street, erected in 1873. This company manufactured a popular, lightweight sewing machine at its works in nearby Newark, New Jersey. Serving as general offices and salesrooms, the Union Square building was the center of a lucrative North American merchandising empire that included not only the machines themselves, but also paper dress patterns and a quarterly publication, the *Fashion Review*.[31] The architect of the building, Griffith Thomas, took advantage of the obtuse angle where Broadway met Fourteenth Street, highly unusual in the Manhattan grid, to design a continuous, heavily ornamented cast-iron and glass facade with an elaborate rounded corner pavilion surmounted with a mansard roof and a dome in the Second Empire Style.[32] Though it was praised in the newspapers, the redoubtable architecture critic Mrs. Schuyler van Rensselaer described this building tartly as "an elaborate vulgarization of palatial magnificence."[33] Inside, the store displayed not only the latest sewing machines, but also models wearing the latest fashions copied (like the building) from those seen in France and London. A row of competing sewing machine businesses soon opened their own showrooms on Union Square East between Fifteenth and Sixteenth Streets. This included one of the most enduring names in the business, the Singer Sewing Machine Company.

Just as the department stores and luxury good showrooms brought new people to the area, including not only shoppers but also store employees, the construction of theaters and concert halls attracted a diverse audience. In the 1870s Union Square became known as "the Rialto," New York's theater district.[34] Then, as now, the theater was a popular pastime for tourists and locals alike, including all but the very poorest. In 1872, a guidebook writer described the theater going demographic in the following way:

> There are usually from 50,000 to 100,000 strangers in the city, and the majority of these find the evenings dull without some amusement to enliven

3.4 Domestic Sewing Machine Building, Broadway and 14th Street.

> them. Many of them are persons who come for pleasure, and who regard the theaters as the most enjoyable of all the sights of the city; but a very large portion are merchants, who are wearied with buying stock, and who really need some pleasant relaxation after the fatigues of the day.[35]

The origins of the Rialto lay in the early 1850s when a group of private citizens solicited subscriptions for a large public concert hall as an alternative to the Astor Place Opera House. Sited at the city's former social center, this building was tainted by the memory of the Astor Place Riot of 1849, when a rivalry between two actors, the American Edwin Forrest and the Englishman William Charles Mcready, improbably escalated from a disagreement over the correct method of performing Shakespearian roles into a full-scale street battle involving thousands of people, twenty-five of whom were killed.[36] The Astor Place Opera House could not escape its association with this tragedy, and soon afterward New Yorkers sought to erect an alternative theatrical venue. Opened in 1854 on Fourteenth Street between Irving Place and Third Avenue as the Academy of Music, this building was deliberately designed as a democratic institution with only a few private boxes and seats available at a wide range of prices. Designed in the "Rundbogenstil" (round-arched Gothic) style by architect Alexander Saltzer, it was unadorned and rather dour on the exterior. But inside it was renowned for its excellent acoustics. After a difficult start (the large size of the auditorium made it difficult to fill for every performance), the Academy of Music became the social center of New York following the Civil War. It staged not only opera, but also plays, with opening nights flooded by members of the upper ten, always in full evening dress. The academy also hosted society receptions, including one for the English Prince of Wales in 1860, and grand balls, some of a decidedly licentious variety. Notoriously indecent and reported on in salacious detail by the popular press, so-called French or masked balls were designed to allow society men to consort with scantily costumed women of the *demimonde*, observed from the safety of a gallery by their more adventurous lady companions.[37]

The construction of the Academy of Music spurred the establishment of several other theaters in the immediate neighborhood. In 1866 the Steinway and Sons piano company expanded its showrooms to include a concert venue, Steinway Hall, fronting onto Fifteenth Street.[38] Designed for musical concerts, it was also hired out for lectures, including a reading by the foremost author of the day, Charles Dickens, as part of his American tour of 1867–68. This event was so popular that more than 150 people, "including two women," queued outside all night to buy tickets.[39] Nearby Irving Hall, Nilsson Hall, and the Union Square Theater, which opened in the old Union Place Hotel, provided a variety of popular diversions.[40] If the shows on offer at these venues did not appeal, there was always the Hippotheatron, also known as "Lent's New York Circus," opposite the Academy of Music on Fourteenth Street. Opened in 1864, this curious octagonal structure, clad in corrugated iron and entered through a monumental archway, offered circus-style acts such as horseback riders, clowns, acrobats, and trained dogs and monkeys. Heated by steam and notoriously drafty, it was used throughout the year, offering Christmas pantomimes such as "Bluebeard," the thrilling story of a wife-murdering aristocrat, complete with fairies suspended from the trapeze wires. It was also a venue for billiard tournaments. This building was taken over by the circus impresario P. T. Barnum in 1872 and burned down later that year.[41]

Along Fourteenth Street, saloons and oyster houses satisfied the appetites of the theater-going crowds. Locally supplied, oysters were a form of early fast food popular with New Yorkers. Speaking of her visit to the city in the early 1850s, the curious and daring Englishwoman Isabella Bird wrote:

> The amount of oysters eaten in New York surprised me, although there was an idea at the time of my visit that they produced the cholera. . . . In the business streets of New York the eyes are confronted continually with the words 'Oyster Saloon' painted in large letters on the basement story. If a stranger's curiosity is sufficient to induce him to dive down a flight of stairs into a subterranean abode, at the first glance rather suggestive of robbery, one favorite amusement of the people may be seen in perfection. There is a counter at one side, where two or three persons, frequently black, are busily engaged in opening oysters for their customers who swallow them with astonishing relish and rapidity. . . . Some of these saloons are highly respectable, while others are quite the reverse.[42]

From the saloons of Fourteenth Street, the boisterous atmosphere flowed over into the park, which began to gain a somewhat louche reputation after dark. The park's comfortable benches and overgrown trees provided shelter for out-of-work actors and, as a popular magazine put it, "more or less disagreeable idlers, varying in distinction from the tramp to the slightly overcome tippler."[43] It was also frequented by what a contemporary guidebook called "professional beggars," who gathered there in hopes of earning a few cents:

> Broadway, and especially Fourteenth Street, Union Square, and the Fifth Avenue, are full of them. They represent all forms of physical misfortune. Some appear to have but one leg, others but one arm. Some are blind, others horribly deformed . . . the greater the semblance of distress, the more lucrative is their profession. Women hire babies, and post themselves in the thoroughfares most frequented by ladies. . . . They hang on to you with the utmost determination, exposing the most disgusting sights to your gaze, and annoying you so much that you give them money in order to be rid of them.[44]

Beggars were not the only ones to seek a living in the environs of the park. Other guidebooks referred, in more or less explicit terms, to the prostitutes who would mix with the Broadway crowds after dark. Fashionably dressed, they would procure customers and escort them back to furnished rooms or nearby brothels. One contemporary guidebook listed over forty houses of prostitution in the vicinity.[45]

By 1870 Union Square was finished as a residential district exclusively for the wealthy. The outlet for both Broadway and the Bowery—the fashionable- and functional thoroughfares of nineteenth-century New York—it no longer marked the elite end of town, an escape from the city, but was a center of commerce equal to Lower Broadway. Though the goods on display in local showrooms were luxury items that only a few could afford, the entertainment to be had at theaters, concert halls, saloons, oyster houses, and brothels were within reach of most. In response to these changes, the city authority responsible for public parks began a campaign to renovate Union Square. Since 1857 all New York City parks had come under the control of the state-run Board of Commissioners of Central Park directed by President Andrew H. Green. That changed when the Tammany Hall–controlled city government created a new Department of Public Parks independent of state control. Better attuned to the desires of their working-class constituents than the old Board, the new Parks Department began an expensive program to improve the city parks, motivated by a desire to make them more egalitarian. Accompanying the transformation of the Square from a residential to a commercial center, this change of administration resulted in a significant alteration to the form of the park and its intended purpose.

Popularizing Public Parks

While Union Square thrived as a commercial and entertainment Mecca in the late 1860s, the park at its center was suffering from overcrowding and neglect. In this it was not alone. All of the so-called downtown squares drew unfavorable comparisons with the enormous eight-hundred-acre park being constructed north of the city between Fifty-Ninth and One Hundred and Sixth Streets. Designed as an escape from the pressures of urban life and as a prompt for real estate development in the parts of the grid still sparsely developed, the new Central Park was of a different scale. In comparison, the older parks seemed undersized, shabby, and out of date. City Hall, and Union and Madison Squares, the journalist Junius Henri Brown wrote in 1869, "have been so much neglected that they have lost most of their attractions. . . . The downtown parks have of late years, especially since the opening of the Central, been given over up to disreputable loungers, children and nurses—those of our citizens requiring recreation and fresh air going to the Central to find them."[46] Union Square could hardly compete with this spacious new attraction. Now fully grown, the trees created a dark and gloomy interior where criminals and prostitutes took advantage of the leafy canopy to ply their trades. A heavy iron fence, some thought, was "more suited for a cemetery than a pleasure park," compounded the sinister effect.[47]

Central Park was planned to counter this gothic seclusion. Designed according to a new philosophy of park design, it was to be healthy, educational, and morally improving.[48] Speaking of the new enterprise, the renowned landscape designer Andrew Jackson Downing claimed, "It is republican in its very idea and tendency. It takes up popular education where the common school and ballot box leave it, and raises up the working-man to the same level of enjoyment with the man of leisure and accomplishment."[49] Central Park was a solution to the problem of the grid, with its focus on private property and individualism. It was necessary to construct such a park in New York, Downing argued, to temper the competitive spirit of business that dominated social interactions in the city with a more refined sense of community. The park was intended to be a powerful force for social and moral improvement, available to all. "Out of this common enjoyment of public grounds, by all classes," he wrote, "grows a social freedom, and an easy and agreeable intercourse of all classes."[50] For the wealthy it would provide a place for gentle recreation and social interaction, a relief from the pressures of commerce that otherwise drove them. For the lower ranks it would be a form of education: exposure to nature in the form of a large city park would instill in them an aesthetic appreciation and an understanding of good taste. In this way the park would contribute to the formation of a better, more refined citizenry.

A grand scale was an essential component of this democratizing function. The park had to be very large to accommodate its diverse uses, much larger than any already existing. Downing called the downtown city squares "little door-yards of space—mere grass plats of verdure," simply too small and too few to accommodate the population of the midcentury metropolis.[51] Closely boxed in by houses and commercial buildings, they did not provide room for civilizing contact with nature. In contrast Downing offered up the example of rural cemeteries such as Greenwood in Brooklyn, Mount Auburn in Massachusetts, and Laurel Hill near Philadelphia which he thought offered the scale and sensibility to foster democratic feeling. It was this schema that Olmsted and Vaux followed in their winning "Greensward" design for Central Park. But the creation of the monumental new park did not mean the abandonment of its predecessors. The downtown parks that the creators of Central Park held in such low esteem continued to attract more and more people as the city grew at a rapid rate. Planned as the centerpieces of residential areas, they were increasingly surrounded by commercial activity, and as a consequence their purpose and design had to be reconsidered.

Besides being shapers of Central Park, Olmsted and Vaux were also responsible for renovating Union Square, making of it a quite a different kind of democratic landscape. Their involvement was the indirect result of a short-lived but radical reorganization of the municipal government under the larger-than-life politician William "Boss" Tweed, the powerful Grand Sachem or leader of the Tammany Society. After Democrats gained control of the New York State Assembly and the Senate in the 1869 elections, Tweed, a state senator, seized control of the various commissions that ran New York City. Early in 1870 he put into effect a new city charter that did away with many of these commissions, replacing them with city-controlled departments whose heads were appointed by the mayor. On paper this was a rationalized and streamlined approach and it initially received support from both sides of the political divide.[52] Ominously, however, this charter allowed the city to borrow large sums of money by issuing bonds for urban improvements. The boss of Tammany Hall was now the boss of the city, and he had almost unlimited funds at his disposal. Two of the newly created municipal departments—Public Works and Public Parks—were especially lucrative. Naming himself head of Public Works, Tweed concentrated on the development of the Upper East Side, a huge effort involving grading land, building roads, and the establishment of sewer and drainage networks. Tweed found a way for this to profit Tammany supporters, largely working and middle-class German and Irish immigrants.[53]

While the new Tammany-controlled Department of Public Parks benefited supportive contracting companies, it also saw its mandate as a political one. When Tammany Hall took control of public parks by disestablishing the state-controlled Board of Commissioners of Central Park, it gained authority over not just the partially completed park but also a sizable part of the physical landscape of the city. Established in 1857, the Central Park Commission had gained broader and broader powers until it acted as a form of city-planning authority. By 1870, it controlled not only Central Park but also the smaller parks in New York City, the undeveloped northern sector of Manhattan, and the parts of southern Westchester that would become the Bronx. Under the direction of two Tweed associates, lawyers Peter B. Sweeny and Henry "Judge" Hilton, the Tammany Department was heavily critical of the old Board of Commissioners of Central Park, mostly made up of the Republican elite. Where the commission had worked by and large for the benefit of land-owning capitalists, they claimed, they would extend largesse to less well-off New Yorkers. The adversarial relationship between the two groups was apparent in the department's first annual report, published in 1871, in which decisions made by the former administrators were constantly called into question.

Though Central Park was intended to be, and is now celebrated as, a democratic landscape, the majority of Democratic politicians and their constituents regarded it with suspicion. From the early years of its existence, it was the subject of conflict, from basic debates about its character (was it to be a romantic, "natural" landscape or a populist pleasure grounds?), to the way it was built and administered. Sweeny and Hilton, along with the landscape architect Ignaz Pilat, moved ahead energetically with the work at Central Park in ways that appalled the park's founders and supporters, including the editors of the *New York Times*. First they greatly increased the number of workers employed to build it, increasing their salaries and improving their working conditions, a move that was characterized as wasteful. Rather than sharing Olmsted's vision of a rustic and romantic landscape, they preferred a more conventional park, trimming his naturalistic plantings and introducing formal flower beds laid out in conventional arabesque shapes. Olmsted vigorously opposed these changes, arguing that the tidying up of the landscape and the construction of buildings within it harmed the park's essential purpose as an escape from the city, in effect urbanizing it. The *Times* agreed with Olmsted, attacking the department on two fronts: it was spending an outrageous amount of money and in the process ruining the original vision of Central Park.[54] In its criticism, the *Times* personalized the debate with a series of ad hominem attacks on Sweeny and Hilton that exposed the issue of class. While the members of the old parks Board were men of "cultured taste" and the "highest integrity," the *Times* editors argued, their successors lacked the education and aesthetic sensibility to shepherd this great public works project to fruition. Sweeny was described as a "vulgar demagogue," and Hilton an "impertinent, self-conceited, unprincipled lawyer," "notoriously a man of bad taste," a man obsessed with French fashion who had to be talked out of his worst excesses by those who worked for him.[55] The newspaper was particularly contemptuous about their championing of practicalities such as the erection of "earth closets," or public toilets. When the Department of Public Parks was created, the *Times* wrote, "the vulgar, tawdry, catch penny tastes of the [Tweed] Ring became manifest in all the parks of the city."[56]

When the *Times* called Sweeny and Hilton's efforts at improving the city's parks vulgar, they were correct in an essential sense. Although they were undeniably corrupt, spending huge amounts to benefit themselves and their associates, the two men also acted out of desire to make parks more accessible, pleasant, and functional for ordinary people. Besides reorienting Central Park further along the spectrum from wilderness to man-made, they also undertook an ambitious program to renovate the downtown parks, parks that had suffered from neglect under the supervision of a commission that believed them to be hopelessly deficient. The new board members were pointed in their commentary on this issue:

> The members of the present Board, having long been residents of the City of New York—some of them having been born here, and most of them having lived here the greater portion of their lives—all felt a sensitive regard for the eminent public demand that these parks should be converted from the neglected, repelling, and unpleasant places that they had been for many years, into breathing spots that should afford pleasure to the people frequenting or passing them, and to the masses who have not the means of frequent access to Central Park. . . . The small squares or open places of the city, consisting of triangles and odd pieces of ground, will all be converted into plots agreeable to the surrounding neighborhood, instead of leaving them offensive spots, the resort of vile characters for improper purposes, as had been the case of late years.[57]

This criticism was not just rhetoric. The state of the downtown squares had been a source of embarrassment for the previous decade. In 1867 an essay in the *Round Table*, a popular journal, commented on the air of neglect that surrounded them. In its efforts to complete Central Park, the author wrote, the city ought not to forget that these smaller parks also served a purpose: "There are many people within our city limits to whom a visit to the Central Park is the rarest of luxuries, who live and die in dens and kennels where poverty spawns disease without ever knowing, except from hearsay, the beauty of field and forest and river. . . . To such as these the city squares are almost an absolute necessity, the one delight of many a darkened life."[58] The *Times* wrote along similar lines, and at first gave the Tammany administration grudging praise for its work in this area. But over time, as it became apparent that a great deal of money was being spent, the newspaper withdrew its support. By 1871 the Department of Parks project to improve the state of the downtown squares was swept up in criticism of the lavish spending of the so-called Tweed ring. In the eighteen months it was under the control of Sweeny and Hilton, the Department of Public Parks lavished $6.25 million on twenty-four city parks. After Tweed was ousted, the *Times* detailed these expenses with horrified glee: over four hundred thousand dollars was spent at the Battery and Washington Square alone, and even tiny parks such as those at Duane and Beach Streets in Lower Manhattan were improved at costs of three and five thousand dollars each.[59] The total spent led the *Times* to offer the satirical suggestion that, given the amount spent, the surface of these parks should be carpeted with "greenbacks, not grass."[60]

For all the money spent, the changes were modest, with the exception of City Hall Park, which was in a particularly bad state following its use as military barracks during the war. The improvements consisted of general maintenance (such as repaving and new planting) and the erection of structures and buildings intended for public convenience, including drinking fountains, horse troughs, urinals, and the euphemistically named "cottages" or restrooms, for ladies and children. Seemingly unexceptional, these restroom buildings were a controversial political statement in a city where such public conveniences were rare. Their construction in public parks allowed people of all classes access to the same basic amenity, side by side, segregated only by gender. Along with the construction of restrooms, other practical changes undertaken by the Parks Department also had a symbolic dimension. These include the dismantling of the iron railings that surrounded many parks, throwing them open at all times of day and night, and the creation of free events such summertime concerts held in music pavilions erected for this purpose at the Battery, and in Washington, Tompkins, and Madison Squares.[61]

Seemingly practical, the construction of restrooms, the dismantling of fences, and the provision of musical concerts in purpose-built pavilions were the first shots in a class war fought on the grounds of the city's public parks. At the same time, the Tammany–controlled Parks Department also took steps to dictate the use of public parks in ways that the old Board had not considered. Most significant of all was a new requirement established in 1871 that the permission of the Parks Department commissioners be obtained by any group wishing to organize a gathering in any city park. This was followed a year later by a requirement that the permission of the Police Department also be sought if the meeting was to infringe on public streets. These regulations, little commented on at the time they were implemented, gave the city enormous power to control the use of public parks and were prophetic of changes to come.

Tweed's fall was swift. It began with outrage over a public demonstration, the Orange march of July 1871 in which sixty people were killed in skirmishes between Protestant and Catholic Irish Americans.[62] Tweed's enemies saw this disastrous parade as evidence that he could not control the fractious urban populace. Using public outrage as a lever, his opponents set to work to push him out of office, beginning with a *New York Times* campaign that shone a harsh light on Tweed and his associate's corruption. This journalistic crusade was greatly aided by the graphic artist Thomas Nast's cartoons of Tweed, which depicted him as a greedy ogre.[63] Soon afterward Tweed lost the support of bankers as the city's excessive loans began to come due, upsetting financial stability. In September of 1871 a meeting at the Cooper Union (organized in part by Samuel Ruggles) led to the formation of the "Executive Committee of Citizens and Taxpayers for Financial Reform of the City," a group tasked with choking off Tweed's power. Informally known as the "Committee of Seventy," this group named former Central Park Commissioner Andrew H. Green as the city comptroller, a position he used to institute draconian austerity measures. Tweed's public works and public parks programs came to an abrupt halt. In October he was arrested on charges of corruption. The following November the majority of his supporters were ousted in elections and the defeat of the Tweed Ring was complete.

Olmsted and Vaux's Plaza

In early 1872 Sweeny and Hilton were forced to resign and the Board of Commissioners of the Department of Public Parks was reconstituted under new leadership, with Olmsted and Vaux reappointed as landscape architects. On assessing the state of the city parks, Olmsted's immediate concern was to complete work on Central Park according to his original plan, maintaining his naturalistic vision and fighting off suggestions that large buildings be included. At the same time he and Vaux took seriously their review of the downtown parks, including Union Square. The Tweed-backed Department had included a landscaping plan for the Square in its 1871 annual report, a plan ascribed to Engineer-in-Chief M. A. Kellogg and Acting Landscape Gardener E. A. Pollard. This plan followed the new fashion for the picturesque that Olmsted had helped establish, but in a highly stylized manner, replacing the straight paths with curved ones and including the kind of arabesque-shaped flower beds that Olmsted abhorred. It also made the park more open and accessible, removing the iron fence and perimeter of trees, widening the paths, and cutting back the planting. However, few of these changes had been made: some trees and shrubs had been removed, the sidewalk was repaved, and Hilton had personally overseen the dismantling and auctioning of the iron railing surrounding the park.[64] Hilton had also ordered the

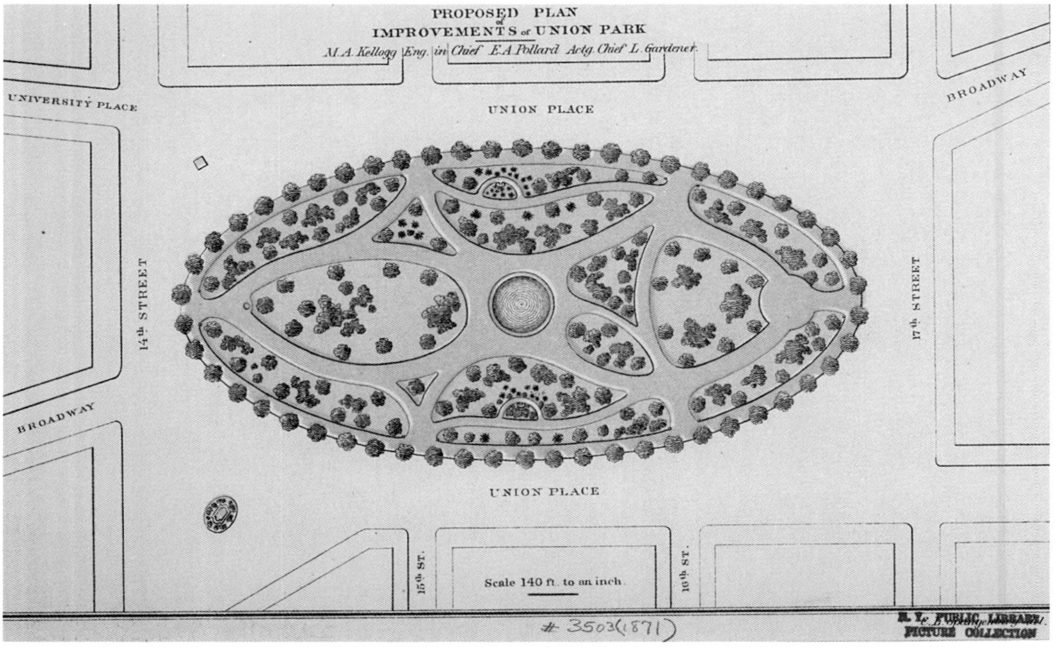

3.5 "Proposed Plan Improvements of Union Park," *New York City Department of Parks Annual Report, 1870* (New York: [s.n.], 1871).

construction of a new fountain replacing the Croton memorial. One of a number of costly fountains he had planned for the downtown parks, it was decorated with vases of alternating pink and green granite. When asked to review the work that had been done under the direction of Sweeney and Hilton, Olmsted and Vaux offered a bold suggestion, one that would alter the Square's associations for decades to come. Recognizing and reinforcing its unique urban character, they created a space specifically designed for mass meetings. In this they may have been influenced by work they had done in Brooklyn, then a separate city from New York.[65]

Many scholars have described a contradiction between Olmsted's democratic impulse and the elite activity he imagined taking place in his parks.[66] But far from being obsessed with the pastoral, he understood very well the need for urban parks to respond to their specific locations and to accommodate different kinds of activities. In an 1870 speech, "Public Parks and the Enlargement of Towns," he noted the advantage of supplementing large parks "rich in landscape attractions" with "numerous small grounds so distributed through a large town so that some one of them could be easily reached by a short walk from every house," particularly if they were connected by a system of roads or boulevards.[67] In other words, in his later career as a landscape architect he was thinking beyond the design of individual parks toward larger park systems, systems in which different parks could serve different purposes, with the parts connected together to form a larger whole. While far more modest than their work on Central Park, Olmsted and Vaux's proposal for Union Square reveals their pragmatic side, in particular their willingness to accommodate particularly urban uses of small city parks.

Olmsted was intimately familiar with the Square when he took over this project in early 1872. As a founding member of the Union League Club he had been a frequent visitor to the old League clubrooms in the Parish mansion at the northwest corner: from the porticoed front steps he witnessed many of the patriotic meetings that took place there during the Civil War. As first executive secretary of the United States Sanitary Commission, he had seen the transformation of this urban oasis into a Metropolitan Fair visited by thousands. Olmsted and Vaux's initial assessment of the park in Union Square is contained in a letter of March 13th, 1872, to Henry G. Stebbins, the new president of the Department of Public Parks. In this letter they describe the change in the character of the surrounding neighborhood and the consequence of that change for the park, which was now under threat from the crowds who regularly blocked the surrounding streets and trampled the plants.[68] After the Civil War the use of the Square as a staging area for public celebrations and protests became increasingly at odds with its original design as a place of repose. They noted these events were not ad hoc but highly organized, involving the construction of platforms around the base of the statue of Washington which often blocked the streets for days at a time. If anything, the Square was too successful as a public space.

In their report to the Commissioners, Olmsted and Vaux recognized that it would no longer be enough to offer "a refreshing gleam of simple greensward under an umbrageous grove to those who pass by on the outside."[69] As the Square assumed a central role in the city's civic affairs, its use for mass gatherings would only increase. The two men presented the parks commissioners with two options: replacing the fence and plantings making them sturdy to enough to resist encroachment by large crowds, or accepting the use of Union Square for public meetings and finding a way to accommodate them. Unless the department intended to actively prevent public meetings from being held there (which was regarded as difficult if not impossible), it was only prudent to plan for future mass meetings, continuing the Tammany plan to make the park more accessible.

Most significantly, Olmsted and Vaux suggested creating a separate area specifically for public assembly, a third space between the street and the park. Widening Seventeenth Street and flattening the northern end of the

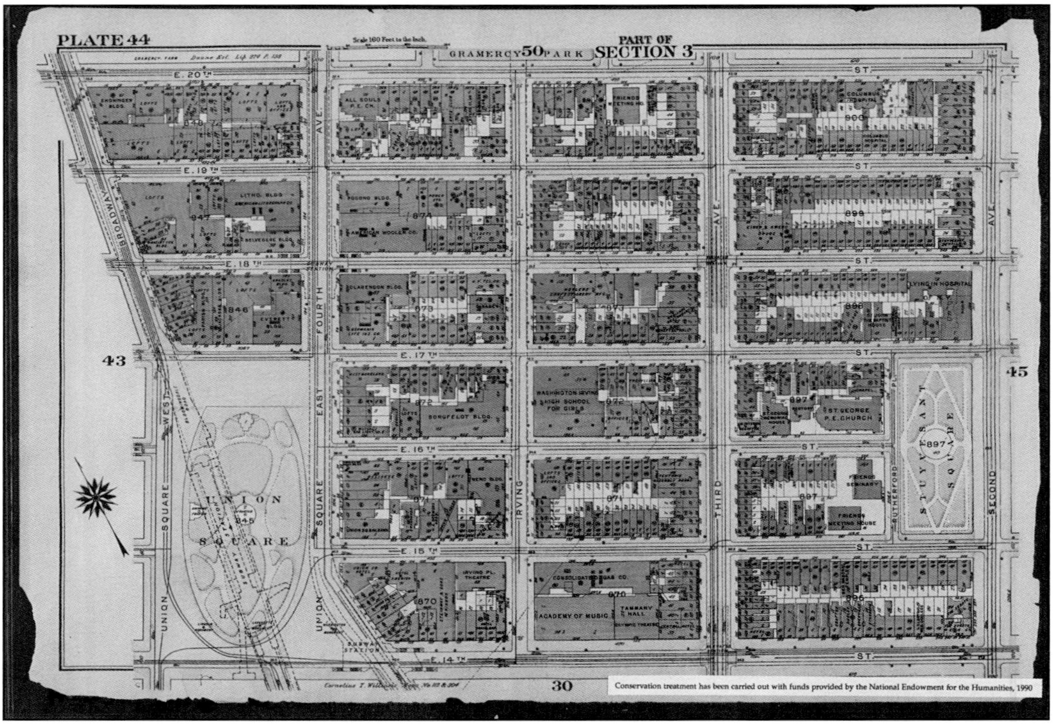

3.6 The new form of Union Square following Olmsted and Vaux's 1872 alteration, as depicted in *Atlases of New York City*, Section 3, Plate 44 (New York: G. W. Bromley and Co., 1916).

elliptical park, they created a 300-by-100-foot paved area set aside for this purpose. While their approach was more pragmatic than ideological, it formalized the growing use of Union Square as an active public space rather than a place of quiet contemplation. Labeling it a "muster ground," Olmsted and Vaux were explicit in intending this space to replace the Washington memorial as the main gathering point in the Square. In their words it was designed to "meet the public requirements of mass meetings, which had previously led to the frequent erection of temporary stagings, booths, tents, flags, staffs and lighting apparatus, of a character inconvenient, unseemly and dangerous, on the southeast part of the Square."[70] The Board of Commissioners agreed with this proposal, stating, "Twenty thousand persons can stand in the new ground without interrupting or being incommoded by the streetcars and omnibuses. . . . The whole space may be fully illuminated by substantial fixtures. The arrangements are adapted to allow a military column or other procession passing the platform to be reviewed from it by any guest of the city."[71] In support of the muster ground, Olmsted and Vaux designed a rustic building in the Swiss style, known as "the cottage," between Seventeenth Street and the park to the south. As its name suggests, the cottage was a version of the kind of practical amenity that the Tammany Parks Department had built in many other city parks. However, it was intended from the first to serve a greater purpose, not only a bathroom, but also a stage for speeches. In November of 1872 the *Commercial Advertiser* reported that "the cottage has been so placed on the north end of the Square, facing Seventeenth Street, that it commands a view of the space wherein thousands of people may gather without causing inconvenience to travel or discomfort to themselves. . . . There will be a rostrum in front from which speakers may address the multitude."[72] The designers reinforced the separation between the plaza and the park by providing a screen of ornamental columns that extended across the width of the park on either side of the building. These columns supported a row of 140 "oxyhydrogen" lamps enclosed under glass globes. A new technology, these lamps provided about sixteen times the illuminating power of regular gas streets lamps and were praised for their brilliant white light, "almost like sunlight."[73] Less than six months earlier the New York Oxygen Gas Company had arranged for the temporary illumination of Madison Square Park using such lamps, and announced that it was about to enter into contract to illuminate all the city streets by this method. This row of lamps, a feature of many contemporary images of the muster ground, facilitated nighttime meetings. In a short period of time the cottage and the open space in front of it took on practical and symbolic importance as the stage for many passionate political speeches, a function it would serve well into the twentieth century.

As a site for political rallies, the plaza came to symbolize the ideal of democratic action and the constitutionally sanctioned principle of free speech. But its origins lay in a different impulse—the desire to control what was seen as a volatile urban populace. The presence of "muster grounds," or military parade grounds, was considered normal in American cities at this time. Olmsted and Vaux included them in several of their park system designs, the one in Buffalo, New York, for example. They were considered a necessary component of urban control. In the original 1811 plan, the parade ground was by far the largest public space designated. At nearly 240 acres extending from Twenty-Third to Thirty-Fourth Streets and from Third to Seventh Avenues, it was the most outstanding feature on the map besides the grid itself.[74] Tied to a series of existing arsenals, the parade ground was considered a vital urban amenity in the years following the Revolution and in the lead-up to the War of 1812. However, with the threat of foreign invasion reduced and the cost of land rising quickly, it was reduced in size, first to eighty-nine acres and then to less than seven acres, before being sub-

3.7 "Anarchism in New York: The Cottage in Union Square from which the Open Air Meeting of the 'Unemployed' Was Addressed," 1893.

sumed into Madison Square in 1837. Around this time Washington Square became the primary parade ground in the city.

With no standing army, New York City depended on the National Guard, a volunteer militia controlled by the state, to defend it in times of war and internal conflict. The use of the militia as an urban peacekeeping force was common and its presence was inscribed into the urban infrastructure in the form of parade grounds and armories built to house its various companies. As we have seen, the Civil War saw a huge increase in military activity in New York City, with many city parks, including City Hall Park and the Battery being converted to use as barracks. But even in peacetime columns of mounted soldiers were regularly seen, called out not to defend the city against invaders, but also to repress internecine conflict. The bloody tangles of the midcentury were many, including the Astor Place Riot of 1849, the Draft Riots of 1863, and the Orange Parade Riot of 1871. In 1854 the English traveler Isabella Bird noted her host's blasé attitude about the regular occurrence of "election riots."[75] In response to the scale of the violence, the city drastically increased its police force and frequently chose to bring in militia companies to suppress conflict. These companies were based in heavily fortified armories built in emulation of medieval castles, which loomed over city streets, serving as highly visible symbols of order and control.[76] Often located in or near immigrant neighborhoods, these structures were built to monitor and suppress working-class dissent. The Lower East Side was a locus of particular concern for middle-class New Yorkers, who saw it as an incubator of the revolutionary movements then active in Europe.[77] The ethnic violence that raged between Irish American Protestants and Catholics in the summers of 1870 and 1871 resulted in broad support for an infrastructure of permanent military preparedness, including the conversion of public parks into parade grounds. At its first meeting in 1870 the Tammany–controlled Department of Public Parks noted the need for "a piece of ground suitable for parades, reviews and drills of all arms of the service."[78]

Tompkins Square Park between Avenues A and B, and Seventh and Tenth Streets, is the most well-known example of a public park turned military encampment. It opened in 1835, part of the same campaign to create attractive residential squares to ornament the city and encourage real estate development that led to the founding of Union Square. The park was initially well maintained, with trees, shrubbery, comfortable seats, and a fountain, all protected by an iron fence. But while Union Square was a neighborhood for wealthy and well-established New Yorkers, Tompkins Square was in an area occupied by middle-class immigrants from Germany. Hardworking and moderately well off, they appreciated the park as a place to relax and socialize. Besides its popularity as a place for leisure, Tompkins Square was also a site for political meetings. In the wake of the German revolution of 1848, both types of use became worrisome to municipal authorities; segregated by ethnicity from the rest of the city, the crowds that gathered there seemed to represent an irreversible social splintering, one that might harbor and even encourage revolutionary activity. By the late 1840s Tompkins Square, dry and almost barren of vegetation from heavy use, was also "used for the exhibition of military tactics," in the words of a contemporary guidebook.[79] In 1866 the city converted it into a parade ground for the First Division of the New York National Guard, uprooting the few trees and shrubs that remained and paving the ground in the hope that the constant presence of this highly visible martial force would repress any challenge to the status quo. This barren ground was to become the site of bitter conflicts between labor groups, the police and the National Guard, culminating in the "Tompkins Square Riot" of 1874 discussed in the next chapter.

The accepted use of public parks for military exercises, especially those in areas heavily populated with new immigrants, is the context in which

Olmsted and Vaux's proposal for a muster ground at Union Square must be seen. Strangely, however, although they used this term to describe the space they created, they did not mention military uses in their description of it, and the Parks Department specifically noted that it was not intended for military purposes. How did Olmsted and Vaux imagine this muster ground being used? Although there is no record of their specific intention, their work in Brooklyn provides a suggestive precedent. In early 1865 Vaux had been asked by James S. T. Stranahan, President of the Prospect Park Commission, to consider plans already drawn up for a great park in the center of Brooklyn.[80] In response he persuaded the Commissioners to purchase additional land in order to extend its scope, and he invited Olmsted to help him. Building on their work at Central Park, Olmsted and Vaux planned a city park in the pastoral tradition. Prospect Park had similar constitutive elements to Central Park: a "greensward," woods, a lake, and separate circulation paths for different kinds of traffic. By the time the two men had finished their work, the park was more than an autonomous element of landscape design; it was the centerpiece of a larger urban park system made up of a series of green spaces, each appropriate for the specific neighborhood in which it was situated.

The 1861 legislation creating Prospect Park included a requirement for a parade ground, which Olmsted and Vaux saw as valuable open space not only for military drills but also for the kinds of "exertive" or "gregarious" recreation that Olmsted believed desirable within certain kinds of city park.[81] Olmsted was largely disdainful of sports, believing them devoid of intellectual dimension and tainted by the immorality of gambling. But like many Victorians he saw military style exercises as a valuable way to build character and cooperation among men of all classes.[82] In 1869 the parade ground at Prospect Park was complete: Vaux designed a cottage or lodge adjacent to it for use by athletes as well as militia. It is possible that Olmsted and Vaux imagined that some form of recreational formation drilling might happen in Union Square as well. A more interesting possible precedent is Washington Park (now Fort Greene Park), which Olmsted and Vaux designed in 1867, including a space specifically designed for public meetings.

Located on an area of high ground east of Brooklyn Heights used as a redoubt during the Revolutionary War, Washington Park was created in 1847.[83] However, by 1867 it had fallen into disuse and the Board of Commissioners of Prospect Park, under whose jurisdiction it fell, was considering its future. Olmsted and Vaux were asked to look into the matter. In a report to the president of the board, the designers argued that the site, with its "fine prospect and pure air, combined with [the] extended and varied character of [its] surface," was naturally advantageous and ought to be preserved and improved upon as a public park rather than sold off.[84] They submitted a plan that included two distinct areas with winding paths laid out in the picturesque manner, two open grassed areas for use as girls' and boys' playgrounds, and a large octagonal-shaped paved area to the northwest. Near the busiest and most densely populated part of the neighborhood, this was labeled "open area for public meetings." Of this last feature they wrote:

> We accordingly set off this area, a space of 370 feet in diameter, which will give easy standing room for a mass meeting of thirty thousand persons. The whole of this ground will have a regular slope towards the north end, which furnishes a suitable location for the display of fireworks, and is provided in the center with a "rostrum" for public speakers, to which may be attached, if thought desirable, convenient accommodations for the seating of guests of the city, or for committees.[85]

Adjacent to this open area, and connected to it via a set of broad steps, was a monument to the Revolutionary War and a "saluting ground." The memorial was to be a tomb holding the remains of the so-called Prison Ship Martyrs, nearly twelve thousand American prisoners of war who died on British prison ships anchored in nearby Wallabout Bay. A simple granite tomb was erected on the high ground of the park in 1873.[86] In their report, Olmsted and Vaux argued that this memorial tomb overlooking the meeting ground was to be "at all times a conspicuous object, well calculated . . . to aid in establishing the real solemnity of the duty which meetings ostensibly held for political and patriotic purposes should always have in view."[87] In other words, it would temper the mood of public gatherings, acting as a constant reminder of the sacrifices upon which the nation was founded.

The connection Olmsted and Vaux drew between a space dedicated to public meetings and a war memorial that moderated the activities taking place there could also be applied at Union Square. Here the muster ground to the north was counterbalanced and complemented by the patriotic statues of Washington and Lincoln to the south. As at Washington Park, their plan was to provide a space for orderly and calm public gatherings modeled on the nostalgic ideal of the colonial New England town green, a space overlooked by inspirational statues of figures signifying the common national culture. If the urban populace could not organize itself in an orderly way, they hinted, these spaces might also be used as military marshalling areas. Speaking of Washington Park they noted, "Although the space is not large enough for the practice of military maneuvers, it will serve for

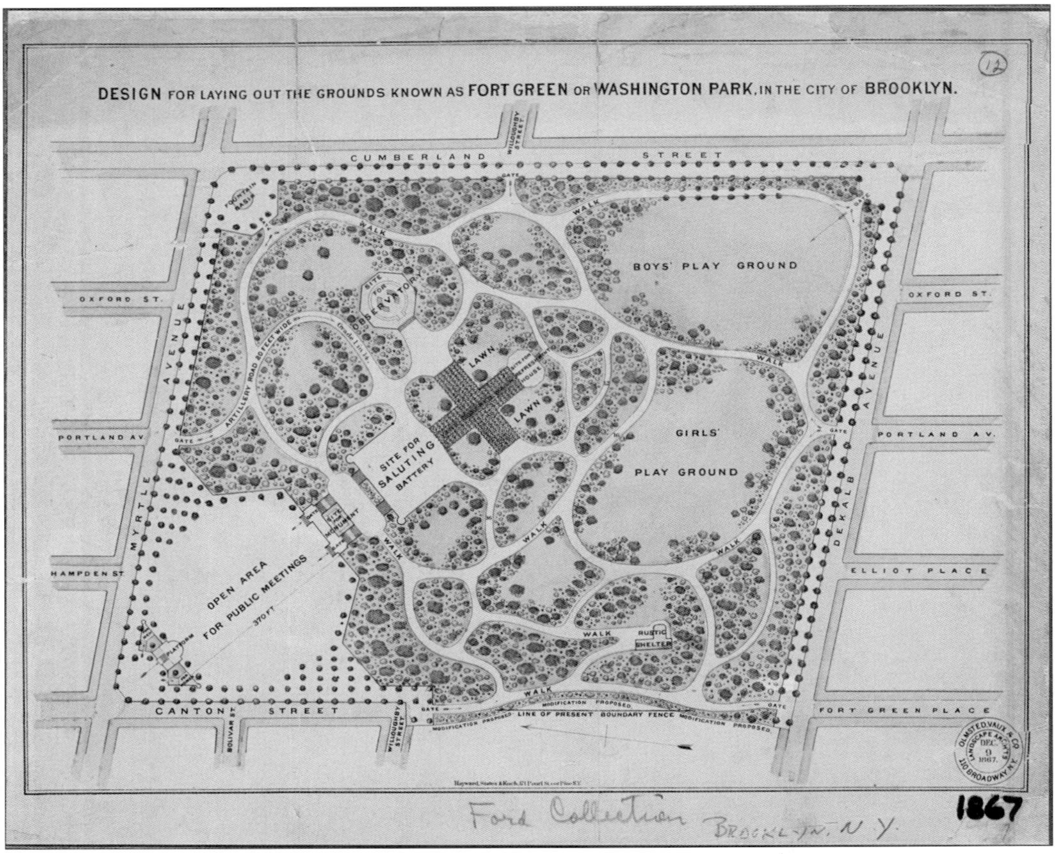

3.8 "Design for Laying Out the Grounds Known as Fort Greene or Washington Park, in the City of Brooklyn," 1867.

the parade and drill of a regiment, and for a marching review of a division or larger body. It would, on any occasion of necessity, be a convenient and suitable position to place and hold in readiness for service a large or small body of troops."[88] The designers did not need to specify what they meant by an "occasion of necessity" in times of urban insurrection, the open space could be given over to military use. Though they were not voiced directly, these comments applied equally well to Union Square. While the muster ground was ostensibly set aside for democratic use, it also anticipated the need for martial law.

After it was completed in late 1872, newspapers began referring to the paved area to the north of Union Square as the "plaza."[89] During the Civil War years huge crowds had gathered around the statue of Washington on the southeastern edge of the park to express civic unity and commitment to the defense of the nation. From the mid-1870s the plaza became the new focus for public events. By 1878 the *New York Times* noted that it was "the scene of so many popular demonstrations during the last few years that people center here by instinct on extraordinary occasions."[90] As we will see in the next chapter, generally understood as a dedicated forum for public action, the plaza lent legitimacy to any crowd who gathered there. Beginning in the early 1880s, it became a prime site for gatherings organized by New York's labor unions, a place where the labor movement could proudly present a public face, imitating other civic celebrations that took place in the same space.

Union Square counters the romantic vision of the mid-nineteenth-century urban parks movement that dominates discussions of Olmsted's work. In particular, it contradicts the belief often incorrectly attributed to Olmsted, that urban parks should be places of leisure and repose alone, and illustrates the coexistence of another concept of the public park as a space of democratic action. At Union Square Olmsted and Vaux built on the model of a popular public park established by the Tammany-led Parks Department to create a different kind of democratic landscape, not a semi-naturalistic setting for promenading, but an open space where the urban crowd could organize and show itself: here it was not statues of inspirational figures, or picturesque nature, but the populace itself that represented the American ideal. Olmsted and Vaux gave physical expression to the ideal of public space as a place for the mass formation of urban citizenry, a place where the crowd could express its common identity and beliefs. It offered the spectacle of human figures as a kind of mass urban ornament, the highly visible and emotionally charged manifestation of a self-organizing, self-policing polis. In its new form, the Square was truly a civic space, a "theater adequate to the utterance of the national voice," as Samuel Ruggles had proudly proclaimed it, an urban space sanctioned for the exercise of democracy. What Olmsted and Vaux did not anticipate, however, was that the space they had created would come to represent the voice of dissent, a stage for those who challenged the dominant order in American society. By the turn of the twentieth century, the plaza, Ruggles's "theater," was a platform for pageants not only of patriotism but also of protest.

4

The People's Forum, 1872–1886

In April 1873, the elite Seventh Regiment of the National Guard formally inaugurated the plaza Frederick Law Olmsted and Calvert Vaux had created at the northern end of Union Square. This was to be "a parade and review ground for the National Guard in this city."[1] In the summer of that year the guard staged a grand parade of all its divisions; eight thousand men marched up Fifth Avenue from Ninth Street to Union Square. The *New York Herald* reported that the reviewing stand stood "on the northern end of the Little Gothic cottage and fronted the broad street with Belgian pavement (Seventeenth Street originally, but now widened and philologically harmonized into the Grand Plaza), and it was decorated with a profusion of flags and banners."[2] According to the *Herald*, the transformation of Union Square was now complete:

> No longer do we behold a dull, inane Union Square, with sickly gas lights and wooden benches, but A BROAD OPEN PLAZA, brilliantly lighted, and a lively, agreeable lounging place by day or by night, at the very center of the population of the island. UNION SQUARE may now be termed the center of the city, the nucleus of its metropolitan life, displaying the endless and varying nebula of mind, body and estate, native and foreign, to our shores.[3]

Though the Square was now considered the "nucleus" of metropolitan life, its public use was heavily restricted. A year after the Seventh Regiment held their review, the Parks Department enforced a new policy: a permit must be granted for the use of the plaza. While police and military parades were common, no permit was issued to any other group for several years.[4] In its earliest incarnation, in response to the urban disorder of the 1870s, the plaza at Union Square was utilized for shows of force. But within a short period massed ranks of working people would appropriate it for parades and pageants that dwarfed those of the National Guard.

During the nineteenth century the rapid growth of the American economy, the expansion of national and global markets, and new methods of production led to huge changes in the geography of New York City. Increasingly dominated by the garment trade, the tenements and loft buildings of the Lower East Side and SoHo became components of a massive urban-industrial machine.[5] The concentration of low-level and semi-skilled workers living and working in Lower Manhattan, most of which comprised of immigrants from Europe, spawned new kinds of workers' groups, challenging the authority of older craft organizations. In response to low wages, long hours, and poor working conditions, industrial workers' unions staged strikes accompanied by mass meetings and demonstrations. Initially these meetings took place in small public squares near workers' homes, such as Tompkins Square and Rutgers Square, followed by parades to the traditional venue for airing public grievances, the steps of City Hall in the crook of Broadway and Park Row. Prompted by the new use of Union Square for important public gatherings, labor groups chose the plaza as the site for meetings that signaled a sharp economic and philosophical divide between the city of production and a city of consumption.

Perfectly poised between the manufacturing district below Fourteenth Street and the Ladies' Mile shopping district, Union Square would become a favorite site for union meetings. During the 1880s Olmsted and Vaux's plaza, designed especially to accommodate civic gatherings, became a significant national center for the American labor movement. On September 5, 1882, a new organization, the Central Labor Union (CLU), staged what they called a Monster Mass meeting to celebrate Labor Day. This unprecedented event was a physical enactment of the power of the labor movement, the corporeal expression of the political strength of a new class of industrial workers. The meeting was to be far more than a labor holiday; it was a political experiment, a show of strength ahead of the November elections when the CLU would put up its own slate of candidates. The meeting was preceded by a parade extending the length of the city from City Hall Park to Bryant Park, concluding with a military style review from the cottage at Union Square. A highly successful amalgam of tradition and innovation, the first Labor Day parade was a masterstroke of public relations. Framed as a workers' celebration, it incorporated elements from socially inclusive civic celebrations dating back to the Erie and Croton parades of the early nineteenth century but was dedicated to the promotion of one particular class. In appropriating this sanctioned form of parade, and utilizing a space set aside by the city for public gatherings, the organizers avoided the negative connotations of past workers' demonstrations such as the disastrous Tompkins Square Riot of 1874. The Labor Day parade was intended as a positive celebration of the unity of labor and its potential as an independent and autonomous political force. In choosing the plaza at Union Square as the culmination of its parade, the CLU extended the reach of working-class New York from its traditional locale in the tenements, loft buildings, and saloons of the Lower East Side into the commercial heart of the city. Flexing its muscle with a spectacular piece of mass choreography, the union overcame the undesirable image of the working-class demonstrations of the past, and proudly proclaimed its right to the city.

Although they did not involve physical changes to the structure of the Square, the labor and political meetings that took place there in the late nineteenth and early twentieth centuries are important to historians of urban form for two reasons. Firstly, they may be considered a form of design in the sense sociologist Henri Lefebvre intended when he described the idea of the social production of space; here the working class co-opted Olmsted and Vaux's plaza, along with the established ritual of the civic parade, for their own purposes of self-organization and self-representation. Secondly, the size and success and these labor meetings (reflected in the wide publicity given to them in newspapers and the popular press) directly prompted an attempt to physically reshape the Square in an attempt to constrain the activities taking place within it during the first two decades of the twentieth century.

The Industrial Landscape of Lower Manhattan

On the 1811 Commissioners' Plan, Houston Street represented the dividing line between old New York to the south and the city of the future to the north. By the middle of the century, Fourteenth Street had come to mark a different sort of geographic and social divide, one between classes. In 1911 the economist Edward Ewing Pratt described the area south of Fourteenth Street as "the district of extreme congestion of both population and manufactures."[6] One historian has estimated that around the turn of the twentieth century, half of the city's population lived within four miles of City Hall.[7] Beginning in the early nineteenth century, the dense network of streets in Lower Manhattan comprised a system of industrial production dependent on human labor massed in close proximity. This human labor was the engine that powered the city's highly productive manufacturing businesses. As labor historian Sean Wilentz has noted, "The high cost of Manhattan real estate and the inaccessibility of water power precluded much mechanization or centralization of work."[8] Instead the focus was on reducing labor costs by tapping into the enormous and continually replenishing pool of new immigrants, housing them closely together in a network of tenement dwellings.

The city had been a national center of garment manufacturing since the early nineteenth century. While the actual work of mass-producing ready-to-wear shirts, pants, and dresses was not mechanized until the 1870s when rotary cutting and sewing machines were invented, garment manufacturing was already semi-industrialized, dependent for its scale and efficiency on the minute division of labor. This was achieved via the infamous "sweating" system: fabric was cut in manufacturing workshops then taken by contractors to so-called outside workers who partially assembled the pieces together in small-scale shops or inside their own homes.[9] These pieces were then taken back to the "inside" shops where they were transformed into complete garments before being sold to wholesalers. Over time, especially after 1892 when New York State passed a law limiting the practice, manufacturing in residential tenement apartments gave way to purpose-built workshops.

In 1902 Russell Sturgis's *Illustrated Dictionary of Architecture* defined the word "loft" to mean "any upper floor as in a warehouse, when intended to be used more or less as one large workshop or storage place, and hence, open throughout without elaborate finish."[10] The idea that the loft was restricted to the upper floor of a building was already an archaic use of the term. By the middle of the nineteenth century manufacturers were already commissioning the construction of multistory loft buildings in Lower Manhattan. While single-story manufacturing buildings had existed throughout the country from the early nineteenth century, this new version was an adaptation designed to exploit Manhattan's high real estate costs and narrow plots.[11] New kinds of material-handling systems—conveyors, chutes, hoist ways, and freight elevators—were developed to maximize efficiency. From the 1850s, block after block of five to ten story loft buildings were constructed south of Houston Street, on either side of Broadway between Chambers and Eighth Streets. Inside these lofts, armies of unskilled and semi-skilled laborers, many of them young women and children, worked six days a week, up to ten hours a day.

Industrial workers were in special need of protection because their jobs were both dangerous and precarious. Ineligible to join craft unions, so-called piece workers had no guarantee of employment from week to week. Their hours and working conditions were unregulated. In response, special groups dedicated to organizing and assisting the emerging industrial labor force began to emerge. By 1850 there were more than eighty labor organizations in New York City. Most of these were not unions but "cooperatives" and "benevolent societies" formed around a specific trade, many segregated by ethnicity. In the Lower East Side Irish and German groups organized meetings in spaces both formal, such as union halls, and informal, such as saloons and bars. They also met on Bowery street corners and in nearby parks such as Tompkins Square and Rutgers Square at the junction of Rutgers and Canal Streets, a popular location for nineteenth-century labor meetings that was destroyed during the construction of the Manhattan Bridge in the early twentieth century. These places may be described as forms of "counter-public sphere," places where people outside the privileged social and economic classes organized themselves as a unified civic group with common beliefs and interests.[12] The meetings held there served to articulate interests and ideas not heard in more traditional arenas of political discourse.

In the prosperous years following the Civil War, efforts to improve the lives of working men and women coalesced around the eight-hour movement, or lobbying for the enactment of legislation restricting the length of the working day to eight hours. The movement became the central cause of trade unions around the country, and "eight hours" became the rallying cry at labor meetings, demonstrations, and parades staged in Lower Manhattan during this period. Although organized efforts to restrict the length of the working day had begun as early as the late eighteenth century, in the mid-nineteenth century ten- to twelve-hour working days were still the norm in mills and manufacturing shops.[13] Following the Civil War, labor organizers made analogies between the eight-hour movement and the abolitionist cause: black slaves working in the southern cotton fields had been freed, and now it was time to free industrial workers from what union organizers called "capitalistic slavery."

In their efforts to achieve a universally recognized eight-hour working day, labor groups adopted the format and choreography of earlier civic celebrations to gather support. By this time the grand civic parades common in the first part of the century had become rare: the elaborate funeral procession accompanying the coffin of President Lincoln in 1865 and the 1876

4.1 "Union Square, New York, July 4, 1876."

celebration of the American Centennial were two of the last of this type the city would ever see.[14] However, the form and choreography of such events—including the arrangement of the participants in militaristic "ranks" or "divisions," the participation of marching bands, and the use of symbolic images and slogans pasted on brightly colored banners and transparencies—lived on in increasingly elaborate trades union parades. These parades served two functions: they communicated their message to the wider public and those in authority, and they encouraged increased union membership by presenting an image of union men as a strong and unified social group. In a tradition well established by the middle of the century, the various divisions of the parade, made up of members of different trades, would march from the union halls along the Bowery to nearby Rutgers Square or Tompkins Square Park, where they would fall in line and proceed in massed ranks to City Hall Park. In this way they bridged between the working-class districts of the Lower East Side and the center of civic power.

Following the success of the Sumter rally and the other Civil War–era massed gatherings, Union Square became an increasingly popular as a site for labor demonstrations. In April 1866, the Workingman's Union held an evening meeting there, urging the state legislature to pass a law limiting the workday to eight hours. A bold attempt to gain the attention of well-off New Yorkers, it took place on the south side of the Square near the statue of Washington. Although the New York State legislature passed an eight-hour law that year, it had little practical effect. In 1872 trades unions staged a series of meetings calling for recognition of the eight-hour day, meetings that led to a prolonged citywide general strike.[15] The strike began in May when a loosely organized coalition of different unions including the Plasterers and Painters unions, as well as the Typographical Union, the Workingmen's Union, and the Internationalists (a politically oriented labor group affiliated with European Socialists), organized dual demonstrations in City Hall Park and Union Square. At City Hall speeches were given from two podiums—one for German speakers and one for English—both decorated with blue and gold ribbons and "built with taste and skill by striking upholsterers."[16] Members of the crowd waved the red flag, a symbol of the international socialist movement. A four-page tract distributed to the crowd of about three hundred called upon workingmen to "combine themselves with each other to accomplish the normal eight hour working day and to secure the means of superior happiness, not only for ourselves, but for our descendants."[17] Aimed specifically at corporation laborers (city workers employed by the Parks and Public Works departments), who had seen their wages reduced, the Union Square meeting was somewhat smaller, but significant in that it definitively extended the geography of labor meetings north of Fourteenth Street.[18] As a result of these meetings, one thousand journeymen piano makers employed by the Singer Sewing Machine Company resolved to strike for an eight-hour day. This strike action quickly expanded to include clothing cutters, carriage painters, slaters and roofers, and journeymen bakers. Soon nearly two-thirds of the manufacturing workforce of New York City was refusing to work. In June the strikers chose Union Square, the center of the piano trade, as the site of a giant rally attended by forty thousand workingmen. Fearing this mass meeting would become violent, local businesses petitioned the state to supply "two or three regiments of infantry, divided up into detachments for patrol duty in the streets, and to guard public and private buildings which might be selected as objects of attack by the mob."[19] Ultimately the strike was ineffective, and the striking men returned to work under the ten-hour system. Expressing relief at this outcome, *Scientific American* called the strike a "great uprising" and claimed that its ultimate goal was "to revolutionize the entire relations of capital and labor."[20] Though it was not successful, this strike prompted the belief that a significant portion of the industrial workforce had become permanently militant.

Middle-class fears about labor unrest were compounded during the

1870s as the national economy descended into a deep recession. New labor demonstrations were accompanied by violent confrontations between workingmen, police, and militia, confrontations that would prompt city leaders to effectively criminalize large-scale labor meetings and pass new laws strictly controlling the use of public streets and parks. In September 1873 the New York Stock Exchange was forced to close after a series of bank failures. In the following months many companies went bankrupt and the manufacturing and building construction industries collapsed. This was the beginning of an international depression that lasted nearly a decade. While trades union had come together over the eight-hour cause, in the wake of a drastic economic collapse they were motivated by a more immediate and desperate issue: devastating unemployment.[21] In response, labor leaders took to the streets to demand the city provide relief in the form of a public works campaign involving city-sponsored building projects. The most famous of these demonstrations resulted in what is known as the Tompkins Square Riot, a violent clash between unemployed workingmen and police. While far less deadly than previous urban conflicts such as the Orange Parade Riot, this was a landmark event, not least because it produced a new civic policy toward the control and use of public space: the preemptive suppression of any public meeting deemed a potential threat to public safety.

Though little remembered today, it was a rally at Union Square that precipitated the notorious meeting at Tompkins Square. At nine o'clock on the morning of January 5th, 1874, about four hundred men gathered at the southern end of the Square for a meeting organized by the Workingmen's Central Council (WCC). This meeting had none of the pomp and ceremony of previous events and far more urgency: there were no flags or banners, and an upturned barrel served as the speaker's rostrum. Peter J. McGuire of the United Brotherhood of Carpenters and Joiners was the first to address the crowd from atop the barrel: he demanded immediate enforcement of the eight-hour law, the abolition of the contract system under which the city government operated, and a reduction in house rents for the unemployed.[22] Following McGuire's speech, Theodore A. Banks, another activist in the eight-hour movement, exhorted the crowd to form a column and march to City Hall "and there demand of the Board of Assistant Aldermen that work be given them on the public works, and to take no refusal."[23] If this demand was not met, he said, they would parade every day until it was granted.

Emboldened by this meeting, labor organizers agreed to hold a second meeting at Tompkins Square on January 13th, from whence they would again march on City Hall. As we saw in chapter 3, Tompkins Square was already a highly politicized space in the 1870s. No longer a green park, it had been paved to discourage social use and also to service military parades; nevertheless, it continued to serve as a place for political discussion and demonstration. Under legislation issued by the Tweed administration in 1871, Parks Department permission was necessary for any gathering within a city park. Representing the Committee on Public Safety, a group lobbying for unemployment benefits, McGuire applied for and was granted a permit for a meeting beginning at 11 a.m. Suspicious of McGuire and fearing an outbreak of violence, the Police Department asked the Parks Department to revoke the permit and made it known that they intended to prevent the meeting taking place.[24] At 10 a.m. a crowd of three thousand people had gathered and assembled around the banner of the Tenth Ward Working Men's Organization. At 10:15 a.m. a squad of mounted police rode into the crowd brandishing truncheons in an attempt to disperse it. In the ensuing melee a police sergeant was struck on the head and forty-four men, almost all recent immigrants, were arrested and charged with disorderly conduct, inciting to riot, and assault. In a humiliating parody of the intended parade, the police marched the arrested men through the streets to the Essex Market Police Court for arraignment. As with other similar events, reaction was drawn according to class lines. Those arrested claimed they had peaceable intentions and were provoked into violence only in an effort to defend themselves. Characterizing the confrontation as a riot, the *New York Times* denigrated the participants as "Communists, Internationalists, demagogues, and evil-disposed persons," and the arrested men as "malcontents," representatives of the "worthless section of the community."[25]

The labeling of the demonstration organizers as "Communists" built on an established narrative in which working-class urban communities were regarded as threats to national stability, justifying a brutal police and military response. To the specter of a working-class uprising, business-friendly commentators added the suggestion of conspiracy and sedition: according to conservative newspapers, labor organizers were not initiating meetings and parades for the sake of their own members, but as a way to promote a foreign political agenda, communism. This negative characterization was influenced by the example of the European revolutions of 1848 and reinforced by the Paris Commune of 1871.[26] In the United States, both socialism and communism were associated with attacks on private property, with opposition to religion, and with disdain for law and order. In this context, labor organizers, particularly immigrants fleeing the failed German revolution, were criticized as "public enemies" intent on importing seditious ideas from across the Atlantic. Using the language of public health, newspapers described radical political philosophies as a disease and the Lower East Side

4.2 "The Red Flag in New York—Riotous Communist Workingmen Driven from Tompkins Square by the Mounted Police, Tuesday, January 13th, 1874," *Frank Leslie's Illustrated Newspaper* (January 31, 1874).

as a dangerous incubator of un-American activity. According to this point of view, any gathering of working-class men was a threat to social stability: stirred up by the wild ranting of foreign demagogues, the irrational and suggestible crowd might resort to mob violence. For those attempting to curtail this apparent threat, one solution was the strict control and policing of public space.

Following the so-called Tompkins Square Riot, city authorities were determined that the Square should not become a locus for working-class organization. The event cemented an unofficial municipal policy that discouraged the popular use of public spaces for political meetings of any kind. As urban historian Lisa Keller has written:

> The . . . riot proved to be a marker in the establishment of clear rules for what was "acceptable" public behavior. Rather than see free speech and assembly as a healthy outlet for political dissent, a way of stemming public violence and thwarting revolution, authorities and propertied classes saw it as a conduit for that revolution, encouraging lawlessness, instability and chaos. Officials discouraged popular use of public space except for parades, recreational use, or nonthreatening events.[27]

While the police had the ability to deny permits for public gatherings, they had seldom withheld permits in order to preemptively suppress political gatherings. After the events at Tompkins Square, this practice became routine. This policy enshrined in law a contemporary assumption about the correct use of public space, an assumption summarized by a *New York Times* editorial of 1877. In reference to another gathering of "Communists" at Tompkins Square Park, the *Times* argued that the right to peaceable assemblage must not be allowed to overshadow the original function of public squares or parks as places of "ornament, health, and recreation." The preservation of these functions should be the role of the city authorities, the *Times* opined. This was especially true when the assembly is "aimed at the subversion of social order," and where "a pestilent and dangerous section of the population was gratified."[28] The consequences of this attitude may be seen in the way the city treated Union Square during the same period. Where Tompkins Square was all but obliterated as a functioning social space, the plaza at Union Square was transformed into a showcase of urban order, given over to highly choreographed displays of police and military power.

Order and Disorder

During the 1870s Union Square presented a somewhat contradictory image as a public space. After it was completed in 1872, Olmsted and Vaux's plaza hosted a number of police and military parades, spectacles designed to display the authority of the city over its populace. At the same time the adjacent park became known as a haven for tramps, indigent men made homeless during the bitter depression years. The first public event staged at the plaza, on November 25th, 1872, utilized all the tools of Victorian pageantry and iconography to establish an image of Union Square, and by extension the city as a whole, as a stronghold of stability and lawfulness. This event came at the end of a tumultuous year, one in which the city experienced fears of mob riots breaking out once again and talk of another general strike. It involved the presentation of a ceremonial flag to the New York City Police Department "as a mark of the appreciation of the bravery and discipline displayed by them during the riots of 1863 and 1871."[29] (That is, the draft riots and the Orange Parade riot.) This flag was intended to be displayed at police reviews and at funerals of policemen who lost their lives on duty. Proposed by Colonel Henry S. Olcott, a respected Civil War veteran and lawyer, this private initiative followed the model of the Washington Memorial project, with the flag as the civic offering rather than a statue. Lead by Olcott, a few socially prominent citizens raised money for a symbolic gesture, claiming to act on behalf of all New Yorkers. In this case a self-nominated Citizen's Committee set up a fund, soliciting small sums from private individuals. Though the organizers were anxious to avoid the appearance of sectarianism, there was an obvious political message behind the exercise: when the police "defended" the city during the draft riots of 1863 and the Orange Parade riot of 1871, their opponents were not a foreign invading force but working-class New Yorkers. Led by an honor guard of mounted police, the Citizen's Committee paraded the flag from police headquarters downtown to the newly constructed plaza where it was formally handed over to Police Commissioner Joseph Bosworth. Of dark blue silk, the flag measured 6′ × 6′6″, in size, and was bordered with a gold-colored silk fringe and supported by a lance mounted by a brass eagle with spread wings. On one side was embroidered the coat of arms of the city of New York, and on the other the motto "The Citizens of New York to their Brave Police. 1863—July—1871. Faithful until death." Following this ceremony it became a tradition to review the annual police parade from the plaza at Union Square, and each year this ceremonial flag led the parade.

With the plaza established as a site for demonstrating civic authority, the park itself was falling into decline. Under the austerity budget imposed on the city after the rout of the Tweed regime, expenditure on public parks was heavily restricted. During the years of national depression and limited city spending, the only significant changes to the park itself were the installation of a new statue on the east side and a drinking fountain on the west. The statue of the Revolutionary War hero General Lafayette by French sculptor Frédéric-Auguste Bartholdi, presented in 1876 on the occasion of the centenary of American Independence, has been described in chapter 2. Its unveiling was accompanied by a parade of police, military, and firemen in yet another display of civic power.[30] The gift of a private citizen, Daniel Willis James, the so-called James fountain was installed in 1881. Sculpted in Germany by Karl Adolf Donndorf, the fountain sat on a granite and bronze pedestal complete with lions' heads spouting water, and was topped by a relief sculpture depicting a mother with two children holding a pitcher of water.[31] James intended the fountain as a philanthropic example to other wealthy New Yorkers: at a time of economic hardship it provided a source of clean water. Though the gift was well intentioned, it was criticized from both aesthetic and practical points of view: on one hand it was considered too "academic" as a work of art and on the other it was placed too high for horses and dogs to drink from.[32] It is doubtful that the Parks Department would have accepted such a gift at a time of greater civic prosperity. As realized the James Fountain was not particularly useful; nor did it fit the precedent of patriotic heroes set by the earlier statues.

The military parades and the installation of new ornaments was not enough to stop the decline of Union Square during the deep depression of the mid-1870s. Though the streets surrounding it were crowded with shoppers by day and theatergoers into the evening, the park gained a reputation as a dangerous place at night. As unemployment peaked, many single men and some women took to sleeping on park benches after dark. In 1875, the editor of *Appleton's Journal* condemned the presence in Washington, Union and Madison Squares of

> idle and dirty vagabond[s] . . . [b]leary-eyed and bloated topers, ragged and vicious tramps, soiled and untouchable wretches of all kinds. . . . A slightly better class—that is, a class just above begging and vagabondage—go there to smoke their rank pipes, to eject their filthy tobacco juice . . . and to help to their full degree to render the places noisome and offensive.[33]

Because of this nuisance, the editor noted, these parks were no longer suitable for respectable women. Seen as illegitimate intruders, tramps were an unwanted presence, depriving the rightful users of the park their peace and respite. It was the nightly task of the park police to rouse sleeping tramps by slapping the soles of their feet with a sturdy nightstick. When the "tramp problem" became especially great, they were rounded up en masse, arrested on charges of vagrancy and sentenced to a term at the workhouse on Blackwell's Island in the middle of the East River.[34] This draconian practice was justified as a valid effort to reduce crime. Robberies were common in parks, and tramps were often blamed, though they were just as likely to be victims of violence as perpetrators. In the summer of 1876, for example, a man sleeping in Union Square was attacked by a pack of six men and boys, who poked his eye out with a stick, a gruesome injury that caused his death three days later. This was the most vicious of several attacks that took place in Union Square during 1876 and 1877.[35]

For some commentators, the tramp problem pointed to a larger and more pernicious threat: they were the most visible portion of a growing underclass of men unable to find work. During a time of national crisis, these indigents became symbols of a sinister threat to national stability: the anarchic and combustible energy of working-class men released from traditional social bonds and not engaged in productive labor. In 1877, during the worst of the drawn-out depression years, the *New York Times* editorialized that the rapidly expanding industrial economy had produced a new class of Americans characterized by their reckless disinclination to live normal lives protected by attachments to stable jobs, home, and family. This class, the *Times* warned, was increasingly dangerous: "When a great riot, like that in Pittsburg, breaks out, the tramps gather from afar, like eagles to the carcass. As they don't care for consequences, nothing short of an immediate and violent death frightens them from a work of destruction."[36] Here, the editor referred to a series of violent strikes during the summer of 1877. Beginning in Pennsylvania, railway workers across four states struck against pay reductions, causing huge disruption to the nation's rail network. These strikes soon spread to other trades. In response to corporate pressure, police, local militia, and federal troops were called out, and hundreds were injured and killed on both sides.[37] Nationwide, newspapers reinforced a narrative that these work stoppages and bloody confrontations represented a threat to the stability of the American republic. Inflammatory press coverage stoked fears that a "great rebellion" was beginning.

Following a pattern established earlier in the century, newspapers refused to believe that American workers might challenge the economic system that had caused such hardship; instead they placed the blame on dangerous foreign influences. In his assessment of the volcanic social disruption, Allan Pinkerton, founder of the Pinkerton National Detective Agency, an organization that played a role in repressing the strikes, pointed to the influence of European Communism. Pinkerton drew a direct connection between striking workers, tramps, and the 1871 Paris Commune in his book, *Strikers, Communists, Tramps and Detectives* (1878). Like the opinion writers at the *New York Times*, he saw underemployed industrial workers as the catalyst for the importation of communism into the United States. Seeing the strikers' dissatisfaction with the results of unchecked capitalist expansion, he argued that a transient and reckless class, holding no stake in the preservation of the national economy, would just as soon overthrow as contribute to it.

Reinforced by this rhetoric, by the end of the decade public opinion had been mobilized against the labor movement. In response, unions began to marshal their own publicity campaign. Denigrated and delegitimized in the press as dangerous and irrational mobs, and restrained in their actions by brutal police practices and strict civic policies outlawing public meetings, they planned a different form of self-presentation, one that combined the peaceful and celebratory traditions of the artisan and civic parades of the early nineteenth century with a new political agenda. The themes that characterized this mobilization of labor power were prefigured at a rally in

Union Square held for the Californian labor organizer Denis Kearney.[38] A powerfully built Irish American, Kearney had acquired a national reputation for thunderous oratory following a series of speeches given at an outdoor plaza near San Francisco's City Hall known as the "Sandlot." The spokesman for the Workingmen's Party of California, Kearney's chief preoccupation in these speeches was the economic threat presented by Chinese immigrant labor. Soon afterward he embarked on a countrywide tour urging American born workers to come together as a political force, united in opposition to this form of competition. This tour took him as far as the East Coast; in September 1878 handbills appeared addressed to "To the Workingmen of New York City," announcing that Kearney would speak in Union Square at a meeting to be held "sand lot style"—that is, without pomp and ceremony.[39]

Kearney's rabble-rousing reputation preceded him. While the park commissioners granted his supporters a permit to hold a meeting (one of the first given to such a group under the strict new policy), the city prepared accordingly: 250 policemen were stationed around the periphery of the plaza; a reserve force of 150 stood nearby in front of the Academy of Music on Fourteenth Street; and a party of mounted police was stationed between Fifteenth and Sixteenth Streets on Irving Place. The Seventh Regiment stood in readiness at their arsenal and members of the militia mingled with the crowd. The meeting was also closely observed by a group of German American Socialists leery of Kearney's nativist message, and by representatives of Tammany Hall. But if Kearney was disturbed by all this attention he did not show it. At 8:00 p.m. he arrived at the plaza, took off his coat, and leaped up onto a small wooden platform erected opposite the Everett House Hotel. From there he began to address the eight thousand men gathered before him. Kearney's oratory was masterful. In the era before electronic sound amplification, "he spoke slowly and with sufficient strength of voice to be heard by nearly all in the assemblage, taking pains to turn his face from side to side of the plaza while speaking, and thus holding the attention of all parts of the crowd."[40] His colorful speech was full of virulent attacks against capitalists, including the evil "monopolists" who ran the city's railway companies. He also denounced the press, as well as politicians, criticizing the Democratic and Republican parties equally. His message was not a demand for violent revolution, however, but a call for workingmen to utilize their numeric superiority at the ballot box. The time had come, he said, for a working-class political movement to rise up and seize power through established democratic channels. If a popular uprising was going to succeed in any country, he said, it would happen in the United States. After traveling all over the globe, he concluded, "I have seen that America is the workingman's heaven and the Stars and Stripes is the flag of freedom."[41] In other words, the true patriot was the native-born American worker who claimed his democratic rights.

Kearney also praised Union Square as a site entirely fitting for the formation of a populist political movement. "I was informed that if a hall was hired tonight it would cost $250," he said. "But here we are, occupying a hall given to us by God almighty, with a splendid roof over our heads and a splendid lamp [pointing to the moon] to give us light."[42] With his speech Kearney rehearsed the themes that would reappear in the first Labor Day parade of 1882: the urgent need for working people to realize the political power they held because of their superior numbers; references to the American tradition of righteous revolution and workingmen as the true patriots; and the argument that American parks and squares were to be utilized to the fullest, as places of democratic action. Hastily organized and highly contentious, Kearney's meeting was viewed with deep suspicion by city authorities and by many members of the labor movement. By contrast, the organizers of the first Labor Day aimed at conciliation. In widening their constituency to include workers of all ethnicities, and in broadcasting a seemingly simple and peaceful message celebrating the contribution of labor to American society, they created a sympathetic event praised across all sectors of New York society.

The First Labor Day Parade

Adapting the choreography of earlier artisan parades and civic celebrations, the first Labor Day parade, on September 5th, 1882, created a new tradition copied around the country and also a new symbolic association for Union Square.[43] Though it was presented as a peaceful and orderly demonstration of the fraternity of workingmen, those who planned it had larger ambitions. The parade had a dual message, one for union members and another for the wider public who witnessed it. To outsiders it was intended as a celebration of the unity of labor in a broad and abstract sense. To insiders it advertised the potential of the united labor movement as an independent and autonomous political entity. More than a workers' holiday, it was the first shot in a campaign to demonstrate the political power of the working class. In choosing Union Square for the formal review of the parade, the labor movement took Kearney's metaphor to its logical conclusion. They transformed the plaza, the "Hall given to us by God almighty," into a forum of the working people. In doing so they attached to themselves the language and symbols of patriotism that had so often characterized large gatherings held there. In

4.3 "New York City—Grand Demonstration of Workingmen, September 5th: The Procession Passing the Reviewing Stand at Union Square," *Frank Leslie's Newspaper* (September 16, 1882).

contrast to the turbulent 1870s, when mass meetings of working New Yorkers often communicated a confrontational and aggressive message, theirs was calm and orderly. In adopting the pageantry of earlier civic celebrations, along with their site, the labor movement lent itself social and political legitimacy. Beyond this, the parade extended the geography of the working class beyond its traditional locale in the Lower East Side into the chief public space of the city. Uniting the Lower East Side and the commercial and residential districts to the north, it displayed a positive image of working people and their contribution to civic life. Flexing its muscle with a spectacular piece of mass choreography, the union movement overcame the negative associations of previous labor rallies and proudly proclaimed its right to the city.

The parade was organized by a newly formed organization, the Central Labor Union of New York and Vicinity (CLU). The CLU exemplified a new kind of workers' association, one not dependent on traditional craft unions but on the idea that industrialization had fundamentally altered the relations between workers and their employers. Founded in 1881, the CLU was an umbrella organization uniting many small unions divided by trade and ethnicity.[44] Beginning with fourteen trades groups, it quickly expanded to over fifty, including the elite typographers, stonecutters, carpenters, and furniture makers, as well as painters, blacksmiths, clothing cutters, and shoemakers, along with unskilled sales clerks and day laborers. In a practical sense the CLU helped individual unions by settling disputes with employers and raising strike funds. Its membership was politically eclectic, including socialist and communist radicals, as well as more conservative labor organizers dedicated to reform within the democratic system. Together they had experience as members of the Workingmen's Union and the Irish-dominated Knights of Labor. Reflecting this diversity, the group's aims were broad, covering all issues of general concern to labor during this time: support for an eight-hour day; the abolition of child and prison labor, and the sweating system; equal pay for men and women; and the abolition of conspiracy laws that made union organization illegal.

Already successful in lobbying the city government on behalf of city workers, the CLU was about to enter a new phase, putting up its own slate of candidates in the upcoming November elections. In the CLU's publication, *Truth*, two of its leaders—George Block, a member of the Bakers Union, and Matthew Maguire of the Machinists and Blacksmiths Union—described the organization as "an industrial rather than a political party."[45] They aimed to challenge the two-party system by uniting the combined force of labor into a single voting block. Besides promoting specific goals such as wage increases and the realization of the eight-hour day, the CLU was designed to unite numerous small and ethnically divided workers' organizations into a single powerful unit. In this way it had the effect of strengthening the union movement, encouraging new immigrants to join a group in which they had not previously seen a place for themselves. If it was to be successful in the elections, the CLU had to transform the negative image of organized labor into something more palatable to middle- and upper-class New Yorkers. One of the chief aims of the monster meeting was to erase the memory of the confrontational and sometimes violent labor meetings of the 1860s and 1870s. Calm and orderly, it would overturn the stereotype of the working-class "mob" born out of the carnage of the draft riots and the bloody Orange Parade, as well as the contentious meetings that had taken place in Tompkins Square. Now that the country had emerged from economic depression, money was flowing once again and work was plentiful. The CLU was anxious to present the combined forces of labor as willing and able to achieve their aims through peaceful negotiation and through the electoral process. As historians Michael Kazin and Stephen J. Ross have noted, the parade's success lay in "building, inspiring and mobilizing a labor movement, and courting a mass public whose opinions about that movement could help legitimize and advance its reputation and power."[46]

The September 5th parade was staged in conjunction with the Knights of Labor annual convention in New York City. In August the CLU announced plans for the parade at Science Hall at 145 East Eighth Street. Block reported on arrangements for "one of the greatest labor demonstrations ever seen in this city."[47] Overseen by Grand Marshal William McCabe of Typographical Union no. 6., the demonstration would consist of a parade marching in three divisions. The first, consisting of unions from Brooklyn, Jersey City, and those below Canal Street, would assemble at City Hall Park. The second, comprising unions on the east side above Canal Street, would form at Cooper Union. The third, made up of unions on the west side above Canal Street, would meet at Washington Square. At 10:00 a.m. sharp the first division would begin to march up Broadway. At Fourth Street the second division would fall in, followed by the third division at Waverly Place. From there the line would move up Broadway to Fourteenth Street, around the east side of Union Square to the plaza where it would be reviewed. From there it would proceed up Fifth Avenue to Reservoir Square at Forty-Second Street (now Bryant Park), where the marchers would be dismissed and retire to a picnic at Wendel's Elm Park on the far Upper West Side. The chairman concluded the meeting by calling the actions of the union "the starting point of a great victory for the working masses."[48] Later that week the CLU issued a circular addressed to "the Working People of New York, Brooklyn, Jersey City and Adjacent Cities," asking for the participation of every labor union in the "monster street parade and a grand picnic."[49] Issued from the CLU headquarters at Front Street in Brooklyn, the circular was signed by Block and Maguire. All manufacturing shops were asked to close in order that union members could attend. Though it was later celebrated in the press as a peaceful and orderly demonstration of the fraternity of workingmen, it is clear from the pages of the *Truth* that the intentions were far more confrontational. Block was combative in his use of language: "Let us on that day show labor at its full strength," he wrote. "Let us give thereby a warning to those who fatten on our blood and marrow and who use our children's blood and youth to keep their fathers in bondage."[50]

The monster meeting was a publicity tactic as much as a holiday celebration. The CLU knew that a large gathering would attract substantial press coverage. Its leaders actively sought the attention of sympathetic journalists, hoping to counteract the negative publicity the labor movement had received in mainstream newspapers, especially the *New York Times*. Above all the Labor Day parade represented a new form of public ritual, a civic ceremony presenting an image of labor as indispensable to continued prosperity, a powerful and peaceful force within American society. Mimicking the kinds of mass parades favored by other civic clubs and organizations, and occupying the politically charged space of Union Square, the parade was an unmistakable statement about the future of American democracy, one in which the labor movement aimed to galvanize its numerical advantage in order to play an active, if not leading, role.[51] Speaking in explicitly militaristic terms, Block called the parade "the review before the battle."[52] That battle, of course, being the one that dominated American society in the late nineteenth century: the fight between labor and capital.

Despite claims for its uniqueness, the monster meeting was not without precedent. The CLU had already organized two mass meetings in Union Square during the summer of 1882, both of which served as opportunities for the group to show its strength and reveal its political intentions. The first was a reception for Michael Davitt, one of the leaders of the Irish National Land League, a group that sought Irish home rule and relief of the oppression of Irish agricultural workers.[53] Though somewhat lacking in execution, the evening reception for Davitt was a dress rehearsal for the monster meeting held later that fall. As at the Kearney rally, a platform was erected in front of the Everett House, illuminated this time not by the moon but by calcium lights.[54] After some confusion a permit had been granted for the reception by the Parks Department. Wary of trouble, the police deployed a large contingent of men around the space in front of the podium, keeping it clear until the reception started. Following tradition, the procession, made up of members of the Freight Handlers, Boilermakers, Longshoremen, Cigar Makers, and other unions marching in ranks, paraded from their downtown meeting halls to the plaza where they heard speeches by Davitt and Robert Blissert of the Tailor's Union. Both men repeated the same message: though their movements were radical, they were committed to achieving them via peaceful means. The events organized by the CLU were not only opportunities to voice that idea, but also forums to demonstrate it, showing New Yorkers that the union was made up of civilized and rational men capable of effective self-organization.

At a second, smaller, meeting of 1882, called in support of the freight handlers' strike, the union made clear its intention to speak for all its members by staging a multilingual assembly. In addition to the main stand where speeches were made in English, they arranged a series of improvised stands mounted on "trucks" (horse-drawn carts) on either side of the plaza, from which speeches were delivered in Russian, Italian, German, and also

"Hebrew" (as the newspaper reports had it).[55] This effort to accommodate members of all the dominant ethnic groups that made up the working class of the city went a long way to overcome the tensions between older and newer immigrant groups that had divided the labor movement earlier in the century. With these two meetings, the CLU demonstrated its strong links to international workers' movements, its recognition of the diverse ethnic makeup of its own members, and its determination to claim political power. The Labor Day parade cemented these ideas in a grand piece of urban theater, equal in every way to the Croton parade and the great Sumter rally.

September 5th was a Tuesday. As the CLU had requested, workshops and stores throughout the city were closed. From early morning huge crowds began to gather along the route, including 250,000 in Union Square alone. Headed by a company of mounted police, then a group of women bearing flags, twenty thousand men marched in the line, representing 150 labor organizations.[56] Wearing the regalia of their trades, they were accompanied by bands playing the Marseillaise and other rousing tunes. They held banners inscribed with mottoes: "All Men are Born Alike and Equal," "Labor Built the Republic and Labor Shall Rule It." In Union Square the parade passed in front of the cottage where labor leaders including Terrence V. Powderly of the Knights of Labor, Maguire, and Blissert, reviewed the massed ranks. Though there was some criticism of the event in the press (the *Christian Index* called the organizers "contemptible demagogues" and the marchers "dupes"), the general reception was positive.[57] The *Irish World*, a strong supporter of the CLU, concluded that the demonstration pointed "to the good time coming when envy, jealously, and bickerings shall cease forever, and all our industrious people stand shoulder to shoulder in the struggle with the triple-headed monster, interest, rent and profit."[58] The *Herald* credited the CLU with putting on a spectacular show, and praised the participants for being well dressed and well behaved. Calling the parade "hugely successful," it concluded that the event should give the unions confidence they would succeed at the ballot box. Even the generally unsympathetic *Tribune* reported favorably on the positive atmosphere of the parade, saying it ably demonstrated the "strength and *esprit de corps* of the trade and Labor organizations."[59] In this way organized labor was officially recognized as an equal participant in the political life of the city, with the same rights to public self-presentation and self-expression as any other civic group. The parade was so successful that a similar one was held in Union Square the following fall, and in other cities around the country, while Labor Day soon became an officially recognized national holiday. In 1884 the CLU decided to observe the first Monday in September as Labor Day every year. Supported by national labor organizations and by politicians who recognized the power of the unions as a united voting bloc, it became a national event by 1886. Oregon became the first state to make Labor Day a holiday in 1887, and in 1894 President Grover Cleveland designated it an official federal holiday.

Besides establishing a national tradition, the Labor Day parade created a new connotation for the plaza at Union Square as an important locus for labor meetings. In the years to come a familiar routine would be followed: after the proper permits had been acquired, printed handbills and press advertisements would announce a meeting, the podium at the cottage would be decorated with banners and flags, including the Stars and Stripes. Chairs would be provided for those scheduled to address the meeting, along with other dignitaries, and tables would be set up for press reporters. Massed ranks made up of different union groups would assemble outside Lower East Side union halls and march to Union Square. Accompanied by bands playing patriotic tunes and the ever-present Marseillaise, they would brandish banners and transparencies printed with labor mottoes and wave red flags. The next day detailed reports, including transcriptions of the primary speeches, would appear in the major newspapers, even those not generally supportive of labor. These events served to almost completely transform public opinion about the labor movement and its claim to public space, at least temporarily. The identification of Union Square as a legitimate forum for working-class political speech would continue well into the twentieth century.

Following the triumph of Labor Day, the CLU achieved its greatest political success in the mayoral election of 1886 when it supported the candidacy of the hugely popular social activist Henry George.[60] George ran under the banner of the United Labor Party (ULP), the political arm of the CLU. The ULP campaigned on a platform of better pay, hours, and working conditions, along with an end to police restrictions on peaceable assemblages. George's candidacy has been called "the most significant political moment in New York labor history."[61] For a brief moment the possibility of radical social and political change led by the labor movement seemed real, and Union Square was the space in which this change was demanded. Just before the election, on the last day of October, George's supporters staged a massive evening rally. Contemporary reports describe the splendor of the scene, and the hope it embodied. Starting from Great Jones Street and the Bowery, a torch-lit parade made up of members of many trade organizations marched up Fourth Avenue to the plaza. Cementing its links with the Labor Day parade, the Grand Marshal was William McCabe. Permission had been granted to those living along the line of the march to decorate their windows with

4.4 Labor Day Parade, Union Square, 1887.

banners and lights. From the veranda of the cottage, George reviewed the marchers, which was again illuminated for the occasion with calcium lights. Though the night was rainy, the parade was so large that it took an hour and a half to pass the reviewing stand, marching in ranks of eight to twenty men. The next day the *New York Times* reported:

> Torches, Chinese lanterns, banners, transparencies, and other parapherna-lia of a political parade began to appear on the streets near the upper end of the Bowery early in the evening, and the air was filled with the sounds of fife and drums, brass bands, and a cheering populace, for quite an hour

> before the time to start. . . . Occasionally a silk banner drooped in the rain, or some shining device out of the ordinary, such as the banner of the brass-workers, burnished like brass, or a pretty transparency carried by the plumbers, who made of all the finest display, on which was emblazoned "You Knighted We Stand." The Cuban Society carried lanterns giving a soft red light, very pretty in effect, and District Assembly no. 49, Knights of Labor, made a brilliant display of fireworks and torches. The broom-makers swung aloft a broom four stories high, to which Mr. George raised his hat while everybody yelled with delight.[62]

After leaving Union Square, the procession turned south again, back to what the newspaper described as the labor movement's own territory, finishing at Tompkins Square.

When the official election results were tallied George came second, receiving almost sixty-eight thousand votes to the Democratic candidate Abram S. Hewitt's ninety thousand. (The young and politically untested Republican Theodore Roosevelt received a mere six thousand.) Despite its loss, the ULP celebrated its entry into the political process as a great victory, believing it would continue to grow in strength and one day claim the ultimate prize: the presidency. However, this was not to be. In the 1887 local elections the ULP stood candidates again, with public support from George, who was still a popular figure. But this time they competed not only against Democrats and Republicans, but also against the newly formed Progressive Labor Party (PLP), a socialist group that promoted a transatlantic culture of working-class unity rather than a specifically American idea of democracy. The entry of the PLP onto the political scene represented a fracturing of the labor vote from which the larger movement would never recover. In the next two decades more militant splinters of the political working class would emerge, all organizing meetings in Union Square as a way to publicize their message. As these groups competed for attention, their messages became more extreme, leading to further efforts to repress such events altogether.

A single event in the 1887 election campaign, a meeting to ratify the ticket of the PLP, illustrates the themes that would come to dominate discussion of the right to public assembly in New York City during the next twenty years. During the course of the meeting, police suddenly drew their clubs and began hammering blows on the crowd in an attempt to disperse it.[63] One of the organizers of the meeting, Sergei Shevitch, a Russian journalist active in socialist politics and the editor of the German language labor newspaper *New Yorker Volkszeitung* (New York Peoples' News), later testified before the New York State Senate:

> On the evening of the 8th day of October, 1887, at Union Square, a lawful meeting of peaceable citizens held under the auspices of the Progressive Labor Party and numbering about 4000 persons was violently and brutally dispersed by a large force of police under the command of Captain Riley in the presence of Police Commissioner Voorhis. Many persons, including women, were severely clubbed, the speakers and officers of the party on two trucks in the middle of the Square were violently thrown down and beaten, and American flags and trade banners were torn and destroyed, and the citizen who then addressed the meeting from the platform of the cottage was threateningly ordered by a policeman to stop his speaking.[64]

The sudden and brutal assault was premeditated, Shevitch claimed. The following day Henry George condemned the attacks a "gross outrage." Though they were his opponents, the PLP had "as good a right as any American citizens to peaceably meet and to express their feelings and wishes."[65] Prefiguring an argument frequently deployed over the next two decades, George accused the New York City police force of anarchic behavior, of not obeying the law of the land. The *New York Tribune* published an editorial essentially agreeing with George, though from a different political perspective: "It is a mistake to give these people any real grievance such as they undoubtedly had on Saturday night. . . . So long as they keep within the bounds of the law, the Socialists have the same right of peaceable assemblage and free speech as any other persons."[66] Nothing could be more to the liking of the socialists, nor win them more recruits, the paper suggested, than to deprive them of their right to free speech.

Mindful of this criticism, the police took a different approach when the PLP held another meeting the following week, organized by the socialists to condemn the police for withholding their constitutional rights. Eight thousand attended the meeting, which followed the by now usual stagecraft and choreography of marching bands, a profusion of red flags, and three stands erected on different sides of the plaza. The crowd held aloft transparencies referring to police violence: one depicted a police club brandished over the stars and stripes. Others said, "We need no public insulters but public protectors"; "Down with police. Free speech forever. Workingmen, defend your freedom."[67] The police were present in force, but careful not to interfere. Copying tactics used by the British in Ireland, they sent official stenographers to record the words of the speakers, making it clear that they would "prosecute any orator who should abuse the right of free speech by inciting the multitude toward any criminal act."[68] Addressing the crowd, Shevitch condemned the actions of the police in the strongest terms, telling them the law and the constitution had been trampled into dust. He went further, claiming that the repression of public meetings was part of a larger state conspiracy to deprive working men of their rights:

> We are gathered peacefully, every man is his own policeman. The only element that has proven itself riotous is the police. The clubbing was not a mistake, it was part of a systematic plot inaugurated by those that do not work and rob the product of other's work. Ever since 1874 we have seen a long series of outrages against free speech. There was the Tompkins Square attack, the shooting of the rioters in 1877, the police murders in Chicago last year, and the murders by the Pinkerton men in East St. Louis and Jersey City.[69]

Near the end of the meeting Col. Richard Hinton, a Civil War veteran and prominent socialist, read from the Constitution the sections relating to freedom of speech, the press, and the right of citizens to assemble and petition for redress of grievances. The citation of the Constitution was to be echoed frequently in the following decades. Though the New York City labor movement was never again as united as it was in the early 1880s, its various factions continued to come together in Union Square. During the next twenty years, as the challenge to the accepted political order became more and more provocative, debate about the exact meaning of the freedom of speech and assembly guaranteed under the First Amendment, and about what kinds of gathering could and should be tolerated in public parks and squares, assumed larger and larger national importance.

5

The Home of Discontent, 1886–1917

When thousands of working-class New Yorkers marched around Union Square in triumphant assembly in 1882, they claimed one of the city's premiere public spaces as their own. For the next fifty years, unions and political groups used the Square as a stage for elaborately choreographed presentations of working-class power and solidarity designed for both internal and external audiences. However, the unity and common purpose that characterized the first Labor Day parade did not last. Within a decade, radical groups splintered away from the mainstream wing of the labor movement. From 1890 they began a new tradition, the celebration of May Day, which challenged the supremacy of Labor Day as the primary date in the workers' calendar. On this day socialist and anarchist orators gathered in Union Square to reject moderate labor goals such as the eight-hour day and to argue instead for the complete overthrow of capitalism. As May Day grew in size and radical political philosophies gathered support, Union Square acquired a reputation as a forum for anti-American ideas, a ground zero of immanent revolution. Beginning in the 1890s, anarchists staged new forms of protest in Union Square, refusing to accept sanctioned norms of public behavior. Their purposeful noncompliance with the rule of law was intended as a political statement. In response, police put extreme pressure on political meetings of any kind, denying permits, infiltrating the activities of meeting organizers, censoring speeches given from the cottage, and breaking up demonstrations by force.

After the turn of the twentieth century, political meetings in Union Square became key tests for the free speech movement, with liberal commentators decrying attempts to suppress them as a violation of the fundamental rights of American citizens. The detonation of a bomb in the Square in 1908 created a public debate over the issue of free speech as newspaper articles and journalistic commentaries struggled to make sense of the new era of urban terrorism. Influenced by a progressive municipal administration, the Police and the Parks departments fundamentally changed their attitude regarding mass meetings. Parks Commissioner Charles B. Stover and Police Commissioner Arthur Woods promoted a reformed attitude to the control and use of public space, arguing that the role of the police was to protect rather than repress public speech, even when it was highly contentious. This attitude anticipated a new judicial approach toward the Constitutional rights to freedom of speech and freedom of assembly initiated by the Supreme Court in 1919. In this way Union Square was momentarily transformed from a highly dangerous public space, the literally explosive home base of a nationwide anarchist threat, into a fragile test case for progressive attitudes to the protection of public assembly for the purpose of political expression.

This attitude was short-lived in its effect, however. During World War I and its aftermath, the idealistic view of public life and public space envisioned by progressives was abandoned. Between 1914 and the early 1920s fears of an immigrant-led revolution saw hundreds of foreign-born activists rounded up and deported. Political activity in Union Square was harshly repressed as the violent action espoused at antiwar and Industrial Workers of the World (IWW) meetings engendered a less optimistic view of the urban crowd. As protestors continued to claim the Square as a site of radical protest, the local government attempted to reclaim it as a symbol of patriotism. Civic authorities refused permits for May Day rallies, deeming them seditious. They countered public displays of pacifism with a series of counter-spectacles designed to promote the war effort. During the war years, visitors to Union Square were confronted with the absurdist spectacle of an ersatz battleship, the USS Recruit, sitting in the middle of an enlarged suburban garden. Intended as a navy recruiting station, this construction was far larger than necessary for that modest purpose. Sitting squarely in the middle of a public space strongly associated with antiwar protests, the

Recruit was a blunt propaganda tool intended to quash pacifist activism and bolster local support for nationalism.

May Day and Labor Day

While the popular press celebrated the inaugural Labor Day parade as a praiseworthy civic event, one that showcased the dignity, pride, and economic contribution of working-class New Yorkers, a decade later labor gatherings in Union Square had acquired an entirely different, more sinister, association. By the early 1890s the mass rallies that regularly occurred there were seen as auguries of violent social disintegration—literally a descent into anarchy. The image of Union Square as the place where an inflamed urban populace might put the spark to the powder keg of revolution was cemented in an apocalyptic novel, *Caesar's Column* (1890). Written by an eccentric politician named Ignatius Donnelly, under the pen name Edmund Boisgilbert, the book described a fictional and highly dystopian New York City one hundred years in the future. In 1988 the city is ruled by a capitalist oligarchy that has corrupted the courts, the newspapers, and the ballot box. In response, the "Brotherhood of Destruction," a confederacy of destitute former industrial workers has taken control of the city and begun to destroy it. An Italian immigrant, the demonic Caesar Lomellini, directs the mayhem from his barricaded fortress in Lower Manhattan. From here, members of the brotherhood loot the Wall Street banks, then rampage uptown to murder scores of wealthy people inside their palatial mansions. Lomellini orders his men to pack the slaughtered bodies of capitalists and their families into wooden boxes, pour cement over them, and create out of these grisly building blocks a colossal column in the middle of Union Square. Riding up Broadway, now deserted by all but the angry mob, the narrator observes the result:

> The shops had all been broken open; dead bodies lay here and there; and occasionally a burned block lifted its black arms appealingly to heaven. As we drew near Union Square a wonderful sight—such as the world had never beheld—expanded before us. Great blazing bonfires lighted the work; hundreds of thousands had gathered to behold the ghastly structure, the report of which had already spread everywhere. . . . The men of intellect were doing the work; the men of muscle were giving the orders.[1]

At the center of this mayhem, overshadowing the statues of Washington and Lincoln far below, stood Caesar's Column, a ghastly parody of the

Roman victory column. The narrator provides an epitaph to accompany the horrific spectacle:

> This Great Monument is Erected by Caesar Lomellini, Commanding General of the Brotherhood of Destruction, in Commemoration of the Death and Burial of Modern Civilization. It is composed of the bodies of a quarter million of human beings, who were once the rulers of this city, or the instruments of the rulers, of this mighty but alas ruined city. . . . By the very own instruments of their own wickedness had they perished; and here they lie sepulchred in stone, and heaped around explosives as destructive as their own lives. . . . Should civilization ever revive on earth, let the human race come and look on the towering shaft, and learn to restrain selfishness and live righteously.[2]

In other words, Union Square is the beginning of the end of the world, and Caesar's Column is its monument.

Donnelley, a supporter of the labor-friendly Populist Party, was acutely aware of the economic and social inequality he saw around him. With his novel he sought to illustrate in lurid detail the potential consequences for the city and the nation if the powerful continued to neglect the suffering of the poor in their greedy quest to collect the benefits of industrial expansion for themselves. While he was generally sympathetic to the aims of the labor movement, his barbaric vision exploited popular fears prompted by the increasingly angry demonstrations taking place in Union Square. An urgent warning, his novel prefigured apocalyptic language about the possible consequences of such meetings employed in the popular press over the next two decades. In many articles and editorials around the turn of the twentieth century, the Lower East Side was depicted as a malignant part of the city, one that fostered radicalism like a cancerous tumor. In this literature Union Square was the place where the seditious talk fomented by immigrants from Germany, Russia, and Italy in the streets, saloons, and union halls, took on a highly visible and even more dangerous aspect.

The annual May Day march became the primary signifier of potential revolution. Like Labor Day, May Day grew out of the eight-hour movement and was based on the same principle, that a single, simultaneous show of force by massed crowds of workers in cities and towns across the country could not be dismissed in the way that smaller-scale local strikes and demonstrations had been. The Federation of Organized Trades and Labor Unions (FOTLU), a militant offshoot of the Knights of Labor, were the founders of the event. Tired of the lack of progress on the legislation of the eight-hour

5.1 "Soc alists Meeting in Union Square, New York, May 1st, 1908."

day via the political system, in 1882 federation members, including the Irish American carpenter Peter J. McGuire, one of the organizers of the so-called Tompkins Square Riot, proposed that workers enforce it themselves.[3] Two years later the federation's convention supported a resolution calling for a line in the sand: on May 1st, 1886, workers across the country would stop work after eight hours. If employers refused to accept this, they would respond with a massive national work stoppage. While the reason for choosing this particular date is unclear, labor historian Philip S. Foner speculates it may relate to the construction trades calendar in which May 1st marked the beginning of the spring construction season, a day on which employers signed workers to contracts and unions collected their dues.[4] While Labor Day was seen as a largely peaceful celebration of the contribution of American workers to the national economy and officially sanctioned in a number of cities, May Day was less benign. A circular, printed and distributed by the Federation, made this clear: "Arouse, ye toilers of America! Lay down your tools on May 1, 1886, cease your labor, close the factories, mills and mines—for one day in the year. One day of revolt—not of rest!"[5]

Although many labor groups, including the powerful Knights of Labor, did not support it, the idea of a general strike on May 1st, 1886, gained momentum: trades union and socialist groups planned gatherings in cities all over the country. The largest of these was held in Chicago, where ninety thousand marched up Michigan Avenue. In New York nearly ten thousand marched in a torchlight procession up Broadway to Union Square, where speeches were made from two stands, one featuring German speakers and the other English. (A permit had not been granted for speeches from the cottage, so these platforms were erected on the edge of the plaza near Broadway.) The *New York Sun* reported that members of local unions marched behind banners, with 3,400 members of Baker's Local No. 1 heading the demonstration.[6] Music, fireworks, and the novelty of electric lighting drew twenty thousand spectators. Though the event passed peacefully, the police were prepared with nearly a thousand officers marshaled nearby. Few in the crowd would have been aware of this: only the small cohort needed to hold the crowd back from the stands was visible. The rest were massed inside nos. 8, 12, and 52 Union Square, private buildings hired for the evening by the police. Police Superintendent William Murray oversaw proceedings from temporary headquarters in a building at Fourth Avenue and Seventeenth Street. Just in case his men needed extra motivation, his staff office was decorated with the flag presented to the police by the people of the city after the riots of 1863 and 1871.

Though the May Day parade was praised in the press for its orderliness, it was also deliberately provocative. Drawing heavily on American history and on the principles laid out in the Constitution, the speakers praised the workers as true inheritors of the republican spirit and criticized capitalists as traitors to it. They repeated themes by now common in labor demonstrations: the nation was on the cusp of a new revolution, one in which workers would emancipate themselves from the tyranny of capitalism; the strike and the public meeting were legally protected actions; and any attempt on the part of the police to repress them was illegal. Speaking from the German stand, journalist-activist and editor of the *New Yorker Volks-Zeitung*, Sergei Shevitch, declared, "Comrades, I heard this evening as I came to the forum of the people that the kings of capital were sick with fear." Noting that hundreds of policemen were watching the meeting, he asked, "Why is this? Are we not citizens of this Republic? Indeed you pay for this surveillance which is so irksome to you." Referring to a recent strike by workers at a Brooklyn sugar refinery, he said,

> Your brothers have been arrested and the weapons with which you wage a peaceful and a righteous warfare are called illegal. And the answer to this illegal action is this great assemblage here tonight. . . . Such a magnificent

demonstration as this is useful in the extreme. It tells capital with what a mighty power they have chosen to take up the cudgels. It inspires them with fear.[7]

Evoking the American Revolutionary tradition, John Frunz, also a journalist for the *New Yorker Volks-Zeitung*, declared that the nationwide meetings on May 1st 1886 would be remembered forever as the "second Declaration of Independence."[8]

Any political traction gained by the first May Day demonstrations was destroyed, however, by an event that took place in Chicago three days later: the bombing at Haymarket Square in which several policemen were killed. While the practice of anarchist attentat, or violent political assault, had not yet traveled across the Atlantic, the bombing in Chicago was widely interpreted as the beginning of an American campaign. The Haymarket bombing and the subsequent trial of the accused conspirators had a devastating effect on the labor movement. Seen as potentially seditious, all forms of labor organization were repressed. Mainstream unions were anxious to distance themselves from the rhetoric of their more radical affiliates. May Day was not celebrated again in the United States until 1890 when, despite its wholly American origins, it had acquired a strong association with the international socialist movement.

In the beginning May Day was an expression of the commitment of a certain sector of American workers to the revolutionary cause. Three years later the idea was revived in Europe at the 1889 International Socialist Congress in Paris (the so-called Second International). Modeled on the American event, the Congress called for worldwide May Day parades on May 1st, 1890. The American Federation of Labor (AFL) was not enthusiastic about the idea because May Day had become closely linked in the popular imagination with the Haymarket bombing. Instead the AFL continued to promote Labor Day as the true American workers' holiday. Rejecting the language and symbolism of international socialism such as the red flag and the Marseillaise, they adopted patriotic songs and the Stars and Stripes. However, many immigrant-based workers' groups wanted to preserve May Day as a way to achieve the aims of the labor movement without the delay or compromise necessary when working within the existing political system. They also favored May Day as a way to promote connections between labor movements in the United States and Europe. Throughout the 1890s the Socialist Labor Party (SLP), an offshoot of the Workingmen's Party, organized May Day parades in New York City. Attracting tens of thousands of participants, these parades rivaled Labor Day in size and splendor. The national economic depression that lasted from 1893 to 1897 lent particular poignancy to the anti-capitalist rhetoric espoused from the cottage at the plaza during these years. In 1894 national outrage over the calling out of the army to suppress the Pullman railway strikers near Chicago gave fuel to the American Socialist movement. That year SLP leaders Daniel De Leon and Lucien Sanial gave speeches rejecting the eight-hour day as too limited a goal, proposing instead the creation of a cooperative commonwealth in which workers would retain the wealth they produced.[9] On May Day 1895 the French-born journalist turned radical Sanial described workingmen as white slaves and argued that May Day was the time when "the masses should rise up and demand their own."[10] Denouncing anarchism, he urged the use of the political system to bring about social revolution.

The May Day parades of the 1890s were an opportunity for previously underrepresented people to show themselves publicly. They included members of new immigrant groups, including Italians and Eastern European Jews, who supplemented the German Americans who had dominated the labor movement since the early nineteenth century, and also women. Union Square had been associated with women's rights since 1866 when the Eleventh Annual Women's Rights Convention was held at the Church of the Puritans. From the 1870s the headquarters of the Women's Suffrage Association was located on Sixteenth Street, just off Union Square. Members of this group called for "freedom of the individual" as well as freedom for the masses.[11] Those who attended these meetings were largely "blue stockings," educated women from the higher levels of society; but as the century moved on, a wider range of people became involved in the women's movement. In the 1890s SLP-sponsored May Day parades were notable for their inclusion of female socialists, who participated on equal footing with men, not just as spectators or symbolic figures.[12] Though they were politically active through social channels, prior to this time the only large-scale public participation of women in civic events had been in temperance parades, a genteel cause believed suitable to the female sensibility. From 1895, when a thousand female members of ladies' garment workers unions marched in the second division of the SLP's May Day parade, until after the turn of the century, women played an active role in socialist demonstrations in Union Square. They were particularly visible because of their festive dress, including red sashes and large hats covered with elaborate paper flowers. Calling for recognition as citizens and equal rights, labor demonstrations intersected with suffrage parades, both politically and as staged publicity events. In 1905 America's first suffragette parade marched up Broadway to Union Square; another significant suffrage demonstration was staged there in 1910, with

5.2 "Girls in Labor Parade, May 1st, 1909."

women wearing bright sashes marching in rank, headed by a band playing the Marseillaise.[13] Whether staged by immigrant workers or by women, the meetings in the Square could no longer be dismissed as discontented exhibitions by a vocal minority.

Despite their new inclusiveness, the violent talk associated with May Day meetings blunted much of the goodwill built up by the Labor Day and other parades. Though it had grown out of the American labor movement and represented the diversity of American workers, by 1900 May Day was identified in the mainstream press as an un-American celebration. Rather than the forum of the people invoked by Ruggles, Kearney, and Shevitch, Union Square was now seen as a dangerous place, one in which incendiary political ideas promoted in overcrowded Lower East Side saloons might spill out and find a wider audience. While the organizers of Labor Day had been careful to adopt the controlled and regimented form of earlier civic parades, May Day was messier and more provocative. In response, the police worked actively to suppress it, fearful that radical talk would inflame a disgruntled proletariat and result in the unleashing of acts of violence.

Anarchist Speech and the Threat to the City

In the 1890s, as a series of bomb attacks and assassinations in Europe gripped the international press, New York and Chicago came in for particular attention as potential anarchist incubators.[14] With little evidence to support their claims, mainstream American newspapers and magazines began to print articles warning that anarchist violence was spreading to the United States—that the fierce battle between labor and capital that had begun in the late 1870s was about to come to a terrible conclusion.[15] In the rhetoric of epidemiology popular at the time, cities densely packed with immigrant workers were described as places where dangerous foreign ideas could spawn and spread, infecting and inflaming the native population. New York City was of particular concern because of the huge numbers of Russian Jews who began to arrive from Eastern Europe, many fleeing the Russian pogroms of 1881–82. Prompted by the racialist understanding of human behavior dominant in the nineteenth century, some journalistic commentators argued that Jews were genetically predisposed toward anarchism because of the decades of repression they had suffered. This attitude is evident in a description of a cloak makers' union parade held in New York in July 1890 published in the *New York Herald*. Though the *Herald* was generally sympathetic to the labor cause, the language it used to describe the event suggested that the participants were both racially distinct and inferior. "Dark hatted, dark whiskered and pale faced Polish Hebrews; sad looking patient men, the hereditary effects of centuries of oppression showing plainly in their gait and expression," they appeared to the *Herald* reporter incapable of independent action, fit only to blindly follow their leaders.[16] In this paranoid environment, newspapermen saw conspiracies everywhere, especially in union meetings held in working-class halls and saloons. Failing to distinguish between the philosophy of anarchism and the tactic of direct action, many commentators saw any expression of anarchist thought as an immediate threat to the stability of the nation. In this context the mass meeting, where union leaders enjoined crowds to reject the exploitative capitalist system, was viewed with a great deal of suspicion.

As a subgroup of the labor movement, the anarchists were a small minority and not much tolerated.[17] While a tradition of anarchist thought in the United States extends back to the individualist anarchists of the early nineteenth century, the anarchist groups appearing in industrial cities such as New York and Chicago were largely made up of immigrants with ties to the anarchist movement then thriving in Europe. Although they recognized no form of authority or organization, so-called communistic anarchists (as opposed to individualist anarchists) were attracted to the labor movement as a mechanism through which to bring about general insurrection. Influenced by events in Europe, they came to advocate what they called direct action against the economic power of the state, known as "propaganda of the deed," in the form of sabotage and strikes. While most concentrated on mobilizing workingmen and women, a small group argued for the violent disruption of the capitalist system, including the use of dynamite against specific targets, and in the most extreme case "attentats," or politically motivated assassinations. Seeking publicity for their cause, American anarchists became a visible presence at public meetings, and in doing so they attracted a new level of police attention.

In New York City the anarchist movement began as a splinter group of German socialists. They met at a saloon on East First Street owned by Justus Schwab, who had been arrested during the 1874 Tompkins Square Riot. Although anarchists did not believe in hierarchical power structures, the de facto leader of the group was a bookbinder turned journalist named Johann Most. Forced out of Germany and then imprisoned in England because of his radical beliefs, Most arrived in New York in 1882 where he founded an anarchist newspaper, *Freiheit* (Freedom). He also published books including *Science of Revolutionary Warfare: A Little Handbook of Instruction in the Use and Preparation of Nitroglycerine, Dynamite, Gun-Cotton, Fulminating Mercury, Bombs, Fuses, Poisons, Etc.*, (1885), which advocated total social revolution by violent means and included instructions in bomb making.[18] In addition to his revolutionary writing, Most undertook wide speaking tours across the country which laid the groundwork for a national anarchist organization. With his distinctive appearance and fierce and uncompromising speeches, Most personified the anarchist threat to the United States. His impressive girth, bottle brush hair and extravagant beard made him easily caricatured: during the 1880s, cartoon images depicting hairy, wild-eyed and bomb-brandishing anarchists were popular fodder for mass-market journals and magazines.[19]

On May Day 1892 anarchists disrupted the established choreography of the labor rally, introducing violent rhetoric and bringing the message of anarchism to a wider audience. Organized by the Central Labor Union, the May Day speeches were dedicated to the eight-hour cause. As usual the principal speakers addressed the crowd from the cottage while two trucks were set up as makeshift rostrums, one on either side of the plaza. The meeting was tense from the start: the CLU was now split into factions and the more conservative wing, strongly opposed to anarchism, had forbidden Most or any of his associates to participate. The speeches had hardly started when catcalls began: all at once a group of his supporters charged one of the trucks and seized possession of it. In a second, the *New York Herald* reported, they "hoisted a slim little sharp faced woman to the position vacated by [the CLU speaker]. It was Miss Goldman, one of Most's friends, and in a torrent of

German she denounced God and government, while the crowd cheered her to the echo."[20]

"Miss Goldman" was Emma Goldman. Born into a middle-class family in the province of Kovno, part of the Russian Empire, in 1869, she was one of the wave of immigrants who found work in the garment industry.[21] After settling first in Rochester, she left an unhappy marriage for New York City where she rented a room on Suffolk Street and earned her living sewing women's dresses called "shirtwaists." Desirous of a larger role in life, she joined the circle of the Pioneers of Liberty, an anarchist organization made up of Russian Jewish garment workers that met at Sach's Café, also on Suffolk Street. Goldman soon came to the attention of Most who acted as her mentor, publishing her writing in his newspaper and helping perfect her public persona. Though she was one of several women active in the anarchist movement, Goldman stood out among her female peers, and Most was quick to exploit the propaganda value of a young woman with a powerful voice. With relentless drive and charisma, and unafraid to address large crowds, she delivered blunt and passionate speeches in German, English, and Russian. Becoming a public figure through her association with Most, Goldman gained further notoriety when she publicly defended her friend and lover Alexander Berkman, a fellow anarchist jailed for attempting to assassinate Henry Clay Frick, the chairman of the Carnegie Steel Company, in July 1892.[22] Though Goldman did not reveal her personal connection (it was discovered much later that she had supplied the gun used to attack Frick), she publicly offered Berkman her vigorous support.[23]

Following her debut speech in 1892, Goldman became a regular at Union Square and was soon included in rumors of anarchist plots. In 1893 newspapers reported on an alleged conspiracy by a gang of anarchists based in Maspeth, Long Island, to detonate a bomb in the Square on May Day. This was to be "a repetition of the Haymarket massacre in Chicago," the *New York Times* reported.[24] Both Most and Goldman publicly denied any involvement, arguing the story was the fabrication of a police informant under pressure to give up his friends as murderous conspirators. Despite the untruth of this rumor, Goldman was watched closely when she took the platform at a mass meeting for the unemployed on August 21st, 1893. This meeting had begun at Golden Rule Hall on Rivington Street with a parade of nearly a thousand people, many brandishing the iconic black flag representing anarchism. At 8:00 p.m. when the parade reached the Square, the plaza was packed, the crowd observed by 450 nervous policemen and park police. Two hundred additional policemen stood in reserve along Sixteenth Street with clubs drawn. As usual, the main addresses came from the cottage, with supplementary speeches given from trucks at either side of the plaza.

This time Goldman did not have to force her way in front of the crowd: she was given a place of honor on the main platform. As others spoke, she could be seen pacing back and forth. The audience began to call for her, and soon she launched into a speech given in her passionate style, switching easily back and forth between German and English. Aware that most of the speeches would be in German, the police had posted German-speaking officers in attendance. They were deputized to make notes of what was said and to immediately arrest any speaker inciting the crowd to violence. While almost every address included radical exhortations, it was Goldman who attracted the most attention. Building on the patriotic associations of the venue, she began by contrasting the historical past of Union Square as a representation of the highest aspirations of American democracy with the abject industrial and commercial landscape surrounding it. "Do you not believe that Thomas Jefferson, John Brown and Wendell Phillips would be ashamed today if they could see thousands here in this city asking for bread?" she said. "While you have nothing to eat the rich are living in great luxury."[25] Advising the crowd not to expect the government to provide relief because politicians were nothing but servants of capitalism, she directed her audience to "demonstrate before the palaces of the rich," only a block away on Fifth Avenue. As various newspapers reported, she then told the crowd: "You want bread and you are hungry. Well go and ask the rich. They won't give it to you? Then take it. Take it by force if you can't get it peaceably."[26]

Spoken from the rostrum at Union Square, Goldman's fiery words led to a notorious legal trial at which the principle of free speech was put to the test in court. She was not arrested immediately, however. Perhaps fearing the reaction of the large crowd, the police let her go. Eleven days later after her speech, following days of cat and mouse as police and journalists hunted for her in the Lower East Side meeting halls and saloons she was known to frequent, Goldman was arrested in Philadelphia. Extradited back to New York City, she was charged with inciting a riot. The trial, which began in the Court of General Sessions on Center Street on October 4th, 1893, became a national sensation.[27] Abraham Oakey Hall, a lawyer and former mayor of New York, took Goldman's case pro bono because he believed she was the victim of police persecution. In his defense, he tried two tactics: first, he pointed out discrepancies in the official police record of her speech. But his second tactic was riskier. Quoting the section of the penal code that allowed for "peaceable assemblage of lawful purposes of protest and petition," he argued that his client had committed no crime.[28] Pointing out that the relevant permits had been obtained from the Parks Commission, and that the meeting had been peaceable, he argued that no law had been broken. Unmoved, the jury found Goldman guilty and she was sentenced to one year in the women's penitentiary on Blackwell's Island.[29] Seemingly unconcerned, she left the heavily fortified courthouse smiling at the crowd who had come to see the most dangerous woman in America.[30]

Though unsuccessful, Hall's defense prompted a new interpretation of the rights to freedom of speech guaranteed in the First Amendment to the Constitution. As the legal scholar David Rabban has noted, before World War I American courts were openly hostile to legal claims to the right of free speech.[31] Although libertarians of all kinds frequently claimed this right, it was almost never successful as a legal defense. The thirty years from the 1890s to the end of World War I saw tremendous social instability; as a result public speech critical of the government was heavily repressed. In the case of legal action against anarchists such as Goldman, the courts were especially biased in favor of the rights of the state as opposed to the rights of the individual. Judges and the police took a particularly hard line on public meetings that might devolve into riotous behavior. Because of this precedent, although he argued it eloquently, Hall's defense was bound to be a losing one.

Following her release from prison in 1894, Goldman made fun of the police and lawyers for trying to stop her from speaking, reasoning that her gender and small stature meant she should not be considered a threat. She was welcomed by a rowdy bunch of three thousand supporters gathered at the Thalia Theater on the Bowery. "I have come back to you after having served ten months in prison for talking," she told the appreciative crowd.[32] More seriously, she sought to turn attention away from anarchist violence toward the violence inflicted by the state and by private security forces like the Pinkerton agency, actions downplayed or unreported in the mainstream press. "Compared with the wholesale violence of capital and government, political acts of violence are but a drop in the ocean," she wrote in 1910.[33] While Goldman found little sympathy among the general population, her arrest fostered a growing alliance among radical political groups, labor organizations, and progressive social reformers for the cause of free speech. This alliance led to the formation of the nonpartisan Free Speech League and made Union Square a test case for changing social and judicial opinion on the issue.

5.3 "[Alexander] Berkman [speaks at Socialist meeting], Union Square, May 1st, 1908."

The Fight for Free Speech

The vast majority of political meetings held in Union Square in the 1890s and 1910s were organized by groups dedicated to social change via the electoral process and the courts, groups such as the Central Labor Federation (formerly the CLU), the United Hebrew Trades, and the Socialist Labor Party (SLP). However, the Police and Parks departments became increasingly fearful that these meetings might degenerate into mass rioting or worse. The crackdown on public meetings in Union Square reached new heights after the assassination of President William McKinley in 1901. If Berkman's failed attack on the capitalist Frick in 1892 inaugurated the American anarchist scare, the politically motivated murder of the president created paranoia on a national scale. It didn't help Goldman that McKinley's assassin, Leon Czolgosz, claimed to have been inspired by her. Though she declared no knowledge of him, Goldman further inflamed her critics by defending his actions. In the wake of McKinley's assassination, radical political speech was harshly repressed, whether in public or in private. As Goldman's biographer Paul Avrich put it:

> Public outrage and fear reached a far greater intensity than it had after the Haymarket affair or the attack on Frick. Anarchists were hunted, arrested and persecuted throughout the country. Homes and clubrooms were raided and possessions confiscated. Many anarchists lost their jobs and lodgings were subjected to violence and abuse.[34]

Across the country the general sentiment was toward complete suppression of anarchist rhetoric, both verbal and published. Robert A. Pinkerton, cohead of the private Pinkerton Detective Agency, dismissed what he called the "fetish of free speech," arguing, "As for open fulminations, these should be placed entirely under the ban, and the police should be given practically unlimited powers to deal with the men and women concerned."[35] While acknowledging the vast majority of American anarchists were harmless, he also called for the forcible deportation of any person caught preaching the principles of anarchy to an "anarchist colony" to be established by the government on one of the islands of the Philippines, newly under the control of the United States. New York State went some way to implementing these recommendations when it enacted the Criminal Anarchy Law in 1902. This law, one of the first in the country, made it a felony for anyone to advocate, verbally or in writing, the forcible overthrow of the government or political assassination. Punishable by a fine of five thousand dollars or up to ten years' imprisonment, the law included a clause making it a felony to "voluntarily assemble with any group formed to advocate or teach such doctrines." Under these vague terms, simply calling for a strike was grounds enough for imprisonment and the owners of public halls could be held liable if they allowed their property to be used for radical political activities.[36] The Criminal Anarchy law also led to creation of a specialist police "Anarchist Squad" in 1903. Sometimes known as the "Bomb Squad" or the "Italian Squad," it was formed to disrupt public meetings, infiltrate anarchist groups, and block the distribution of anarchist publications. Founded five years before the Federal Bureau of Investigation, the squad was one of the earliest groups in the country tasked with the systematic covert surveillance of potentially criminal organizations.

With anarchist and even socialist speech now effectively illegal, the police and city authorities began to question the validity and safety of Union Square as a forum for public meetings. Given the frequency with which they included speakers with anarchist and socialist affiliations, as well as their high public profile, union gatherings came under particular pressure. In the early years of the twentieth century, the police used the heightened powers provided by the new law to restrict mass meetings via legal means (the refusal of permits) and through the use of physical intimidation. Violent clashes between crowds and police, including the indiscriminate clubbing of meeting-goers by mounted police, became common. In response, in May 1902 the Free Speech League, a precursor to the American Civil Liberties Union, was founded by a cross-section of liberals, progressives, and radicals including Goldman herself.[37] The league provided legal support for those arrested under the new laws and lobbied the police and the courts to uphold the Constitution. While the league's officers were careful to explain that their organization was committed to the protection of free speech from all political perspectives, cases involving socialists and anarchists took up most of their time.[38] Beginning in 1905, they were frequently called upon to defend members of a new and militant labor organization, the Industrial Workers of the World (IWW). Formed in Chicago in opposition to traditional labor groups, especially the American Federation of Labor (AFL), the IWW claimed to represent the true proletariat, unskilled workers.[39] The founders had no interest in working within the economic and political system. Rather, they believed in direct action such as strikes and sabotage, in order to spur the collapse of capitalism.

From the first the IWW made free speech one of its principal causes.[40] Active particularly in industrializing towns in the American West, the group began a campaign of civil disobedience, mounting soapboxes on street corners and speaking to whoever would listen. From the time of its founding the group organized its own meetings in Union Square, with general support from anarchists and socialists, at least at first. In 1906 the IWW held a meeting there in support of striking miners in Colorado, one that followed the same format as hundreds of earlier labor demonstrations. Beginning from various locations in the Lower East Side, three separate ranks of marchers joined together in front of the cottage on the plaza to listen to speeches.[41] Using patriotic imagery and rhetoric, including the Stars and Stripes and references to the coming of a second American Revolution, IWW members characterized those who opposed their right to be heard as traitors to the Constitution, and to the country itself. Echoing rhetoric heard over and over during these years, they contrasted the supposed illegal activities of their own members with the activities of the police and the courts in repressing labor protest.[42]

Late in 1907 rallies in support of the unemployed were staged all around the country, closely monitored by the police. The country had entered another economic depression following a stock market crash in October of that year. The result was a severe contraction of industries including manufacturing and mining. In March 1908 the Conference of the Unemployed,

5.4 "Taken 20 Seconds after Bomb Thrown," March 28, 1908.

a group of labor unions with close ties to the SLP, resolved to organize an impressive demonstration at Union Square to demand relief for the unemployed. As the organizers would later emphasize, they planned the event in an orderly and legal manner, applying for the proper permit from the parks commissioner. This permit was first granted, then revoked on the grounds that such a large gathering would cause damage to the park.[43] The conference appealed this decision and it was again denied. However, handbills had already been posted advertising the meeting. At 2:00 p.m. on March 28th, the time appointed for the meeting to begin, three hundred police on foot and horseback were deployed around the perimeter of the plaza, struggling to hold back a crowd estimated at thirty thousand people attempting to push their way into the empty space.[44] After a fruitless half hour, the police decided to clear the streets. Mounted officers charged the crowd, clubbing them and pushing them backward. At 3:00 p.m. a bomb was detonated near the central fountain. One man was killed instantly, one was seriously wounded, and a police officer was injured when he was blown against a tree. Soon afterward a correspondent for the Bain News Service recorded gory photographs of the bleeding men receiving aid, photographs that were sent over the wire to newspapers around the country.

The 1908 Union Square bombing caused a news media sensation and intensified the already overheated public debate about the threat of anarchism to the stability of the country. Even though the aborted meeting was organized by a socialist organization, very few journalistic commentators drew any distinction between the political doctrines of socialism and anarchism. The bombing was lumped together with two other anarchist "outrages" committed within five weeks in different places around the country.[45] The day after the explosion the *New York Times* reported that the bomber was a "Williamsburg Anarchist," a twenty-two-year-old Russian immigrant named Selig Silverstein, whose homemade bomb had exploded prematurely, seriously injuring him and killing an accomplice.[46] Several newspapers printed rumors that letters from Emma Goldman had been found in Silverstein's Brooklyn apartment. From Chicago, where she was on a speaking tour, Goldman denied any knowledge of the bombing and accused the police of instigating a plot to incriminate her on the same spot where she had been arrested fifteen years earlier.[47] In fact the bombing was atypical as an act of anarchist violence because it did not target a specific symbolic figure, such as Frick or McKinley. As an attack in which innocent people were highly likely to be injured, it had more in common with the notorious Haymarket bombing for which anarchists always blamed the police. Goldman and others believed Silverstein to be an unwitting patsy. There was no doubt that the young man had a useful profile from the point of view of the police: a search of his apartment uncovered his membership card to the Anarchist Federation, an organization founded by Alexander Berkman.[48] Blinded and missing an arm, Silverstein lay severely injured in Bellevue Hospital for almost a month before dying on April 28th. While many reports claimed that he was unable to speak, the police claimed he had made a full confession, apparently telling them he had manufactured the bomb using the brass knob from a bedstead. The *Daily People*, an SLP newspaper, was skeptical about this confession.[49]

The 1908 bomb explosion triggered a national debate about access to, and control of, public space. For their part the police immediately announced that no more permits would be issued for political meetings in Union Square. While the annual May Day parade was allowed, the red flag was barred and the crowd was monitored by an extremely high number of police. Deeply troubled by both the bombing and the police reaction to it, the leaders of the SLP, the organizers of the aborted meeting, tried to distance themselves from the actions of the bomb thrower, and at the same time suggested that the police shared some of the blame for the affair. Shortly after the event, members of the Unemployed Conference of the City of New York held a meeting at the Rand School of Socialism on East Nineteenth Street, at which they drew up a statement denying any "complicity in the crime committed by some irresponsible, or insane individual." Further, the statement read: "[Union Square] and other parks and squares in and about the city have been placed at the disposal of the citizens of New York for over forty years, for purpose of public assemblage." In denying the permit, the park commissioner had demonstrated "official arrogance in placing at naught the constitutional rights of citizenship of the municipality, for the gratification of his personal whims. Have then the people no right of assemblage, as provided by Article I of the first amendment of 1791 of the Constitution? . . . If so, then these boasted rights of free speech and free assemblage are a delusion and a farce."[50] SLP leader Morris Hillquit expanded on this theme in a speech on April 10th. Though the penal code prohibited certain kinds of meetings—when those assembled have intent to commit unlawful acts by force, those which disturb the peace, and when violence or lawlessness was threatened—this was not the case on March 28th. Hillquit claimed:

> If there was an unlawful assembly in Union Square on the 28th day of March, it was the large assembly of mounted and unmounted police. . . . It had gathered with intent to commit an unlawful act by force, namely to prevent citizens from the exercise of a constitutional right by clubs. They assembled in a manner to disturb the public peace, by committing a savage assault upon a peaceful public. They violated the Penal Code and they violated the constitution, and they did so openly and defiantly, and cynically proclaimed that the club is mightier than the constitution.[51]

One month later another SLP leader, Robert Hunter, put the issue in broader terms. He issued a pamphlet addressed to Governor Charles Evans Hughes, Mayor George B. McClellan and Police Commissioner Theodore Bingham, asking them to consider "whether or not the right to issue permits for mass meetings shall be used to suppress the right of peaceable assembly instead of merely regulating that right?" If such actions are to be officially sanctioned, he said, "then civic freedom and inviolability of persons in New York City no longer exist."[52]

Contemporary publications reveal some sympathy for these ideas beyond the ranks of anarchists, socialists, and labor organizers. Among progressive thinkers a theory emerged that the expression of free speech might in fact counter violent acts rather than promote them. Three days after the Union Square bombing, the *New York Times*, always suspicious of mass meetings of working people, published a letter arguing in favor of allowing large assemblies in public places.[53] Citing the Constitution and the positive example of Trafalgar Square in London, the letter writer argued such spaces acted as a safety valve, allowing extremists to harmlessly blow off steam. By contrast, he continued, when policemen attacked citizens they could only expect to be met with more violence. The progressive weekly magazine, *Outlook*, made a similar point in April 1908, stating, "There are some subjects on which free speech may be dangerous, but none on which repression of speech is not more dangerous."[54] The *New York Tribune* criticized the police for preventing the meeting from occurring and other newspapers compared their actions in riding into the crowd to that of brutal Russian Cossacks. Making this case, the *New York Evening Post* argued, "To prevent anyone speaking on behalf of anarchy is to give to the cause of anarchy the most formidable weapon it has ever possessed."[55] Although one historian has described the legacy of the 1908 anarchist scare as one of "increased distrust, suspicion and bitterness between the varied elements of American society," the liberal sentiments of these newspapers point to one positive outcome, the emergence of a new attitude toward free speech and access to public space.[56]

In New York City this new attitude was apparent not only in newspaper columns but also in official city policies. In 1910 Charles B. Stover became parks commissioner. Appointed by reformist Mayor William Gaynor, Stover brought a progressive agenda to the management of city parks.[57] A former Presbyterian minister and something of an ideologue when it came to municipal reform, he had little experience as a civic administrator but an almost fanatical passion for improving the lives of the urban poor. In 1886 he had founded the Neighborhood Guild in the Lower East Side, one of the first settlement houses in the country, modeled on similar settlements in London's East End. In the 1890s he had led a private effort to create a series of children's playgrounds in the area, playgrounds that were taken over by the city in 1902. When it opened in 1903 the Seward Park playground at East Broadway and Essex Street was the first municipally sponsored playground in the United States. Its purpose was to socialize and improve the health of poor immigrants by providing outdoor play spaces for their children. As parks commissioner from 1910 to 1913, Stover continued to focus on the creation of parks and playgrounds in poor neighborhoods, organizing the first Bureau of Recreation within the Parks Department.

Stover was also committed to the realization of Mayor Gaynor's pet project, a "big open air meeting place in the central part of the city for public meetings, a sort of Manhattanese Hyde Park" (a project the *New York Times* labeled an "amiable delusion").[58] Immediately following his appointment, Stover suggested that the plaza at Union Square was perfectly suited to this purpose, declaring it would be "remodeled and thrown open to public meetings of all sorts without the red tape of securing permits."[59] Speaking to newspaper reporters at his new office in the arsenal in Central Park, Stover declared that New York had too long been without a meeting place for the people in the style of Hyde Park and Trafalgar Square in London:

> At present, there is no place where people can assemble and talk over the questions of the day. Now, if people want to do that, free speech you know is guaranteed them under the constitution. There is no reason why people from the east side should be refused permits to hold mass meetings in some park of convenient access. This sort of thing has been an institution in England for years. And far from fomenting disorder it has been the means of preventing it. There has not been for some time any such happening there as the unfortunate affair in United States between the police and a mass meeting of the unemployed some two or three years ago.[60]

Stover concluded optimistically, saying that Police Commissioner William Baker had promised his complete cooperation, and it was quite likely that soon anyone would be able to hold a meeting at the plaza.

Stover's tolerant attitude was tested by the events of 1912–14 when Union Square was again the site of huge demonstrations during yet another period of economic depression.[61] These began when the IWW organized rallies in support of striking silk workers in Paterson, New Jersey, in June 1912.[62] Though large and boisterous, these rallies were generally orderly, carefully staged to elicit the sympathy of the middle-class office workers and shoppers who witnessed them. They were notable for including large numbers of children (representing the hardship of industrial action on worker's families) and young women (representing the increasing organization of female garment workers). In the spring of 1913, the Square hosted several parades organized by the Ladies' International Garment Workers' Union whose headquarters were nearby at 32 Union Square.[63] Red-sashed young women marched in line, carried banners and transparencies, and sang the Marseillaise in the traditional fashion, publicly proclaiming their rights as workers and as citizens. Their actions drew attention to the dismal working conditions in the loft buildings that now surrounded the Square. The horrifying and highly publicized fire at the nearby Triangle Shirtwaist factory two years earlier had led to calls for labor reform and strengthened the union movement by adding hundreds of women to its ranks. These demonstrations were permitted by the Parks Department and overseen by a large number of police officers who observed the crowds closely but did little to restrain them.

Stover's term as park commissioner ended in 1913 when he suffered a nervous breakdown and was forced to resign. The following year his efforts to allow greater freedom of speech in city-owned parks were tested by a decisive event, one in which Goldman and Berkman were the primary protagonists. In March 1914 the pair addressed a crowd in Union Square at a meeting of the newly revived Conference of the Unemployed. Goldman's speech was similar to the one she had delivered on the same spot twenty-one years earlier. Referring to the recent series of "church invasions" in which unemployed men occupied neighborhood churches demanding food and shelter, she told her audience: "Go to the churches. Go to the hotels and restaurants, go to the bakeshops and tell them that they must give you something to keep you from starving."[64] Afterward she and Berkman led a parade up Fifth Avenue all the way to the committee's headquarters' at 107th Street. Though the police closely observed the march, again they did nothing to stop it.

Soon afterward another group, the Central Federated Union, received a permit to hold a meeting at the plaza on Saturday, April 4th, 1914. Rumor soon spread that the IWW and the so-called Berkman-Goldman group of anarchists would attempt to crash it. Warned earlier in the day of the planned disruption, Commissioner McKay put four hundred police in and around the Square and ordered reservists to stand ready at police stations in all parts of the city. The CFU meeting was called for 3:00 p.m. When this time arrived, at least six thousand people had gathered, but only a few hundred were members of the CFU. Closely watched by police, Berkman arrived accompanied by Lincoln Steffens, a journalist and supporter of the Free Speech League. Berkman mounted the steps to the cottage, but instead of giving a speech he simply announced that a meeting of the unemployed would be held the following Saturday. Then he and Steffens left. In an apparently prearranged signal, two men held aloft black flags, and the crowd began to move in the direction of Fifth Avenue. Mounted policemen standing in line across the western edge of the plaza quickly blocked them. Seeing the way was barred, IWW organizer Joe O'Carroll ordered the crowd to turn and march down to Rutgers Square. As soon as he did so police ordered the crowd to disperse and mounted officers rode into the crowd brandishing clubs. Many were hurt and nine men were arrested.[65]

The *New York Times* was triumphant: "The outgoing Police Commissioner McKay has given new proof of his efficacy and his understanding of the danger of permitting these people to defy the law."[66] The courts and the newly elected Mayor John P. Mitchel, however, took a different position. At the trial of two of the men arrested during the melee, the magistrate was lenient, releasing them on the grounds that they had done nothing unlawful, and warning the police officers not to interfere with the right to free speech.[67] After the trial the young reform-minded mayor told reporters:

> I wish to reiterate that there is no IWW "situation." Some people who are out of work have tried to hold meetings to discuss their condition and that is entirely lawful. Some persons have tried to capitalize on the situation but that is lawful so long as they do not engage in disorder. I want the police to take all necessary steps to prevent breaches of peace and law; on the other hand I want to re-emphasize the point that there must be no unnecessary clubbing.[68]

Three days after the debacle, Mayor Mitchel followed up his words with action when he installed a new police commissioner, Arthur Woods, who took an entirely different attitude to public meetings than that of his predecessor, McKay.

On first appearance Woods was an unlikely candidate for the job: rather than rising through the ranks of the police force, his last position had been secretary to the mayor.[69] Born into a well-to-do family and educated at Harvard, he lived with other well-off bachelors at the Harvard Club on West Forty-Fourth Street. Despite this plutocratic background, Woods had experience with police work and he was deeply committed to Mitchel's reformist agenda. Dissatisfied with a career teaching English literature at Groton, the elite prep school, he had contemplated a career as a missionary before following in the footsteps of famed police reporter Jacob Riis, taking up journalism as a means to publicizing social ills. As a reporter for the *New York Sun*, Woods published his firsthand observations of the desperate living conditions of the urban poor. This experience, together with passionately held views on the need for police reform, led to his appointment as a deputy under Police Commissioner Theodore Bingham from 1907 to 1909. During this time Woods witnessed the fallout of the 1908 bombing at Union Square: increasing distrust between the police, labor groups, and other working-class political organizations. As commissioner, he aimed to better relations between these groups, following through on Bingham's largely unsuccessful efforts to reduce the common practice of frequent and arbitrary police violence.

At his investiture, Woods was mindful of the "riot" that had taken place at Union Square only days before, and he cited the disastrous police response frequently in explaining his attitude toward public meetings. Giving testimony before a federal Commission on Industrial Relations in 1915, he said:

> Free speech and free assembly are constitutional rights, and as I understand it the local authorities have the right to regulate those locally, but not in such a way as to destroy them or abrogate them, and really only in such a way as to preserve them. For instance in New York we [do] not merely permit free speech and free assemblage and picketing, but we protect it.[70]

Describing the turbulent meetings that had taken place in Union Square in the months leading up to his installation as police commissioner, Woods noted that violence was perpetrated by both sides, and that the actions threatened by various political groups were partly the result of anger at the denial of their right to free assembly. After he took office, he said:

> [I] quite changed the policy, the methods, and the orders given to the police. There was on the following Saturday a very small police force evident, although there were enough police available that if violence had resulted we would have handled the situation. Very few police were there. I had personally given them their instructions, and told them they were to afford the assemblage its full rights; that they were to interfere only if the traffic was seriously impeded, and if incitement to immediate violence was present.[71]

The result, he claimed, was a peaceful meeting of many thousands of people addressed by members of the IWW, socialists, and anarchists, concluding with one of the speakers calling for "Three cheers for the cops!"[72] It should be noted, however, that Woods did not give radical groups totally free reign. Rather, he transferred police energy from the overt monitoring of their public activities to covert surveillance of their private ones: while publicly proclaiming their rights to free assembly and free speech, he continued the efforts of previous police commissioners to secretly infiltrate their activities via specialist police units, including new versions of the Anarchist Squad, the Police Bomb Squad (founded in 1914), and the Industrial Squad (founded in 1917).[73]

Though groups such as the IWW, the SLP, and the anarchists were still considered threats to civic and national stability, under progressive civic administrations in early twentieth-century New York City these organizations were offered unprecedented freedom to hold large meetings in public parks, supported by an emerging belief that the suppression of free speech was more dangerous than the alternative. Encouraged by Mayors Gaynor and Mitchel and implemented by Parks Commissioner Stover and Police Commissioner Woods, the city offered the nation an early testing ground for a new interpretation of the constitutional rights to freedom of assembly and free speech. The policing strategies implemented in Union Square and other city parks between 1910 and 1914 were cemented by legal decisions made by the Supreme Court in the years immediately following World War I. The extreme repression of political speech during the war had led progressives to defend the right to dissenting political speech, seeing it as an essential component of democracy. Soon after the war, the idea that free speech, no matter how unpopular, was a safety valve for social and political dissent became generally accepted, and the belief in an essential connection between the protection of free speech and the successful continuation of American democracy was strengthened. By 1914 the plaza at Union Square, created by Olmsted and Vaux as a physical space specifically set aside for public meetings, was supplemented by official city policies that protected the rights of all citizens to gather and make public speeches there. For a brief time, officers of both the Parks and the Police departments were directed to allow such meetings (provided they did not impede public safety or incite immediate violence), and to protect the rights of speakers to be heard. The association between Union Square and political dissent established in the last decade of the nineteenth century had become officially sanctioned. However, although public and official opinion about the danger represented by political speech had changed, the physical space in which this speech took place was coming under threat. In the early years of the twentieth century, Union Square underwent a dramatic change as civic and military authorities tried to transform it into a center of patriotism rather than pacifism. This transformation began with its total destruction.

Wartime Park

Though the old plaza and the streets around it continued to be an active site for political meetings after 1914, Union Square Park was all but destroyed as a place of peaceful reflection. Beginning in 1900 the park was dug up, section by section, in order to create a transit hub for the new citywide subway system. Parks Department annual reports from 1912 to 1914 detail the transformation of the park into a giant construction site.[74] Much of the plaza was covered with unsightly sheds and the wood-framed cottage was in disrepair. The park itself was a muddy mess, with a great strip cut through it and trees and plantings removed. Sections were fenced off and boarded up as the new subway station was constructed underneath. In 1916 the new BMT subway route was opened, including a new terminal at Union Square connecting it to the existing IRT line. An impressive transit amenity had been created, but the park itself was destroyed and the plaza remained conveniently littered with construction materials.

With the plaza, the traditional venue for dissent, out of commission, the local and federal governments tried to reclaim Union Square as a site of conventional patriotism. Just as New Yorkers had been ambivalent about joining the Civil War, the city was bitterly divided in its reaction when the war in Europe began in July 1914. Progressives and conservatives supported American participation, seeing it as an important move toward global democracy and the furthering of American interests. Opposition to American involvement came from diverse groups including religious pacifists and radical communists. In New York resistance to the war was especially strong within the Socialist Party and the union movement. Running on a pacifist platform, the Socialist Party had success in the 1917 mayoral election; their candidate Morris Hillquit, a labor lawyer and active member of the garment workers union, came second, beating out the Republican candidate. As part of his campaign, Hillquit condemned the war as a capitalist-fueled power grab benefiting only the ruling classes.[75] There was truth to Hillquit's claims: with Wall Street financiers including J. P. Morgan financing the Allies, the war was bringing huge economic benefit to the city's bankers.

Socialists and anarchists staged regular antiwar protests on the periphery of Union Square between 1914 and 1917. For the federal and state governments, these events were yet another sign that immigrant-dominated political groups were a dangerous political force, and that New York City, and the Lower East Side in particular, was a nursery for foreign subversives, "the enemy within," in a popular phrase of the era. As the home to a large number of political dissenters, conscientious objectors, and pacifists, the city was seen as the weak link in national self-defense. President Woodrow Wilson voiced this concern directly in his 1915 State of the Union Address, when he denounced disloyal foreign-born citizens:

> I am sorry to say that the gravest threats against our national peace and safety have been uttered within our own borders. There are citizens of the United States, I blush to admit, born under other flags but welcomed under our generous naturalization laws to the full freedom and opportunity of America, who have poured the poison of disloyalty into the very arteries of our national life; who have sought to bring the authority and good name of our Government into contempt, to destroy our industries wherever they thought it effective for their vindictive purposes to strike at them, and to debase our politics to the uses of foreign intrigue.[76]

Antiwar gatherings stoked fears that New York City, with its large population of immigrants, was vulnerable to enemy infiltration. Wilson urged the use of legal mechanisms to purge the country of this insidious threat. As the war in Europe intensified, the federal government cracked down on radical activity and radical speech. While permission to hold May Day rallies in Union Square was suspended in 1916, pro-war advocates were allowed to organize public meetings in support of the war effort. Besides these ephemeral events, the Parks Department instituted other forms of spatial propaganda.

The first of these was a 75-by-25-foot "Demonstration Garden," built in the southeast corner of the Square in 1916. Sitting at the very center of New York City, the garden was an advertisement for urban decongestion and the benefits of suburban living. At a time when the population of the Lower East Side was already in decline and the outer boroughs were being opened up for development (aided by the construction of new subway lines), there were undoubtedly ideological reasons to encourage the resettlement of the working-class population outside the inner city.[77] Removed from unsatisfactory lives in crowded tenement buildings, enjoying the space and amenities of suburban housing, immigrants would become assimilated into the "American" way of life and be less inclined to question the economic and political system. As part of this broader effort, the Demonstration Garden was intended to educate potential suburbanites about the pleasures of horticulture. Throughout the summer of 1917, the Farm Garden Bureau (a division of the Parks Department) provided representatives to answer questions about garden design, proper care of lawns, use of fertilizer, and growing vegetables.[78] In 1928, when the garden was demolished to make way for further subway work, Parks Commissioner Walter R. Herrick reported that newly minted commuters had found the garden a "Mecca for needed information."[79] In this way, the department employed Union Square to promote the values of home ownership during World War I, helping to dilute the working-class solidarity created in the segregated and overcrowded Lower East Side.

In June 1917 the United States entered the war in Europe. A month prior, the federal government had enacted the Selective Service Act which required all men aged between twenty-one and thirty to register for military service. The presence of an active antiwar movement in the city gave rise to acute anxiety about how eligible men might react.[80] Though the real war was being fought far away in France and Belgium, a propaganda war was underway in New York with little expense was spared to win it. Under Mayors John P. Mitchel and John F. Hylan the New York City government, acting

5.5 "Recruit," Union Square, ca. 1917.

in close collaboration with federal agencies and private groups, began an extraordinary campaign to commandeer public space and erect patriotic monuments throughout the city. These included an extensive replica of the French trenches and the display of a captured German U-Boat in Central Park, and the erection of temporary triumphal arches along Fifth Avenue. At the same time that city authorities severely restricted the public expression of antiwar sentiment, these structures served as the backdrop to highly choreographed patriotic events.

Just as it had during the Civil War, Union Square became an important site for the expression of the pro-war message. While in 1861 crowds gathered around Henry Kirk Brown's statue of George Washington, in 1917 a larger and much more unorthodox structure became the focus. Early that year the *New York Times* reported that Mayor Mitchel's Committee on National Defense was putting into action "various plans for promoting recruiting for the army and navy, and in particular the construction of a replica battleship in Union Square, which will become the headquarters for recruiting for the navy in this general territory, and which we believe will serve as a very material stimulus."[81] This plan, a grandiose expansion of the common practice of locating recruiting stations in public parks, was

5.6 USS Recruit in Union Square, ca. 1917.

to bring the reality of war directly home to the people of New York and to encourage young men to enlist.

On May 1st, 1917, the traditional May Day rally was held in Union Square. A month later on Memorial Day, the USS Recruit was formally launched when Mrs. John P. Mitchel, the wife of the mayor, smashed a bottle of champagne across its bow, observed by Parks Commissioner Cabot Ward, two hundred boys from the American Junior Naval and Marine Scouts who formed a guard of honor around the ship, and a large crowd of onlookers.[82] Constructed by the George A. Fuller Company, the wooden ship was a miniature of a navy dreadnought, two hundred feet long and forty feet wide. Under the supervision of Commander C. A. Adams, it housed

> a spacious waiting room for recruits and applicants, physical examination rooms, both fore and aft; doctors' quarters, shower baths, and numerous other accommodations for officers and men. . . . The main deck will be fitted out after the fashion of a battleship from turrets to awning rails. A number of machine guns have been sent over from the Brooklyn Navy Yard, which will be manned by regular gun crews prepared to give instruction.[83]

A public monument erected in the service of national military objectives, the Recruit was a contemporary version of the ancient Roman *naumachia*, an amphitheater built to host a mock sea battle staged for mass entertainment. Eighty-seven real sailors were employed to mimic the work they would be doing at sea, including cleaning and inspecting the vessel and completing various drills and exercises. The Recruit was docked at Union Square for two years, and during that time it played host not only to enactments of naval routine, but also to numerous special events including film screenings projected onto its hull, a vaudeville show featuring Gilbert and Sullivan operettas, and a demonstration boxing match. All of these events were designed to attract crowds and to inspire them with patriotic feeling.

For the three years between 1917 and 1920, New Yorkers passing through Union Square were presented with the bizarre sight of a giant battleship seemingly about to plow through a suburban garden, a surrealistic reminder of dangers overseas and the need to protect domestic life at home. In the summer of 1920, the Recruit was broken into pieces and moved to Luna Park at Coney Island.[84] As a recruiting station, it had been a huge success: it was claimed that at least twenty-five thousand men had signed up for the navy onboard the Recruit. With the mock battleship broken up and carted away, Union Square was ready to be invented anew, remade as a public park suitable for the modern age. This reconstruction invoked the neoclassical geometry and imagery of the City Beautiful movement. Significantly, it involved the removal of the historic statues to more prominent locations. Where Washington and Lincoln had formerly occupied positions on the periphery, they were now positioned on a central axis, reinforcing the Square's association with the heroes of the American republic and telegraphing a warning to those who sought to revive more rituals of radicalism.

6

City Beautiful Civic Center, 1898–1933

In the 1840s the founders of Union Square had imagined it might one day be a civic center equal in importance and grandeur to City Hall Park. Around the turn of the twentieth century it seemed possible to realize that goal: following the construction of Olmsted and Vaux's formal plaza at the northern end, reformist city administrations and civic groups imagined a new form for the Square, a form that would enhance its identity as a public meeting place rather than an urban retreat. The ambitious goal to make Union Square the center of Manhattan's centerless grid was part of a much larger urban planning project. In 1898 the consolidation of New York City into five boroughs with Manhattan as the hub provided the impetus to reconfigure the newly enlarged city based on contemporary principles of city planning. With its location at the nexus of several important streets and its already established reputation as a place for civic meetings, Union Square was the ideal test case for the implementation of City Beautiful ideas. For those sympathetic to the progressive era project to transform the restless and polyglot urban crowd into a unified American public, the large labor meetings that took place in the plaza were hugely suggestive. In the wake of the free speech movement, these meetings demonstrated the possibility of a self-organizing working-class demographic willing and able to participate peacefully in the governance of the city and the country.

Prompted by a progressive municipal administration and by City Beautiful planning philosophy, Union Square was reimagined as modern civic center between 1900 and 1932. Tied into the wider metropolis by a network of new roads and public transit routes, planners hoped to visually articulate its centrality through the language of baroque city planning and neoclassical architecture. This period saw the most significant physical changes to the Square since it was established one hundred years earlier. From 1900 it was torn up piece by piece to make way for two subway lines and a concourse connecting them, part of the unified underground rapid transit system being constructed throughout the city. Above the ground roads were rerouted and buildings resited. The skyline rose as building developers began to erect tall loft buildings along the side streets. Ambitious plans to remake the park were proposed, with Olmsted and Vaux's plaza expanded and transformed from a modest staging area into a major public space, reinforced by the construction of a magnificent new courthouse on the east side of the Square. Building on the legacy of radical meetings, these efforts aimed at the same time to repress them.

These efforts were redoubled during the Depression years. From the turn of the century Union Square became known as a destination for bargain shopping. Across the country, with the economy facing an unprecedented slump, business and property owners placed their hopes in retail space, and in women shoppers in particular, to prop up the economy. In response to the shifting economic landscape, local storeowners increased their efforts to attract shoppers from the suburbs and even uptown, people who might previously have turned their noses up at tables of merchandise offered cafeteria style. In other cities and towns, business owners embarked on efforts to remodel shop fronts in the new modern style. In Union Square improving the intangible attractiveness of the neighborhood became the primary concern. Working in concert with the Parks Department, local businessmen, led by Samuel Klein of Klein's department store, staged patriotic events designed to counter radical activities. The culmination of these efforts, the Centennial celebration of 1932, unveiled a completely renovated Union Square, one designed explicitly to suppress radical political activity and to reinforce a new image of American public space.

The Crowd Becomes the Public

By the turn of the twentieth century Union Square had acquired a somewhat Bohemian reputation. In the popular imagination the Square was the place where the social worlds of uptown and downtown intersected. On weekdays it was filled with women taking a break from their shopping, nurses with their charges, gentleman idlers, theatrical types seeking employment, as well as tramps and other loiterers. Regular nightly meetings of radical groups of all stripes were still held at the plaza, and at the southern end of the park soapbox orators gathered large crowds around them. The polyglot and ethnically diverse crowd that gathered in and around Union Square was portrayed in contemporary journalism, literature, and art as the face of modern America. At the same time an idea that this diverse and dynamic populace was in need of positive influence if not direct control began to emerge in the new discipline of sociology, as well as in political science and urban planning.

As we saw in the previous chapter, the socialist and anarchist gatherings that took place in Union Square during the first two decades of the century were frequently portrayed as portents of a larger threat to national stability. The urgent need to transform the restless and potentially anarchic urban crowd into an organized and rational public was central to the writing of American sociologist Robert E. Park. Derived from his observations of life in New York and Chicago, his writing is part of a large body of American scholarship attempting to come to terms with the rise of mass culture around the turn of the twentieth century.[1] After studying philosophy with John Dewey at the University of Michigan, Park began his studies of the crowd working as a journalist in the emerging industrial cities of the Midwest. There he observed recent immigrants from diverse geographic backgrounds, loosened from their traditional social groupings, and struggling to form new relations, often resulting in unstable and fractious communities. Park's work was part of a tradition of sociological study originating in Europe. In France the physician Gustav Le Bon had initiated the scholarly study of crowds with his pessimistic book, *The Crowd: A Study of the Popular Mind* (1895).[2] Le Bon warned that the crowd was pliable, irrational, and emotionally sensitive, highly susceptible to manipulation by skillful demagogues preaching revolutionary politics. But where Le Bon regarded the emergence of the modern crowd as a portent of social devolution, prefiguring the breakdown of civil society, Park saw its potential. Framed by the context of American democracy, he believed, individual thought could be collectivized in a positive manner, with the fickle opinion of the crowd swayed and stabilized through rational public discourse. Park's writing supported the progressive era project to elevate the masses into a civilized public through democratic reforms and the influence of strong leaders. In response to the individualism and extreme inequity of the laissez-faire era, progressives sought to create new forms of social cooperation by reinforcing loyalty to the state. For Park, the press was to be the site of this transformation: in the right hands it would present reasoned arguments about contemporary affairs, with a balanced and synthetic presentation of opposing ideas. In this way he believed the print media had the power to overcome the sway of emotions exhibited on the streets. However, others continued to believe in the potential of public space as a viable site for the formation of rational and informed collective opinion.

Building on the Enlightenment belief in the power of monumental public buildings and urban spaces to foster new forms of civic life, early twentieth-century social reformers, city planners, and architects sought to redefine the physical space of the city according to progressive political ideals.[3] If grid cities such as New York and Chicago were anonymous and alienating, the inhospitable creation of commercial interests, the answer was to reconfigure them centered on new civic monuments with which all citizens could identify. Supported by newly created civic traditions such as holidays, pageants, and parades, these monuments would imbue the urban masses with a sense of collective endeavor and loyalty to one another. For progressive planners the most significant of these modern monuments was undoubtedly the governmental center. Providing a place for the urban crowd to gather together—not in the form of an unruly mob, but as a rational and unified body—it was to be the built embodiment of progressive politics. These ideals coalesced in the City Beautiful movement. Influential promoters of City Beautiful thinking such as the Rochester journalist Charles Mulford Robinson provided practical advice on the correct design and configuration of such centers. Robinson especially praised the creation of centrally located administrative complexes in which municipal buildings were grouped together for both ease of access and monumental effect. In his ideal American town, these buildings would face an open plaza modeled on a "common," derived from a typical New England village.[4] Robinson's nostalgic proposal to transform the modern industrial city via the installation of such a space reflected his desire to return to the nation's political roots, an imagined era of collective political purpose.

Noble in aspiration, the City Beautiful was difficult to realize in practice. Many American towns and cities were built on a grid. While this planning form was now reviled for its unattractiveness and inefficiency, in most cases city governments had little power to implement large-scale changes to it. Although some cities such as Detroit and Chicago were partially reconfigured, comprehensive change was difficult to achieve.[5] With its rigid street grid and weak municipal government, New York City was particularly problematic in this regard. After the consolidation of the five boroughs in 1898, it had become the largest city in the world after London. Both city authorities and social reformers were increasingly convinced that the grid laid out in 1811, a plan designed to accommodate almost unimaginable urban expansion, was now severely limiting the city's ability to operate efficiently.[6] Around the turn of the twentieth century, unofficial proposals to radically remake the New York City grid proliferated, supported by private organizations including the Architectural League and the Municipal Art Society.[7] For example, in 1904 architect Ernest Flagg proposed combining Broadway and Central Park together to create a grand boulevard lined with trees on each side, one thousand feet wide and more than ten miles long.[8] This linear and formal parkway would be both a monumental public space and organizing circulation spine.

Without substantial financial backing and lacking a powerful municipal planning authority these grandiose visions had little hope of being realized. In the late nineteenth century the Tammany Hall–controlled city government had little power and no inclination to take on grand urban projects. However, the possibility of comprehensive city planning was advanced in 1902 when Seth Low, the former president of Columbia University, was voted into the mayor's office with a mandate to do away with Tammany corruption and to put city management on a professional rather than a political footing. The establishment of a permanent civil service would mean the elimination of patronage appointments, placing important decisions in the hands of trained managers, economists, doctors, social workers, and engineers rather than political appointees. Beyond this, multiple state and civic agencies would be consolidated into fewer, larger agencies, with the presumption that they would work more efficiently and collaboratively. The challenge for these agencies was the scale of the city and the diversity of its occupants. Low's administration faced the problem of controlling the urban growth caused by economic speculation without inhibiting the capitalist engines that drove the city.

The early focus of City Beautiful planning in New York City was one of the few areas that the city had complete control over: City Hall Park. For over a decade architects, journalists and city historians had been agitating to have this park improved and identified as an important national landmark. In 1895 the *New York Times* art critic Royal Cortissoz had recommended its preservation as a "souvenir of history."[9] In 1902 the Municipal Art Society of New York, a private group of influential citizens, advised Mayor Low to clear the park of all buildings except City Hall and to acquire a large amount of land to the north and east for the construction of new administration buildings.[10]

When the city accepted City Hall Park as a historic landmark worthy of preservation in 1910, some were concerned that this would come at the cost of its public function. The journalist Herbert Croly was particularly critical of the preservation plan, seeing it as creating a static showpiece rather than a real center for political activity.[11] A leading progressive thinker, Croly was critical of City Beautiful planning in general, regarding the civic center ideal as romantic and unrealistic. In order to create a communal spirit, more than just charming historical pageantry was needed, he believed: people had to feel that their participation in the political process was meaningful. Even the most enthusiastic supporters of the City Hall plan realized it was located too far south to be of much use as a city center. In this sense another public park, one that occupied the geographic center of the city and sat at the nexus of many major streets, one already serving as a forum for large public meetings, seemed to offer richer possibilities.

Starting at the turn of twentieth century, City Beautiful planners hoped to transform Union Square from a London-style square (green, private, and enclosed) with a small plaza attached, into a grand scale, classically inspired public square. For example, in 1898 architect Julius F. Harder had proposed enlarging Union Square and making it the center of a radial series of grand diagonal avenues with a new City Hall sited in the middle.[12] The creation of a comprehensive rapid transit system for New York City, which entailed remaking the Square entirely, seemed to offer an opportunity to achieve this goal. The Square featured as a major transportation hub in almost all speculative plans for elevated train or subway routes made during the nineteenth century.[13] As we saw in chapter 1, early mass-transit systems were surface-level ones: horse-drawn streetcar lines were introduced in 1833, running up Broadway from Prince Street to Union Square, and then north on Fourth Avenue (now Park Avenue South) to Twenty-Third Street. As the city grew, entrepreneurs were eager to realize the potential of elevated and subterranean travel and plans for private transportation lines connecting the various parts of New York City began to appear. In 1847, John Randel Jr. (the man responsible for surveying the 1811 grid) put forward a contentious proposal for a railway line elevated above Broadway and running on a continuous loop from Bowling Green to Union Square, displaying his plan in the form of an enormous model twelve feet wide and forty feet long.[14] This plan was rejected by the city because of the negative effect it would have on the street underneath. While an elevated line was established in 1860, running along the western edge of Manhattan as far north as One Hundred and Twenty-Ninth Street in Harlem, most private proposals had little hope of being realized because they required the purchase of too much land. In

1866 New York State appointed a commission to look into the creation of a rapid transit system for New York City, and in 1868 the New York City Central Underground Railway Company was created by an act of legislature. The company proposed a route from the Battery up to Fourteenth Street with its northernmost terminus at Union Square.[15] This line was never realized because of the expense of buying up a great deal of private property.

By the 1870s the pressure to improve New York's transportation system was felt acutely in Union Square where the proliferation of streetcar lines inevitably led to conflict, and traffic congestion had become a major problem. In 1874 two private companies—the Cross Town Road and the Bleecker Street Company—put forward competing and incompatible plans for a cross-town rail system along Fourteenth Street. The Department of Parks objected to both because the construction of tracks inside the park would create a dangerous confluence of streetcars and public gatherings.[16] At the southern end of the Square, the tight turn that streetcars were required to make from Broadway onto Fourteenth Street earned the nickname "dead man's curve" because of the high number of traffic accidents occurring there.[17] In 1896 the city debated a proposal to do away with the curve by running surface streetcars directly through the park. Although the streetcar line was to be covered by a landscaped tunnel, the Parks Department Board ultimately rejected this plan.[18]

If elevated tracks shaded the streets in unappealing ways, and surface streetcar lines impeded traffic, the answer was to go underground. In the 1890s the state and city governments began to work in partnership with private companies to construct a comprehensive subway system. In 1891 New York State passed the Rapid Transit Act, initiating the construction of an electric underground railroad, a true "Metropolitan Railway for New York" modeled on the one in London.[19] This system would comprise three lines: a central one running up Broadway from the Battery to One Hundred and Fifty-Fifth Street and down Third Avenue; and one each running up the east and west sides of the island to Twenty-Third and Seventy-Second Streets respectively, where they would join the main Broadway line. After some debate a proposal for municipal ownership of the system was rejected in favor of private operators. While the Board of Rapid Transit Commissioners drew up the plan, actual construction and operation was put out to tender to franchisees: the first two were the Interborough Rapid Transit (IRT) and the Brooklyn Manhattan Transit (BMT) Companies. The mid-1890s saw discussion about how Union Square would accommodate station stops: some argued for the redesign of the park to incorporate street-level cars, but most agreed that submerging the lines was the best solution. The implementation of subway lines necessarily meant the complete destruction of Union Square. Work began on the tunnels in 1900 when an area at the northern end was fenced off for construction, and it would last more than a dozen years. In 1904 Mayor McClellan opened the first subway line in New York, with Union Square as a stop; it ran from City Hall to Grand Central Station, across to Times Square, and up Broadway to 135th Street. The plaza end of the Square was not fully restored until 1918. While hugely disruptive, the turmoil created by this protracted construction presented an opportunity: the chance to create a true civic center after the City Beautiful model on the important site at Broadway and Fourteenth Street. The Municipal Art Society (MAS) was to be the primary promoter of this transformation.

Founded in 1893 by a group of artists and their patrons, and inspired by the splendor of the World's Columbian Exposition in Chicago, the MAS was the chief voice of the City Beautiful movement in New York City. Its motto was "To make us love our city, we must make our city lovely."[20] Elected in 1901, Mayor Seth Low was a keen supporter. In 1902 he commissioned an unofficial report on city planning from the society, which focused on circulation and the creation of monumental buildings. Buoyed by the society's vision, in 1903, Low created an official "New York Improvement Commission" and charged it with drawing up a comprehensive city plan. Though Low was defeated in the November election by George B. McClellan, the commission continued its work. When it issued its final report in 1907, New York City had its first comprehensive urban planning document in almost one hundred years.[21] Heavily influenced by MAS ideas, the focus of the report was a major new civic precinct to be built north of City Hall. It also included a bold concept for the redevelopment of traffic networks in Lower Manhattan developed by MAS member and sculptor Charles Lamb. As the chair of the MAS committee on "thoroughfares," Lamb proposed turning Union Square into a giant star shape, the paved confluence of a series of diagonal streets, with the statue of Washington at the center.[22] Though this proposal was presented as an attempt to improve traffic circulation, there is no doubt that the resulting form had an aesthetically pleasing monumentality. Lamb intended the intersecting pathways through the Square to be used for civic processions, culminating in a classical forum on the site of the plaza at the northern end, equipped with a monumental speaker's platform. Invoking the examples of Trafalgar Square and Hyde Park in London, he sought to monumentalize the political rallies already taking place there, greatly expanding on Olmsted and Vaux's vision.[23] Remaking Union Square using formal, neoclassical geometry rather than the existing curving pathways, the MAS answered contemporary criticism of its layout. No less an authority than Charles Mulford Robinson had singled out Union Square, claiming that its meandering paths were "an example both of ineffective and of positively wrong planning." He also claimed, somewhat enigmatically, that "the wrong portion is paved."[24] With their redesign, Lamb and the MAS hoped to transform a place of rowdy protest into a site for far grander and much more genteel displays of civic pageantry.

The model of the classical forum as the ultimate public space was hugely appealing to City Beautiful planners. Even as the movement's focus on aesthetics over functionalism began to be criticized in the 1920s, the forum remained a desirable precedent because of its democratic associations. In 1920 the New York critic John Taylor Boyd sketched an idealized "Gathering Place in Town Plans" in *Architectural Record*. Boyd described the necessity for open space in democratic societies:

> As one aspect of the life of such communities we have countless public meetings, where people foregather collectively, not to transact business directly, but for celebration and stimulation; with ceremonies, addresses, commemorations, inaugurations, pageants, in which the whole people formally but democratically and spontaneously, delight to join.[25]

Seeing democracy as a kind of public performance, he called for the design of a forum or stage for its enactment. Boyd believed that the functional requirements of such spaces necessitated a form different from that of traditional urban parks. Since civic centers were intended for public gatherings, not private leisure activities, he argued, and they should be formal, rather than picturesque in character, "any great masses of green cut up the crowds and they detract from the impressive effects of that colorful pattern of crowds and processions. . . . The simpler the setting, the better. Neither elaborate architecture nor elaborate naturalistic parks are needed."[26] His ideal model, the football stadium, was borrowed not from any landscape tradition but from a built artifact of emerging mass culture.

Lamb's proposal to remake Union Square in the form of a giant star received a favorable response when it was presented to the Parks Department in 1903. Ironically this plan was rejected by Samuel Parsons, a former employee of Calvert Vaux, whose vision of Union Square as a public space Lamb wished to enlarge.[27] Parsons had been superintendent of parks for a decade in the 1890s and in 1902 Mayor Low named him the Parks Department landscape architect. Devoted to his mentor Vaux, he dedicated himself to preserving the picturesque vision of city parks established fifty years earlier. Feeling the pressure from City Beautiful advocates who frequently offered unsolicited advice to the department, Parsons was moved to defend his own vision for New York City's small parks, one that centered on the now old-fashioned beds of flowers arranged in semi-naturalistic ovals set within a larger lawn.[28] He maintained the view that such planting was desirable because it offered working-class park users contact with nature and a relief from the heat and crowding of the city. After initially supporting Parks Commissioner Charles Stover's plan to popularize city parks, including the creation of children's play areas and sports facilities, he came to oppose it, claiming that it was impossible to maintain plantings and trees if children and athletes were allowed to run free.[29] On this basis he also vetoed Lamb's plan for Union Square, a plan that would have meant the elimination of most of the planting.

While the Parks Department ultimately rejected the MAS proposal to turn Union Square into a monumental and formal civic center, alternative plans to remake it as a major City Beautiful set piece were proposed. Between 1903 and 1913 the state legislature and the New York City Board of Estimate considered relocating the New York County Court House from Foley Square, just north of City Hall in Lower Manhattan, to Union Square. If realized, this plan would have replaced the collage of individually conceived commercial buildings with a backdrop of unified administrative buildings. Lawyers and politicians had long sought to replace the existing Court House north of City Hall. Notorious for the high cost of its construction, it was a symbol of the corruption of the Tweed era, and the reform administration was anxious to see it demolished. In 1905 State Senator Nathaniel Eisberg sponsored a bill to build the New York County Court House in either Union or Madison Squares, with a new public square to be constructed on land directly adjacent.[30] By January of 1907 the Board of Estimate declared it had chosen a site for the new courthouse on the eastern side of Union Square, between Fourteenth and Seventeenth Streets, from Fourth Avenue to Irving Place.[31] Shortly afterward, the Justices of the Supreme Court voiced their support for this idea. The Square would become a new legal center, complementing the new municipal center being developed near City Hall.

It was heavy-handed symbolism to place the County Court House directly facing the site favored by anarchist and socialist groups for their vocal public demonstrations. These groups openly questioned the validity of the United States government and its legal system. For conservative politicians, however, the courts were the proper place to seek social change, not the streets. They did not concur with the liberal agenda for public space put forward by planners such as Lamb and Boyd. The *New York Times* came out in support of the courthouse plan as a monument to the tax-paying public. Fronting onto Union Square, the courthouse would provide an "object of pride and admiration for the citizens whose money erected it," the editors claimed.[32] Despite the support of Senator Eisberg and the *Times*, however, many members of the legal community were less than enthusiastic about the location, considering it too remote from the municipal buildings in Lower Manhattan. A few months later, in May of 1907, the Board of Estimate abandoned the plan because of the high cost of purchasing land. There was also lingering discomfort about moving the courthouse to what was becoming a rather down-at-heel shopping and entertainment district. Surrounded by department stores, hotels, and theaters, Union Square seemed to present a tawdry atmosphere for the transaction of civic business. And although they were not voiced publicly, there were possibly also concerns about safety. These fears were to be realized the following year. The new County Court House was built instead at Foley Square, the alternative civic center being constructed just north of City Hall Park.

The Loft and Shopping District

Though it never became a center of civic administration or a courthouse precinct, the area around Union Square did undergo a significant architectural transformation in the first two decades of the twentieth century. During these years everything seemed unstable, even the ground itself. The plaza, the lawn, and Parsons' beloved bedded plants were all torn up. Behind them, five-story buildings erected in the middle of the nineteenth century were demolished and a series of towers sprang up as a backdrop to the turmoil. Around 1890 the garment industry (or "needle trades") had begun to move north of the Fourteenth Street divide, into new mercantile structures along the west side of Union Square and Lower Fourth, Fifth, and Sixth Avenues. At the street level a new kind of department store appeared, replacing the older luxury stores. As the Federal Writers' Project *New York City Guide* noted in 1939,

> The business center had shifted, or rather split, leaving a great gap between downtown and uptown New York, into which the young needle trades rushed like a tide. Besides cheap rents—real estate values had fallen rapidly—the neighborhood offered two great advantages to the industry: it was on the outskirts of the fashionable shopping center, and it was near the plentiful and cheap labor supply—the immigrant families of the Lower East Side.[33]

6.1 "Union Square West, Nos. 31–41, Manhattan," 1938. The Decker Building is second from the left.

In 1890 the architect R. H. Robertson completed the imposing Lincoln Building, designed in the Romanesque Revival style, at nos. 1–3 Union Square West.[34] Next door, at no. 5, William H. Hume and Sons built the neoclassical Spingler Building in 1896, replacing the Spingler Hotel, which had been damaged by fire and demolished. While both were decorated in a manner befitting their prestigious address, they were intended primarily to house the workshops and showrooms of manufacturing businesses. To cite just two examples, the Lincoln housed the Eyelet Buttonhole Attachment Company. Incorporated in 1888, this company was patentee and manufacturer of the Eyelet Buttonhole Attachment, advertised as "the only attachment that makes a perfect eyelet end buttonhole." A sewing machine attachment, it was "so easily worked that two or three buttonholes a minute can be made by a six-year-old child."[35] Charles E. Bentley, manufacturer, importer, and jobber of specialties in decorative art needlework, had his offices, salesroom, and factory in the Spingler. Here 150 women and men produced "decorative art needlework, unique designs in printed drapery silks, painted and embroidered novelties, linens, plushes and embroidery materials," all in the hot and humid atmosphere created by the latest in steam-powered machinery.[36]

One of the most curious buildings constructed in this period is the tall and narrow Decker Building at 33 Union Square West. Completed in 1893 as a showroom for the Decker Piano Company, it replaced the company's earlier building on the same site. While attributed to the architect Alfred Zucker, architectural historians have argued it is the work of Zucker's employee John Edelmann, a Chicago architect who was friend and mentor to Louis H. Sullivan.[37] Predominantly Venetian Gothic in style, it incorporates eclectic ornamentation, including Moorish motifs, which were commonly used in buildings associated with leisure and entertainment though seldom so intricately. More than its elaborate style, however, what makes the Decker Building unique is Edelmann's complex biography. After working in large architectural firms throughout the Midwest, he came to New York around 1887, pursuing a commitment to radical politics. In 1892 he founded the Socialist League, and in 1893 he became publisher of *Solidarity*, an anarchist periodical. Writing in *Engineering Magazine* at the same time the eleven-story Decker Building was being designed, he was highly critical of the new American building type, the skyscraper, calling it an unwelcome aestheticization of capitalism: "If this is to be our future, well may we regret our rude and buoyant youth, ere we had bought accomplishment, high aims and subtle insight to the service of the prevailing money cult."[38] Soon after the Decker was completed, overlooking the plaza at Union Square, Edelmann was a participant in radical meetings held there, standing alongside Emma Goldman who mentions him in her memoirs as a "gifted architect and publicist," perhaps referring to his work with *Solidarity*.[39] Unusually for his profession, Edelmann was both responsible for the construction of a capitalist monument and at the same time deeply critical of the system that had produced it.

Despite the rhetoric in the plaza, the capitalist machine drove forward. In 1903 the *New York Times* reported that the area bounded by Union Square and Twenty-Third Street, Fourth and Sixth Avenues was experiencing a building boom as new structures were erected to house the various branches of the wholesale trades.[40] This flurry of construction was only expected to intensify when the Fourth Avenue subway opened the following year offering a direct connection to the nearly completed Grand Central Station. Supported by this new transportation link, the Fourth Avenue corridor between Union Square and Twenty-Third Street was touted as a future center of the wholesale trade. The incursion of wholesale and manufacturing businesses and new real estate demands in the district produced a hybrid building type. The area was already home to several recently completed office buildings including the Bank of the Metropolis at 31 Union Square West (1902–3) by Bruce Price, and the Union Square Savings Bank at 20 Union Square East (1905–7) by Henry Bacon.[41] Designed in the neoclassical style, these were fairly conventional buildings with retail banking and stores on the ground floor and rental office space above. In 1910 *The American Architect* described a new form of commercial building appearing along what is now Park Avenue South:

> A distinctive type of business building on a large scale (partly loft and partly office building) is being developed in New York in that section of Fourth Avenue between Union Square and Park Avenue. The development of the district is part of the northward march of wholesale textile industry on Manhattan Island.[42]

The most prominent of these loft-office hybrids was the seventeen-story Everett Building built in 1908 on the prestigious site of the old Everett House Hotel at the North West corner of Union Square.[43] The loft designation was a valuable one because the law allowed such buildings to cover 90 percent of their lot with no height restriction. The neoclassical building designed by architects Goldwin, Starrett, and Van Vleck had a base of polished and carved granite, lower stories of Indiana limestone, and upper stories of glazed terracotta. Inside it contained the features of a manufacturing building: large floor plates, minimal columns, and plentiful windows. With Portland cement floors, it was sturdy enough to bear the weight of heavy machinery. It was also serviced with ten elevators, five for passengers and five for freight. While the rear provided north light for manufacturing and show rooms, the south side of the building overlooking the Square was set aside for offices. Before it was completed, the *New York Times* reported that "six or eight of the most important firms in the city dealing in woolens and other dry goods have already engaged to take entire floors in the new building."[44] The Everett Building was recognized in the architectural press as a pioneer of the loft-office type, a wholly new form of American invention.[45] Two years later it gained a partner. In 1910 work began on the twenty-one-story Germania Life Insurance Building by architects D'Oench and Yost, directly across Fourth Avenue from the Everett.[46] Also in the neoclassical style, it was designed as headquarters for an insurance company but like the Everett it contained large open spaces for use as manufacturing salesrooms. The building was notable for its impressive four-story mansard roof topped with a large electric sign bearing the building's name. Six years after that Union Square lost two of the original townhouses built by Samuel Ruggles, when nos. 36 and 38 Union Square East were demolished to make way for stores, leaving only two of the original row standing.[47] With the construction of these two prominent skyscrapers, and the destruction of almost all of the original east side

6.2 Everett Building, Fourth Avenue and E. 17th Street, ca. 1910.

townhouses, the character and scale of the Square was dramatically altered. While much of the city north of Union Square benefited from a commercial building boom during the 1920s, older businesses to the south and east suffered.

With the west side given over to grand new high rises, a different kind of business moved in to fill the commercial vacuum on the quieter east side.

When he opened his eponymous business in 1905, Samuel Klein began the transformation of Union Square into a mecca for bargain shopping. The son of Polish Jewish immigrants, Klein followed his tailor father into the garment trade, training as a fabric cutter.[48] In the late 1890s he had opened his own wholesale business on Bleecker Street manufacturing women's skirts. Capitalizing on the decline in real estate prices, he moved his company to a building on the east side of Union Square and from the 1920s continued to expand into a series of contiguous buildings. At his death in 1942, Klein's estate controlled most of the buildings on that side of the Square, including the prominent Union Square Hotel. S. Klein specialized in a new kind of self-service retailing. Instead of employing large numbers of salespeople, patrons sifted through goods laid out on tables and racks, taking clothes to try on in communal dressing rooms. As a budget retailer it competed with Hearn's (James Hearn and Son), an older style department store operating from premises on Fourteenth Street between Fifth and Sixth Avenues, and Ohrbach's, which had opened in 1923 at Broadway and Union Place with an erratic inventory of irregular and overstocked merchandise.[49] Selling clothing and household goods to New Yorkers on modest incomes, these stores were famous for the deep discounts they offered during their coordinated seasonal sales. With the establishment of the bargain department stores and the construction of prominent loft buildings, the character and scale of the Square was dramatically altered. A new urban landscape was created: towering loft-office buildings filled with workers in the needle and printing trades and new retail establishments designed to serve budget conscious shoppers.

The mercantile district that emerged between Union Square and Twenty-Third Street in the first decade of the twentieth century was one of the prompts for urban reformers urging the city to adopt stricter building regulations. In 1911 the city's Committee on Congestion of Population presented its annual report to Mayor William J. Gaynor. One of the chief issues of concern was "excessive congestion and a lack of proper air, lighting and ventilating facilities," in some of the blocks north of Fourteenth Street, owing to the construction of loft buildings.[50] Noting the clearly apparent shift of scale between these buildings, fourteen stories high or more, and the older, six-story mercantile houses built along Mercer, Greene, and Wooster Streets in SoHo, the committee called for restrictions on the height of loft buildings and on the permissible lot coverage. This report was part of a larger movement to restrict the size and deployment of tall buildings throughout the city.[51] Pointing out the dangers of overcrowding presented by the forest of towers, critics argued for strict controls on these gargantuan new

6.3 Walker Evans, Street Scene in Front of S. Klein-on-the-Square Department Store, Union Square East, New York City, September 1937.

buildings. The problem was not tall buildings themselves, but the way in which they seemed to be constructed with no thought of their relationship to their neighbors, to the street, or to the city as a whole. Urban reformers longed for some kind of order. In 1908 the *New York Times* asked: "Why not make the new American metropolis, which is being created by remodeling old New York, a city that is not only great, but architecturally beautiful?"[52] But the problem was the one that had bedeviled urban reformers for the last hundred years. In the absence of a dictator, or an emperor as in Paris, the creation of architectural and urban harmony via grand scale construction was virtually impossible. Private property owners must either acquire huge parcels of land or cooperate, something they had shown little interest in doing before. Herbert Croly recognized this problem in an excoriating review of the city's 1907 plan. Explaining why City Beautiful ideas had little chance of success in America, he used New York City as an example.[53] Although the municipal government had the will, it had very little money and less power to enact large-scale planning. Dependent on the favor of real estate interests to maintain their power, politicians had little incentive to enact restrictive building regulations. If any changes were to occur, they must be with the cooperation of business interests.

This was the case in 1916 when the city enacted a wide-ranging zoning law. As with other urban improvements, this law was prompted by agitation on the part of influential and wealthy private citizens.[54] Around the turn of the century a group of property owners and retail merchants with an interest in lower Fifth Avenue formed the Fifth Avenue Association in order to lobby against the proliferation of manufacturing businesses north of Washington Square Park. In particular they sought to prevent loft buildings from encroaching on high-end Fifth Avenue stores. Members of the association believed that the "occupation of and the congestion of the sidewalks on Fifth Avenue by the great crowds of workers in the clothing trades was beginning to be a serious menace to the retail trade."[55] The 1916 law entailed a reframing of City Beautiful ideals away from aesthetics and toward more practical concepts of urban function and management. Under the law the city was divided into zones, and building height was limited according to the zone. The zoning envelope, which restricted building volume, was created to preserve the flow of light and air to the streets. After the enactment of the law, lofts were banned on Fifth and Sixth Avenues, and the garment district was pushed further west, to Seventh Avenue and beyond.

The Centennial

While not as far reaching as the new zoning law, the remaking of the park at Union Square was prompted by a similar process: local businessmen urging the city to act on order to promote or preserve an area's distinct identity. With the Recruit dismantled and removed to Coney Island, and the subway construction nearing completion, preparations were made to begin the park's long-delayed renovation. When the new BMT subway line opened in 1928, the transit terminus underneath was the largest in Manhattan, accommodating fifty million passengers annually.[56] With the major subway lines converging there, Union Square was one of the most accessible points in the city. While Manhattan was losing population to the outer boroughs and to newly developed regional centers in New York, New Jersey, and Connecticut, it continued to be an important business and cultural center for the wider region. The *New York Times* noted that "probably nowhere else in town is there such a concentration of building as is going on around Union Square at the present time."[57] The completion of the subway terminus underneath allowed for the creation of an aesthetically conservative, yet ambitious relandscaping project above. Though the design and planning work was undertaken by the city Parks Department, the renovation of the Square was completed with the aid of local businessmen. When the new park was officially opened as part of a highly choreographed civic spectacular, a new narrative of the Square and its history was rolled out.

In the early 1920s Klein organized his fellow department store presidents and other local business owners into a voluntary organization, the Fourteenth Street Association of Business Leaders, with the general aim of protecting and promoting business interests.[58] The association was one of many created in the interwar years that engaged in coordinated marketing campaigns on behalf of local stores while also lobbying the city for financial assistance and favorable legislation. As art historian Ellen Wiley Todd has noted in her study of the culture of Union Square during this period, these efforts were ideological as well as financial. Klein and his peers described the neighborhood's commercial success in terms of strengthening American values: the goods sold at local department stores were both symbol and agent of the better standard of living available to new immigrants, engendering in them a patriotic attachment to their new country along with new forms of behavior and new ways of thinking.[59]

From the first the association was deeply involved in the renovation of Union Square, seeing it as a vital part of the project to rededicate the area to healthy American consumerism. For much of the 1910s and 1920s the park in the center of the Square was nothing more than a series of muddy construction pits surrounded by untidy wooden hoardings. During the construction of the underground concourse in the late 1920s, the entire surface was raised three feet, supported by a granite retaining wall. The statues were removed from their locations and put in storage. In 1927 the Municipal Art Society began to agitate for influence in the design of Union Square and the city Art Commission gave approval for the work to begin.[60] Like many other urban improvements conceived during this prosperous period, this project came to an abrupt halt in 1929. During the Depression renovations dragged on, and newspapers published ongoing complaints about the continual delays. The park was so debased that the *Herald Tribune* drew a grim comparison between its muddy and furrowed state and the trenches of France and Belgium.[61] Echoing criticism made about corruption in the Parks Department during the Boss Tweed era, the newspaper hinted the entire beautification project was a Tammany Hall boondoggle with well-connected contractors getting rich off the seemingly never-ending work supplied by Mayor James J. "Jimmy" Walker.[62] A popular party machine Democrat, Walker rode the wave of the city's prosperity. Though he had improved many public services including sanitation, hospitals, and parks, by the late 1920s his administration was tainted by rumors of corruption.

The association between the seemingly endless delays at Union Square and questionable management practices in Walker's City Hall was cemented by the erection of a new Tammany Hall building on the corner of Union Square East and Seventeenth Street. Designed in the neocolonial style by architect Charles B. Meyers, this grand structure replaced the old Tammany Hall building on Fourteenth Street when it was demolished to make way for the monumental Con Ed building in 1927.[63] Not content with stamping its authority over the city via its grand new headquarters, Tammany Hall also erected a monument inside Union Square itself in the form of a decorative flagpole. Commissioned by the Tammany Society, the flagpole was intended as a memorial to longtime Tammany boss Charles F. Murphy. However, since this honor would place Murphy, a dubious character in the eyes of many, on equal footing with Washington, Lincoln, and Lafayette, this controversial proposal was soon abandoned.[64] Renamed the Liberty Flagpole, it was reimagined as a commemoration of the sesquicentennial of the Declaration of Independence. In 1864 Samuel Ruggles had invoked the Forum of Trajan in his patriotic description of Union Square. The Liberty Flagpole was the Tammany version of this imperial monument. Designed by sculptor Anthony de Francisci, the bronze relief around the base was inscribed with a quotation from Thomas Jefferson: "How little do my countrymen know what precious blessings they are in possession of and which no other people on earth enjoy."[65]

In erecting these twin monuments, Tammany Hall was competing for the loyalty of working-class New Yorkers. After the repression of the war years, the annual May Day parade was revived in the 1920s. Maintaining its reputation as the center of America's radical movement, Union Square was home to the headquarters of unions, radical political groups, and left-wing publications such as *Call*, *Mother Earth*, and the *New Masses*. In 1927 the Communist Party of the USA (CPUSA) relocated its national headquarters from Chicago to 26–28 Union Square East, promptly painting the facade of the building red and draping it with slogan-bearing banners.[66] The ground floor housed the offices of the party's newspaper, *Daily Worker*, and the popular Cooperative Cafeteria where cheap food was sold and radical talk encouraged. The crowd that gathered on the sidewalk outside the building, talking from noon until late into the evening, was a favorite subject of artists and writers.[67] For journalists at the *New York Herald Tribune*, this crowd was visible evidence of the success of fifth columnists, communist agents carrying out plans laid by "the ruling committee in Moscow."[68] Before long fear of

6.4 Communist Party Headquarters and the *Daily Worker* newspaper, 26–28 Union Square East, ca. 1930.

Soviet infiltration culminated in a confrontation between police and communist protesters, one that gave added impetus to efforts to remake Union Square, both physically and symbolically.

Adhering to the liberal policies put in place in the 1910s, the Police and Parks departments generally granted permits for political rallies. However, as these demonstrations gained in size and fervor, Mayor Walker and Police Commissioner Grover Whalen grew increasingly nervous. In March 1930 a huge demonstration organized by Worker's International Relief, an organization backed by both communists and socialists, brought matters to a head. This rally was one of many planned across the country to draw attention to the desperate condition of the unemployed. In advance of the demonstration, Walker and Whalen issued statements outlining a strict policy toward possible public disturbance: while lawful public assembly would be respected, rioting and lawlessness would be put down by force.[69] In particular, any attempt to march on City Hall would not be tolerated. Fourteenth Street was the demarcation line below which the crowd would not be allowed to pass. Following this hostile and uncompromising rhetoric it is hardly surprising that the resulting demonstration, one of the largest ever held in Union Square, ended badly. Whalen placed his men as if for war: he personally directed two hundred policemen and fifteen mounted police from a temporary police headquarters set up in the cottage on the plaza. Emergency crews equipped with gas, tear bombs, and fire hoses were held in readiness. After about three hours of fiery oratory, the leaders of the demonstration were offered the chance to meet privately with the mayor at City Hall. Whalen later noted that he had offered to drive them downtown in his personal car. When the leaders rejected this offer, saying that all would meet the mayor or none, a group of about two thousand broke away from the larger crowd and attempted to march south in violation of the police permit. Police and firemen turned their fire hoses on the crowd, initiating one of the worst riots in the history of the city.[70] The *Herald Tribune* described the scene:

> For fifteen minutes the Square was a battleground with charging horses, swinging clubs, flying bricks, thumping fists, and screaming women as 500 police in uniform and plain clothes subdued the raging Communists. More than fifty persons were injured, at least fifteen requiring medical care. Thirteen arrests were made, including the five leaders of the demonstration which was staged as part of the Moscow-directed world-wide Soviet protest on unemployment.[71]

Following the riot five of the meeting organizers were arrested. Although the whole event lasted no more than fifteen minutes, the repercussions reverberated in national newspapers for weeks afterward.

Echoing the response to the anarchist demonstrations of 1914, public opinion was divided. Many commentators were appalled by the aggressive tactics used by the police, seeing them as a suppression of civil liberties. Arguing that these tactics served only to embitter the crowd, they made the case for open access to public spaces as necessary social safety valves. Meanwhile others demanded a strict crackdown on public demonstrations.

6.5 Unemployed American protesters running through Union Square pursued by tear gas–wielding police, March 6, 1930.

Following the melee, the New York City Chamber of Commerce petitioned the city for a complete ban on public demonstrations in Union Square. Two years later the Broadway Association, a business group, lobbied the police commissioner to banish demonstrations to a far-flung spot where they would not be a nuisance, "the marginal street facing the East River between Nineteenth and Twenty-Third Streets."[72] The association argued their case on the basis that "the Union Square demonstrations have 'demoralized the business atmosphere' of that area and humiliated the property owners, frequently causing tenants to refuse to renew their leases."[73] Despite these draconian suggestions, newspaper editorials were generally agreed that public gatherings of this type were best tolerated, that it was better not to suppress them entirely, making martyrs of the communists. Though Union Square had become a dreary place, editorialized the *New York Times*, it served a useful function as the Home of Discontent, America's version of Hyde Park in London. The *Times* concluded by quoting the political philosophy of Thomas Jefferson: Union Square was a place where "error of opinion may be tolerated" because "reason is left free to combat it."[74]

While businessmen and newspaper editors debated the future of the Square, the Parks Department was at work giving it new shape. In May 1930 the Board of Transportation returned management of the Square to

6.6 Union Square, aerial view, ca. 1944.

the Parks Department, which took on the task of relandscaping the barren surface at an anticipated cost of $125,000. When the department published a plan by chief landscape architect Julius V. Burgevin, the Square's orientation and symbolism was radically altered.[75] Raised up three feet above the surrounding streets, the new Union Square was an artificial platform of lawns, plants, and statuary disguising subway entrances and vents. Echoing early twentieth-century City Beautiful visions, it was classically ordered and symmetrical with a single straight path down the center and the Washington and Lincoln memorial statues relocated along this axis. These statues would be once again the focus, replacing the massed ranks that had dominated it in the early years of the twentieth century. The MAS had insisted upon a grand approach from the south side of the park upwards toward the statue of Washington.[76] This approach consisted of five steps, each fifty feet wide, elevating the statesman above any crowds gathering at his feet. This newly landscaped space was designed as a forum for public receptions. The northern end of the Square was also altered; in the new plan it was not elevated but depressed. Given over to parking since the 1920s, by 1930 it was referred to in Parks Department drawings as a parking space.[77] Olmsted and Vaux's neo-Gothic cottage was demolished, replaced by a neoclassical stone and concrete building designed by Parks Department architect Charles Schneider. This new park pavilion was not a place for public address, but a rather more prosaic public amenity, a combined bandstand and "comfort station" or public bathroom.

In April 1932 Union Square celebrated its centennial. Formally remade, its political associations were recast in new terms. The remnants of Olmsted and Vaux's plaza and cottage were replaced by a watered-down version of a City Beautiful public park. Supported by local business groups such as the Broadway Association, the goal of the centennial was to rebrand Union Square as an thoroughly American space, one in which the former ethnic and political allegiances of new immigrants were rejected in favor of a unified national spirit and identity. Planned by the Union Square Centennial Committee made up of local business leaders and Tammany Society officials, the centennial was intended to renew patriotic spirit and to celebrate the renovated park as a representation of American democratic values, while at the same time renouncing the latest role of the Square as a center of radical political activity. Announcing the event, the committee's chairman, A. M. Player of the Everett Investing Company, owners of the Everett Building, told the press that, because of its historical background, Union was "the center of true Americanism . . . and not to be associated with radical activities because of the groups which at times have used it as a meeting place."[78] The centennial celebration was the result of years of effort on the part of the Parks Department, working in concert with local business leaders, to repress the Square's radical reputation.

Heavily underwritten by the Fourteenth Street Association, the two-week centennial program featured a dedication ceremony for the new bandstand and a historical pageant sponsored by Tammany Society complete with actors in 1832 dress. Though the landscaping was not yet finished, they did their best to put on a good show on top of the large dirt oval. Echoing the great civic celebrations of years gone by, department stores and other buildings were draped with American flag bunting. Storefronts displayed prints showing historical images of Union Square.[79] A mass chorus of high school students sang patriotic songs and three hundred dignitaries attended a formal luncheon inside the S. Klein store. In his centennial proclamation, Mayor Walker reinforced the association between the Square and the American Revolution, urging the, "reawakening of the spirit of those early pioneers of every race and religion who, from Revolutionary times down to our own days, were associated in one way or another with the development of this great city as it is centered about this historical spot."[80] In case there was

6.7 Celebration of the 100th anniversary of the founding of Union Square, April 1932.

any doubt as to the underlying message, the centennial program concluded with an "Americanization" meeting staged by the Veterans of Foreign Wars. At the meeting members of the Police Academy demonstrated military maneuvers, including the art of handling a pistol and disarming prisoners, and the Police Rifle Regiment performed a riot drill. The *New York Times* reported:

> For more than 30 minutes the policemen went through a series of intricate drill maneuvers in a fashion that would have done credit to a West Point Battalion, with the crowd applauding at every interval. The crowd was frightened when the riflemen pointed directly into it as they pressed the triggers on their repeating rifles, but the guns were not loaded and no casualties resulted. A bayonet charge into a mythical crowd ended their exhibition.[81]

Onlookers could not mistake the intended message: future displays of public dissent in Union Square would be met with force. Prompted by events

6.8 Base of Flagstaff looking toward Union Square West.

such as these, the image of a renewed Square cleansed of communist association appeared in the newspapers. The *Herald Tribune* was pleased to report that

> Union Square, for so long the step-child among city parks, is slowly but surely becoming the Manhattanites ideal of a garden spot—a playground of concrete adorned with Grecian colonnades, surrounded by banks and shaded by skyscrapers. Vestiges of its Communist and subway eras are disappearing. . . . Thanksgiving sun shone yesterday on a Union Square full of new, radiantly clean concrete. At the north end the columns of a miniature Greek temple were rising. . . . The Communist aura is now but a memory.[82]

In the process of its 1920s-era renovation, Union Square Park was remade as a memorial to national political values: its role as a place for active political gatherings was consigned to history and its reputation as a center of labor activism was actively repressed. The symbolism of the new Union Square could not have been clearer: it was a memorial to the nation created by the revolution and the Civil War. Whereas Ruggles, along with Olmsted and Vaux and progressive-era city planners such as Lamb, had seen the Square as a place in which the democratic process would be actively practiced, it was now fixed as a passive memorial to American democracy.

With this renovation complete, the physical form of the Square was fixed for the next fifty years. The inauguration of Fiorello La Guardia as mayor in

1934 ushered in a new era of civic politics and new strategies of urban design. La Guardia's parks commissioner, Robert Moses, had grand ambitions to reshape the metropolitan landscape, ambitions that did not involve tinkering with the downtown parks. But while the lawns, plaza, and statuary were left untouched, Union Square continued to assume an important role as a center for political action during World War II and in the postwar era. With the goal of bringing shoppers back to the area, local retailers (working in close collaboration with city authorities) attempted to transform it from a center of protest into a place to celebrate the virtues of American patriotism. Dominated by business interests, civic groups tried to banish the Square's radical reputation once and for all, rendering the soapbox orators who gathered there on warm weekend afternoons nothing more than a curiosity, a nostalgic memento of old New York.

7

Cold War Park, 1934–1965

In the decades between the Depression and the urban and fiscal crises of the 1970s, Union Square lost its status as a center of the city's social life. The businesses offering mass-market luxury to middle-class customers in the early years of the twentieth century gave way to bargain shopping emporiums, and the raffish glamour associated with theatrical first nights and urgent late-night political meetings faded away. Which is not to say it was not busy: the subway interchange served millions every year and local shops and offices were seldom vacant. But by the 1960s it had become almost a historical artifact, a shabby reminder of its former self, propped up by commuter crowds but of little relevance to the larger forces reshaping the rest of the city. This transformation was not particular to this square in this city, but part of a much bigger picture. The pressures of postwar population decline, demographic change, decentralization strategies, and economic disinvestment on older American cities are well known, as is the dramatic reshaping of the network of metropolitan landscapes that took place in the 1950s and 1960s. New York City Parks Commissioner Robert Moses is the figure most closely associated with the concept of urban renewal: under his name this term has come to be associated with the wrecking ball and the bulldozer, with large-scale earthworks, wholesale demolition, and the rapid expansion of the city beyond its nineteenth-century periphery. This chapter tells the story of a parallel, less strategic and more tactical form of urban revival.

While local and government agencies did not include Union Square in their plans for the wholesale destruction and remaking of New York City, the Square became a focus for another kind of urban renewal. Aligned together under the banner of the Fourteenth Street Association, and supported by the Parks and Police departments, local business owners put in place a comprehensive plan to bring middle-class shoppers and residents back to the historic center. Soon after the war ended, they began small-scale efforts to revive the area, starting with a program of public events aimed at overturning the Square's radical reputation. This was part of a nationwide movement, one with its own New York City twist: across the country collectives of downtown business owners worked in concert with municipal authorities to staunch the flow of capital to the suburbs and the regions, experimenting with different ways to maintain the attractiveness of downtown shopping districts. In some places this involved pasting a veneer of modern design over nineteenth-century storefronts to make them seem more up-to-date. In the case of Union Square, between the 1930s and the 1950s the Fourteenth Street Association, a private group made up of local business owners attempted to maintain the commercial value of their businesses and properties by creating a new kind of public space in the heart of New York City: one in which the celebration of American political identity was linked to the rapid expansion of consumer society.

The association's key tactic was to counter May Day parades with newly manufactured patriotic events, driving away one kind of crowd and attracting another. Even though the parades were much smaller after the war, the Square's lingering radical reputation was believed to be off-putting to the most desirable class of consumers: white, middle-class women. Supported by municipal authorities, the association actively repressed demonstrations of working-class immigrant pride and replaced them with a host of newly invented and seemingly apolitical celebrations including Flag Day and Loyalty Day. Designed to make the Square less threatening to the new class of suburbanites, these events promoted adherence to shared national values and a pan-ethnic, classless idea of "Americanness." In their efforts to promote a new, patriotic association for Union Square, the association used tactics of display and publicity derived from advertising: marketing ploys such as decorative display windows and theatrical events tied to annual sales leaked out of the stores and into the public park at the center. These spectacles pointed the way toward a new era, one in which physical public space was tied to, and then gradually usurped by, the ethereal public space of the electronic media. Although earlier demonstrations had always had a media component (dating back to international distribution of images Civil War–era gatherings), these had always been secondary to the need to persuade a local audience. As the televised draft-card burning ceremonies that took place in the Vietnam era demonstrate, as the century drew to a close, the importance of physical public space began to recede as the public space of mass media grew.

The Decline of the Square

In 1950 New York City was enormous, one of the largest cities in the world by any measure. However, the economic tide that brought a huge influx of businesses and immigrants to the city around the turn of the twentieth century was ending.[1] Beginning around 1910, a host of problems endemic to the nineteenth-century city, including inefficient traffic systems, the unsuitability of older buildings for modern manufacturing, and population decline, prompted city planners to argue for wholesale urban decentralization and decongestion. According to planning theory, networked rather than centralized patterns of development were preferable for reasons of both productivity and defense. Put on hold by the economic depression of the 1930s and curtailed by the single-minded focus on military production during World War II, this philosophy resulted in the radical reshaping of the urban landscape after the war ended. Federal policies encouraging private car and individual home ownership led to the rapid growth of the suburbs, supported by a vigorous highway building campaign. Using the persuasive term "blight," the federal government gave municipal authorities the power to declare whole city sections obsolete, allowing them to seize and demolish property to make way for grandly scaled office and housing blocks, along with new parks and highways. Regionally, an improved public transportation system and the development of new centers of commerce and industry at the urban periphery in Long Island, New Jersey, and Connecticut resulted in the exodus of thousands of working-class New Yorkers from Manhattan. While not immediately apparent uptown—Times Square still served as a signifier of desirable, if risqué, nightlife in songs, movies, and books up until the mid-1960s—the result of this disinvestment and the resulting flight from the center was soon visible downtown. Once seen as essential to public health, inner-city parks were now thought of as outdated, ineffective, and even as places of national vulnerability. Their ability to provide access to fresh air and to nature was puny in comparison to suburban living, and at the same time the electronic media increasingly usurped their function as public meeting spaces.

As the commercial nucleus of Manhattan moved north toward midtown and the urban populace spread further out, beyond the confines of the five boroughs into the ever-expanding metropolitan periphery, Union Square lost its allure as a retail and entertainment center for the whole city. Its historic tie to the social world of the Lower East Side and SoHo became a liability as those neighborhoods fell into further decline. In 1940 the Works Progress Administration Guidebook to New York State described Fourteenth Street as "the poor man's street of the city."[2] In the dense grid of streets below this demarcation line, the tenement houses that had provided homes for immigrant workers for a hundred years could no longer compete with the affordable and accessible housing becoming available in the suburbs. The extreme population density that characterized Lower Manhattan in 1910 fell steadily until it was nearly halved by the middle of the twentieth century.[3] Declining in value and poorly maintained, the aging buildings were crumbling: decaying tenement buildings did not meet contemporary living standards. The office towers and apartment buildings created during the building boom of the 1920s were more than the city needed or could afford during the lean years of the Depression. With the population declining and the tax base reduced, the city had less and less to spend on maintenance and, as a result, public streets and parks were neglected.

In 1934 Union Square came under new control when Mayor Fiorello La Guardia appointed Robert Moses the new commissioner of parks. In histories of twentieth-century New York City, Moses has assumed mythical proportions, and is held accountable for everything from the destruction of historic tenement buildings to the racial segregation of the city and even the phenomenon of white flight itself. But even allowing for the exaggerations of historical narrative, his powers were immense. In his first position of authority, influenced by progressive-era urban reformers like Charles Stover, Moses continued the program to build play and sports grounds in the densest parts of Manhattan where local people were poor and had fewer amenities. Soon afterward he extended the scale of this program to the construction of large recreational spaces in the underdeveloped outer boroughs.[4] He also oversaw the restoration of Bryant Park at Forty-Second Street and Sixth Avenue. Created on the site of the former Croton Reservoir, by the early 1930s this was an unattractive dirt lot, urgently in need of attention. Moses was happy to take credit for the renovated park, a classical-style design featuring a large central lawn surrounded by low plantings and park benches. But when it came to the city's nineteenth-century showpieces, Union Square, Washington Square, and Tompkins Square, the ornamental green spaces in the heart of Manhattan, his attitude was at best ambivalent. As the products of nineteenth-century urbanism, they held little interest for him, seeming to represent the city's past rather than its future. In his oversight of the downtown parks, he combined two central beliefs: that the densely built fabric of the city must be opened up in favor of fast, efficient automobile circulation, and that the genteel, Victorian style park, was hopelessly anachronistic in the modern age. The fresh air and access to nature it provided was inconsequential in comparison to the benefits of suburban living accessed quickly and efficiently by new highways connecting downtown with the residential periphery.

When Moses first became parks commissioner, Union Square had been recently renovated, so there was little reason for him to focus attention on it. It did, however, serve as a model for a controversial plan to alter Washington Square a few blocks to the south. Like Union Square, Washington Square had been improved in the early 1870s under the Tweed-sponsored parks program with curving, picturesque walks and large shade trees planted, according to Tweed's politicized rhetoric, for the benefit of all New Yorkers, not just the wealthy who could afford carriages. Little else had been done in the intervening sixty years, apart from the erection of a monumental triumphal arch to commemorate the centennial of Washington's inauguration as President. In 1935 Moses proposed radical changes: in an effort to promote better automobile circulation he proposed rounding off the corners and widening the surrounding streets to create a park-like traffic circle somewhat similar to Union Square, which had been converted from a square to an ellipse in the mid-1830s, also to improve traffic circulation. Moses's plan was not realized because of the curtailment of Parks Department activities during World War II. Drawing on generous federal subsidies available for highway building and the postwar "think-big" attitude toward city planning, he revived the idea in the early 1950s, tying it to an ambitious vision for three new expressways connecting Manhattan to Long Island and New Jersey. His plan was to build a four-lane roadway through the middle of Washington Square, extending and connecting Fifth Avenue south to the proposed Lower Manhattan Expressway at Houston Street, which linked the Holland Tunnel with the Manhattan and Williamsburg bridges. The proposed bifurcation of Washington Square was part of a major urban renewal project that included the demolition of several blocks of housing between the Square and Houston Street, to be replaced by tall apartment towers. Within the park a roller-skating rink and playground would supplement existing plantings. The story of Moses's defeat at the hands of the Washington Square Park Committee, a group of local residents including the journalist and activist Jane Jacobs, is well known.[5] In the so-called Battle for Washington Square, both sides employed the rhetoric of democracy: Moses's opponents argued that the Parks Department was acting unilaterally, without proper consultation with the park's everyday users. Against this opposition he argued that the desire to keep the Square in its historic configuration was reactionary and elitist. Those who stood in the way of his plans, he said, "insist on keeping Washington Square as it was years ago, with lawns and grass and the kind of landscaping which goes with big estates or small villages. These people want the square to be quiet and artistic, and they object to the noise of children playing and to other activities that we proposed."[6] But Moses was soon to find that it was he who was regarded as backward, relying on an increasingly unpopular vision of the city's future, one that disregarded its past. During the years-long battle for Washington Square, the genteel park became shorthand for opposition to the blunt instrument of urban renewal. In 1958 his plan was abandoned, and traffic was banned from Washington Square Park forever.

While Union Square was not similarly targeted under the Moses regime—he could hardly argue that it impeded traffic since Broadway swung easily around its western flank—his actions impacted its use in other ways. Soon after becoming commissioner, Moses issued a press release announcing the scope of his future efforts: thirty-seven new playgrounds were to be opened and a further twenty-one were planned for completion by 1940. The only mention of Union Square was a brief note about an East Side memorial, a ten-foot-high granite column commemorating soldiers from the Lower East Side who had died during World War I. Erected by the Parks Department in 1934, this monument was dedicated in 1936.[7] For the remainder of Moses's twenty-seven-year term as commissioner of parks, Union Square barely featured in Parks Department documents and reports. While his gardening staff worked conscientiously year after year, planting trees and flowers according to the season, his treatment of the Square signaled other priorities. Although city authorities made no attempt to remake the space of Union Square following the 1932 renovation, however, they increased efforts to control how that space was used. In their attempt to repress May Day marches and other political demonstrations in Union Square, they employed two familiar tools: permits and traffic.

In 1941 the long-running debate about free speech flared up again as the Parks Department announced new guidelines for the issuance of permits for events in public parks. Victor S. Gettner of the New York City Civil Liberties Committee wrote to Moses protesting the new regulations, citing a then-recent Supreme Court case (*Hague v. C.I.O.*, 1939) that gave "recognition to the fact that parks are dedicated for public meetings and that any unreasonable prohibition of such meetings in parks is unconstitutional."[8] In response Moses argued that permits had always been required for gatherings in city parks. While no attempt was ever made to censor the content of the speeches made there, he said, permits could be refused to people of "vicious and irresponsible character with a recent record of creating racial, religious and other animosities among our people."[9] He noted that in their decision the Supreme Court had upheld "the need for proper regulation of the right to public assemblage in parks."[10] While few gatherings were planned for Union Square during the war years, these new laws were put to the test in the summer of 1950 when the New York Labor Conference for Peace applied for a permit for a public rally to protest US military intervention in Korea. The police department denied the application on the grounds that it represented an "unreasonable hazard to the public."[11] In an accompanying press release the Parks Department maintained that while Union Square was specifically set aside for public meetings, this one was declined because it might result in serious public disorder. When the rally went ahead anyway, mounted police charged into the crowd, beating them back, and thirteen people were arrested.

While the Parks Department respected the letter of the law with regard to public meetings in city parks, it also made subtle changes that restricted their use for this purpose. In the case of Union Square, Moses fell back on his favored urban improvement strategy: prioritizing automobile traffic. In 1942 the Parks and Police departments submitted a plan to the City's Board of Estimate creating a parking area along Seventeenth Street between Union Square West and Union Square East. Separated from the street by a line of trees, this parking area was intended as an amenity for shoppers and commuters, and also for safety purposes.[12] The logic of this curious proposal (which brought cars into what was historically a pedestrian area in order to prevent traffic accidents) was not explained. However, it was successful: the parking lot was created and, to the dismay of many, by 1949 the Parks Department had turned it into a storage space for impounded cars.[13]

The transformation of Olmsted and Vaux's plaza into an automobile dumping ground was not accidental: it accentuated and helped facilitate the idea that the Square's glory days of passionate rhetoric, rippling seas of red and white banners, and rousing music were gone for good. In 1940 a guidebook described Union Square as "America's open-air center of radical propa-

7.1 Vehicles are lined up at the "auto pound" along the edge of Union Square Park, 1949.

ganda, the district of liberal and trade-union ferment."[14] But by the time the United States entered World War II those days were on the wane. The huge May Day parades that made it famous were coming under intense pressure, suffering from dwindling participation and threatened by the restrictive policies of the Police and the Parks departments. From a practical point of view, it no longer made sense to hold May Day or Labor Day celebrations in Union Square because downtown was no longer home to the majority of workers.[15] Although many unions continued to rent office space in the area, increasingly their members were dispersed to the outer boroughs. Attendance at May Day slowly decreased from a high point of over one hundred thousand in 1933 to a fraction of that number twenty years later. This decline was due as much to political events as it was to demographic changes. In 1942 May Day parades were suspended for the duration of the war. When they were revived in 1946, they came to signify something sinister to many Americans: the insidious global influence of the nation's Cold War enemy, the Soviet Union.

Immediately after the war, the cacophony of dissenting voices that rang through the Square on May Day in the early years of the century harmonized to a single voice, that of the Communist Party of the United States (CPUSA). Although some union members continued to take part in the parade, this was in defiance of the American Federation of Labor (AFL), which banned its members from participating. Rather than a celebration of working-class pride or union affiliation, May Day became intensely politicized, the most visible expression of American Communism. Recently demobbed soldiers marching in the parade were condemned in the press for wearing their uniforms: how could they show pride in the American military and at the same time support the political regime of America's greatest enemy, newspapers asked?[16] A few years later, with American Communism weakened by the imprisonment of a number of its national leaders, organized labor (the AFL and the Congress of Industrial Organizations) tried to seize back control of the May Day parade from the CPUSA.[17] On May 1st, 1950, twelve thousand people marched down Eighth Avenue from Thirty-Ninth Street to Seventeenth Street, then east to Union Square where the waiting crowd numbered a few hundred. The banner at the head of the march read "Peace-Jobs-Civil Rights." Other banners protested the use of nuclear weapons and called for peace with the Soviets and an end to Jim Crow laws. The march was quiet and orderly. But this effort to broaden the May Day march to focus on wider labor and civil rights issues was not enough to recover its past importance. The early 1950s saw the last of the large May Day meetings in Union Square and labor's national holiday never regained its position as a central event in the New York calendar.

With its role as staging area for labor celebration and protest severely curtailed, the Square seemed irrevocably diminished. In 1958 Isidore Wisotsky, a Russian émigré and fervent supporter of the International Workers of the World, compared the Union Square of his youth with its present-day banality: "Along Seventeenth Street, where roaring thousands once streamed from every part of the city for turbulent political meetings, there stood an array of parking meters. The robot coin collectors looked like so many headstones marking the place which once, like London's Hyde Park, had been a world symbol of free speech."[18] Wisotsky did note, however, the continuation of soapbox oratory, a tradition in which small groups gathered to listen to political speeches delivered by speakers standing on makeshift podiums made of empty grocery cartons. So benign was this practice that the police tolerated, even managed it: each speaker would be allowed his allotted time, and then gently or firmly moved on, as necessary. Postwar guidebooks frequently commented on this antiquated custom, describing the speakers as eccentrics rather than serious political dissenters. With Union Square's homegrown radicalism in remission, attention turned to a different, vastly more horrifying threat.

Downplayed in guidebooks as a quaint anachronism, Union Square took on a different role in popular journalism as a symbol of American vulnerability to nuclear attack. Sitting at the approximate geographical center of the city, it was an irresistible target in narratives of atomic destruction, perhaps subliminally because of its elliptical shape. In 1950, *Time* magazine published a lengthy description of what it called "The Horrendous Hypothesis":

> Suppose that on an overcast, autumn morning, a Russian bomber carrying an atomic bomb the equivalent of 50,000 tons of high explosives swept through the stratosphere above New York and dropped its missile. Suppose that the bomb was timed to explode half a mile in the air over Union Square. Within a radius of one mile of Union Square (Ground Zero), the city would appear to have been struck by a giant fist. Within that radius would be the lofty Empire State Building, the Metropolitan Life Insurance Building; the teeming cliff dwellings of Peter Cooper Village and Stuyvesant Town; Klein's department store; Fourteenth Street's subway complex; a labyrinth of gas mains, water lines, telephone cables, electric wires; 55 elementary schools, high schools and trade schools; 17 universities and private schools; twelve of the city's hospitals. Whole sections would be obliterated. Within a second zone, ¼ mile wide, the destruction would be only a little less complete. In that area would be Times Square, Rockefeller Center, Hell's Kitchen, the Metropolitan Opera House; the Holland and Queens vehicular tunnels, the Williamsburg Bridge, the Pennsylvania and Grand Central stations. Many more buildings would be wrecked by the explosion, and gutted by fire. In the zone beyond, destruction would be—as atomic scientists describe it—'severe.' As the mushroom cloud drifted off, in the cluttered, congested, trapped island of Manhattan, storms of fire would lick furiously across the stricken city.[19]

Within a few minutes, the author continued, New York City would be reduced to "History's Biggest Pile of Rubble," with the intersection of Broadway and Fourteenth Street as the white-hot center of the surrounding devastation.

This rhetorical attack was part of a larger mobilization effort. The hypothetical annihilation of Union Square was intended to communicate the immediacy of the nuclear threat to the American public and to prompt them to be prepared. In May 1941 President Franklin D. Roosevelt had created the Office of Civil Defense with the aim of making cities and states responsible for organizing their own welfare in the event of attack.[20] From the first this federal unit had a strong connection to New York City: its first head was

Mayor Fiorello LaGuardia. In 1949 President Harry Truman's National Security Resources Board identified 140 American cities as potential targets for atomic strike and issued a lengthy set of directives to local governments instructing them to mobilize the civilian population. State by state, Civil Defense units organized drills marshaling hundreds of thousands of volunteers to provide first aid, decontaminate chemical weapons, and fight fires, in the event of nuclear attack. On January 28th, 1953, the New York City Office of Civil Defense undertook a communications exercise based on the hypothetical scenario that eight nuclear bombs had been released over the United States, one aimed at Union Square. Escalating the statistics given in *Time* magazine, the *New York Times* enumerated the devastating consequences of such a detonation: "Theoretically 86,400 people were killed by the bomb, 38,400 were seriously wounded and 76,800 less so, and 278,400 were left homeless."[21] The threat of nuclear attack and its apocalyptic consequences gave further impetus to the movement for urban decongestion that had begun earlier in the century.

The blueprint for urban dispersal had been established before the war with the publication of the multivolume *Regional Plan for New York City and its Environs* (1929). This comprehensive report represented a philosophical change in thinking about the basis of urban design, away from the symmetry and monumentality of the City Beautiful ideal toward concern with the provision of infrastructure and the segregation of urban functions. In the ambitious agenda of the *Regional Plan*, Manhattan was to retain its role as the center of New York City's economic and social universe while much of the city's manufacturing and residential functions were to be dispersed to the periphery.[22] Factories and dormitory suburbs were encouraged in Long Island, New Jersey, and Connecticut, and new rail and road links were planned to connect the various parts of the sprawling megalopolis together. While the Depression and World War II stalled the implementation of the plan, it remained the guiding document for city and regional planners into the postwar era. After the war politicians and developers, enabled by economic prosperity and increasing powerful federal laws, united to implement a far-reaching program of urban renewal in many northeastern cities. Using the power of eminent domain (legal rights given to the government to seize private property for public use), large sections of New York City were cleared of tenement blocks along with the remnants of the hundred-year-old grid. In their place tall apartment buildings and spacious new roadways were constructed. As chair of the mayor's Committee on Slum Clearance as well as parks commissioner, Moses played a significant role in this process. As his authority grew he combined the building of new parks with other responsibilities including the creation of new highways and bridges. Famously, he argued for the expansion and rationalization of the city, placing special emphasis on new automobile connections between the central city and its expanding periphery. The thousands of acres of green space he created between 1934 and 1961 were often conceived of in concert with grand infrastructural schemes.

Despite its generally neglected state, this process of urban renewal never threatened Union Square directly. As a major transportation hub, it retained an important function within the larger circulation network being constructed across the city, and it served as a commercial hub for local renewal projects. Only a few blocks to the east along Fourteenth Street, on land previously occupied by a series of enormous gas storage tanks and tenement buildings, the Metropolitan Life Insurance Company built two giant residential apartment complexes during the 1940s. Stuyvesant Town and Peter Cooper Village were built as part of an effort to clear land identified as "blighted," and to encourage white, middle-class people to remain living in the center of the city. In one way these buildings were twentieth-century versions of the mid-nineteenth-century development boom that had produced Union Square. The Square was improved, or landscaped, in the 1840s as an amenity for those who lived in the neighborhood and as an enticement for new residential development. A planted green space set apart with an iron fence and framed by new streets, it was available for gentle recreation to all who those lived in the narrow townhouses sitting side by side around it. In their architecture and landscaping, Stuyvesant Town and Peter Cooper Village represented the modernist version of the same idea, one with a different scale and relationship between residential buildings and open space. Built according to the "superblock" model introduced to the United States in the 1920s—which melded the American Garden City ideal of mass housing set within landscaped grounds with modernist urban planning principles introduced in Europe—skyscraper apartment blocks were placed within a spacious park rather than around its edges. Variations of superblock planning were proposed, in the second volume of the *Regional Plan*, which suggested removing industrial buildings along the East River and the construction of a landscaped East River Drive, in the hope that this would inspire the demolition of the nearby tenements.[23]

Between 1945 and 1969, large swaths of New York City, particularly along the eastern edge of Manhattan, were remade according to this new urban planning model.[24] Built as green sanctuaries in an increasingly crowded city, older parks such as Union Square, Washington Square and Tompkins Square were supplemented by acres of newly built green space. In theory the landscaped grounds of Stuyvesant Town and numerous contemporaneous mass housing developments rendered the older parks less necessary to the livability of the postwar city. However, when considered not only as a residential amenity but also as a vital place for the enactment of public life, they only gained in importance.

Union Square USA

Nationwide postwar trends toward urban deindustrialization, the growth of the suburbs, the ghettoization of inner cities, and cuts in local government spending led to the decline of historic city centers.[25] Downtown businesses such as the department stores along Ladies Mile began to lose customers to regional centers, in particular to the suburban shopping mall. Developed by architect and Austrian émigré Victor Gruen, the shopping mall was an American version of the walkable market square he had left behind in Europe, brought up-to-date and made appealing through the application of modern design principles.[26] Influenced by Gruen, several early experiments with the shopping mall typology were built in Long Island and New Jersey. Owing to the city's enormous size these malls complemented rather than competed with the established shopping districts in Manhattan: in the 1950s the owners of large department stores around Union Square would seem to have little to fear from their suburban competitors. The Square's reputation as a destination for budget shopping, built up since the turn of the twentieth century, remained strong and the local subway station was heavily used, bringing thousands of shoppers into the area each day. In 1958 a guidebook described the area as being "well known for low prices on all needs and for years it has been considered the bargain area for the city. It is the place where credit terms are easy, and 'shopping around' is the normal buying pattern."[27] However, this did not stop local business owners joining their national counterparts in worrying about the threat of suburbanization to their future profits. Such a threat required collective action: for the first time downtown needed a marketing campaign. The urban historian Alison Isenberg has described the "proliferation of organizations, committees, and publications that singled out the problem of downtown survival" in mid-twentieth-century America.[28] These groups attempted to lure affluent workers and shoppers back to traditional urban cores via the creation of mass-transit systems; easy traffic routes and parking buildings; the modernization or demolition of old building stock; and the creation of safe, clean, and controlled shopping areas, spaces that mimicked the attractions of the neighborhood shopping district and the shopping mall.[29] As Isenberg notes, these efforts were in many ways directed to the ideal shopping mall customer: white, middle-class women.

> The explicitly woman-centered commercial aesthetics appearing in suburban shopping centers captured the imagination of downtown investors too. . . . So for downtowns as well as suburbs, the goal of attracting affluent suburban shoppers guided decisions about parking, accessibility, building appearance, and the general commercial "atmosphere."[30]

The concept of consumerism as the savior of historic downtowns was linked to broader ideas of good citizenship. In the postwar era, individual consumption was equated with the national interest: to increase personal consumption was to bring greater affluence and greater equality for all citizens, affirming the values of the nation's founders.[31] In these terms, the owners of the mass-market department stores surrounding Union Square felt entitled to claim a stake in its political associations, appropriating them for their own purposes.

As we saw in chapter 6, the Fourteenth Street Association, first organized in the 1920s in order to lobby for greater municipal investment in public transport, had a huge influence on the design of Union Square Park and the management of the activities that went on inside it. The association engaged in coordinated marketing campaigns around the seasonal sales, hosted musical concerts and holiday festivals, including the annual lighting of a giant Christmas tree, and paid for small-scale improvements to the park such as street cleaning and the installation of new lighting and street furniture. Beyond these seemingly benign activities, the group also fought a long campaign to overturn the Square's historic association with leftist politics. In a continuation of efforts dating before the 1932 centennial celebration, the association built on smaller events such as National Americanization League rallies and commemorations of Lincoln's birthday at the foot of Lincoln's statue organized by the National Republican Club.[32] The sentiment behind these events gained traction after the war when anti-communist feeling was widespread.

In 1953 the Police permit for the traditional May Day march organized by the People's May Day Committee was revoked in State Supreme Court after lobbying by the West Side Association of Commerce, the Catholic War Veterans, and representatives of businesses situated along the customary route down Eighth Avenue, from Thirty-Ninth to Seventeenth Streets and east to Union Square. Upholding the decision, Police Commissioner George Monaghan announced he would not "subject New Yorkers to the sight of

7.2 Union Square, East Side between 14th and 16th Streets.

the red flag of communism while American blood is being split in Korea."[33] However, the police did not veto the traditional rally in Union Square for which a Parks Department permit had already been issued. Emphasizing a message of diplomacy, the organizers were anxious not to provoke a response from the large number of policemen on hand. The rally went ahead in wet weather, with the moderately sized crowd gathered at the plaza under a painting of President Dwight Eisenhower shaking hands with Soviet Premiere Georgi Malenkov, emblazoned with the word "peace" in red letters six feet high.[34] The meeting opened with the playing of "The Star-Spangled Banner," and speakers were subdued in their support of Soviet Russia, emphasizing instead that the labor movement sought global unity above all. But despite this careful presentation of the workers' holiday, this would be the last large May Day rally held in Union Square for many years. The next year the police again refused a permit for the May Day march, citing a possible threat to public order. While the Parks Department granted a permit for a static rally, it was overshadowed by another, much larger one planned to do away with May Day for good.

From 1953 the Fourteen Street Association began its direct assault on the May Day tradition. In the process, the plaza, already compromised by the presence of cars and parking meters, became further diminished as a forum for mass political meetings. That year the association announced a "monopoly of Union Square by loyal American citizens thus making the historic site unavailable for the rabble-rousing elements at times most coveted by those elements."[35] As a kind of warm-up event, it staged a Flag Day parade along Fourteenth Street from Avenue C to the plaza. Established in 1893, Flag Day (June 14th) celebrated the adoption of the American flag by the Second Continental Congress in 1777, and was intended to signify the unity and common purpose of American culture and society. At a ceremony in the plaza's pavilion, Jan Mitchell, chairman of the Fourteen Street Association, called for a "re-dedication of the park to the flag."[36] Mitchell's rhetoric was unambiguous, overblown and prescient in the context of current events. Five days after the Flag Day parade, an emotional crowd of five thousand people gathered along Seventeenth Street at a "prayer meeting" protesting the execution of Julius and Ethel Rosenberg, the New York couple convicted of passing atomic secrets to the Soviet Union. Standing in the street because a permit was denied for a meeting in the plaza, the crowd listened solemnly to speakers who denounced the executions as political murder and cried out in horror as the executions were announced.[37]

Inflaming this highly charged atmosphere, the Fourteenth Street Association planned a full-fledged attack on May Day. In March 1954 Mitchell announced plans for what he called a Loyalty Day fete to be held in the Square on May 1st.[38] The origins of holiday lay in Loyalty Day programs began in the 1920s as one of many "Americanization" activities designed to counter events organized by political groups such as the IWW.[39] In New York City the Veterans of Foreign Wars (VFW) staged Loyalty Day parades throughout the five boroughs after the war. In the words of Brooklyn Borough President John Cashmore, they were intended to "emphasize the evil of communism and the menace this godless and brutal totalitarianism clearly constitutes to our peace, freedom and security."[40] Loyalty Day was recognized by Congress in 1955 and made an official holiday in 1958. Celebrated with large gatherings from 1954 to the early 1960s, Loyalty Day in Union Square was explicitly labeled an "Anti-Red" rally. The subtext of the event was to make the Square more welcoming to the consumer diaspora, shoppers who had moved beyond Manhattan to the suburbs. Through events such as Loyalty Day, the association aimed to revive Union Square, overturning its historic association with leftwing causes and giving it a new symbolic meaning, one in which patriotism was conflated with consumerism. It was of course no accident that it was planned for the 1st of May; the event was designed to finally obliterate the already mortally weakened May Day tradition.

Mitchell's interest in the area derived from his own business interests. He was the owner of Lüchow's, a popular German restaurant located on East Fourteenth Street between Third and Fourth Avenues. A Latvian immigrant, he had started out as a waiter before working his way up in the restaurant business. Established in 1882, Lüchow's had been a favorite of the theater crowd until World War I when anti-German feeling cut into its popularity. Taking over the restaurant, Mitchell revived it by reinventing immigrant food for the mid-twentieth-century palette. Inspired by the restaurant's heyday in the 1890s, he created spectacular food-centered festivals designed to remind patrons of a gemütlich Lower East Side of days gone by.[41] But if the revived Lüchow's was an exercise in nostalgia, Mitchell had an entirely different goal when it came to Union Square itself. Rather than celebrating its working-class history, he wanted to completely repress its former identity and turn it into a particularly New York version of an all-American town square.

The Loyalty Day campaign was ideological, with both political and economic imperatives, and it received the full support of city authorities. When the Provisional Committee for the Sixty Ninth Anniversary of May Day applied to the Police and Parks departments for a permit to gather in Union Square on May 1st, 1954, they were denied on the pretext that the Fourteen Street Association had already been granted one to gather on that spot at the usual hour. After the committee complained to Mayor Robert F. Wagner and Parks Commissioner Moses, a compromise of sorts was reached: the association received a permit to occupy the Square for eight hours from 10:00 a.m. to 6:00 p.m., while May Day organizers were allowed access to the plaza for the ninety minutes between 6:30 and 8:00 p.m.[42] The organizers attempted to persuade city authorities and the public of the historic civic importance of their rally: the chairman of the United Labor and People's May Day Committee Leon Straus argued May 1st was "a labor holiday, not a business holiday."[43] But the imagery and rhetoric of May Day was out of step with the dominant mood of the times.

Like May Day, Loyalty Day entailed the vigorous wielding of nationalistic symbols: the Stars and Stripes, marched ranks of veterans, and the authority of citizenship itself. Tied into popular culture, it included music, dancing, games, and sack races for children (supervised by John J. Downing, the recreation director of the Parks Department), and also appearances by sports and entertainment celebrities such as Milton Berle, the hugely popular comedian, and clowns from the famous Ringling Brothers Barnum and Bailey Circus.[44] The highlight of the day was an "Americanization" ceremony during which immigrants received their citizenship. To mark the day, Manhattan Borough President Hulan E. Jack renamed Seventeenth Street "Union Square USA."[45] Well covered in the press, the fete was a public relations coup: ten thousand were estimated to have attended. In the following years the association escalated its efforts. With the continued support of the Parks Department, Loyalty Day celebrations were held annually in Union Square from 1954 until the mid-1960s. By 1959, when the organizers included a "Salute to Alaska and Hawaii"—the newest two states—and an exhibition of American flags dating to colonial days, the annual Union Square USA brand had taken over not only Union Square, but also the identity of May Day itself: presenting a proclamation to Mitchell, Mayor Wagner renamed May Day as Union Square USA Day.[46] In renaming the holiday, the Fourteenth Street Association reclaimed the symbolic association with patriotism the Square had long held, but in a passive sense. In a 1961 *Newsday* article, the journalist Robert Mayer described the result as the "decline of the Square as America's bustling marketplace of ideas."[47]

Following the success of Loyalty Day, Mitchell continued his efforts to revive Union Square as another kind of marketplace, creating a unique shopping experience tied to the Square's historic past. In April 1955 he announced the formation of the Union Square Merchants and Property Owner's Association, an organization designed to "promote and revitalize the Fourteenth Street and Union Square area."[48] With an impressive annual budget of $150,000, the association hoped to continue the work of the Fourteenth Street Association. One of the group's first projects was the creation of a new kind of department store known as "The Fair at Union Square" in premises that had recently been vacated by Ohrbach's. The previous year Ohrbach's had relocated to Herald Square at Broadway and Thirty-Fourth Street in order to be closer to its main competitors, Macy's and Gimbel's. The move followed a rebranding exercise by the Madison Avenue advertising

7.3 Clown Frankie Saluto races children in Union Square during USA Day celebrations, 1955.

agency Doyle Dane Bernbach: seeking to shake off the store's bargain basement reputation, the agency gave Ohrbach's a new tag line: "High fashion at low prices."[49] The move left vacant its former premises, a series of five buildings on the south side of Fourteenth Street between Broadway and University Place. Mitchell took over redevelopment of the site. Launching his new venture at a formal luncheon at Lüchow's, he described the Fair at Union Square as a vertical version of the suburban shopping mall.

The Fair, as it became known, was to operate on a cooperative model. It would include an international food market in the basement and two hundred rental stalls leased to independent merchants on the first and second floors, along with five restaurants and refreshment stands.[50] Like the shopping center, it would feature not only shopping opportunities but also attractions such as a carousel, auctions, and even antique shows. Significantly, the wares for sale in the rental booths were designed to mimic the products sold in nearby tenement districts in years gone by: mussels, strudel, and other specialty items associated with early twentieth-century immigrant life. Sold at attractive discount prices, they would appeal to uptown residents and suburban dwellers wanting to experience the heady culinary culture of Delancey Street without the bother of navigating the crowded streets of the Lower East Side. To add to the convenience, the store was to stay open until 9:00 p.m. on weekdays, and customers were to be offered reduced rates at nearby parking lots and garages. The Fair opened in October 1955 with 150 merchants selling goods at rental stalls.[51] Though it lasted only a short time (it was replaced by a Mays Company store in 1964), this venture set an important precedent as one of the earliest themed shopping environments. A decade before the SoHo cast-iron district was designated a Historic Landmark, Fourteenth Street was already being sold as an authentic experience of old New York, packaged for easy consumption by locals and visitors alike.

With Loyalty Day established as a major event and the wider Union Square area rebranded as a unique shopping environment, one that exploited and sanitized its immigrant heritage, a group of veteran's associations put forward an audacious proposal to concretize the Cold War symbolism of Loyalty Day. In 1962 the Veteran's Memorial Building Fund of New York County held a press conference to announce a fundraising campaign in support of a major war memorial project. The group told the audience of journalists they were raising seven million dollars in order to build an eighteen-story-high glass and stainless steel tower on a site donated by the Parks Department: the plaza at the northern end of Union Square.[52] As grand and as politically freighted as the unbuilt George Washington monument of 1843, this gargantuan monument to military power would have completely reoriented the Square, this time in the direction of the domineering new tower. Like the Washington monument, it combined educational and memorial functions. Elliptical in plan, the tower was flanked by two five-story wings. The tower was to house offices of veteran's organizations, an auditorium, convention hall, library, public lounge, restaurant, and an observation deck. The polished black granite facades of the base were to be inscribed with a quotation from the Gettysburg address: "It is rather for us the living here to dedicate ourselves that these dead shall have not died in vain."[53] In keeping with mid-twentieth-century planning preoccupations, the structure would incorporate parking for three hundred cars in its basement.

While it may have had some chance of being realized during the paranoid atmosphere of the 1950s, by the early 1960s anti-communist feeling was less urgent and there were other reasons to oppose this quasi-fascistic structure. Sidestepping its political message, the *New York Times* condemned the proposal as an "atrocity," not only because of the unwelcome incursion of private interests into public space, but also because it was simply in very bad taste.[54] Though the proposal remained unrealized, a miniature echo appeared a year later in 1963, when twelve missiles were set up on the northwest corner of Union Square park as part of an exhibit during Armed Forces Week, with military personnel on hand to explain the missile's working and uses to interested civilians.[55]

One of the Fourteenth Street Association's last efforts was the so-called Check-a-Child playground built adjacent to the plaza on the south side of the centennial pavilion.[56] Dedicated on May 1st, 1967, by Parks Commissioner August Heckscher, it was funded through a ten-thousand-dollar donation from the association. Designed by architect Richard Dattner and planned in conjunction with a series of adventure playgrounds in Central Park, the Check-a-Child playground was another amenity intended to make the area attractive to shoppers.[57] At a cost of twenty-five cents per child, mothers could "check" their child into the park for a three-hour period, where they were supervised by Parks Department employees, "giving mothers free time to spend shopping, lunching or just relaxing," as the department's press release put it.[58]

While some version of the traditional May Day celebration continued to occur into the late 1960s, participants dwindled to a few hundred and they were increasingly focused on civil rights and antiwar messages, rather than the overt encouragement of socialism or communism. Influenced by the counterculture flourishing in nearby Greenwich Village, folk singers replaced union bands as music providers. Perhaps because of the relatively soft tone of these demonstrations and their notably diminished size, the Parks Department put up little opposition to their staging. In a 1968 letter to Mrs. Louis S. Auchincloss, president of the Park Association of New York City, Commissioner Hecksher noted that while mass gatherings were very seldom permitted in Central Park, Union Square was one of the locations set aside by the department as "Forum Areas . . . where demonstrations, protests, etc. can properly take place."[59] One of the last meaningful protest activities to take place in the Square during this era was a draft-card burning. Significantly, this event was staged not only for a corporeal audience but also for a virtual one observing via press cameras: their presence a sign of the way in which political protest was beginning to change, with physical space ceding importance to the public space of the airwaves.

On November 6th, 1965, five men associated with the antiwar Committee for Nonviolent Action ascended a wooden platform erected for the purpose in the plaza of Union Square, read statements protesting the United States' military action in Vietnam and the federal law concerning the draft, then set their draft cards alight using a cigarette lighter.[60] Because the deliberate destruction of a draft card had recently been made a federal crime punishable by up to five years in jail and a fine of ten thousand dollars, the

7.4 Veterans and reservists line up on a platform in Union Square to await their turn to drop their military service discharge and separation papers on a fire, in a basket. Seventeen men added their papers to the fire in a protest against the war in Vietnam, as about five hundred spectators looked on. March 25, 1966.

incident attracted a considerable amount of media attention. Two of the men had originally tried to burn their cards a week earlier in front of the federal courthouse in Foley Square, but the crush of journalists had been too great to complete the task. At a press conference held at the Commodore Hotel in midtown, they announced their plan to burn the cards at a rally at Union Square, claiming the burning required a more dignified atmosphere. Reporters were supplied with a diagram of the Square, biographies of four men who planned to destroy their cards, and copies of the required permit from the Parks Department. When put into action, the spectacle was slightly absurd: though the crowd was more tightly controlled (press were kept back thirty feet), a protestor wielding a fire extinguisher got close enough to douse the burning cards. Once dried, the cards were again ignited while members of the 1,500-strong spectator group sang "This Little Light of Mine." Though FBI agents observed the spectacle, they did not try to stop it. Away from the press cameras, four of the men were subsequently arrested, and three were indicted.

As the presence of the press cameras in 1965 suggests, electronic media began to overturn the importance of traditional civic spaces for political speech and action. The broadcast image of protest began to assume more power than the protest itself. Even while the physical fabric of New York City was in the process of being renewed, the ways in which it was used began to change: the city was being transformed from a center for the production of physical objects into a center for the production of images. As a result, new models of public space began to emerge. In the postwar years, cultural commentators argued that the telephone, radio, and television would be the new mechanisms through which to share ideas. Some, including America's foremost modern architect, Frank Lloyd Wright, believed that the growth of electronic media would negate the need for cities altogether, that the ethereal, immaterial, and dispersed network of telecommunication would provide the new public sphere.[61] While that extreme vision did not eventuate—people still feel the need for physical proximity and social interaction—the availability of new forms of communication and ways of working did begin to alter the profile of historic urban neighborhoods. Working under the banner of the Fourteenth Street Association, the alliance of private and public interests that created the Loyalty Day fete in Union Square operated with a certain expectation about the purpose and design of public space. To revive the local economy, they purposefully emulated the allure of the suburban shopping mall experience, providing amenities such as pedestrian-friendly sidewalks, plentiful seating, and a clean, appealing street environment. In turn, the work of the association paved the way for a further transformation of Union Square. This transformation, which began in the early 1970s, hinged less on the revival of a once vibrant commercial center, making it newly attractive to distant suburban consumers, and more on the creation of a local neighborhood hub desirable to a new class of urban residents.

8

Renewal, Revitalization, and Place Making, 1966–1998

Along with the rest of New York City, Union Square Park suffered during the 1970s. But despite being dilapidated and run-down, it did not evoke an image of urban blight in quite the same way as other areas: in fact the neighborhood around it was doing quite well in relation to the city as a whole. As financial deregulation began to free up money for private real estate development in the early 1980s, and a new municipal administration supported localized renewal, the Square was a prime target for redevelopment. Following years of financial austerity, the municipal government rewrote its planning regulations to encourage private real estate investment. Along with other undercapitalized neighborhoods such as the Lower East Side and the Hudson River waterfront in Manhattan, Union Square began to thrive again. This rejuvenation followed a new model of urban renewal: the rejection of large-scale, comprehensive planning projects implemented by the city and financed by federal funding in favor of a decentralized approach, with an emphasis on civic policies encouraging private investment to revive selected areas. Propelled by New York City's transformation from a manufacturing hub into a service center for the new global economy, the changes that took place in and around the Square in the last two decades of the twentieth century might be described as a process of economically and culturally driven re-urbanization, or gentrification. This transformation was dependent on the revival of commerce, and on the reemergence of Union Square as middle-class shopping and entertainment center.

In describing the turnaround of ideas about urban renewal in New York City between the mid-1970s and the early 1990s, many authors foreground the work of local community activists like the journalist Jane Jacobs. While it is true to say that the late twentieth-century approach to what might be called the re-urbanization of New York City reflected many of Jacobs's ideas, such as retaining older buildings and backing neighborhood-led development, it also could not have been achieved without the support of government at all levels. Targeting specific sections of the city, the municipal government turned away from wholesale demolition and grand infrastructural projects in favor of regulatory changes (tax breaks and zoning changes) designed to encourage private real estate development. Coinciding with a demographic shift which saw the return of a small but significant number of the white middle-class to the inner city (first bohemians working in or around the art scene, then so-called yuppies in the language of the day—young, upwardly mobile, urban professionals), the city once again attempted to renew Union Square, albeit with a new profile as a neighborhood amenity that supported the economic growth of the area, rather than a civic space in the traditional sense.

For some critics, the renewal of the economic and urban landscape placed new and undesirable constraints on the public function of the Square, privileging the commercial characteristics of the market square over the civic ones of the political forum. Seen through a longer lens, the assertion that the most recent reinvention of Union Square reflects a significant increase in the influence of the interests of capital is debatable. It could be argued that the late twentieth-century coalition of private and public interests that reshaped the Square during this period simply echoed and refined practices dating back to the 1840s—practices in which the imperatives of democracy and commerce were inextricably intertwined. At the same time the uniqueness of their form and methods of operation must not be discounted: attention to the history of this particular place helps us understand the ways in which methods of private-public cooperation were revised in the late twentieth century.

Building on a tradition of civic-business alliances established in the 1920s, renewal efforts began with relatively modest efforts to make Union Square Park more attractive by programming cultural events such as musical concerts. These efforts gained traction with the founding of the Union Square Greenmarket in 1975. A major case study in the planning strategy of "place making," the highly successful Greenmarket gave the Square a new identity as a source of locally grown food and a locale for fashionable restaurants. These ad hoc renewal efforts took on a more concrete form with the publication in 1976 of a New York City Department of Planning report entitled *Union Square Street Revitalization*. Coinciding with the rise of the historic preservation movement, and with a new interest in contextual design, the report proposed reinforcing the architectural and urban qualities of the nineteenth-century Square in order to retain and reinforce its unique morphology. Starting in the 1980s, the Parks Department began a major renovation of Union Square Park with the goal of driving out socially undesirable users such as vagrants and drug dealers. Though the Square's radical past was acknowledged, it was as a compelling but safely historical referent, a selling point for new residents. In 1984 day-to-day management of the Square was given over to the Union Square Partnership, New York City's first business improvement district. In the process Union Square was reconceived not as a civic or national center, but as a "neighborhood" that had been "saved."

Neighborhood Revitalization

The geographic and economic restructuring that accompanied American deindustrialization hit New York City hard in the 1970s. In 1975 the national fiscal crisis reached a point when the city could no longer finance its budget. The flight of middle-class workers to the suburbs and the huge reduction in well-paying industrial jobs meant a declining tax base, increasing debt, and not enough money to cover municipal salaries and basic services. At first the federal government refused to help out. When President Gerald Ford gave a speech refusing to help bail out the city from near bankruptcy, an infamous headline in the *New York Daily News* read: "Ford to City: Drop Dead."[1] As a result the city made severe cuts to public works and social services leading to the erosion of the urban infrastructure and a rapid decline in quality of life for millions of New Yorkers. Seen as an expendable public amenity, the city's park system suffered especially badly. Funded almost entirely from municipal tax revenues, it was a visible symbol of the dire state of the city's economy. After Moses's departure as commissioner in 1960, the Parks Department lost much of its power, becoming drastically underfunded and suffering from quickly rotating leadership into the mid-1970s. All the parks suffered as a result. Lawns were reduced to mud and dust, fences and statues were covered in graffiti, broken play equipment was left unrepaired, and crime was rampant.

Like its bigger cousin, Central Park, Union Square Park was overgrown and littered with trash. Guidebooks recommended tourists avoid both. In 1976 the *New York Times* noted Union Square had become a habitat for "an assortment of derelicts, drug addicts, panhandlers and prostitutes who daily are attracted to Union Square's crossroads confluence of shoppers and commuters and to high concentration of methadone or alcohol treatment centers nearby."[2] The city recognized the problem but could do little to solve it. When Mayor Abraham Beame took office in 1974, he had optimistically budgeted six hundred thousand dollars toward the redevelopment of the park, the first significant money to be spent since the early 1930s. But because of extreme financial pressure, and at a time when the city was divesting itself of parkland elsewhere in order to rid itself of the maintenance burden, these funds were rescinded and the deterioration intensified.[3]

The general sense of decline was not helped by the state of surrounding buildings, in particular those on the eastern side of the Square. For years this side had been dominated by the S. Klein department store, the bargain hunter's paradise. Housed in a series of eleven haphazard buildings, including the old Union Square Hotel, the store looked more and more decrepit as the twentieth century drew to a close. Desperate to turn around the image of his store, in 1972 the chairman of S. Klein's commissioned a group of students from Parsons School of Design, located nearby at 66 Fifth Avenue, to come up with a cohesive "environmental concept" for their storefront, consolidating the mismatched windows and attracting new customers. Working in partnership with the Parks Department, the Metropolitan Transit Authority, the Institute of Architecture and Urban Studies, and what remained of the Fourteenth Street Association, the students extended their study to take in not only the storefront but also the whole of the park and subway concourse below.[4]

Presented publicly in the spring of 1973, the students' ambitious proposal called for a dramatic new stainless steel facade and signage for the S. Klein store, which dominated the east side of the Square, along with colorful new graphics for the subway. Prefiguring later suggestions, it also eliminated the car-parking area to the north of the Square, integrating it back into the park. But despite the support of the Community Board, this proposed rejuvenation came to nothing. In 1975 S. Klein closed for good, leaving May's on the south side of Fourteenth Street as the last department store on the Square's periphery. The boarded-up store remained empty for over a decade, an obvious symbol of economic decline and urban deterioration. The vacant site attracted plenty of interest but little activity. In 1976 a wealthy Argentine developer named Julio Tanjeloff offered another grandi-

8.1 Parsons' student project to redesign the facade of S. Klein Department Store on the east side of Union Square, 1973.

ose plan for the site, imagining it as the hub of an affluent shopping district once again. With a flair for publicity, Tanjeloff announced his proposal accompanied by an architectural model showing the buildings completely reclad in stucco and polished stainless steel.[5] An electronic newsboard above the entranceway would announce the day's specials. But these plans did not eventuate either, and the store remained boarded up and neglected until 1980. Proposals for the renewal of the wider Union Square area remained in the realm of optimistic architectural models and renderings.

Part of the problem was that no single entity was in charge: the management of Union Square overlapped several city agencies and community boards (although it was in Community Planning District 5, it bordered Districts 2, 3, and 6), with none having ultimate responsibility. Responding to lobbying by Community Board 5, in 1976 the New York City Department of Planning aggregated earlier proposals into a report entitled *Union Square Street Revitalization*.[6] Prompted by earlier studies and funded by a grant from the National Endowment for the Arts, this report focused on the area bounded by Twelfth and Nineteenth Streets, and Fifth and Third Avenues; it was unsparing in its description of the problem as "bleakness, difficult access, underutilized play area, nonfunctioning fountain and a general lack of attractive activity centers. For the most part the park today is a gathering space for indigent men whose presence further tends to discourage others from enjoying quiet moments within the walled open space."[7] Around the edge, it was lined with vacant stores and "honky tonk establishments"; underneath the large subway station was "one of the busiest but most unattractive in the city . . . maze-like, with poor lighting, bad signage, low ceiling and bad smells from food stalls."[8] Relatively modest in its recommendations, and implemented only in part, the report is significant because it unites and demonstrates three concepts central to urban planning and design in America during this period. The first is a new understanding about the relationship between part and whole; the second is recognition of the social and economic utility of historic architectural and urban forms; and the third is a new relationship between public and private agency.

From the mid-1960s, urban planners came to see the city not as a complex singular entity with a central heart that must be preserved in order for the system to survive but as a series of semi-autonomous units. In contrast to systematic and totalizing modernist strategies involving wholesale demolition and rebuilding, planners focused instead on individual neighborhoods. Giving up the desire to restructure and revive the whole, they accepted partial decay as fundamental to the late-modern urban condition. While was it possible (perhaps even desirable) for some parts of the city to die, other parts might be saved. Using the analogy of triage, urban planners were advised to provide help in places where it might do some good and leave the rest to their fate.[9] Inevitably this new model, moving away from a unitary approach to one in which the state focused on cofinanced efforts with private actors in targeted sectors, led to inequitable results. In some areas, such as the South Bronx, a neighborhood's "natural" death was hastened by the tactical withdrawal of city services.

A test case for this approach, Union Square represented the other pole; still economically viable, it showed signs of life. The median income of residents was higher than the city average and building vacancy rates were relatively low. In the biomedical terminology that dominated discussions of urban renewal, it was an ailing area capable of being revived. "Cities contain many centers and communities rich in history and a sense of place," the authors of the 1976 report wrote. "We seek to develop prototypical techniques by which the particular character of these areas can be reinforced so as to assist in their preservation through increased safety, use and enjoyment."[10] In other words, if newly developed techniques of renewal worked here, they might also work elsewhere; and if enough of those neighborhoods were also revived, both socially and economically, these localized transformations might be collaged together, saving large sections of the city, if not the whole.

The 1976 report promoted the idea that historic urban forms, in particular narrow streets lined with older mixed-use buildings, had an important and ongoing value to the community.[11] While modernist city planners believed the original New York City grid fundamentally unsuitable for twentieth-century purposes, the report emphasized the desirability of retaining and reinforcing historic architecture and the existing street pattern. By the late 1960s the concept of urban renewal was gaining new meaning as alternative visions of future urban life were imagined: the ideal of the modern city foundered on a sense that valuable forms of city and social life were being lost or obliterated. While there was no absolute consensus about the correct approach, as they saw one project after another fail to meet its aims, critics of modernist urban renewal began to question the collective wisdom of urban planning and management professionals.[12] Several of the city's ambitious plans for modernist urban renewal projects in Lower Manhattan had been stymied. These plans were part of a vast urban renewal agenda managed by David Rockefeller's Lower Manhattan Development Office; they included projects for the renovation of Washington Square Park (1955–56), the renewal of part of the West Village (1961), and creation of the Lower Manhattan Expressway (mid-1960s). These older methods of renewal were now denigrated as too big, expensive, bureaucratic and slow, and unlikely to achieve their original aims. Instead, a new generation of critics and urban reformer activists pointed to the still-vibrant street life of neighborhoods such as Greenwich Village, comparing them negatively to a host of disruptions caused by wholesale demolitions, the construction of highway systems and high-rise apartment complexes, and other large urban projects. In response the city began attempting a different approach, encouraging preservation of the existing city fabric in some areas, and emphasizing small-scale changes with a greater level of local community involvement.

The third and final concept underpinning the 1976 report was the suggestion that the primary role of the city was to encourage private investment. This attitude toward city management (later labeled "neoliberal") promoted a particular relationship between public and private agency, one in which the city government acted as facilitator, assisting and encouraging neighborhood renewal by private groups (both commercial and nonprofit) working together collaboratively. This new approach began during Mayor John Lindsay's administration. Elected in 1966, Lindsay was one of a number of mayors elected across the country around the same time on a reformist platform.[13] Rejecting the idea that urban renewal was purely a matter of physical reconstruction, he promoted a strong component of social reconstruction, believing this was the best way to deal with the current urban crisis. With financing from the federal government, he created neighborhood-scale agencies such as community boards made up of local residents and business owners. These agencies supplemented the ad hoc community rebuilding efforts already underway, including modest efforts to clean up existing housing stock rather than demolishing it. Part of a broader reaction to the authoritarian nature of planning, these agencies introduced strategies of community participation, enlisting people to help in the design of their own neighborhoods, a process later incorporated into the profession through practices such as advocacy planning.[14]

The question of public-private cooperation was significant because in 1976 the pool of public funding available to prop up the ailing economy and decaying physical infrastructure was rapidly drying up. In the depths of an economic recession, the Department of City Planning needed to think creatively: hampered by budget constraints, with very little state or federal funding available, it could not afford to fund major planning studies or to pay for major infrastructural changes out of its own purse. Instead the department concentrated on inexpensive short- and medium-term proposals to encourage nascent signs of economic growth. This involved both design and legislation. The *Union Square Revitalization* report effectively aggregated the results of previous studies into four main recommendations: the rehabilitation of the park, increasing its size by reincorporating Olmsted and Vaux's plaza which had been used for parking since the 1940s; the modernization of the subway hub beneath it; the rerouting of street traffic to ease congestion; and (most significantly) the introduction of zoning inducements to encourage building owners to upgrade their properties.

The report grouped its recommendations into three phases: short-term proposals costing almost no money; medium-term proposals with modest budgets, but for which funding was presently unavailable; and long-term proposals which would have to wait for a radical change in the economic situation.[15] In the first category, the city proposed getting rid of parking spaces and widening the sidewalks, removing the barrier hedge around the park's perimeter, and installing new paving and seating. The report also recommended the integration of commercial activities such as small boutiques into the subway mezzanine, and the relocation of subway turnstiles so that the underground concourse could be accessed freely. The drive to increase ease of movement included ambitious ideas: the construction of an elevated pedestrian link across the facade of the S. Klein buildings, for example, with the goal of protecting pedestrians from automobiles and bad weather; and a repetition of the frequently voiced proposal to build an enormous parking garage under the plaza at the north end of the park. Augmenting the green space of the park, this garage would be topped by volleyball and basketball courts, along with two café terraces on either side of the existing pavilion.

With its small budget, the Parks Department could not afford to implement any of these proposals. In late 1976, Charles F. Luce, board chairman of Consolidated Edison, and Dr. John R. Everett, president of the New School for Social Research, announced the formation of the Fourteenth Street–Union Square Area Project. A consortium of local groups such as the Union Square Park Community Coalition, this group aimed to raise $1.5 million to implement some of the report's short-term recommendations. Luce and Everett each pledged fifty thousand dollars per year for three years.[16] Adopting "Sweet 14" as its slogan, it focused on organizing events in the park. Its first project was a lunchtime concert series that took place during the summer of 1977, with performances by a gospel choir, Dixieland, and Cuban salsa bands, and a demonstration of Dominican folk dancing. The events were announced with orange and black posters bearing the slogan: "We're trying to bring out the natural spirit and zest of this great area. We're making [Fourteenth Street] the livingest street in town!"[17] This initiative extended the latest Parks Department efforts. When Lindsay became mayor in 1966, he disestablished the old department and created in its place the Parks, Recreation and Cultural Affairs Administration (PRCA), which packaged responsibility for libraries, museums, and performing arts groups together with the Parks Department and recreation programs.[18] Throughout his administration, the PRCA, under Parks Commissioner August Hecksher, pursued efforts to "upgrade Union Square Park by programming," in the words of the PRCA's Publicity Department. In 1968 these programs included a concert by New York–based electronic rock group, the Silver Apples, and two other rock bands, which occurred in conjunction with an aerial light sculpture by artist Frosty Myers.[19] In 1970 the city co-sponsored the multimedia Astro-Fest, an astrology-themed festival arranged in twelve areas corresponding to the signs of the zodiac and featuring "bongos, bagpipes, dancers and a mime troupe."[20]

The new approach to urban renewal was to focus on small areas, using modest and inexpensive techniques such as concerts and festivals to attract people and investment. The harder part was giving these areas fresh cultural meaning. The authors of the 1976 report had recognized this, aiming to make a renewed Union Square "the element which unifies the character of the community, strengthens the sense of place, and brings residents and visitors together to experience the positive qualities of city life."[21] Critical to this approach was the reinforcement of the neighborhood's identity, not just as a transportation hub and budget shopping district, but as a destination with Union Square Park its functional and symbolic center. With its radical history all but erased and the unabashed patriotism of Loyalty Day unappealing to a new generation of urban dwellers, the park had no natural community. Focusing on cultural programming, Sweet 14 aimed to change that. At the same time, the city began a different initiative, the introduction of temporary greenmarkets in various parts of the city, which was to have more substantial and long-lasting results at Union Square than any musical concert.

Loft Conversions and the Greenmarket

Concluding that the attempted megascale functional and infrastructural urban realignments of the immediate postwar period were hopeless, in the 1970s planners and designers focused instead on strategies of local "place making," the creation of an appealing identity for older sections of cities hollowed out by the forces of decentralization and disinvestment.[22] The elusive "sense of place" was a unique combination of physical and social markers that set one area apart from another in a positive sense. Motivated by a desire to humanize the city, planners and designers were fascinated by the ways in which historical elements, particularly historical building typologies, reinforced ideas of community through a common understanding of, and shared association with, familiar urban features.[23] Sociologists of city life, the journalists Jane Jacobs and William H. Whyte were important figures in this movement. Both published books describing the positive attributes of New York City's nineteenth-century fabric, books that were hugely popular with nonspecialist readers and also highly influential on practitioners of urban renewal.[24] Most significantly, Jacobs and Whyte overturned the long-standing belief in the causal relationship between the crowding endemic to the nineteenth-century city and social and public health problems, a link enshrined in modernist city planning philosophy. Instead, they argued for the value of urban density, that the close interaction of the crowd would recoup social capital in the form of greater community cohesiveness. Inspired by these ideas, planners, architects and community groups across the country sought to preserve and adapt historic buildings and neighborhoods for new uses, retaining the unique character of particular urban places while at the same time reinventing them for new generations. However, as these practices became pervasive, tensions appeared between optimistic visions of community-based renewal and critics who argued "sense of place" is often code for one group's need for safety and protection—that renewal is another word for segregation.

For practitioners of place making, New York's SoHo serves as an exemplar, offering a model for historic preservation and adaptive reuse emulated in cities across the country and the world. The story of SoHo's "rebirth" has been told many times.[25] In the 1950s this densely built industrial zone was still an active manufacturing area but more and more businesses were moving out to larger premises on the urban periphery. With declining demand, and the threat of demolition from the proposed Lower Manhattan Expressway, rents were low. Attracted by the large, open floor plans, high ceilings, and plentiful light, a new generation of New Yorkers took over the stock of mid-nineteenth-century cast-iron loft buildings. Artists began to create live-in studios, residing illegally because the area was still zoned for light industry. Initially, SoHo was an inconvenient place to live: basic services like household garbage collection did not extend there; the neighborhood lacked amenities such as grocery stores; and the remaining manufacturing businesses generated lots of noise. But the environment changed quickly. In 1969 the Expressway project was abandoned and in 1971, supported by Mayor Lindsay, the City Planning Commission changed the zoning law making it legal for those designated "artists" to live in SoHo. In a few short years SoHo became internationally known as a center of art production. Art galleries, boutiques, restaurants, and stores opened up, and loft living became fashionable. In 1974 *New York* magazine called it the "most exciting place to live in the city."[26]

The city actively supported the recycling of historic manufacturing buildings into fashionable residences through rezoning, including its J-51 program.[27] Created in 1955 in response to a severe shortage of moderately priced rental housing, this program provided tax benefits in exchange for upgrading substandard tenement buildings. Twenty years later, at a time when many commercial and manufacturing buildings were underused or empty, Mayor Abraham Beame's administration amended the program to include the conversion of commercial buildings into residential ones. With its stock of underutilized loft buildings, real estate developers saw Union Square as a profitable continuation of the trend that had begun south of Houston Street. Prompted by the success of SoHo, and supported by the city, they hoped to extend the market for loft apartments north of Fourteenth Street. With the incentive of this expanded J-51 tax program, many of the loft-office hybrid buildings around the Square were converted in the same way. Redeveloped, these conversions were highly desirable for the city because they increased the tax base and brought money into the local economy in the form of consumer expenditure.

Without the concentrated aesthetic appeal of SoHo's streets lined with cast-iron buildings, Union Square's appeal was more intangible. Boasting a smaller number of landmarked buildings, the Square had its own star power in the form of a series of artists' studios, most famously Andy Warhol's Factory, where his "art-workers" produced silk-screen paintings and films under the Warhol name. Housed on the sixth floor of the Decker Building from 1967 to 1973, then in another building on the corner of Broadway and Seventeenth Street, the presence of the factory gave the area substantial cultural capital. Real estate investor David Teitlebaum, who specialized in recycling loft buildings, built on this association when he was granted a zoning variance to convert 31 Union Square West (architect Bruce Price's ornate neoclassical Bank of the Metropolis) for residential use in 1975.[28] Teitlebaum's entrepreneurial project incorporated not only regular loft apartments but also four floors of dormitory space for students from nearby Parsons School of Design, ushering in a wave of dormitory construction in the area dominated by New York University in nearby Washington Square.

As the manufacturing economy gave way to the information economy, what had once been a meeting space for industrial workers to discuss political ideas gave way to a recreation space configured for an entirely new class of working New Yorker. More likely to be affluent college students or members of the desk-bound "creative class" than the artist-producers of SoHo, the second generation of loft dwellers appreciated the gritty industrial chic of their new homes but also wanted easy access to the kinds of amenities found uptown and in the suburbs.[29] Although poorly maintained, the park in the middle of Union Square had huge potential. Such an open green space was found in only a few other Manhattan neighborhoods. The area continued to attract affluent residential tenants even in the depths of the economic crisis. As the authors of a Department of City Planning report discovered, while the population of New York City fell from eight to just over seven million between 1970 and 1980, the population of the Union Square area increased by more than 10 percent in the same period.[30] Most of the increase was in the twenty-five to forty-four age bracket, which made up nearly half of the district's population. The people who lived near the Square were wealthier than those in New York City as a whole, and this difference only increased between 1970 and 1980. Well-educated white-collar professionals, they were drawn to the unique atmosphere of downtown, but at the same time they were not willing to suffer the deprivations of the SoHo artists who rode freight elevators and survived without garbage collection or hot water. They sought not only a better class of apartment building, but also the kinds of public amenity that accompanied more affluent neighborhoods.

The Union Square Greenmarket was just such an amenity: not only a useful source of fresh fruit and vegetables, but also a nostalgic, late twentieth-century version of the traditional market square, a nod to a past that had never existed, at least not on that site. The Greenmarket was one of several opened across the city in 1976 under the umbrella of the Council on the Environment of New York City, a nonprofit citizen's group supported by the city and housed in City Hall. The others were located in the Brooklyn Academy of Music parking lot, at One Hundred and Second Street and Amsterdam Avenue, and at Fifty-Ninth Street and Second Avenue. The New York City Greenmarkets offered urbanites the chance to buy fresh produce directly from local farmers. Operating one day a week during the summer months, the Union Square Greenmarket was set up on the plaza, with about a dozen farmers selling their wares directly from the back of their trucks. Under the direction of Barry Benepe, who had trained as an architect and planner, they were envisioned as much more than a practical resource; they were agents of urban regeneration, offering pleasurable communal activity in the heart of inner-city neighborhoods.

From an urban design point of view, farmers' markets had huge benefits: they were cheap and easy to set up, requiring little investment and basically no site improvement; and they lent a wholesome and desirable aura to areas perceived as dangerous and unattractive. There was no need for a specially prepared site—all that was needed was space to park a truck and room in front for a trestle table. And because so little was invested, there was not much at stake if they failed to attract customers. In his research into the recovery of historic urban centers, William H. Whyte was particularly enthusiastic about the potential of food as a catalyst for other urban functions: "If you want to seed a place with activity, the first thing to do is to put out food," he wrote. "This particular form of commerce has restored the kind of intimate, personal exchange that the city has lost over the years."[31] In his book, *City: Rediscovering the Center* (1988), Whyte proposed that new city zoning guidelines mandate the provision of facilities such as food cart vendors in all new plazas and parks. Shopping for fresh food in an outdoor setting, seeing and smelling displays of colorful vegetables and fruits, was not only a deeply pleasurable experience, he believed; it was also essentially sociable. In these terms the Union Square Greenmarket was hugely successful. While the Parks Department had achieved only limited success with the cultural

8.2 Union Square Greenmarket, ca. 1976–78.

events they programmed for Union Square Park in late 1960s and early 1970s, the Greenmarket's regular presence and affordable offerings made it attractive to a larger section of the population over a longer period of time.

Although it needed the authority and active support of the city to get off the ground, the Union Square Greenmarket was soon held up as an exemplar of community-driven urban renewal. A powerful place-making tool, it was a catalyst for other social activities and for further economic development. Besides shoppers, the Greenmarket attracted people who might not otherwise come to Union Square, drawn by the urban spectacle. While the produce sold was not necessarily cheaper than in a regular store, customers were happy because they felt they were participating in an authentic urban experience: an entirely satisfying sensory and sociable encounter.

This was "real" food, gratifyingly fresh and unpackaged. Buying it involved interaction with wholesome people—farmers—and safe social exchanges with others. As sociologist Sharon Zukin has pointed out, the provision of localized urban experiences built around food soon became a major tool of gentrification.[32]

The Greenmarket appeared to give Union Square something it had lacked since the political protests were driven out in the1950s: a clear identity. The area around the Square soon became known as a fashionable gastronomic destination, a site dedicated to food as a form of leisure. By 1981 when the Greenmarket entered its sixth season it had doubled in size, hosting thirty farmers.[33] By 1984 it was open year-round. Union Square's reputation as a foodie mecca was cemented when restaurateur Danny Meyer opened the Union Square Cafe on Sixteenth Street and Union Square West in October 1985. As Alison Perlman has noted, Meyer's restaurant was at the forefront of a new trend, featuring high quality produce from local sources, accompanied by equally high prices, but notable for its relaxed atmosphere (at least compared to the white tablecloth establishments found uptown).[34] Suited to their unfussy, up-and-coming locations, the Odeon in Tribeca and the Union Square Cafe began a trend for so-called casual fine dining restaurants across the country. As financial deregulation brought money back into the city after years of decline, the square mile connecting Union Square and the Flatiron district was one of the first specialist gastronomic sites directed at the new class of discerning urbanite. In Ronald Reagan's America, New York's Red Square became the center of a thriving culture based on the display, preparation, and consumption of food. By the late twentieth century, the Greenmarket and the restaurant culture that grew around it seemed to return to Union Square the sense of place it had lost when it ceased to be a center of Bohemian life in the 1940s.

It mattered little that Union Square's new identity was not a revival of a quaint but forgotten historic function but a wholly invented one: although it had been a center for fashionable dining in the second half of the nineteenth century, and for a short period the site of a flower market, the Square had never been a public food market. Nevertheless, the Greenmarket gave the Square something vitally important to the strategies of place making: authenticity, a sense of providing a "real" urban experience. Those who praised the Greenmarket contrasted it positively with what they saw as inauthentic forms of urban renewal proliferating elsewhere; for example, the "festival marketplace" typology popularized by the developer James Rouse through projects in Boston, Baltimore, and other postindustrial cities.[35] These were underutilized nineteenth-century markets, renovated and revived (and in some places re-created) in order to bring new life to run-down waterfronts. Although conceived with the sincere goal of reviving declining urban neighborhoods, the festival marketplace typology was criticized, particularly by academics, as a cynical exploitation of urban nostalgia in order to increase developer profits, and as a distressing commercialization of the public realm. In contrast, the Union Square Greenmarket seemed more genuine: it did not involve the creation of faux architecture (as in the South Street Seaport in Lower Manhattan, for example), and it was open to the public, with no restrictions on access. For many authors, farmers' markets such as the one in Union Square represented the return of a lost urban ideal, a vision of late twentieth-century community—one that would help overcome the deep social, racial, and economic divisions present in American cities.[36]

Behind this sunny vision, the promotion of Union Square as a hub of so-called foodie culture exposed the tensions inherent in demographic and economic change. As with other, supposedly less authentic, forms of urban renewal, the success of the Union Square Greenmarket depended on the continuation of urban segregation. Despite the rhetoric of inclusion and democracy that surrounded it, the Greenmarket had a prophylactic role. Although modest in its form and not mimicking the nostalgic architecture of the festival marketplace typology, it catered to the same demographic market: middle-class whites. As they returned to the area, others were driven away. During the 1970s and early 1980s, panhandlers, prostitutes, and the homeless were on the raw end of municipal policies that reduced funding for social services and made rental housing, even the meanest Single Room Occupancy building, less and less available and affordable. Vilified in the media, the disproportionally Hispanic and African American population of poor and homeless people was cast as a cause of urban decay rather than its victims. As Whyte observed, the perception of crime caused by the presence of "undesirables" in public places is greater than the reality.[37] In fact such places are relatively safe during the hours when people are using them. However, many business people did not differentiate between various kinds of street people, lumping the homeless, addicts, and criminals together and seeking to banish them from view. Spurred by the cultural anxiety of the time, practitioners of place making drew a line around a selected site and narrowly defined who belonged there and what might happen inside it.

Along with the efforts of Sweet 14, the Greenmarket was lauded for driving out not only criminals but also panhandlers, rough sleepers, and the few remaining political speechmakers. In 1979 Sweet 14 started a "clean and green" spring cleanup program in the park directed at clearing out not only rubbish and overgrowth, but also people, replacing them with fresh-faced new occupants, particularly shoppers. The group's coordinator claimed: "If you have people actually using the area, they will replace the derelicts. We want to remove the visual barriers like tall hedges so that people can see inside. Drug dealers like privacy."[38] State Senator Manfred Ohrenstein, a supporter, noted that

> there are almost no soapbox orators in Union Square anymore. The park benches that were once witness to the activities of Mensheviks, Bolsheviks and Trotskyites have now been taken up by community planners concerned with cleaning the subway stop, rerouting traffic around the park and opening a restaurant within it. . . . When Union Square is renovated, I think it will be more like a mall, with shopping around the park and people using it as a place to pass through or rest in for a couple of hours in the spring or summer. . . . The best deterrent is not cops but people. If you had a shopping population there, addicts and peddlers wouldn't hang around.[39]

Dressed in the rhetoric of authentic urban place making, the late twentieth-century renovation of Union Square depended on the encouragement of social homogeneity and the repression of deviant activity of any kind, whether real or perceived. Even while upholding laws that protected the right to free speech and free assembly, it privileged an essential sameness, a common agreement on how to think and act, one that did not allow for different opinions and behaviors.

The Virtues of Density

Though successful, Sweet 14's efforts were not transformational: in order for Union Square's much touted revitalization to be realized completely, bigger moves were necessary. To realize Union Square's potential, planners and developers agreed, not just the park but also the surrounding buildings needed upgrading. And it was not enough to renovate existing buildings; the zoning laws would have to change to encourage the construction of new buildings, a practice known as "upzoning."[40] A new mayoral administration made this a possibility. Coming out of the financial crisis of the 1970s, with money available for building projects again, the New York City planning commission came under intense pressure to support private development. Elected in 1977, Mayor Ed Koch made this one of the primary goals of his administration.[41] In response to the city's dire financial predicament, he cut the city payroll and social welfare programs. He also followed a growing trend in municipal governance practices, reducing expenditure on public works and focusing instead on activities that would stimulate real estate development.[42] As we have seen, the city's business elite have had a close involvement in the affairs of the municipal government throughout the history of New York City, particularly in times of crisis such as the Civil War and the period following the collapse of the Tweed-backed administration. Once again private funding was seen as vital to the survival of public life. Through legislative and planning changes Koch made it profitable to invest in urban development. For twenty years the city had already subsidized the real estate industry in the form of tax abatements. The next step was to loosen zoning regulations and allow private groups to have increasing influence in the management of public spaces.

In the early 1980s, during Koch's second term, the city entered an era of permissive planning: building projects were regularly granted special permits to exceed the height and setback regulation allowed under the existing zoning law. Responding to lobbying, the Department of City Planning held a series of consultation meetings with Community Boards and other civic groups, and in 1984 proposed rezoning Union Square via the creation of a special zoning district (SZD). An amendment to the designation laid out in the 1961 zoning law, SZDs allowed for special circumstances within the greater urban whole. The concept was first employed in 1974 when the Special Clinton District was created on the West side of Manhattan's midtown.[43] The Fourteenth Street Union Square Local Development Corporation was the primary driver behind the Union Square SZD.[44] Created in 1980, the corporation grew out of Sweet 14. A subsidiary of the Public Development Corporations created in the 1960s, local development corporations were quasi-independent municipal entities aimed at encouraging private development. As proposed, the SZD would cover all properties fronting onto Union Square (fifty-two in total). It provided guidelines for building development in the area, guidelines that acknowledged the Square's social importance and preeminent location. In keeping with contemporary urban design thinking, it supported a contextual approach to urban and architectural design, one that preserved the Square's historic architecture and morphology, reinforcing it through the replication of historicist forms and decorative elements.

In particular the SZD emphasized the reinforcement and improvement of the street wall around the Union Square, marking it as a unified urban space with a strong visual presence. Most buildings facing the Square were constructed prior to the height and setback restrictions imposed in the 1916 zoning code. Consequently, they were built right up to their property lines and were tall compared to the fabric of the surrounding area. But clusters of much shorter, five-story buildings could also be found. The Department of City Planning considered this a problem: "These structures defining the Square's perimeter fail to contain the Square as a strong, unified urban space. Gaps and lack of continuity in street wall heights are detrimental to the Square's overall urban design because the irregularity is readily perceived across the open vistas available through the park."[45] Under the new zoning designation, development was to be compatible with the higher nineteenth-century norm. Significantly, the SZD did away with the so-called "plaza bonus" introduced in 1961, where extra floors were allowed in exchange for the provision of privately owned public spaces (commonly known as POPS).[46] Though few buildings in the area took advantage of this benefit, even the possibility was considered problematic for an area directly adjacent to a city park. Under the SZD no plazas or setbacks were allowed, and continuous street walls were mandated to a minimum of eight-five feet and a maximum of 125 feet. The SZD also encouraged building density closer to nineteenth-century norms by increasing the floor area ratio (FAR), from six to ten for commercial buildings. Created as part of the city's 1961 zoning regulation, the concept of FAR, a maximum ratio of lot area to building height, allowed the city to control the density of development on a neighborhood-by neighborhood basis.[47] According to the Department of City Planning, increasing the local FAR would help return Union Square to the "qualities of enclosure associated with a nineteenth-century park-square."[48] As the *New York Times* put it,

> to understand fully what the rescue of Union Square would mean, the observer has to imagine how it once resembled London's handsome Belgravia and Mayfair residential districts. By insisting on the eight-story rise directly from the sidewalk, the planners hope that modern apartment house builders will produce a contemporary echo of the walled-in space that gives the small squares of London and America's older cities their pleasing sense of order and scale.[49]

When it came to the preservation of older buildings, the authors of the SZD plan were encouraging but vague. This became an issue during the mandatory public review process, with several objectors voicing concern that development might lead to the demolition of historically significant buildings. After revision the SZD report identified a number of architecturally significant buildings and signaled a general desire for their improvement. It also encouraged the removal of postwar modifications such as the retrofitted facades that obscured the original storefronts of the Lincoln and Decker buildings on the west side of the Square. Over the next few years, several structures around the Square were given landmark protection status in order to preserve the ornate turn-of-the-century architectural character of the area. In 1988 several buildings on the west side were landmarked, including the Decker Building, the Bank of the Metropolis, and the Lincoln and Germania Buildings. The Union Square Savings Bank was added in 1996.[50]

The SZD also presented an opportunity to secure the kinds of public improvements the city was not able to provide, including the renovation of the long-problematic Union Square subway station. As part of the SZD, private developers were required to contribute to the improvement of the subway station: for example, the construction of new subway entrances within private property lines was mandatory for any new development fronting onto existing subway entrances. In addition, developers could receive an FAR bonus up to twelve in return for implementing functional improvements to the subway station approved by the Department of City Planning, the Transit Authority and the MTA. In this way the city was gradually transferring responsibility for updating a vital part of the city's transportation infrastructure into private hands.

Besides these functional and aesthetic changes, the primary goal of the SZD was to encourage the rapid redevelopment of the derelict S. Klein site, which had long been an embarrassing eyesore. In its report the Department of City Planning wrote that the development of this site "will have a stabilizing influence by attracting new residents and projecting a sense of permanence and confidence in the area."[51] Under the existing zoning plan the site could be built up to a maximum of six stories for commercial purposes and three for residential which was not enough to attract any serious developer. Not only did the SZD significantly raise the allowable height for the whole area, it also contained a special dispensation for the S. Klein site allowing the construction of an even taller building there.

The developer William Zeckendorf Jr. was the chief beneficiary of this provision. A major developer in his own right, Zeckendorf was son of one of the leading developers of the postwar period. William Zeckendorf Sr. was a strong believer in the power of private investment to stimulate the regeneration of the urban core. A master of public relations, he invested millions of dollars of his own money in grand-scale urban renewal projects in New York City and other historic centers.[52] With similar ambitions, Zeckendorf Jr. had expressed interest in buying the S. Klein site as early as 1980. In July 1983 he acquired a two-year option to buy it from Rapid American Corporation, which had purchased it from the Klein estate.[53] From the first Zeckendorf made it clear that his purchase was dependent on a zoning change allowing him to construct a much taller building. Contingent on the approval of the SZD, his architects, Davis Brody and Associates, drew up plans for the eponymous Zeckendorf Towers, a mammoth, one-million-square-foot complex made up of four seventeen-story apartment towers sitting atop a seven-story podium. The podium contained space for shops, movie theaters, and a restaurant on the ground floor, with five floors of offices above. Introducing more than six hundred new apartment units to Union Square, it boasted expansive views over the park and was completely plugged into the infrastructure of the city, incorporating retail stores on the ground floor and two new entrances to the subway station at the street level.

The scale of Zeckendorf Towers attracted considerable criticism. Several community groups, including Community Board 6, expressed concern that it would lead to overcrowding and overdevelopment as others sought to cash in on the area's new desirability. These groups proposed a compromise solution—a lower FAR that was still higher than the one allowed under the existing zoning code—but to little effect. In November 1983 the Department of City Planning submitted a draft report recommending the creation of the Union Square special zoning district. In order to win approval for the SZD, the city reduced the allowable FAR to eight for most sites around the Square. But Zeckendorf Towers was so important to the proposal that the FAR remained at ten on the crucial southeastern corner. In anticipation of a positive decision, the S. Klein buildings were demolished in 1984. After a public review process, the SZD and the permit for the Zeckendorf building were both approved at the same Board of Estimate meeting in January 1985.

Zeckendorf Towers opened in September 1987, a pastiche of the monumental art deco skyscrapers built in Manhattan during the 1920s. Some questioned whether the giant building that loomed over the eastern side of the Square was in keeping with the neighborhood. But others praised it as an economic engine; the complex was widely credited with pushing the long sought-after renewal of the area into hyperdrive. Of course, no single building, no matter how colossal, can effect such a change all by itself. One might point to other nearby projects, such as the restored Palladium building on East Fourteenth Street, a theater turned successful nightclub by promoter Ian Schrager, with opulent interior design by Japanese architect Arata Isozaki.[54] Even the SZD was but one of the causes of local gentrification, a small piece of a wider strategy aimed at restructuring the city for new kinds of investment and a new generation of urbanites. However, Zeckendorf Towers became a powerful visual symbol of change. Made manifest by this and other postmodern monuments, the remaking of the city during the last two decades of the twentieth century was not a smooth process. The stock market crash of October 1987 ushered in a recession that caused a sharp decline in the New York City real estate market; however, the economic and aesthetic rejuvenation of the Square and other parts of the city resumed once the economy picked up again in the early 1990s. In the last decade of the twentieth century, a series of retailers and companies opened around the Square, including upscale businesses such as publishers, architects, and graphic design agencies, as well as boutiques and more restaurants. A Rothman's clothing store opened on the northeast corner of the Square; Kiddie City, a children's toys and clothing store opened in the building that once housed S. Klein's Annex; and both an A&P supermarket and a FedEx leased space in the ground floor of Zeckendorf Towers. Plans were underway to transform the former May's store on Union Square south into a vertical shopping mall. All that was left was to remake the park in the image of the new neighborhood.

Defensible Space

Besides the SZD and the construction of Zeckendorf Towers, the restoration of Union Square Park was an essential component of the reinvention of the wider area. After years of drastic budget cuts, beginning in the late 1970s Mayor Koch made the renovation of New York City's devastated park system one of his major projects, a highly visible sign that the city was returning to its glamorous and well-provisioned former status.[55] While he significantly increased public funding for parks, as in other areas he supported this particular urban renewal initiative through partnerships with private entities. Central Park was the new Parks Commissioner Gordon Davis's first target. Supported by wealthy donors who lived on its periphery, he created the Central Park Conservancy to raise funds for the much-needed landscape restoration work and to manage the park from day to day. Although his approach was controversial, seen by some as handing over the city's responsibility to maintain its premiere public space to an elite few, it allowed the kind of comprehensive overhaul the city could never have afforded using public funding alone.[56]

Primed by years of community lobbying accompanied by speculative design suggestions, the Parks Department also began a major overhaul of Union Square, described in its own literature as a "physical and social renovation."[57] Supported by the city's relaxation of property taxes and lenient planning regulations, the Square was undergoing a metamorphosis from a drab and down-at-heel transit hub to a desirable place to live and work. With an emphasis on the creation of a safe, family-friendly amenity, the renovation of the park was designed to reinforce that new character. In 1982 Bronson Binger, assistant parks commissioner, announced a $1.5 million plan for the redesign of Union Square, designed by the landscape architect Hui Mei Grove in association with the Parks Department. Launching the project, Binger said, "The population around the park is changing very rapidly. Some of the warehouse buildings are being turned into lofts and there is a good deal of residential development underway. We are designing the park for a changing population, where instead of people walking through the park on the way to stores or offices the park will be more thoroughly used."[58] Begun under Commissioner Davis, the renovation continued under the new commissioner, Henry J. Stern, and was phased in two parts. Launched in February 1984, phase one included the renovation of the subway entrances, the provision of handicapped access, some repaving and relandscaping, and the provision of new furniture inside the park, including benches, drinking fountains, lights, and a news kiosk. Phase two, which involved closing Union Square West to through-traffic and rehabilitating the plaza, was projected to begin in 1988.

Firmly aligned with the goals of real estate development, the Parks Department plan incorporated the principles of "defensive design" in order to deter illicit activities and drive out the socially undesirable. In the climate of rampant gentrification, the plan was controversial: the geographer Neil Smith has described the deployment of updated landscaping in Union Square as the "aestheticization of the profit motive."[59] The city was hardly shy in acknowledging this. Attending the groundbreaking of the renovation in the spring of 1984, Mayor Koch borrowed from the popular "law and order" rhetoric to make the aims of the project clear: "First the thugs took over," he said, "then the muggers took over, then the drug people took over, and now we are driving them out. We are going to reclaim the parks of this city."[60] With this purpose in mind, the park's designers employed the tactics of what is known as "defensible space." Popularized by architect and city planner Oscar Newman in the early 1970s, the concept was a key part of many late twentieth-century, inner-city urban renewal projects.

According to Newman, design played an essential role in ensuring the safety and security of the urban environment. In contemporary large cities, he wrote, the traditional social codes guiding human behavior had broken down. In order to reclaim control, the design of a space must clearly express to whom it belonged; architecture must become "the physical expression of a social fabric that defends itself."[61] The mechanisms used to achieve this expression included real and symbolic barriers, what Newman described as strongly defined "areas of influence," and improved opportunities for surveillance. Though Newman was largely concerned with the design of housing complexes, his principles were used to inform the design of other parts of the city, most famously the new corporate plazas and atria built during the 1960s and 1970s.[62] In New York City, many of these were built under the POPS program. While these were public in the eyes of the law, and in theory completely open to all, their design often included subtle exclusionary cues in order to keep unwanted people out and to allow for oversight of users' behavior.[63] Designed as internalized environments integrating circulation, stores, and opportunities to pause and rest, projects such as Citicorp Tower on Lexington Avenue featured several layers of defensive design in order to subtly discourage entry. William H. Whyte criticized this strategy as a "war against the street."[64] Even though this era was marked by an impulse toward contextualism in which designers sought greater connection between new buildings and their surroundings, in practice, critics argued, the result was an intentional abdication of the responsibility to design for the public.

Incorporating many of Newman's ideas, the Parks Department took a slightly different approach to defensible space in its renovation of Union Square Park. Here the focus was on the removal of physical and visual barriers in order to increase visibility: this was the control of public behavior via a panoptic effect.[65] After renovation the park was much more open than it had been. Hedges surrounding the park, which screened activities taking place in the interior, were cut down. The new design included the installation of straight east-to-west and north-to south paths leading to a central lawn space, and better lighting in order to discourage undesirable activity. Defensible measures were not restricted to design alone. The Parks and Police departments pledged strong security, including frequent police patrols from 8:00 a.m. until midnight, and the installation of a police booth at the Fifteenth Street entrance signaling perpetual vigilance. At the opening of the renovated park, Inspector Thomas Gallagher of Manhattan South Patrol Borough Command reassured the public that it had been rendered "inhospitable to drug dealers. . . . Whatever police presence we need to throw at it, we will. There are no places now where they can hide, and we just have to keep up the pressure, which we intend to do."[66] Once implemented, these measures were generally regarded as successful: newspaper articles on the turnaround of Union Square Park described people lying on the grass reading, mothers playing with their children, and office workers sharing coffee at café tables.

With the 1980s renovation complete, Union Square had not only a new identity, but also a new narrative to explain how it had come into being. The renovation featured references to nineteenth-century design: the news kiosk constructed on the southeastern corner of the park; the benches, lamps, and drinking fountains were all designed in Victorian-style decorative cast-iron and glass supposedly in keeping with the park's historic character. The park received recognition from the federal government: in 1997 the United States Department of the Interior designated Union Square Park as a National Historic Landmark because of its significance in American labor history.[67] The way in which the Square's historic past has been acknowledged is also controversial: the art historian Rosalyn Deutsche has criticized the renovation as a branding exercise designed primarily to sell the park to potential residents and tenants.[68] There is no doubt developers and local business owners were selective in the way they told the Square's story. According to Deutsche, they presented a partial and biased history, with the past employed as a nostalgic commodity to be sold and consumed. Their marketing literature conjured up images of the Square's historic role as a place of national unity, making an example of large Civil War era gatherings, and suppressed memories of more contentious demonstrations. This effort was another attempt to pacify the Square, remaking it as a peaceful and quiet memorial to long-resolved struggles. In many ways the most recent reimagining of Union Square, begun in the 1980s, had the same agenda as the centennial celebration of 1932: a desire to promote the kinds of gentle urban leisure that appeals to middle-class users (strolling, playing, and shopping) at the expense of more active political gatherings. The tension between those who imagine Union Square as a place for escape from the pressures of urban life and those who see it as a place to intensify, and through intensification to resolve, is one that resonates into the present day.

The sense that the Square's identity was becoming ossified as a historical artifact and that its present-day uses were being curtailed is apparent in interviews with local residents. These interviews reveal both satisfaction that the bad old days of the 1970s were no more, that the drug dealers and homeless people who once camped out in the park had been moved on, but also concern about the future.[69] For longtime residents the signs of gentrification were uncomfortably difficult to ignore: upmarket restaurants, high charges for basic services such as a cup of coffee or dry cleaning, and the telltale presence of "women in silk suits and sneakers," walking symbols of the financial services companies that had replaced manufacturing as the engine of the city's economy.[70] Observing these changes, residents wondered, had the creation of the SZD and the renovation of the park destroyed rather than preserved the historic diversity of the neighborhood?

Underlying this unease was the implementation of a new urban management strategy. Established in 1984, the Union Square Partnership was New

York City's first business improvement district, or BID. Established under state law and in cooperation with the New York City Public Development Corporation, the BID allowed for the special assessment of property within the district, with the additional tax levies used to "stabilize and improve business conditions on Fourteenth Street."[71] While BIDs are controversial, as the history of Union Square reveals, they are hardly unprecedented in their form of organization and operation; nor are they entirely private, being enabled and supported by government at all levels. An expansion and formalization of earlier practices of public-private management, the Union Square Partnership BID was an outgrowth of the Fourteenth Street Local Development Corporation (LDC), itself an outgrowth of Sweet 14, the group established by community leaders and bankers to lobby for renewal in the late 1970s. Along with the LDC, its offices were housed in the Con Ed building on Fourteenth Street, and Con Ed was a major sponsor. The BID paid for private street cleaning (including garbage collection and street sweeping) and minor capital improvements, and promoted shopping activity. It also ran a security office in a storefront on Fourteenth Street from which uniformed guards patrolled the area. When the Parks Department budget shrank in the 1990s, the BID assumed an even greater role in the management and control of Union Square Park.

While critics see BIDs as the sinister result of neoliberal city management practices, they also acknowledge that they are an extension of a long tradition of public-private coalitions. Indeed, the staunchest adherents of the BID argue that they are an inherently American form of civic organization.[72] As political scientist and BID historian Jerry Mitchell puts it, "BIDs exist today because there is little in the American democratic tradition to prohibit the development of innovative administrative devices within localities."[73] Theoretically made up of local people taking charge of their own neighborhoods, they are in keeping with the early forms of loose "citizen-associations" that had characterized American cities since colonial times. The motivation behind them is the assumption that businesses are heavily invested in the success of their own neighborhoods, that the contribution of some of their excess capital is a reasonable request in order to maintain the quality of shared public space.[74] At the same time, there is no doubt that BIDs play an important role in creating a particular idea of what public space should be in the postindustrial city.

BIDs alter public spaces to complement the kinds of private spaces being built around them (office buildings, apartments, shops, and restaurants), and offer the kind of shared environment that affluent people find desirable. However, this is not the same as privatizing them; rather the "publicness" of such spaces, always defined through some type of exclusion, is reformulated in new terms.[75] Delayed by recession from 1987 to 1991, the second phase of the renovation of Union Square illustrates this. When the economy picked up again, so did the controversy: in 1993 the Parks Department constructed two new playgrounds and authorized a café to operate in the sunken courtyard outside the neoclassical pavilion. To be built with the approval of the New York City Art Commission, the Fourteenth Street LDC, and Community Board 5, this was trumpeted as a successful example of public-private partnership working together in the service of improving a shared space.[76] However, neighborhood activists protested the construction of the café, saying the incursion of a private business into the space of the Square was a betrayal of its public nature. The pavilion, built in the 1930s as part of a project to subdue the park's radical reputation through an active campaign of "beautification," was now embraced as a much loved and untouchable public amenity.

Criticism of the alignment of the Parks Department and the BID depends on the assumption that it places control of public space in the hands of private entities at the expense of a strong public authority. Yet, as we have seen in the context of New York City, this strict dichotomy between past and present practice is not easy to substantiate. Part of the long history of the Square, the fragile alliance of public and private interests working together to shape, preserve, and reconfigure this public space continued into the late twentieth century. From the mid-1970s local residents joined forces with business groups, community boards, and city agencies to affect a physical and reputational rehabilitation. As with other renewal efforts across the country, this cooperation was not smooth but involved the recognition and negotiation of mutual interests and the formation of strategic alliances.[77] This study of Union Square supports the contention that the aims and results of public and private action have long been difficult to disentangle. Rather than being unique to the neoliberal era of urban management, throughout the history of New York City the control and management of public spaces has more often been via a loose network of related interests, some governmental and others private, all claiming to represent the public interest while at the same time holding divergent opinions about its nature and purpose.

Which is not to deny that the scale of capital involved has grown, putting pressure on the definition of the public in ways that are legitimately concerning. As the twenty-first century approached and the city became ever more globally connected, the economy of Union Square was increasingly reliant on large-scale, international corporations and large-scale, international retail chains.[78] In 1997 a 3,500-square-foot Starbucks coffee shop opened at the base of Zeckendorf Towers at Union Square East and Fifteenth Street. Other businesses opened in restored historic buildings, including a W Hotel in the Germania Life Building managed by Starwood Hotels, and a branch of Barnes and Noble in a historic building on Seventeenth Street. Demolition and new construction continued: in 1998 a mammoth full-block building housing a Virgin megastore and a fourteen-screen movie theater opened on the southeast corner of Fourteenth Street and Broadway. Planning began for a New York University dormitory building on the site of the former Palladium Theater on East Fourteenth Street. Later that year the city announced a $2.6 million expansion plan for Union Square. Announcing the project Parks Commissioner Henry J. Stern said,

> It's a park in transition. Just as you wouldn't recognize the park of twenty years ago today, in twenty years you will no longer be able to recognize today's park . . . once decrepit, [it] is already considered a major success story of urban revitalization, having helped draw new housing, glittering stores and restaurants, and thousands upon thousands of visitors to what was, little more than a decade ago, a dowdy factory and retailing area.[79]

Designed by Michael Van Valkenburgh Associates and Architecture Research Office in 2004, the so-called North End project was the third and final phase of the project to "restore and rehabilitate" the park begun in the early 1980s. It did not attempt to recreate any particular era with historical exactitude. Rather it involved replacing the current asphalt surface with hex blocks and planting a line of Japanese Pagoda trees between the plaza space and Seventeenth Street. While they nod to history, these two simple and seemingly uncontroversial design moves—resurfacing the plaza and defining its northern boundary with a line of trees—simultaneously reinforce and erode the most storied component of Union Square Park: Olmsted and Vaux's plaza along Seventeenth Street. While Van Valkenberg Associates claimed its design "supports the continued use of this space for large public gatherings," city documents make it clear that the new plaza was not primarily intended for use as a meeting place for large groups.[80] Instead it was an amenity for the Greenmarket and the site of an enlarged children's playground. Together the Greenmarket and the playground came to represent public life in Union Square Park, at the expense of other uses and users.

With the turn of the twenty-first century, this book ceases to describe history and ventures into the realm of current concern. In the present day, Union Square continues to serve as an exemplar, or a cautionary tale, of prevailing attitudes about the purpose, design, and use of public space. The history of this contested site has bearing on enduring questions including, how do legal and social limitations on the use of public space coexist with physical ones? How do we acknowledge historic expressions of public life in a way that preserves their contemporary relevance? And most pressing of all today, at what point do definitions of what is truly public expand and break?

Conclusion

Approaching Union Square from the southeast along Fourteenth Street, a gently raked paved plaza curves away from the street. Supported by a backdrop of trees, it opens up to the north. Most days small groups of people gather on the shallow steps to talk, debate, play chess, dance, and eat, thankful to find a place to pause and rest. At other times the crowd grows larger, converging around homemade signs, and the conversation is louder and more urgent. Following 9/11, this plaza became the focal point for spontaneous memorials and tributes to those dead and missing in the attacks on the World Trade Center. While many people gathered around their televisions in disbelief, others felt the need to express their emotions in the form of tangible public offerings: flowers, photographs, and writings. In turn, these makeshift shrines became fodder for media spectacle as they garnered worldwide attention on cable news channels.

Walking north, we pass the equestrian statue of George Washington who observes the scene. With his right arm extended, the foot of his horse raised as if to move forward, he directs the crowd southward to the Battery and City Hall, historic sites of the city's economic and political power. This convergence of quotidian activity with symbols and sites of authority defines the role Union Square has played in this history of New York City. This small area of parkland, not central but still somehow at the core of a set of ideas, finds itself symbolic of an identity far larger than its modest silhouette would suggest. *Design for the Crowd* began with the intent to examine a specific urban space considered as an artifact or historical object that is both ordinary and familiar as well as monumental and exceptional. The premise has been that both our use and understanding of Union Square is mediated by deeply embedded social norms and expectations: it is a real space with unique physical characteristics containing within it broader ideas, thematics, and ideologies. In different historical periods, different facets of those thematics become brighter or dimmer.

Continuing north along a path lined with trees, we follow the axis created when the Square was renovated during the 1920s. Influenced by City Beautiful principles of order and symmetry, this renovation was an attempt to pacify the Square, to remake it as a peaceful and quiet memorial to struggles resolved long ago. At the end of this path and directly in line with Washington, is another statue, this one of Abraham Lincoln. Draped in a cloak, Lincoln holds a copy of the Emancipation Proclamation lightly under his arm. Together these statues reinforce the Square's association with patriotism: over its nearly two-hundred-year life span, it has come to embody the ideals of American democracy. This association has been affirmed and appropriated by various actors ever since it was first created, from Samuel Ruggles's Civil War–era contention that it had been created specifically as public meeting place (when he knew very well it hadn't); to the Californian labor organizer Denis Kearney's description of it as "a hall given to us by God almighty" in 1878; to the attempted conversion of the park into a progressive era civic forum in the early 1900s; to the restaurateur Jan Mitchell's vow to rededicate the park to the American flag in 1953 during the height of the Cold War.

At the foot of the Lincoln statue, we are forced to turn left or right. The northernmost part of the Square is impossible to access along the central pathway, blocked by a children's playground and a Beaux Arts Pavilion. Hidden from view is a simple rectangular space edged with a border of trees, the formal legacy of the simple yet powerful intervention introduced by Frederick Law Olmsted and Calvert Vaux. In 1872 Olmsted and Vaux were commissioned to complete a renovation of the Square, part of a larger project to popularize city parks. Their great innovation was a plaza intended as a forum for public meetings and celebrations. This plaza organized and gave aesthetic shape to a new kind of urban crowd. Following its construction it was used for all kinds of gatherings, from Fourth of July and Columbus Day parades, to working-class labor marches (including the first Labor Day parade on September 5th, 1882), to mass meetings of the International Workers of the World and antiwar demonstrators during World War I, and gatherings of unemployed workers during the Depression. It became so successful as a forum for political protest that Union Square became known as one of the key sites of American radicalism in the early years of the twentieth century.

Turning left at the statue of Lincoln, we descend slightly into a wide paved street running along the west side of the Square. Facing the renovated storefronts of Seventeenth Street, what remains of Olmsted and Vaux's plaza continues to thrive, though perhaps not in the way they had intended. Here, and along the northern edge of the Square, the popular Union Square Greenmarket operates four days a week, an outdoor marketplace for artisanal food and seasonal produce, with the mass gatherings of past centuries largely disallowed by city regulations. The Greenmarket has become a popular case study of urban renewal. This and other modest efforts were unified and encouraged by the creation of the special zoning district designed to attract mixed-use and residential development, including the Zeckendorf Towers on the east side. Ironically this mammoth development stands on the site of Samuel Ruggles's original row of townhouses and marks a desire to return at least part of the Square to its exclusive residential origins.

For some, the new Union Square represents a sinister conception of public space, one inextricably intertwined with the process of gentrification and with the wider decline of public life. In influential cultural criticism of the 1980s, the glamorous and fortified metropolises of late capitalism (particularly American financial centers) were presented as irrefutable evidence of the rejection of the ideal of an open, accessible, and inclusive public realm; carefully chosen architectural and urban examples were cited in support of an argument about the descent of society into hopeless consumerism. As Reinhold Martin has noted, several key narratives or mythologies underpin this argument.[1] They include the decline of authentic street life; the increased control of public spaces via private interests as part of the neoliberal agenda of city management (referred to in shorthand as the "privatization of public space"); the idea that the public being designed for is increasingly limited and segregated; the rise in creation of "inauthentic" places employing distorted semiotic references to past architecture and urbanism; and the betrayal of historic connections between urban life and citizenship. In this narrative the privileging of the marketplace as the primary forum for public life reduces the possibility of political engagement. The loss of the traditional street and city square means the loss of a stage for debates necessary to an effective democracy. In the worst case, the story goes, private interests have taken over completely. In the best and most optimistic case, public opposition provides a check and counterpoint to the attractions of private control.[2] But when the recent history of Union Square is considered in relation to its past, the limitations of this narrative of epistemic change become apparent.

In New York City comprehensive public control over city planning and urban design has existed in only a few, exceptional periods. At most times public space has been the creation of multiple actors, only a few of them elected to representative office or employed by the city or the state. As the example of Union Square illustrates, even in the early years of the American republic, the ideal of public space—open and accessible to all, unrestricted in its uses—was far from a historical reality. In the early years of the republic, equal access to property was thought to confer a sense of civic responsibility. Within a few decades, however, Manhattan had become a landscape of exploitation, with a small number of landowners controlling access to land and housing. In the nineteenth century the creation of public parks was largely in the power of a few wealthy and powerful individuals—individuals who imagined their collective actions would create benefit not only narrowly for themselves, but also more broadly, for the citizenry as a whole. The results were, predictably, uneven.

Union Square owes its existence and civic importance to many people and organizations and to complex motivations. Although Ruggles, the chief force behind the creation of the Square, was a real estate developer who profited directly from its establishment, he was also one of the loudest and most effective voices arguing for the preservation of its public character throughout the nineteenth century. The identification of Union Square as a privileged public forum was a post-rationalization created during the Civil War following the huge success of patriotic rallies organized by influential private organizations such as the Union League, acting in concert with established political parties. Though this sentiment was given physical form by Olmsted and Vaux acting under the authority of the Parks Department, it was private groups including the Central Labor Union that were most effective in opening up the plaza for public use through the vehicle of parades and demonstrations designed to promote the goals of their members. In the late nineteenth and early twentieth century, the heavy use of police violence to break up these gatherings shows that municipal authorities actively suppressed both informal and semi-sanctioned uses of public property. In time these violent events became so contentious they were employed as tests of the constitutional principles of the rights to free speech and public assembly. Widespread condemnation of police violence led to the founding of the private organizations such as the Free Speech League, the development of new policies and practices by the Parks and Police departments, and the revision of federal laws surrounding free speech. Under the direction of progressive leadership at the Parks and Police departments, the city tried, by and large, to abide by these laws. Finally, the present reinvention of Union Square as a vibrant city neighborhood, with all of the exclusionary practices and new business opportunities enabled by gentrification, is due to the agency of no single group, private or public, but is rather the product of strategic alliances formed between civic and community groups, local residents and business owners, property developers, and the various wings of the city government.

Exiting Union Square at its busy northwestern corner, the opening in the grid closes behind us: Broadway narrows, tall buildings tower over us, and the city resumes its familiar density. Looking back, it is easy to imagine the Square as a stable and timeless opening, an unchanging void within the delirium of the grid. But for the historian and the urban archeologist, Union Square presents a fascinating study of urban design at the small scale, one in which the central figure is itself in flux, a palimpsest continually erased and traced anew—one in which the differences between waste ground and commons, street and square, park and plaza, have been tested and retested through both individual and collective actions. The Square is not just a stage for public life, but a site on which ideas of publicness are imprinted and enacted. Throughout its history this enactment has taken many forms, from the making of maps to the erection of statues, from written reportage to the creation of images and photographs, from the planting of trees and plants to the design of ephemeral street parades and festivals and the setting out of steel barricades. All of these actions overlap with each other, producing a collective and eternally unfinished work of urban design, a stage for, and representation of, our social world.

Notes

Introduction

1. Setha M. Low, "Spaces of Reflection, Recovery and Resistance: Reimagining the Postindustrial Plaza," in *After the World Trade Center: Rethinking New York City*, ed. Michael Sorkin and Sharon Zukin (New York: Routledge, 2002), 163–71.

2. On the importance of corporeality and the nonverbal in mass protest, see Judith Butler, *Notes toward a Performative Theory of Assembly* (Cambridge, MA: Harvard University Press, 2015).

3. Brian McGrath, "Recycling New York City" in *Recycling City: Lifecycles, Embodied Energy, Inclusion*, ed. Lorenzo Fabian, Emanuel Giannotti, and Paola Viganò (Pordenone, Italy: Giavedoni editore, 2012).

4. Naomi Wolff, "The New Totalitarianism of Surveillance Technology," *The Guardian* (August 15, 2012).

5. Andrew Pask, "Public Space Activism," in *Insurgent Public Space: Guerrilla Urbanism and the Remaking of Contemporary Cities*, ed. Jeffrey Hou (London: Routledge, 2010), 227–40; Jonathan Massey and Brett Snyder, "Occupying Wall Street: Places and Spaces of Political Action," *Places Journal* (September 2012).

6. Samuel B. Ruggles, *Union Square and the Sanitary Commission: Address by the Hon. Samuel B. Ruggles, at Union Square, on the Opening of the Metropolitan Fair, April 8th, 1864* (New York: C. A. Alvord, 1864), 11.

7. See, for example, Michael Sorkin, ed., *Variations on a Theme Park: The New American City and the End of Public Space* (New York: Hill and Wang, 1992); Margaret Kohn, *Brave New Neighborhoods: The Privatization of Public Space* (London: Routledge, 2004); Setha Low

and Neil Smith, eds., *The Politics of Public Space* (New York: Routledge, 2006); and Sharon Zukin, *Naked City: The Death and Life of Authentic Urban Places* (New York: Oxford University Press, 2010).

8. Lance Jay Brown and Ron Shiffman, "Introduction," in *Beyond Zuccotti Park: Freedom of Assembly and the Occupation of Public Space*, ed. Ron Schiffman, Rick Bell, Lance Jay Brown, and Lynn Elizabeth, with Anastassia Fisyak and Anusha Venkataraman (Oakland, CA: New Village Press, 2012), xxi.

9. Rosalyn Deutsche, "The Question of Public Space," in *Evictions: Art and Spatial Politics* (Cambridge, MA: MIT Press, 1998), 1–13.

10. Mary Ryan, *Civic Wars: Democracy and Public Life in the American City During the Nineteenth Century* (Berkeley: University of California Press, 1997); Lisa Keller, *Triumph of Order: Democracy and Public Space in New York and London* (New York: Columbia University Press, 2008).

11. Henri Lefebvre, *The Production of Space*, trans. Donald Nicholson-Smith (New York: Wiley-Blackwell, 1992), 14.

12. Roland Barthes, "Semiology and the Urban" (1967), *L'Architecture d'Aujourdhui* 153 (December 1970); Roland Barthes, *The Semiotic Challenge*, trans. Richard Howard (New York: Hill and Wang, 1988), 191–201.

13. Roland Barthes, "The Eiffel Tower" (1964) in *A Barthes Reader*, ed. Susan Sontag (New York: Hill and Wang, 1982), 236–50.

Chapter One

1. John Reps, *Views and Viewmakers of Urban America* (Columbia: University of Missouri Press, 1984), 160; Nat Case, "John Bachmann and the American Bird's Eye View Print," *Imprint* 33, no. 2 (Autumn 2008): 19–35.

2. The origins of the phrase the "upper ten" cannot be ascertained with certainty, but it appears to be an American term that was later adopted in Great Britain. As contemporary newspapers attest, it was in widespread use in New York City in the mid-1840s. In later years publishing houses produced directories and guides of members of the "upper ten," such as Charles Astor Bristed's *The Upper Ten Thousand: Sketches of American Society* (New York: Stringer and Townsend, 1852). The phrase is defined in John Russell Bartlett's *Dictionary of Americanisms: A Glossary of Words and Phrases Usually Regarded as Peculiar to the United States*, 2nd ed. (Boston: Little, Brown and Company, 1877), 729. The area above Fourteenth Street is described as the home of the "upper ten thousand" in numerous contemporary guidebooks, including William Bobo, *Glimpses of New-York City* (Charleston, SC: J. J. McCarter, 1852), 76.

3. Isabella Lucy Bird, *The Englishwoman in America* (London: John Murray, 1856), 368.

4. A row of houses on East Seventeenth Street between Union Square East and Irving Place is the only remnant left of the residential architecture of the 1830s and 1840s. Gale Harris and Jay Shockley, "East Seventeenth Street/Irving Place Historic District Designation Report" (New York: New York City Landmarks Preservation Commission, 1998).

5. On the importance of maritime trade in the early nineteenth-century growth of New York City, see Robert G. Albion, *The Rise of the New York Port, 1815–1860* (New York: Charles Scribner's Sons, 1939); Writers Program of the Work Projects Administration in the State of New York, *A Maritime History of New York* (New York: Haskell House, 1941); David T. Gilchrist, ed., *The Rise of the Seaport Cities, 1790–1825* (Charlottesville: University of Virginia Press, 1967); Simeon J. Crowther, "Urban Growth in the Mid-Atlantic States, 1785–1850," *Journal of Economic History* 36, no. 3 (September 1976): 624–44; and Janet Abu-

Lughod, "The First Growth Cycle to the 1820s," in *New York, Chicago, Los Angeles: America's Global Cities* (Minneapolis: University of Minnesota Press, 1999), 20–30.

6. On Randel's work on surveying the New York City grid, see Marguerite Holloway, *The Measure of Manhattan: The Tumultuous Career and Surprising Legacy of John Randel Jr. Cartographer, Surveyor and Inventor* (New York: Norton, 2013).

7. On the creation of the New York City grid, see Hilary Ballon, ed., *The Greatest Grid: The Master Plan of Manhattan 1811–2011* (New York: Columbia University Press, 2011). See also John Reps, "Checkerboard Cities and Gridiron Plans," *The Making of Urban America: A History of City Planning in the United States* (Princeton, NJ: Princeton University Press, 1965), 294–324; M. Christine Boyer, "The Inheritance of the Grid," *Manhattan Manners: Architecture and Style, 1850–1900* (New York: Rizzoli, 1985), 8–23; Edward K. Spann, "The Greatest Grid: The New York Plan of 1811," in *Two Centuries of American Planning*, ed. Daniel Schaffer (Baltimore, MD: Johns Hopkins University Press, 1988), 11–39; and John R. Stilgoe, "National Design: Mercantile Cities and the Grid," in *American Architectural History: A Contemporary Reader*, ed. Keith Eggener (London: Routledge, 2004), 25–38.

8. Rem Koolhaas, *Delirious New York: A Retroactive Manifesto for Manhattan* (New York: Monacelli, 1994), 13.

9. On the process of urban "regulation" in the context of late eighteenth- and early nineteenth-century America, see Dell Upton, *Another City: Urban Life and Urban Spaces in the New American Republic* (New Haven, CT: Yale University Press, 2008). On eighteenth and nineteenth-century ideas of "urban improvement" in the British context, see S. J. Daniels and S. Seymour, "Landscape Design and the Idea of Improvement 1730–1900," in *An Historical Geography of England and Wales*, ed. Robert A. Dodgshorn and Robin A. Butler (London: Academic Press, 1990), 487–520.

10. Upton, *Another City*, 1. See also Elizabeth Blackmar, *Manhattan for Rent: 1785–1850* (Ithaca, NY: Cornell University Press, 1989), 72–108.

11. On this interpretation of the New York City grid, see David M. Scobey, *Empire City: The Making and Meaning of the New York City Landscape* (Philadelphia: Temple University Press, 2002). This interpretation owes a debt to the work of geographer David Harvey, in works such as *The Urbanization of Capital* (London: Basil Blackwell, 1985) and *Spaces of Capital: Towards a Critical Geography* (London: Routledge, 2001).

12. John Randel, *City of New York, North of Canal Street, in 1808 to 1821* (New York, 1864), 2.

13. David Schuyler makes this argument in *The New Urban Landscape: The Redefinition of City Form in Nineteenth-Century America* (Baltimore, MD: Johns Hopkins University Press, 1986), 20.

14. Don Mitchell, "The End of Public Space? People's Park, Definitions of the Public, and Democracy," *Annals of the Association of American Geographers* 85, no. 1 (March 1995): 117.

15. On Ruggles's biography, see D. G. Brinton Thompson, *Ruggles of New York: A Life of Samuel B. Ruggles* (New York: AMS Press, 1946). See also "An Old New Yorker Gone: The Busy Life of Samuel B. Ruggles Brought to a Close," *New York Times* (August 29, 1881); and John Austin Stevens, *Tribute of the Chamber of Commerce of the State of New York to the Memory of Samuel B. Ruggles: November 3, 1881* (New York: Press of the Chamber of Commerce, 1881).

16. Sebastian Visscher Talcott, *Genealogical Notes of New York and New England Families* (Baltimore, MD: Clearfield Co., 1994), 647. See also Walter Barrett, *The Old Merchants of New York City*, vol. 1 (New York: Thomas R. Knox and Co., 1885), 853–54.

17. Anticipating the development of the area above Fourteenth Street, the city divided the Twelfth Ward into two in 1836, with the section below Fortieth Street designated the Sixteenth Ward. Ten years later this new ward was again divided in half along Sixth Ave, and the easterly portion was designated the Eighteenth Ward. During the 1830s and 1840s the Twelfth, Sixteenth, and Eighteenth Wards were the focus of new development. *A Compilation of the Laws of the State of New York Relating Particularly to the City of New York, Prepared at the Request of the Common Council by Henry E. Davies* (New York: E. Jones and Co., 1857). On the creation of "uptown" New York in the mid-nineteenth century, see Charles Lockwood, *Manhattan Moves Uptown: An Illustrated History* (New York: Houghton Mifflin, 1976); Boyer, *Manhattan Manners*; and Edwin G. Burrows and Mike Wallace, "Life above Bleecker," in *Gotham. A History of New York City to 1898* (New York: Oxford University Press, 1999), 712–34.

18. Sturges S. Dunham, "Bond Street" in *Valentine's Manual of the City of New York for 1917–18*, by Henry Collins Brown (New York: The Old Colony Press, 1917), 207.

19. On Ruggles's founding of Gramercy Park and improvement of Union Square, see John B. Pine, *The Story of Gramercy Park 1831–1921* (New York: Gramercy Park Association, 1921); Burrows and Wallace, *Gotham*, 577–78; Blackmar, *Manhattan for Rent*, 196–204; and Ballon, *Greatest Grid*, 116–17.

20. E. Porter Belden, *New-York: Past, Present and Future* (New York: G. P. Putnam, 1849), 33.

21. Edwin Williams, *New York, as It Is in 1834; And Citizen's Advertising Directory* (New York: J. Disturnell, 1834), 182.

22. *A Compilation of the Laws of the State of New York*, 581.

23. On the changing meaning of the words "improve" and "improvement" during the eighteenth and nineteenth centuries, see Raymond Williams, *Keywords: A Vocabulary of Culture and Society* (London: Fontana, 1976), 132–33.

24. *Document of the Board of Assistants of the City of New York from the 19th of May 1834 to the 12th of May 1835* (New York, 1835), 47.

25. "Commissioner's Remarks," *Map of the City of New York and Island of Manhattan* (New York: William Bridges, 1811), 1; Randel, *City of New York*, 4.

26. "Commissioner's Remarks," *Map of the City of New York*, 1.

27. Ballon, *The Greatest Grid*.

28. "Commissioner's Remarks," *Map of the City of New York*, 1.

29. "Commissioner's Remarks," *Map of the City of New York*, 1.

30. Edward K. Spann, *The New Metropolis: New York City 1840–1857* (New York: Columbia University Press, 1981), 161. Many of the squares and public places proposed by the commissioners were discontinued by acts of the state legislature in the 1820s. The exception was Manhattan Square bounded by Eighth and Ninth Avenues and Seventy-Seventh and Eighty-First Streets. In 1840 the municipal authorities began proceedings to open this square, but in 1864 it was disestablished in favor of the new Central Park. On the general layout of New York City in the period 1825–50, with a special emphasis on the open spaces, or "places of sociability," see Ryan, *Civic Wars*, 26–57.

31. The North American "common," an early urban landscape type, was developed in the early nineteenth century as the social and political focus of New England towns, differing from earlier open spaces in that it was not used primarily for cultivation or agriculture. J. B. Jackson, *Discovering the Vernacular Landscape* (New Haven, CT: Yale University Press, 1984), 129; Joseph S. Wood, *The New England Village* (Baltimore, MD: Johns Hopkins University Press, 1997), 128–33.

32. Boyer, *Manhattan Manners*, 13–15.

33. *Miller's New York as It Is; Or the Stranger's Guide-Book to the Cities of New York, Brooklyn and Adjacent Places and Its Vicinity* (New York: James Miller, 1866), 24.

34. For a summary of these accounts, see Ellen W. Kramer, "Contemporary Descriptions of New York City and Its Public Architecture c. 1850," *Journal of the Society of Architectural Historians* 27, no. 4 (December 1968); 267–69.

35. "Public Squares," *Commercial Advertiser* (December 21, 1831), 1. *Documents of Board of Alderman and Board of Assistants of the City of New York: November 1831 to May 12 1834*, vols. 1 and 2 (New York: The Common Council, 1838), 243.

36. "Public Squares," *Commercial Advertiser*.

37. Ballon, *Greatest Grid*, 103–5.

38. Scobey, *Empire City*, 203; Ballon, *Greatest Grid*, 106.

39. On ideas of public health in early nineteenth-century American urban planning, see John Duffy, *The Sanitarians: A History of American Public Health* (Urbana: University of Illinois Press, 1990); and Martin V. Melosi, *The Sanitary City: Urban Infrastructure in America from Colonial Times to the Present* (Baltimore, MD: The Johns Hopkins University Press, 2000).

40. *Document of the Board of Assistants of the City of New York: Vol. I; From the 19th of May 1834 to the 12th of May 1835* (New York, 1835), 71.

41. *Spectator* (January 20, 1832).

42. "Public Squares," *Commercial Advertiser*.

43. Todd Longstaffe-Gowan, *The London Square: Gardens in the Midst of Town* (New Haven, CT: Yale University Press, 2012), 43–55.

44. Longstaffe-Gowan, *London Square*, 55.

45. "Common Council, Board of Assistant Aldermen," *Commercial Advertiser* (July 29, 1834), 1

46. Longstaffe-Gowan describes the practical and symbolic importance of the enclosure of London's squares with iron railings in *London Square*, 4.

47. *America* (January 17, 1832), 2; *Spectator* (January 20, 1832), 2; *Evening Post* (January 30, 1832), 1; *Albany Argus* (April 17, 1832). See also *Documents of Board of Aldermen and Board of Assistants of the City of New York: November 1831 to May 12 1834*, vols. 1 and 2 (New York: The Common Council, 1838); Samuel B. Ruggles, *Memorial of Samuel B. Ruggles, On the Social and Fiscal Importance of Open Squares in the City of New York* (1878), in *Documents of the Assembly of the State of New York*, vol. 7 (New York: State Legislature), 3.

48. *Document of the Board of Assistants of the City of New York: Vol. I: From the 19th of May 1834 to the 12th of May 1835* (New York, 1835), 64.

49. "Common Council, Board of Assistant Aldermen," *Commercial Advertiser* (June 29, 1834), 1; Document No. 8., July 14, 1834. *Document of the Board of Assistants of the City of New York: Vol. I; From the 19th of May 1834 to the 12th of May 1835* (New York, 1835), 73.

50. "Board of Aldermen," *Evening Post* (November 27, 1833).

51. "Board of Aldermen," *American* (December 26, 1833); "Board of Aldermen," *Commercial Advertiser* (January 14, 1834); "Common Council," *American* (June 29, 1834).

52. *Documents of Board of Alderman and Board of Assistants of the City of New York: November 1831 to May 12 1834*, vols. 1 and 2 (New York: The Common Council, 1838), 243.

53. "Trees," *Commercial Advertiser* (June 5, 1837), 2.

54. *Evening Post* (February 6, 1833).

55. *Evening Post* (March 15, 1833).

56. "Board of Aldermen," *Commercial Advertiser* (February 12, 1833).

57. "The Custom House," *American* (May 8, 1833), 2. "Custom House," *Evening Post* (May 9, 1833), 2.

58. "The Custom House," *American.*

59. *Evening Post* (February 21, 1833); "Harlem Railroad Report," *Commercial Advertiser* (February 19, 1834), 1; Williams, *New York, as It Is in 1834*, 21–22. The New York and Harlem Railroad Company was chartered by a special act of the New York state legislature on the 25th of April, 1831. On the company, and other early streetcar lines, see Harry James Carman, *The Street Surface Railway Franchises of New York City* (New York: Columbia University Studies in History, Economics and Public Law, 1919), 17–32; Joseph Warren Greene, "New York City's First Railroad: The New York and Harlem, 1832–1867," in *New-York Historical Society Quarterly Bulletin*, no. 9 (1926): 107–23; and Roger P. Roess and Gene Sansone, "The Beginning of Public Transportation in New York: Omnibuses and Street Railways," in *The Wheels that Drove New York: A History of the New York Transit System* (Berlin: Springer Verlag, 2013), 53–61.

60. *Evening Post* (March 8, 1833); *Laws of the State of New York, Relating Particularly to the City of New York, Prepared at the Request of the Common Council by Henry E. Davies* (New York: Gould and Banks, 1833), 751.

61. Brinton Thomas, *Ruggles of New York*, 57; Ballon, *Greatest Grid*, 103.

62. On the importance of the Croton Aqueduct for the process of urbanization, see Matthew Gandy, "Water, Space and Power," in *Concrete and Clay: Reworking Nature in New York City* (Cambridge, MA: MIT Press, 2003), 19–76. See also Charles King, *A Memoir of the Construction, Cost and Capacity of the Croton Aqueduct* (New York: Charles King, 1843); George H. Rappole, "The Old Croton Aqueduct," *Journal of Industrial Archaeology* 4, no. 1 (1978): 15–25; and Jeffrey Kroessler, ed., *The Old Croton Aqueduct: Rural Resources Meet Urban Need* (New York: The Hudson River Museum of Westchester, 1992).

63. Williams, *New York, as It Is in 1834*, 23.

64. "The Celebration," *Spectator* (October 15, 1842), 1.

65. On the Erie Canal and Croton Aqueduct parades, see Martha J. Lamb and Burton Harrison, *History of the City of New York: Its Origin, Rise, and Progress*, vol. 3 (New York: A. S. Barnes and Co., 1896), 696–701.

66. Sean Wilentz, "Artisanal Republican Festivals and the Rise of Class Conflict in New York City, 1788–1837," in *Working Class America: Essays on Labor, Community, and American Society*, ed. Michael Frisch and Daniel J. Walkowitz (Urbana: University of Illinois Press, 1983), 33–77.

67. Gandy, *Concrete and Clay*, 32.

68. "The Celebration," *Spectator* (October 15, 1842).

69. "Union Square," by George De Forest Barton, in *Valentine's Manual of Old New York*, by Henry Collins Brown (New York: Valentine's Manual, 1923), 194.

70. "Union Square," in *Valentine's Manual of Old New York*, 194. Porter was Ambassador to Turkey from 1831 to 1835.

71. *Spectator* (February 26, 1845).

72. "Union Square and its Vicinity," *New York Herald* (May 29, 1845), 2.

73. Brinton Thomas, *Ruggles of New York.*

74. When Tighe died in 1896, his house was one of only two left of the original row houses built by Ruggles. It was demolished in 1904; the other, no. 36, stood until 1916. "Sir Richard Tighe," *New York Times* (May 11, 1896). On the other residents of this row, see Brown, *Valentine's Manual of the City of New York for 1917–18*, 238, 285; Boyer, *Manhattan Manners*, 45, 47; and Michael D. Shapiro, "Becoming Union Square: Struggles for

Legitimacy in Nineteenth-Century New York," University of Massachusetts, Amherst (2010), 43.

75. Bird, *Englishwoman in America*, 360.

76. Moses Yale Beach, *Wealth and Biography of the Wealthy Citizens of New York City* (New York: The Sun, 1845), 8. J. Leander Bishop, *History of American Manufacturers from 1608 to 1860*, vol. 3 (New York: Edward Young, 1868), 193.

77. Phelps's house was designed by John B. Snook and Joseph Trench in 1844. Boyer, *Manhattan Manners*, 45.

78. The architect of this house is identified by an 1862 source as "Mr. Hurry," probably William Hurry, who later entered into partnership with John Rogers, practicing as Hurry and Rogers. After Henry's death in 1856 the ownership of these properties was contested as part of a lengthy legal dispute over his will. Joseph Delafield, *The Parish Will Case, in the Court of Appeals, the Statement of Facts and the Opinion of the Court* (New York: D. Appleton and Company, 1862), 19.

79. On the new style for domestic architecture in New York City, see Charles Lockwood, "The Italianate Dwelling House in New York City," *Journal of the Society of Architectural Historians* 31, no. 2 (May 1972): 145–51; and Jay E. Cantor, "A Monument of Trade: A. T. Stewart and the Rise of the Millionaire's Mansion in New York," *Winterthur Portfolio* 19 (1975): 174.

80. Delafield, *Parish Will Case*, 23.

81. Christopher Hoolihan, ed., *An Annotated Catalogue of the Edward C. Atwater Collection of American Poplar Medicine and Health Reform*, vol. 3 (Rochester, NY: University of Rochester Press, 2008), 490.

82. "The Fenians: The Headquarters on Union Square the Moffat Mansion Occupied by the Fenian Men," *New York Herald* (November 18, 1865), 1.

83. "New York in 1847," *Evening Post* (June 8, 1847), 1.

84. "A Druggist's Water Fancy," *Spectator* (July 16, 1845).

85. Delafield, *Parish Will Case*, 19.

86. Delafield, *Parish Will Case*, 23.

87. Renwick's design for Grace Church was criticized by American adherents of the English Ecclesiological movement who assailed the "untruthful" use of materials: Frank Wills, "Reality in Church Architecture," *New-York Ecclesiologist*, no. 1 (April 1848): 8–12; "New-York Church Architecture," *Putnam's Monthly Magazine of American Literature, Science and Art* 2, no. 9 (September 1853): 247; Kramer, "Contemporary Descriptions of New York City," 275–76.

88. "New Buildings in Union-Square—Decker Bros. Piano Ware-Rooms—Tiffany's Building," *New York Times* (March 27, 1870).

89. Abbott was a friend and advisor to Matthew Vassar, the founder of Vassar College, one of the first women's colleges in the United States. He later closed the Spingler Institute and opened another girl's school, the Abbot Collegiate Institute for Young Ladies, on Fifth Avenue and Thirty-Fourth Street. "Abbot Collegiate Institute," *New York Times* (September 7, 1861); "Intercollegiate," *Wellesley Magazine* 8, no. 4 (January 1900): 200.

90. Quoted in Jane Hanna Pease, "Boarding School, 1850s Style," *University of Rochester Bulletin* 10, no. 2 (1950).

91. Bobo, *Glimpses of New-York City*, 76, 166.

92. Upton, *Another City*, 333.

93. Kenneth T. Jackson, *Crabgrass Frontier: The Suburbanization of the United States* (New

York: Oxford University Press, 1985). On the emergence of the American suburb, see also John Archer, "Country and City in the American Romantic Suburb," *Journal of the Society of Architectural Historians* 42, no. 2 (May 1983): 139–56; and John R. Stilgoe, *Borderland: Origins of the American Suburb, 1820–1939* (New Haven, CT: Yale University Press, 1988).

94. "Union Square," *New York Herald* (June 8, 1848), 2. See also, "Improvement of the Park and City Squares," *New York Herald* (March 25, 1848), 1.

95. *Proceedings of the Board of Alderman of the City of New York: January to May 1850* (New York: McSpedon and Baker, 1850), 363.

96. "New-York Daguerrotyped," *Putnam's Monthly Magazine of American Literature, Science and Art* 1 no. 2 (February 1853): 125.

97. On mid-nineteenth-century New York City hotels, see "New-York Daguerrotyped," *Putnam's Monthly Magazine of American Literature, Science and Art*: 359–68; Ivan D. Steen, "Palaces for Travelers: New York City's Hotels in the 1850s as Viewed by British Visitors," *New York History* 51, no. 3 (April 1970): 269–86; Kramer, "Contemporary Descriptions of New York City," 273–74; Boyer, *Manhattan Manners*, 50–55.

98. Steen, "Palaces for Travelers," 275.

99. "Union Place Hotel" (advertisement), *Evening Post* (September 1, 1848); "City Intelligence," *Evening Post* (29 September 1848); "City News," *Spectator* (October 5, 1848).

100. This quotation was reported in the *New York Herald*: "The Everett House," *New York Herald* (September 1, 1857), 2.

101. Brinton Thompson, *Ruggles of New York*, 66.

102. Ruggles, *Union Square and the Sanitary Commission*, 11.

Chapter Two

1. *Proceedings of the Board of Aldermen* (1853), vol. 4, pp. 130, 189; I. N. Phelps Stokes, *The Iconography of Manhattan Island* (New York: Robert H. Dodd, 1918), 1851.

2. On the statue of Washington in Union Square, see James Lee, *The Equestrian Statue of Washington, New York* (New York: John F. Trow, Printer, 1864); Dorothy C. Barck, "Proposed Memorials to Washington in New York City, 1802–1847," *New York Historical Society Quarterly* 15 (1931): 79–90; Agnes Miller, "Centenary of a New York Statue," *New York History* 38, no. 2 (April 1, 1957): 167–73; Jacob Landy, "The Washington Monument Project in New York," *Journal of the Society of Architectural Historians* 28, no. 4 (December 1969): 291–97; and Rebecca Read Shanor, *The City that Never Was: Two Hundred Years of Fantastic and Fascinating Plans that Might Have Shaped the Face of New York City* (New York: Viking, 1988), 197–203.

3. Kirk Savage, *Standing Soldiers, Kneeling Slaves: Race, War, and Monument in Nineteenth-Century America* (Princeton, NJ: Princeton University Press, 1997), 6.

4. Ryan, *Civic Wars*, 76–77.

5. *New York Daily Tribune* (August 17, 1843), 1.

6. Shanor, *The City that Never Was*, 197.

7. Quoted in Shanor, *The City that Never Was*, 198.

8. This request was dated September 30, 1844. *Proceedings of the Board of Aldermen from May 14 to November 18, 1844, Vol. 27* (New York: J. F. Trow and Co., 1845), 532.

9. *Remonstrance and Protest against the Proposed Appropriation of Union Square*, Broadside dated October 4, 1844. Quoted in Michael D. Shapiro, "Becoming Union Square," 66.

10. Ruggles, *Memorial of Samuel B. Ruggles*. This text was written in response to a plan to build an armory in Washington Square.

11. “The Grand Celebration on the Occasion of Laying the Corner Stone of the Washington Monument,” *New York Herald* (October 20, 1847), 1.

12. On Robert Mills’s national monument in Washington, DC, see Frederick Loviad Harvey, *History of the Washington National Monument and of the Washington National Monument Society* (Washington, DC: Norman T. Elliott, 1902); Kirk Savage, “The Self-Made Monument: George Washington and the Fight to Erect a National Memorial,” *Winterthur Portfolio* 22, no. 4 (Winter 1987): 225–42; and Richard Longstreth, *The Mall in Washington D.C., 1791–1991* (New Haven, CT: Yale University Press, 2003).

13. On Brown’s statue and his short-lived collaboration with Greenough, see Nathalia Wright, *Horatio Greenough: The First American Sculptor* (Philadelphia: University of Pennsylvania Press, 1963), 274–76; Miller, “Centenary of a New York Statue,” 167–73; and Wayne Craven, *Sculpture in America* (Newark: University of Delaware Press, 1984), 151–52. On Brown, see Wayne Craven, “Henry Kirke Brown: His Search for an American Art in the 1840’s,” *American Art Journal* 4, no. 2 (November 1972): 44–58; Michele H. Bogart, *Public Sculpture and the Civic Ideal in New York City, 1890–1930* (Washington, DC: Smithsonian, 1997); Thayer Tolles, “Modeling a Reputation: The American Sculptor and New York City,” in *Art and the Empire City, 1825–61*, ed. Catherine Hoover Voorsanger and John K. Howat (New York: Yale University Press and the Metropolitan Museum of Art, 2000), 166–67; and Michael Preston Worley, “Henry Kirke Brown: New Sources for the Work of an American Neo-Classical Sculptor,” *Burlington Magazine* 147, no. 1233 (December 2005): 824–26.

14. “Inauguration of the Statue of Washington,” *New-York Tribune* (July 5, 1856); “Inauguration of the Washington Statue,” *New York Herald* (July 6, 1856), 1; “The Glorious Fourth; Military Processions. Inauguration of the Washington Statue,” *New York Times* (July 7, 1856), 1; “Brown’s Equestrian Statue of Washington, *Frank Leslie’s Illustrated Newspaper* (July 19, 1856), 86.

15. “Statue of Washington by H. K. Brown, Union Square New York” (New York: G. P. Putnam, 1903).

16. Savage, “Self-Made Monument,” 225.

17. Michael Preston Worley, “Henry Kirke Brown,” *Sculpture* (December 2005), 825.

18. “Evacuation Day,” *Encyclopedia of New York City*, ed. Kenneth T. Jackson (New Haven, CT: Yale University Press, 1995), 385.

19. See, for example, James Grant Wilson, ed., *The Memorial History of the City of New-York from its First Settlement to the Year 1892*, vol. 4 (New York: New York History Company, 1893), 209–10; Miller, “Centenary of a New York Statue,” 168.

20. Charles T. McClenachan, *Detailed Report of the Proceedings Had in Commemoration of the Successful Laying of the Atlantic Cable, by order of the Common Council of the City of New York* (New York: Edmund Jones and Co., 1863), 169.

21. From the beginning of the war, New York City played a major role in housing troops and transporting them by sea, not only from the New York area but also from New England. In order to accommodate this function the city built several temporary barracks, the first a four-hundred-foot-long building at the south end of City Hall Park, which housed two thousand troops, and the second a larger complex built in 1863 at the Battery, which housed five thousand. At that time the City Hall Park Barracks was converted into a hospital.

22. On New York’s role in the Civil War, see Sidney David Brummer, “Political History of New York State during the Period of the Civil War,” PhD diss., Columbia University

(1911); Ernest McKay, *The Civil War and New York City* (New York: Syracuse University, 1990); Edward K. Spann, *Gotham at War: New York City, 1860–65* (New York: Scholarly Resources, 2002); Ryan, *Civic Wars*, 168–80; and Steven H. Jaffe, *New York at War: Four Centuries of Combat, Fear, and Intrigue in Gotham* (New York: Basic Books, 2012), 141–76.

23. "Union Demonstration of Merchants," *New York Herald* (April 18, 1861); *The Union Defense Committee of the City of New York: Minutes, Reports, and Correspondence* (New York: Union Defense Committee, 1885), 45–49.

24. "Meeting at the Chamber of Commerce: A Public Meeting to be Held in Union-Square on Saturday," *New York Times* (April 18, 1861).

25. "Meeting at the Chamber of Commerce," *New York Times*.

26. On the use of public spaces for political rallies in nineteenth-century New York City, see Ryan, *Civic Wars*, 94–131.

27. Phyllis F. Field, *The Politics of Race in New York: The Struggle for Black Suffrage in the Civil War Era* (Ithaca, NY: Cornell University Press, 1982).

28. "Republican Mass Meeting in Union Square. Speech of Anson Burlingame of Massachusetts," *New York Herald* (September 25, 1856), 8.

29. "Fillmore Mass Meeting in Union Square: Bonfires, Electric Lights and other Appliances," *New York Herald* (October 22, 1856), 1.

30. "Political Movements: The Houston Mass Meeting; Large Gathering of the People in Union-Square; Washington Statue Illuminated; The Hero of San Jacinto Nominated for the Presidency; Speeches, Address, Resolutions, Music, Fireworks, Guns, and Fun," *New York Times* (May 30, 1860). "Houston Meeting in Union Square," *New York Post* (May 30, 1860).

31. "The Great Mass Meeting in Union Square," *New York Times* (April 20, 1861), 1.

32. *The Union Defense Committee of the City of New York: Minutes, Reports, and Correspondence* (New York: Union Defense Committee, 1885), 5. See also Martha J. Lamb and Burton Harrison, *History of the City of New York: Its Origin, Rise, and Progress*, vol. 3 (New York: A. S. Barnes and Co., 1896), 773–74.

33. "New York for the Union. Great Mass Meeting in Union Square. Largest Gathering Ever Held," *New York Post* (April 22, 1861), 4.

34. This telegram is known as "Dix's American Flag Dispatch." See Morgan Dix, *Memoirs of John Adams Dix* (New York: Harper and Brothers, 1883), 371–75; and David Work, *Lincoln's Political Generals* (Urbana: University of Illinois Press, 2009), 16.

35. "New York to the Rescue," *New York Times* (April 21, 1861); David S. Coddington, *Addresses at the Monster Meeting in Union Square Urging a Union of All Parties for the Union* (New York, 1861).

36. Baker was killed six months later at the Battle of Ball's Bluff in October 1861.

37. Spann, *Gotham at War*, 6. See also Jerome Mushkat, *Fernando Wood: A Political Biography* (Kent, OH: Kent State University Press, 1990), 112.

38. "The Union Forever!" *New York Times* (April 21, 1861).

39. On the Union Defense Committee, see *Reports and Documents of the Union Defense Committee of the Citizens of New York* (Board of Aldermen, September 9, 1861); J. A. Stevens, *The Union Defense Committee of the City of New York* (New York, 1885); John Perry Pritchett, Frances Katzman, and Howard Dellon, "The Union Defense Committee of the City of New York During the Civil War," *New York Historical Society Quarterly* 30 (1946): 142–60; McKay, *Civil War and New York City*, 63, 84; and Sven Beckert, *The Monied Metropolis: New York City and the Consolidation of the American Bourgeoisie 1850–96* (Cambridge: Cambridge University Press, 1993), 116.

40. "The Great Meeting in Union Square, New York, to Support the Government, April 20, 1861," *Harper's Weekly: A Journal of Civilization* (May 4, 1861). "The 'Union' Mass Meeting Held in Union Square, New York on the 20th of April," *Illustrated London News* (May 18, 1861).

41. Spann, *Gotham at War*, 59.

42. *Proceedings at the Mass Meeting of Loyal Citizens on Union Square, New York, 15th Day of July 1862* (New York: George F. Nesbitt, 1862), 19. "The Loyal Meeting; Thirty Thousand Unionists in Council. Union Square Packed with Patriotic Enthusiasts," *New York Times* (July 16, 1862); "Our Great War Meeting. The Voice of New York: Immense Popular Demonstration. Union Square Overflowing," *New York Post* (June 15, 1862), 3.

43. "General Appearance; The Processions at the Everett House; The Stands," *New York Times* (July 16, 1862).

44. "Sumter Anniversary. Great National Demonstration on Union Square," *New York Herald* (April 12, 1863); The Great Meeting Today," *New York Evening Post* (April 11, 1863); "Sumter Anniversary," *New York Herald* (April 12, 1863); "Loyal Mass Meeting," *New York Times* (12 April 1863); "The Meeting of Saturday," *New York Evening Post* (April 13, 1863); "The Sumter Meeting," *New York Tribune* (April 13, 1863).

45. *The Sumter Anniversary 1863. Opinions of Loyalists Concerning the Great Questions of the Times, . . . Brief Report of Proceedings at the Great Inaugural Mass Meeting of the Loyal National League, in Union Square, New York, on the Anniversary of Sumter, April 11th, 1863* (New York: Loyal National League of the State of New York, 1863), 88.

46. Shapiro, "Becoming Union Square," 89–91.

47. On the activities of the Union League Club during the Civil War, see Henry Whitney Bellows, *Historical Sketch of the Union League Club of New York, Its Origin, Organization and Work 1863–79* (New York: Union League Club, 1879), 176–80; and Will Irwin, Earl Chapin May, and Joseph Hotchkiss, *A History of the Union League Club of New York City* (New York: Dodd, Mead and Co., 1952), 9–50.

48. On the culture of these restaurants, see Cindy R. Lobel, "'Out to Eat': The Emergence and Evolution of the Restaurant in Nineteenth-Century New York City," *Winterthur Portfolio* 44, nos. 2–3 (Summer/Autumn 2010): 193–220; and Cindy R. Lobel, *Urban Appetites: Food and Culture in Nineteenth-Century New York* (Chicago: University of Chicago Press, 2014).

49. Bellows, *Historical Sketch*, 53.

50. Bellows, *Historical Sketch*, 176.

51. Shapiro, "Becoming Union Square," 94.

52. On the draft riots, see Iver Bernstein, *The New York City Draft Riots: Their Significance for American Society and Politics in the Age of Civil War* (New York: Oxford University Press, 1990), 67–68; and Spann, *Gotham at War*, 129–31.

53. "The Mob in New York," *New York Times* (July 14, 1863); Leslie M. Harris, *In the Shadow of Slavery: African Americans in New York City 1626–1863* (Chicago: University of Chicago Press), 279–88.

54. Scobey, *Empire City*, 151.

55. Though this group never saw action, it continued to meet regularly until 1865. *Articles of Association of the Stuyvesant Square Home Guard and Rules for Its Government, Its Officers and Members* (New York: Wynkoop, Hallenbeck and Thomas, 1864); Robert Hendry Kelby, *Memoirs of Colonel Andrew Warner* (New York: New-York Historical Society, 1915), 13–14.

56. Frederick Law Olmsted, *The Papers of Frederick Law Olmsted Vol 4. Defending the*

Union: The Civil War and the U.S. Commission, ed. Jane T. Censer (Baltimore, MD: Johns Hopkins University Press, 1986), 15.

57. "The Twentieth U.S. Colored Regiment," *Harper's Weekly* (March 19, 1864), 178.

58. Irwin, *A History of the Union League Club of New York City*, 33–34.

59. *New York Tribune* (March 7, 1864); *New York Herald* (March 9, 1864).

60. McKay, *Civil War and New York City*, 240–43; Spann, *Gotham at War*, 80–81; Shapiro, "Becoming Union Square," 99–100.

61. On the role of women in organizing these kind of civic events, see Beverly Gordon, *Bazaars and Fair Ladies: The History of the American Fundraising Fair* (Knoxville: University of Tennessee Press, 1998), 59–94; and Lisa Tendrich Frank, ed., *Women in the American Civil War*, vol. 1 (Santa Barbara, CA: ABC-CLIO, 2008), 293–95.

62. *New York Herald* (April 4, 1864).

63. *Metropolitan Fair, in Aid of the United States Sanitary Commission* (New York: Charles O. Jones, 1864); "Metropolitan Fair—Grand Opening Yesterday," *New York Times* (April 5, 1864); "The Metropolitan Fair Buildings," *Harper's Weekly* 8, no. 380 (April 9, 1864): 228.

64. "The Metropolitan Sanitary Fair the Branch Establishment on Union Square: The Knickerbocker Kitchen Etc," *New York Herald* (March 16, 1864), 5. *Harper's Weekly* (April 9 and 16, 1864), 228, 246; US Sanitary Commission, *Record of the Metropolitan Fair* (New York, 1867), 12–13.

65. *National Celebration of Union Victories, Grand Military and Civic Procession. Mass Meeting at Union Square, March 6th, 1865* (New York: G. F. Nesbitt and Co., 1865), 6.

66. *National Celebration of Union Victories*, 37.

67. *New York Herald* (April 25, 1865); *Obsequies of Abraham Lincoln in Union Square, New York, April 25, 1865* (New York: The Citizens' Committee, New York, 1865); George Bancroft, *Oration Pronounced in Union Square, April 25 1865 at the Funeral Obsequies of Abraham Lincoln* (New York: Schermerhorn, Bancroft and Co, 1865).

68. *Appleton's Journal* 4, no. 81 (1870): 475; "Lincoln's Statue, Union Square, New York," *Journal of American History* (Jan–March 1917), 126; "Lincoln Statue, Union Square Park, New York City," *Journal of American History* (Jan–March 1921): 18.

69. "Board of Aldermen," *New York Times* (May 2, 1865); "The Lincoln Monument," *New York Times* (April 27, 1865); "The Lincoln Statue: The Work of Art Placed in Position in Union Square; How it Looks," *New York Times* (September 17, 1870), 2; "A Memorial in Bronze: 'Honor to the Noble Dead'; Erection of Lincoln's Statue in Union Square Yesterday," *New York Herald* (September 17, 1870), 5.

70. "Fine Arts the Lincoln Statue on Union Square," *New York Tribune* (October 1, 1870), 12.

71. On issues of race in Civil War commemorative statuary, see Kirk Savage, "The Politics of Memory: Black Emancipation and the Civil War Monument," in *Commemorations: The Politics of National Identity*, ed. J. R. Gillis (Princeton, NJ: Princeton University Press, 1994); and Kirk Savage, *Standing Soldiers, Kneeling Slaves: Race, War, and Monument in Nineteenth-Century America* (Princeton, NJ: Princeton University Press, 1997).

72. *Appleton's Journal* 4., no. 81 (1870): 475.

73. "New York and Vicinity," *The Independent*, no. 28 (September 14, 1876), 15.

74. Savage, *Standing Soldiers, Kneeling Slaves*, 7.

75. See, for example, "The Procession in New-York and at Cypress Hills," *New York Times* (May 31, 1873); "Ceremonies in Union Square," *New York Times* (May 31, 1877); Shapiro, "Becoming Union Square," 160.

76. "Ceremonies at Union Square: Oratory by Mr. Frederick Douglass," *New York Times* (May 31, 1878).

77. Ruggles, *Union Square and the Sanitary Commission*, 8.

78. Ruggles, *Union Square and the Sanitary Commission*, 10.

79. Ruggles, *Union Square and the Sanitary Commission*, 11.

80. Ruggles, *Union Square and the Sanitary Commission*, 11.

Chapter Three

1. "Local Intelligence: The Uptown Movement," *New York Times* (August 20, 1867), 6.

2. This confection was registered with the US Patent Office in 1876. *Official Gazette of the United States Patent Office*, vol. 9 (Washington, DC: Government Printing Office, 1876), 1020.

3. Bird, *The Englishwoman in America*, 361.

4. "Concentration of the Retail Trade at Union Square," *New York Times* (November 21, 1867), 2.

5. Kramer, "Contemporary Descriptions of New York City and Its Public Architecture ca. 1850," 264–80.

6. Henry James, *Washington Square* (New York: Harper and Brothers, 1881), 24.

7. Bristed, *The Upper Ten Thousand*, 17.

8. Burrows and Wallace, *Gotham*, 970.

9. Junius Henri Brown, *The Great Metropolis: A Mirror of New York* (New York: Hartford, 1869), 205.

10. William H, Rideing, "Life on Broadway," *Harper's New Monthly Magazine* 56, no. 332 (January 1878): 243.

11. "The Fenians: The Headquarters on Union Square the Moffat Mansion Occupied by the Fenian Men," *New York Herald* (November 18, 1865); "The Capital of Ireland in Union Square: The Fenian Fizzle," *New York Herald* (January 2, 1866); "The F.B.: Fenian Burlesque," *New York Times* (January 5, 1866). On the Fenian Brotherhood in New York City, see Burrows and Wallace, *Gotham*, 1005; Eileen Reilly, "Modern Ireland: An Introductory Survey," in *Making the Irish American: History and Heritage of the Irish in the United States*, ed. Joseph J. Lee and Marion R. Case (New York: New York University Press, 2006), 96–100; and Shapiro, "Becoming Union Square," 119–22.

12. "The Fenians: Mass Meeting at Union Square," *New York Tribune* (June 26, 1866), 8.

13. Alexander Somerville, *Narrative of the Fenian Invasion of Canada* (New York: A. Lawson, 1866); Hereward Senior, *The Last Invasion of Canada: The Fenian Raids, 1866–70* (Toronto: Dundurn Press, 1991); and Peter Vronsky, *Ridgeway: The American Fenian Invasion and the 1866 Battle that Made Canada* (Toronto: Penguin, 2011).

14. "Fenian Demonstration," *New York Times* (March 14, 1867).

15. James D. McCabe, *Lights and Shadows of New York* (New York: Fabar, Strauss and Giroux, 1970), 486; Burrows and Wallace, *Gotham*, 995.

16. Shapiro, "Becoming Union Square," 129.

17. On the A. T. Stewart and Company and other mid-nineteenth-century department stores in New York City see Winston Weisman, "Commercial Palaces of New York, 1845–75," *Art Bulletin* 36, no. 4 (1954), 285–302; Jay E. Cantor, "A Monument of Trade: A. T. Stewart, and the Rise of the Millionaire's Mansion in New York," *Winterthur Portfolio* 19 (1975): 155–97; M. Christine Boyer, "Ladies Mile: The Rise of a Victorian Amusement District," in *Manhattan Manners: Architecture and Style 1850–1900* (New York; Random House,

1985), 43–129; and Mona Domosh, "Creating New York City's Retail District," *Invented Cities: The Creation of Landscape in Nineteenth-Century New York and Boston* (New Haven, CT: Yale University Press, 1996), 35–64.

18. Cantor, "Monument of Trade," 168.

19. The ironwork in the Stewart store was by John B. Cornell: "Men Who Have Assisted in the Development of Architectural Resources: No. 1, John B. Cornell," *Architectural Record* 1, no. 2 (Oct–Dec 1891): 245. On early cast-iron commercial architecture in New York, see Daniel D. Badger, *Architectural Iron Works of New York: Illustrations of Iron Architecture* (New York: Daniel D. Badger, 1865); Leland Roth, *A Concise History of American Architecture* (New York: Harper and Row, 1979), 120–121; and Margot Gayle and Carol Gayle, *Cast-Iron Architecture in America: The Significance of James Bogardus* (New York: Norton 1998).

20. Schuyler quoted in Robert A. M. Stern, David Fishman, and Thomas Mellins, *New York 1880: Architecture and Urbanism in the Gilded Age* (New York: Monacelli, 2009), 708; Peter B. Wight, "A Millionaire's Architectural Investment," *American Architect and Building News* 1, no. 6 (May 1876): 148.

21. Stern et al., *New York 1880*, 709.

22. On later nineteenth-century strategies of store window display, see William Leach, "Strategists of Display and the Production of Desire," in *Consuming Visions: Accumulation and Display of Goods in America, 1889–1925*, ed. Simon J. Bronner (New York: Norton, 1989), 99–132.

23. "A Palace of Jewels: A Stroll through Tiffany's New Jewelry Store in Union Square," *New York Herald* (November 15, 1870). "Tiffany's New Iron Building in Union-Square: A Magnificent Structure," *New York Times* (December 8, 1868).

24. Again, Kellum's critic was Montgomery Schuyler. Stern, *New York 1880*, 711.

25. Though the building still stands, the cast-iron ornament does not. In 1952 a piece fell off the building killing a passing pedestrian. This tragic accident led the building's owner, the Amalgamated Bank, to strip the facade of its ornament and cover the iron structure with white brick. Later the white brick was stripped away and replaced by a glass curtain wall designed by the French architect Jean Nouvel. John Hill, *Guide to Contemporary New York City Architecture* (New York: Norton, 2010), 92.

26. "New Buildings in Union-Square—Decker Bros. Piano Ware-Rooms—Tiffany's Building," *New York Times* (March 27, 1870); M. Christine Boyer provides maps of the piano and sewing machine showrooms around Union Square in *Manhattan Manners*, 75, 109.

27. The Steinway and Sons piano factory was located between Fifty-Second and Fifty-Third Streets, and Fourth and Lexington Avenues. Thomas Lloyd, *Lloyd's Pocket Companion and Guide through New York City, for 1866–67* (1865), 51–52.

28. Kathryn E. Holliday, *Leopold Eidlitz: Architecture and Idealism in the Gilded Age* (New York: Norton, 2008), 109–10.

29. McCabe, *Lights and Shadows of New York*, 129.

30. James Parton, "A History of the Sewing Machine," *Atlantic Monthly* 19, no. 115 (May 1867): 527–45.

31. *History and Commerce of New York 1891* (New York: American Publishing and Engraving Co, 1891), 98–99.

32. "An Ornament to Union-Square: The Domestic Sewing-Machine Company," *New York Tribune* (June 25, 1873); "Fall Opening of the Domestic Sewing Machine Company," *New York Times* (December 18, 1873).

33. Mrs. Schuyler van Rensselaer, "Recent Architecture in America, no. III. Commercial Buildings," *The Century* 8, no. 4 (August 1884): 511.

34. On the Rialto, see "New York Theaters," *Atlantic Monthly* 43, no. 258 (April 1879): 452–68; "New York Theaters," *Atlantic Monthly* 47, no. 281 (March 1881): 362–71; and John Warren Frick, "The Rialto: A Study of Union Square, The Center of New York's First Theater District, 1870–1900," New York University, 1983; and Boyer, *Manhattan Manners*, 62–73.

35. McCabe, *Lights and Shadows of New York*, 470. This author estimated that together the New York City theaters earned about thirty thousand dollars per night,

36. Burrows and Wallace, *Gotham*, 761–66. See also Nigel Cliff, *The Shakespeare Riots: Revenge, Drama, and Death in Nineteenth-Century America* (New York: Random House, 2007).

37. McCabe, *Lights and Shadows of New York*, 604.

38. Ronald Ratcliffe, *Steinway* (New York: Chronicle, 1989).

39. *Harper's Weekly* 11, no. 574 (December 28, 1867): 829.

40. Irving Hall was on Irving Place between Fourteenth and Fifteenth Streets. Located on Fifteenth Street behind the Academy of Music, Nilsson Hall often cohosted events with the Academy of Music. "The New Union-Square Theater: Description of the Structure," *New York Times* (August 6, 1871). Stern, *New York 1880*, 665.

41. "The Hippotheairon" [sic] *New York Times* (February 6, 1864); "The Hippotheatron" *New York Times* (March 24, 1864); "Hippotheatron" *New York Times* (December 29, 1864). See also, Frick, "The Rialto," 201–7; Boyer, *Manhattan Manners*, 70.

42. Bird, *The Englishwoman in America*, 352. On the history of oyster bars and oyster consumption in nineteenth century New York, see Mark Kurlansky, *The Big Oyster: History on the Half Shell* (New York: Random House, 2007).

43. Rideing, "Life on Broadway," 234.

44. McCabe, *Lights and Shadows of New York*, 803.

45. On the numerous houses of prostitution located around Union Square in the late nineteenth century, see Timothy J. Gilfoyle, *City of Eros: New York City, Prostitution, and the Commercialization of Sex 1790–1920* (New York: Norton, 1992), 210–12, 287.

46. Brown, *Valentine's Manual of Old New York*, 122.

47. George De Forest Barton, "Union Square," in *Valentine's Manual of Old New York*, 194–95. Barton was describing Union Square as it appeared in his youth.

48. On the philosophy and social aims behind the creation of Central Park, see Ross L. Miller, "The Landscaper's Utopia Versus the City: A Mismatch," *New England Quarterly* 49, no. 2 (June 1976): 179–93; Ian R. Stewart, "Politics and the Park," *New York Historical Society Quarterly* 61, nos. 3–4 (July–October 1977): 124–55; David Schuyler, "Cities and Parks: The Lessons of Central Park," in *The New Urban Landscape: The Redefinition of City Form in Nineteenth-Century America* (Baltimore, MD: Johns Hopkins University Press, 1986), 101–25; Melvin Kalfus, "A Philosophy of Urban Landscape Design," in *Frederick Law Olmsted: The Passion of a Public Artist* (New York: New York University Press, 1990), 277–96; Roy Rosenzweig and Elizabeth Blackmar, *The Park and the People: A History of Central Park* (New York: Henry Holt and Co., 1992), 95–120, 121–49; and Matthew Gandy, "Symbolic Order and the Urban Pastoral," in *Concrete and Clay*, 77–114.

49. Andrew Jackson Downing, "The New York Park" (1851) in *Rural Essays*, ed. George W. Curtis (New York: G. P. Putnam, 1853), 152.

50. Andrew Jackson Downing, "A Talk about Public Parks and Gardens" (1848), in *Rural Essays*, ed. George W. Curtis (New York: G. P. Putnam, 1853), 141. Galen Cranz dis-

cusses the political motivations of successive generations of park designers in America in *The Politics of Park Design: A History of Urban Parks in America* (Cambridge, MA: MIT Press, 1982).

51. Downing, "The New York Park," 147.

52. On the Tammany Democrats' nineteen-month control of the city, under the direction of Tweed, and his fall from power, see Burrows and Wallace, *Gotham*, 927–29, 1002–17.

53. On the Tweed-era Department of Public Parks, see *The Papers of Frederick Law Olmsted Vol. 6 The Years of Olmsted, Vaux and Company 1865–74*, ed. David Schuyler and Jane Turner Censer (Baltimore, MD: Johns Hopkins University Press, 1992), 1–45; Rosenzweig and Blackmar, *The Park and the People*, 263–73; Shapiro, "Becoming Union Square," 133–37.

54. See for example; "The Public Parks," *New York Times* (September 4, 1871); "Some Reasons for Reform," *New York Times* (October 4, 1871); "The Public Parks: Expenditures at the Rate of $600,000 Per Year for their Care and Maintenance," *New York Times* (October 19, 1871).

55. "The Public Parks: Outrageous Extravagance of Hilton's Designs," *New York Times* (August 11, 1871).

56. "The Escape of the Central Park," *New York Times* (November 15, 1871).

57. *First Annual Report of the Board of Commissioners of the Department of Public Parks for the Year Ending May 1st 1871* (New York: William C. Bryant and Co., 1871), 43–44, 50.

58. "Our City Squares," *The Round Table: A Saturday Review of Politics, Finance, Literature, Society and Art*, vol. 5 (June 22, 1867), 390.

59. "Parks, Places and Squares," *New York Times* (December 22, 1871).

60. "A Word with Judge Hilton," *New York Times* (July 29, 1871).

61. *First Annual Report of the Board of Commissioners of Public Parks for the Year Ending May 1st 1871*, 387, 411.

62. On the divisive and violent Orange Parades, see Burrows and Wallace, *Gotham*, 1003–17; Mary Ryan, *Civic Wars*, 229–34; and Lisa Keller, *Triumph of Order*, 161–67.

63. On the anti-Tweed campaign, see Burrows and Wallace, *Gotham*, 987–1017; and Mary Ryan, *Civic Wars*, 271–81.

64. "Sale of the Iron Railing at Union Square," *New York Times* (September 10, 1871). The *Times* noted that Hilton's close friend, the department store magnate Alexander T. Stewart had accompanied him to the auction. After his ouster from city government, Hilton would make counseling Stewart his life's work. Harry E. Reeseguie, "The Decline and Fall of the Commercial Empire of A. T. Stewart," *Business History Review* 36, no. 3 (Autumn 1962): 255–86.

65. On the work of Olmsted and Vaux in this period, see *The Papers of Frederick Law Olmsted Vol. 6*, 1–45.

66. See for example Kalfus, "A Philosophy of Urban Landscape Design," 281.

67. Frederick Law Olmsted, "Public Parks and the Enlargement of Towns" (1870), in *America Builds: Source Documents in American Architecture and Planning*, ed. Leland M. Roth (New York: Harper and Row, 1983), 187.

68. This letter is reprinted in *The Papers of Frederick Law Olmsted Vol. 6*, 531–37.

69. *Minutes of the Commissioners of the Department of Public Parks, 1871*. Document 35 (New York, 1872), 2. New York City Department of Parks and Recreation Library, New York.

70. *Third General Report of the Board of Commissioners of the Department of Public Parks for the Period of Twenty Months, from May 1st, 1872 to December 31st 1873* (New York: William C.

Bryant and Co., 1875), 18. New York City Department of Parks and Recreation Library, New York. See also "The New Union-Square," *New York Tribune* (November 14, 1872), 2.

71. *Third General Report of the Board of Commissioners of the Department of Public Parks for the Period of Twenty Months, from May 1st, 1872 to December 31st 1873*, 18.

72. "City Intelligence: 'The Cottage'; An Improvement in Union Square. Ornamental and Useful," *Commercial Advertiser* (November 8, 1872), 3.

73. "Oxyhydrogen Street Lamps," *Scientific American* 27, no. 4 (July 27, 1872), 55–56.

74. Ballon, *The Greatest Grid*, 104.

75. Bird, *The Englishwoman in America*, 384.

76. On the architecture of nineteenth-century New York City armories, see Robert Koch, "The Medieval Castle Revival: New York Armories," *Journal of the Society of Architectural Historians* 14, no. 3 (October 1955): 23–29; Fred L. Israel, "New York's Citizen Soldiers: The Militia and Their Armories," *New York History* 42, no. 2 (April 1961): 145–56; and Robert M. Fogelson, *America's Armories: Architecture, Society and Public Order* (Cambridge, MA: Harvard University Press, 1989).

77. Burrows and Wallace, *Gotham*, 1002–5.

78. "The Public Parks," *New York Times* (May 21, 1870).

79. E. Porter Belden, *New-York: Past, Present and Future* (New York: G.P. Putnam, 1849), 33.

80. On the Brooklyn Park system and Olmsted and Vaux's work there, see Donald Simon, "The Public Park Movement in Brooklyn, 1824–1873," New York University, 1972; Bluestone, "From Promenade to Park," 529–50; *The Papers of Frederick Law Olmsted Vol. 6*, 19–27.

81. Olmsted, "Public Parks and the Enlargement of Towns," 187.

82. Deborah S. Gardner, "Tompkins Square: Past and Present," *Journal of American History* 77, no. 1 (June 1990): 232–38.

83. The site is bounded by Myrtle Avenue, Cumberland Street, Dekalb Avenue, and Canton Street (now Edwards Street). On its early history, see Henry R. Stiles, *A History of the City of Brooklyn*, 3 vols. (Brooklyn, 1867–70), 3: 615–17. On Olmsted and Vaux's design for Washington Park, see Francis R. Kowsky, *Country, Park and City: The Architecture and Life of Calvert Vaux* (New York: Oxford University Press, 2003), 195–96. On the place of Washington Park within the larger Brooklyn Park system, see Bluestone, "From Promenade to Park."

84. "Report Accompanying a Design for Washington Park" (1867), in *The Papers of Frederick Law Olmsted Vol. 6*, 204.

85. "Report Accompanying a Design for Washington Park" (1867), 204.

86. "The Prison-Ship Martyrs: Removal of their Remains to Washington Park," *New York Times* (June 19, 1873). In 1908 a much larger monument, a gargantuan Doric column designed by architects McKim, Mead, and White, replaced it. "For Ship Martyrs' Bones; Being Put in the New Vault Under the Monument in Brooklyn," *New York Times* (September 16, 1908); "Taft and Hughes at Martyrs' Shaft," *New York Times* (November 15, 1908).

87. "Report Accompanying a Design for Washington Park" (1867), in *The Papers of Frederick Law Olmsted Vol. 6*, 205.

88. "Report Accompanying a Design for Washington Park," 204–5.

89. "Union Square," *New York Times* (August 10, 1873), 3; "Our Public Squares," *New York Times* (August 18, 1873), 4. When it was finally finished at the end of 1873, the Parks Department reported that the total cost of the improvements was forty-two thousand dollars. *Third General Report of the Board of Commissioners of the Department of Public Parks*

for the Period of Twenty Months, from May 1st, 1872 to December 31st 1873 (New York: William C. Bryant and Co., 1875), 31, 56.

90. *New York Times* (May 31, 1878).

Chapter Four

1. "The New Review Ground. Inauguration of Union Square Plaza as a National Guard Rendezvous," *New York Herald* (April 10, 1873).

2. "The Division Parade. Inauguration of the New Grand Plaza at Union Square," *New York Herald* (June 4, 1873).

3. "The Movement Uptown," *New York Herald* (June 2, 1873).

4. *Minutes of Proceedings of the Board of Commissioners of the Department of Public Parks for the Year Ending April 30th, 1874* (New York: Evening Post Steam Presses, 1874), 639–40; Shapiro, "Becoming Union Square," 159.

5. Michael Frisch and Daniel J. Walkowitz make this point about the geography of labor in nineteenth-century New York City in *Working Class America: Essays on Labor, Community, and American Society*, ed. Michael Frisch and Daniel J. Walkowitz (Urbana: University of Illinois Press, 1983), xiii.

6. Edward Ewing Pratt, *Industrial Causes of Congestion of Population in New York City* (New York: Columbia University Press, 1911), 118–19.

7. Kenneth T. Jackson, "The Capital of Capitalism: The New York Metropolitan Region, 1890–1940," in *Metropolis 1890–1940*, ed. Anthony Sutcliffe (Chicago: University of Chicago Press, 1984), 328.

8. Sean Wilentz, "Artisanal Republican Festivals and the Rise of Class Conflict in New York City, 1788–1837," in *Working Class America*, ed. Frisch and Walkowitz, 41.

9. On the sweating system, see United States Congress House Committee on Manufactures, *Report of the Committee on the Manufactures on the Sweating System* (1892); Florence Kelley, "The Sweating System," in *Hull House Maps and Papers*, ed. Jane Addams (New York: Thomas Y. Crowell and Co., 1895), 27–45; Jesse Eliphalet Pope, *The Clothing Industry in New York* (Columbia: University of Missouri Press, 1905); Helen L. Sumner, "History of Women in Industry in the United States," *Senate Report on Conditions of Women and Child Wage-Earners in the United States*, vol. 9 (S. Doc. 645, 61st Congress, second session, Washington, DC, 1910); Moses Rischin, *The Promised City: New York's Jews 1870–1914* (Cambridge, MA: MIT Press, 1966), 51–75; Christine Stansell, "The Origins of the Sweatshop: Women and Early Industrialization in New York City," in *Working Class America*, ed. Frisch and Walkowitz, 78–103; and Heather J. Griggs, "'By Virtue of Reason and Nature': Competition and Economic Strategy in the Needletrades at New York's Five Points, 1855–1880," *Historical Archaeology* 35, no. 3 (2001): 76–88.

10. Russell Sturgis, *Sturgis' Illustrated Dictionary of Architecture and Building: An Unabridged*, vol. 2 (New York: Dover, 1989), 782. See also "Loft Buildings," *Architect's and Builder's Magazine* (February 1908), 270–284.

11. On the history of the industrial loft in the United States, see Robert Bruegmann, "Theme and Variation: The Loft Building," in *The Architects and the City: Holabird and Roche of Chicago 1880–1918* (Chicago IL: University of Chicago Press, 1997), 207–17; and Betsy H. Bradley, *The Works: The Industrial Architecture of the United States* (New York: Oxford University Press, 1999), 29–34. On the architecture of New York City's garment district, see New York Landmarks Commission, "SoHo Cast Iron District Designation Report" (1973); and Margot Gayle and Edmund V. Gillon Jr., *Cast-Iron Architecture in New York* (New York: Dover, 1974).

12. Nancy Fraser describes the concept in "Rethinking the Public Sphere: A Contribution to the Critique of Actually Existing Democracy," *Social Text* nos. 25–26 (1990), 56–80.

13. On the eight-hour movement in nineteenth-century America, see Daniel T. Rodgers, *The Work Ethic in Industrial America, 1850–1920* (Chicago IL: University of Chicago Press, 1974); Leon Fink, *Workingmen's Democracy: The Knights of Labor and American Politics* (Urbana: University of Illinois Press, 1983); Roy Rosenzweig, *Eight Hours for What We Will: Workers and Leisure in an Industrial City, 1870–1920* (New York: Cambridge University Press, 1984); David R. Roediger and Philip S. Foner, *Our Own Time: A History of American Labor and the Working Day* (New York: Greenwood, 1989); and Bruce Laurie, *Artisans into Workers: Labor in Nineteenth-Century America* (New York: Noonday Press, 1989). A more general history of the relations between capital and labor in this period is given in Alan Trachtenberg, "Capital and Labor," in *The Incorporation of America: Culture and Society in the Gilded Age* (New York: Hill and Wang, 1982), 70–100.

14. Ryan, *Civic Wars*, 224.

15. Burrows and Wallace, "The Leeches Must Go!," in *Gotham*, 1089–1103.

16. "The Workingmen: Mass Meetings in Union Square and at the City Hall; The Fight to Continue," *New York Herald* (May 28, 1872).

17. "The Workingmen," *New York Herald*.

18. "Meeting of the Corporation Laborers in Union Square," *New York Times* (May 28, 1872).

19. "Progress of the Strikes Opposing Action of the Piano Manufacturers and Their Men," *New York Times* (June 2, 1872); "The Labor Issue; Efforts Being Made for a General Combination of the Strikers. The Great Procession of Monday: Arrangements for all the Trades to Parade-Police Preparations; The Meetings Last Night," *New York Times* (June 9, 1872).

20. "End of the Eight Hour Strike," *Scientific American* (July 27, 1872), 56.

21. Samuel Bernstein, "American Labor in the Long Depression, 1873–1878," *Science and Society* 20, no. 1 (Winter 1956): 59–64.

22. "The Working Men: The Proposed Parade To-Day; The Committee of Safety Endeavoring to Excite a Disturbance; Extensive Police Preparations," *New York Times* (January 13, 1874).

23. "The Unemployed Workingmen," *New York Times* (January 6, 1874). "A Mass Meeting of Workingmen," *New York Times* (January 4, 1874); "Laborers Crying for Work," *New York Daily Tribune* (January 6, 1874); "Workingmen in Council: Adjourned from Union Square to Tompkins Square," *Commercial Advertiser* (January 8, 1874).

24. "The Working Men," *New York Times*.

25. "Defeat of the Communists: The Mass-Meeting and Parade Broken Up; Encounter between the Mob and the Police; Arrest of Rioters; The 'Committee of Safety' before the Mayor; The Rioters in Court," *New York Times* (January 14, 1874).

26. Samuel Bernstein, "The Impact of the Paris Commune in the United States," *Massachusetts Review* 12, no. 3 (1971): 435–46.

27. Lisa Keller, "The Battle over Tompkins Square," in *Triumph of Order*, 180.

28. "The Right of Public Assemblage," *New York Times* (July 27, 1877).

29. "A Flag of Honor for the Police," *New York Times* (July 15, 1872); "City Intelligence: The Police Flag Presentation; The Ceremonies at Union Square This Afternoon," *Commercial Advertiser* (November 25, 1872).

30. "Lafayette at Union Square," *Commercial Advertiser* (September 4, 1876); "The Lafayette Statue: Imposing Inauguration Ceremonies at Union Square," *New York Herald* (September 7, 1876).

31. "Fine Arts: The James Drinking Fountain in Union Square," *New York Herald* (October 25, 1881). *The James Fountain: The Proceedings at the Presentation. Union Square, New York. Tuesday, October 25, 1881* (New York: Anson D. F. Randolph and Company, 1881).

32. "The James Fountain, Union Square: Commissioner Lane's Address. Address of Mr. D. Willis James," *New York Evangelist* (1830–1902) 52, no. 44 (November 3, 1881), 7; "The Fine Arts: The Union Square Drinking Fountain," *The Critic* (1881–83) 1 no. 23 (November 19, 1881), 324.

33. "Editor's Table," *Appleton's Journal* 14 (September 11, 1875): 340–41. Quoted in Julia Rowland Myers, "J. Alden Weir's Essay On 'Modern Life': In the Park of 1879," *American Art Journal* 34–35 (2003–2004): 144–85. See also "Why They Won't Work," *New York Times* (August 18, 1874); "Bummers," *New York Times* (June 21, 1875).

34. "War on Loungers in the Park," *New York Times* (June 18, 1877).

35. "The Murder in Union Square," *New York Times* (July 6, 1876); "Highway Robbery in Union Square," *New York Times* (August 8, 1876); and "A Bold Robbery in Union Square," *New York Times* (April 8, 1877).

36. "A Man and a Brother," *New York Times* (August 24, 1877).

37. On the civil unrest of 1877, see Robert V. Bruce, *1877: Year of Violence* (Chicago: Quadrangle, 1970); Philip S. Foner, *The Great Labor Uprising of 1877* (New York: Monad Press, 1977); Nell Irvin Painter, *Standing at Armageddon: The United States, 1877–1919* (New York: Norton and Co., 1987); David O. Stowell, ed., *The Great Strikes of 1877* (Urbana: University of Illinois Press, 2008); and Michael A. Bellesiles, *1877: America's Year of Living Violently* (New York: New Press, 2010).

38. On Kearney and his national public speaking tour, see Burrows and Wallace, *Gotham*, 1128; Kevin Starr, *Endangered Dreams: The Great Depression in California* (New York: Oxford University Press, 1996), 9–19; Ryan, *Civic Wars*, 285–92; Andrew Gyory, *Closing the Gate: Race, Politics, and the Chinese Exclusion Act* (Chapel Hill: University of North Carolina Press, 1998), 97–194; and John Soennichsen, *The Chinese Exclusion Act of 1882* (Santa Barbara, CA: Greenwood, 2011), 51–59.

39. "Kearney in New York: The Sand Lot Orator to Appear in Union Square," *New York Herald* (September 5, 1878).

40. "Kearney in Union Square: An Assemblage of Thousands," *New York Tribune* (September 7, 1878).

41. "Kearney in Union Square," *New York Tribune.*

42. "Kearney in Union Square," *New York Tribune.*

43. On the 5th September 1882 Labor Day parade, see Estelle M. Stewart, "Origin and Significance of Labor Day," *Monthly Labor Review* 43 (August 1936): 279–84; Jonathan Grossman, "Who Is the Father of Labor Day?" *Monthly Labor Review* 95 (September 1972): 3–6; Richard P. Hunt, "The First Labor Day," *American Heritage* 33 (Aug–Sept 1982), 109–22; United States Department of Labor, *Labor Day: How It Came About, What It Means* (Washington, DC, 1983); and Michael Kazin and Stephen J. Ross, "America's Labor Day: The Dilemma of a Worker's Celebration," *Journal of American History* 78, no. 4 (1992): 1294–1323.

44. *Appleton's Dictionary of New York and Vicinity: A Complete Guide to the City and Neighborhood* (New York: D. Appleton and Co., 1902), 144–46; Burrows and Wallace, *Gotham*, 1090–91; Shapiro, "Becoming Union Square," 168.

45. George Block, "The Central Labor Union and Politics," *Truth* (August 9, 1882); Matthew Maguire, "The Central Labor Union. An Address of Interest to All Labor Organizations," *Truth* (August 16, 1882).

46. Kazin and Ross, "America's Labor Day," 1296.

47. "Taking Political Action: What the Central Labor Union Has Decided to Do," *Truth* (August 7, 1882). "The Central Labor Union," *New York Herald* (August 14, 1882).

48. "Taking Political Action," *Truth.*

49. "Preparing for the Parade: A Circular Issued by the Central Labor Union," *Truth* (August 13, 1882).

50. "Preparing for the Parade," *Truth.*

51. Shapiro, "Becoming Union Square," 170.

52. "Preparing for the Parade: What Was Done by the Central Labor Union Yesterday," *Truth* (September 4, 1882).

53. On the Irish roots of the American Labor movement, see Michael A. Gordon, "The Labor Boycott in New York City, 1880–1886," in *American Working Class Culture: Explorations in American Labor and Social History*, ed. Milton Cantor (Westport, CT: Greenwood, 1979), 287–332; and Kevin Kenney, "Labor and Labor Organizations," in *Making the Irish American: History and Heritage of the Irish in the United States*, ed. Joseph J. Lee and Marion R. Case (New York: New York University Press, 2006), 354–63.

54. "Davitt and the Toilers: A Great Multitude on the Union Square Plaza; Labor in Ireland and America," *New York Herald* (July 6, 1882); "A Reception to Davitt; Trade and Labor Organizations in Union-Square," *New York Times* (July 6, 1882).

55. "Still Demanding More Pay: Open-Air Meeting of the Strikers; A Small Attendance in Union Square," *New York Tribune* (July 20, 1882); "Upholding the Strikers; Mass-Meeting of Labor Unions in Union-Square," *New York Times* (July 20, 1882).

56. "Labor's Dress Parade," *New York Herald* (September 6, 1882); "Laborers in Line," *New York Herald* (September 6, 1882); "Working Men on Parade," *New York Times* (September 6, 1882); "A Labor Demonstration," *New-York Daily Tribune* (September 7, 1882); "New York City: Grand Demonstration of Workingmen, September 5th; The Procession Passing the Reviewing Stand at Union Square," *Frank Leslie's Illustrated Newspaper* (September 16, 1882).

57. "A Great Demonstration," *Christian Index* 60, no. 6914 (September 1882), 11.

58. *The Irish World* (September 16, 1882).

59. *New York Tribune* (September 8, 1882).

60. On Henry George, his involvement with the labor movement in New York, and his 1886 mayoral campaign, see David Scobey, "Boycotting the Politics Factory: Labor Radicalism and the New York City Mayoral Election of 1886," *Radical History Review* 28–30 (September 1984): 287–95; Burrows and Wallace, "The Leeches Must Go!," *Gotham*, 1089–1103; Robert E. Weir, "A Fragile Alliance: Henry George and the Knights of Labor," *American Journal of Economics and Sociology* 56, no. 4 (1997): 421–39; and Edward T. O'Donnell, *Henry George and the Crisis of Inequality: Progress and Poverty in the Gilded Age* (New York: Columbia University Press, 2015).

61. Sean Wilentz, "Artisanal Republican Festivals and the Rise of Class Conflict in New York City, 1788–1837," in *Working Class America*, ed. Frisch and Walkowitz, 64. See also Burrows and Wallace, *Gotham*, 1098.

62. "Reviewed by Mr. George: His Supporters Parading in the Heavy Rain," *New York Times* (October 31, 1886). See also "George's Men with Torches. Twenty Thousand Brave the Rain for the Great Parade: Union Square's Weird Scene," *New York Herald* (October 31, 1886).

63. "Clubbed by the Police: Charging into a Crowd in Union-Square; A Misunderstanding Leading to a Promiscuous Attack on the Progressive Labor Party Meeting,"

New York Times (October 9, 1887); "Policemen's Clubs. They Break Up a Progressive Labor Party in New York," *Daily Alta California* (October 9, 1887). On the police practice of breaking up meetings by clubbing the participants, see Marilynn Johnson, *Street Justice: A History of Police Violence in New York City* (Boston: Beacon, 2003).

64. *Documents of the Senate of the State of New York, 114th Session, 1891, vol. 9, no. 80, part I* (Albany, NY, 1891), 543–44.

65. "Pitching into the Police: Henry George on the 'Outrage' in Union Square," *New York Herald* (October 10, 1887). "Henry George on the Police. He Denounces the Union Square Clubbing," *New York Tribune* (October 14, 1887).

66. *New York Tribune* (October 11, 1887).

67. "No Clubbing This Time: A Great Socialist Mass Meeting in Union Square Denounces the Police," *New York Herald* (October 18, 1887).

68. "No Clubbing This Time," *New York Herald.*

69. "No Clubbing This Time," *New York Herald.*

Chapter Five

1. Edmund Boisgilbert, MD (Ignatius Donnelly), *Caesar's Column: A Story of the Twentieth Century* (Chicago: F. J. Schulte and Co., 1890), 323–24. On Donnelley and other turn-of-the-century apocalyptic visions of New York City, see Max Page, *The City's End: Two Centuries of Fantasies, Fears, and Premonitions of New York's Destruction* (New Haven, CT: Yale University Press, 2008), 23–43; and Nick Yablon, *Untimely Ruins: An Archaeology of American Urban Modernity, 1819–1919* (Chicago: University of Chicago Press, 2009), 147–89.

2. Donnelly, *Caesar's Column*, 329.

3. Philip S. Foner, *May Day: A Short History of the International Workers Holiday, 1886–1986* (New York: International Publishers, 1986), 16. See also Donna T. Haverty-Stacke, *America's Forgotten Holiday: May Day and Nationalism, 1867–1960* (New York: New York University Press, 2009).

4. Foner, *May Day*, 17.

5. Foner, *May Day*, 19.

6. "Hurrah for Shorter Hours," *New York Sun* (May 2, 1886).

7. "New York Toilers in Line: A Great Workingmen's Demonstration in Union Square; Shorter Hours Demanded," *New York Herald* (May 2, 1886). On the strike, see "Strike of Sugar Refiners," *New York Times* (April 22, 1886).

8. "New York Toilers in Line," *New York Herald.*

9. "Socialists Hold a Big Meeting: Twenty Thousand of Them Crowd the Plaza of Union Square," *New York Herald* (May 2, 1894); "Thousands in May Day Parade," *New York Times* (May 2, 1894); "May Day Labor Demonstration: A Street Parade and Socialist Mass-Meeting at Union Square," *New York Tribune* (May 2, 1895); "Red Was Their Color: May Day Parade of Local Labor Organizations," *New York Times* (May 2, 1895). On the Socialist Labor Party, see Howard Quint, *The Forging of American Socialism: Origins of the Modern Movement: The Impact of Socialism on American Thought and Action 1886–1901* (Columbia: University of South Carolina Press, 1953); David A. Shannon, *The Socialist Party of America: A History* (Chicago: Quadrangle, 1967); Seán Cronin, "The Rise and Fall of the Socialist Labor Party of North America," *Saothar* 3 (1977): 21–33; and Frank Girard and Ben Perry, *Socialist Labor Party 1876–1991: A Short History* (Philadelphia: Livra Books, 1991).

10. "May Day Labor Demonstration: A Street Parade and Socialist Mass-Meeting at Union Square," *New York Tribune* (May 2, 1895).

11. "The Women of the Metropolis. Conclave of the Sisterhood in Union Square," *New York Herald* (November 26, 1870).

12. On the role of women of all classes in urban life during the late nineteenth century, see Mary Ryan, *Women in Public: Between Banners and Ballots, 1825–1880* (Baltimore, MD: Johns Hopkins University Press, 1989); Elizabeth Wilson, *The Sphinx in the City: Urban Life, the Control of Disorder, and Women* (Berkeley: University of California Press, 1991); and Daphne Spain, *How Women Saved the City* (Minneapolis: University of Minnesota Press, 2001).

13. "Suffragists Turn Out. Hold the Fort at Union Square When Showers Descend," *Daily People* (May 22, 1910); "The 1910 Suffrage Demonstration in Union Square," *New York Times* (May 29, 1910).

14. On anarchism in late nineteenth-century Europe, see James Joll, *The Anarchists* (London: Eyre and Spottiswoode, 1964); Ulrich Linse, *Organisierter Anarchismus im Deutschen Kaiserreich von 1871* (Berlin: Duncker and Humblot, 1969); Andrew R. Carlson, *Anarchism in Germany*, 2 vols. (Metuchen, NJ: Scarecrow Press, 1972); Jean Maitron, *Le mouvement anarchiste en France*, 2 vols. (Paris: François Maspero 1972–75); Hermia Oliver, *The International Anarchist Movement in Late Victorian London* (London: Croome Helm, 1983); and Richard B. Jensen, *The Battle against Anarchist Terrorism: An International History 1878–1934* (London: Cambridge University Press, 2014).

15. See for example Herbert L. Osgood, "Scientific Anarchism," *Political Science Quarterly* 4, no. 1 (March 1889): 1–36; George N. McClean, *The Rise and Fall of Anarchy in America: From Its Incipient Stage to the First Bomb Thrown in Chicago; A Comprehensive Account of the Great Conspiracy Culminating in the Haymarket Massacre, May 4th, 1886* (New York: Haskell House, 1972); John Gilmer Speed, "Anarchists in New York," *Harper's Weekly* 36 (August 20, 1892), 798–99; Richard T. Ely, "Anarchy," *Harper's Weekly* 37 (December 23, 1893): 1226; Carl Schurz, "Murder as a Political Agency," *Harper's Weekly* 41 (August 28, 1897); Gustavo Tosti, "Anarchistic Crimes," *Political Science Quarterly* 14 (September 1899): 404, 412–17; Francis H. Nichols, "Anarchism in the United States," *Outlook* 68 (August 10, 1901). For an assessment of popular opinion about anarchism in the United States in this era, see Sidney Fine, "Anarchism and the Assassination of McKinley," *American Historical Review* 60, no. 4 (July 1955): 777–99.

16. "Hungry Cloakmakers Parade on Broadway. Two Thousand of Them March in Orderly Fashion to Union Square and Attract Much Attention," *New York Herald* (July 9, 1890).

17. On anarchism in the United States around the turn of the twentieth century, see Paul Avrich, *Anarchist Voices: An Oral History of Anarchism in America* (Princeton, NJ: Princeton University Press, 1996).

18. The original title was *Revolutionäre Kriegswissenschaft: Eine Handbüchlein zur Anleitung Betreffend Gebrauches und Herstellung von Nitro-Glycerin, Dynamit, Schiessbaumwolle, Knallquecksilber, Bomben, Brandsätzen, Giften usw., usw.* (New York: Internationaler Zeitung-Verein, 1885). On Most, see Frederic Trautmann, *The Voice of Terror: A Biography of Johann Most* (Westport, CT: Greenwood, 1980); and Burrows and Wallace, *Gotham*, 1096–97.

19. Most was a favorite subject of cartoonist Thomas Nast. See, for example, *Harper's Weekly* (May 22, 1886).

20. "Most's Angry Friends Charge a Mass Meeting: Central Labor Union Orators at Union Square Could Not Be Heard for Anarchist Howls and Hisses," *New York Herald* (May 3, 1892). "Captured by Anarchists: They Took Charge of a Section of the Eight-Hour Meeting" *New York Times* (May 3, 1892).

21. On Goldman, see Emma Goldman, *Living My Life* (New York: Knopf, 1931); Candace Falk, ed., *Emma Goldman: A Documentary History of the American Years. Volume One: Made for America, 1890–1901* (Berkeley: University of California Press, 2003); Kathy E. Ferguson, *Emma Goldman: Political Thinking in the Streets* (Lanham, MD: Rowman and Littlefield, 2011); and Karen and Paul Avrich, *Sasha and Emma: The Anarchist Odyssey of Alexander Berkman and Emma Goldman* (Cambridge, MA: Harvard University Press, 2012). On the world of Russian Jewish socialists and anarchists in the Lower East Side around the turn-of-the-century, see Daniel Katz, "The Multicultural Front: A Yiddish Socialist Response to Sweatshop Capitalism" in *Chosen Capital: The Jewish Encounter with American Capitalism*, ed. Rebecca Kobrin (New Brunswick, NJ: Rutgers University Press, 2012), 189–214.

22. On the assassination of Frick, see Paul Krause, *The Battle for Homestead, 1890–1892: Politics, Culture, and Steel* (Pittsburgh, PA: University of Pittsburgh Press, 1992); H. W. Brands, "Blood on the Water," in *The Reckless Decade: America in the 1890s* (Chicago IL: University of Chicago Press, 1995), 128–76; and Kenneth Warren, *Triumphant Capitalism: Henry Clay Frick and the Industrial Transformation of America* (Pittsburgh, PA: University of Pittsburgh Press, 1996). On Berkman, see Alexander Berkman, *Prison Memoirs of an Anarchist* (New York: Mother Earth Publishing, 1912); Avrich, *Sasha and Emma.*

23. "Wild Anarchist Talk: Berkmann [sic] Praised at Public Meeting of the Reds," *New York Times* (August 2, 1892).

24. "Eckholdt Gives Particulars," *New York Times* (May 19, 1893); "Did They Plan Massacre? Anarchist Eckholdt Says as Plot Was Laid by 'Reds' against the Police to Take Effect in Union Square," *New York Herald* (May 18, 1893).

25. "Wild Talk in Union Square No Arrests Were Made: A Big Crowd Hears Incendiary Words in Several Languages," *New York Tribune* (August 22, 1893).

26. While she denied using these words at her trial, she later repeated them in her autobiography. "Emma Goldman Denies It All: Says the Detectives Have Wrongfully Reported Her Union Square Speech," *New York Herald* (October 6, 1893); Goldman, *Living My Life*, 122–23.

27. *People of New York v. Emma Goldman*, 28, 31, 29 (Court of General Sessions of the Peace, City and County of New York), October 4, 1893.

28. "Emma Goldman's Denial: She Says She Did Not Counsel Violence in Her Speech," *New York Tribune* (October 6, 1893); Goldman, *Living My Life*, 128.

29. "One Year for Emma Goldman: The Anarchist Receives Her Sentence with Smiles," *New York Times* (October 17, 1893); "Emma Goldman Guilty. Her Speech Decided to Be Incendiary," *New York Tribune* (October 10, 1893); "The Law's Limit," *New York World* (October 17, 1893).

30. As Kathy Ferguson notes, this frequently repeated characterization originates with J. Edgar Hoover, although the actual term he used, referring to both Goldman and Berkman, was "the most dangerous anarchists in America." Ferguson, *Emma Goldman*, 9.

31. David M. Rabban, "The Free Speech League, the American Civil Liberties Union, and Changing Conceptions of Free Speech in American History," *Stanford Law Review* 45, no. 1 (November 1992): 47–114; David M. Rabban, *Free Speech in Its Forgotten Years, 1870–1920* (Cambridge: Cambridge University Press, 1999). See also G. Edward White, "The First Amendment Comes of Age: The Emergence of Free Speech in Twentieth-Century America," *Michigan Law Review* 95, no. 2 (November 1996): 299–392; Geoffrey R. Stone, *Perilous Times: Free Speech in Wartime from the Sedition Act of 1798 to the War on Terrorism*

(New York: Norton, 2004); and Christopher M. Finen, *From the Palmer Raids to the Patriot Act: A History of the Fight for Free Speech in America* (Boston: Beacon, 2007).

32. "Hailed Emma Goldman," *New York World* (August 1894); "My Year in Stripes," *New York World* (August 1894).

33. Emma Goldman, "The Psychology of Political Violence," *Anarchism and Other Essays* (New York: Mother Earth Publishing Association, 1910), 107.

34. Avrich, *Sasha and Emma*, 162.

35. Robert A. Pinkerton, "Detective Surveillance of Anarchists," *North American Review* 173, no. 540 (November 1901): 613.

36. The prosecution of property owners for public speech uttered on their premises lay at the heart of *People v. Gitlow*, New York State (1922), a famous case taken to the Supreme Court by the American Civil Liberties Union. See Mark Lendler, *Gitlow vs. New York: Every Idea an Incitement* (Lawrence: University Press of Kansas, 2012).

37. On the Free Speech League, see Rabban, "The Free Speech League," 47–114; Rabban, *Free Speech in Its Forgotten Years*, 44–76.

38. Theodore Schroeder, *Free Speech for Radicals* (Riverside, CT: Hillacre Bookhouse, 1916), 54–55. Other defenses of Free Speech published during this time include George Pyburn, *The Conspiracy against Free Speech and Press* (New York, 1902); and Theodore Schroeder, "The Lawless Suppression of Free Speech," *Arena*, no. 39 (1908): 696–98.

39. On the Industrial Workers of the World, see Vincent St. John, *The I.W.W.: Its History, Structure and Methods* (Chicago: I. W. W. Publishing Bureau, 1917); Paul F. Brissenden, *The I.W.W.: A Study of American Syndicalism* (New York: Russell and Russell, 1920); Melvin Dubofsky, *We Shall All Be All: A History of the International Workers of the World* (Chicago: University of Chicago Press, 1969); and Fred Thompson and Jon Bekken, *The I.W.W.: Its First Seventy Years 1905–2005* (Chicago: Industrial Workers of the World, 2005).

40. David M. Rabban, "The IWW Free Speech Fights and Popular Conceptions of Free Expression Before World War I," 80 *Virginia Law Review* 1055 (1994); Rabban, *Free Speech in Its Forgotten Years*, 77–128. See also Margaret Kohn, "Weapons of the Wobblies: The Street-Speaking Fights," in *Brave New Neighborhoods: The Privatization of Public Space* (London: Routledge, 2004), 23–46.

41. *New York Times* (March 15, 1906).

42. "Red Flag Mass Meeting. Violent Speeches in Favor of Alleged Slayers of Gov. Steunenberg," *New York Times* (May 6, 1906).

43. "Unemployed to Demonstrate. Mass Meeting on Union Square on Saturday, March 28, 2 PM," *Worker* (March 21, 1908).

44. "Bomb Kills One; Police Escape," *New York Times* (March 29, 1908); "Bombs Thrown: By Whom? One at Union Square; The Other in Telluride," *Daily People* (March 29, 1908); "The Anarchists," *The Independent* 64 no. 3096 (April 2, 1908): 711; *Collier's* (April 11, 1908).

45. Robert J. Goldstein, "The Anarchist Scare of 1908: A Sign of Tension in the Progressive Era," *American Studies* 15 no. 2 (Fall 1974): 55–78.

46. "Bomb Kills One; Police Escape," *New York Times*.

47. "Emma Goldman Blames Police: Queen of Reds Says the Union Square Tragedy Is a Bluecoat Plot," *Chicago Tribune* (March 29, 1908).

48. After thirteen years in a Pennsylvania prison for the attack on Frick, Berkman had been released in 1905. He was arrested on a charge of conspiracy related to the 1908 Union Square bombing but later released because of lack of evidence. Defending himself

in *Mother Earth*, the anarchist journal he had cofounded with Goldman, he claimed no knowledge of it. However, he upheld the right of anarchists to use violence. Alexander Berkman, "Violence and Anarchism," *Mother Earth* 3 no. 2 (April 1908).

49. "Bomb Thrower Tells All: Silverstein Says He Set Off the Explosion with a Cigarette," *New York Times* (April 7, 1908); "Silverstein, Dead Boy Victim of Union Square Outrage, Passes Away: Police to Last Minute Attempt to Exert Incriminating Statement from Him," *Daily People* (April 29, 1908).

50. "Bombs Thrown: By Whom? One at Union Square; The Other in Telluride," *Daily People* (March 29, 1908); "No Act of Ours, Say the Socialists," *New York Times* (March 29, 1908).

51. "Hillquit's Address: If There Was an Unlawful Assembly in Union Square on March 28, It Was the Assembly of the Police," *Worker* (April 11, 1908).

52. "As If They Don't Know. Robert Hunter Explains Bomb Throwing in Union Square to Hughes, McClellan and Bingham," *Daily People* (May 18, 1908).

53. *New York Times* (March 31, 1908).

54. "The Right of Free Speech," *Outlook* 88 no. 15 (April 11, 1908): 813. Other articles exploring this issue include "The Anarchists," *The Independent* 64 no. 3096 (April 2, 1908): 711; "The Union Square Crime," *Public* (April 10, 1908): 37; "The Bomb in Union Square," *Literary Digest* (April 11, 1908): 505; and "Anarchist or Paranoiac?" *Outlook* 88 no. 15 (April 11, 1908): 808.

55. A summary of these various media opinions is given in "A Review of the World," *Current Literature* 44 no. 5 (May 1908): 461. Publications voicing criticism of the behavior of the New York City Police included *The Wall Street Journal*, *The Washington Post*, *The Public*, *The Nation*, and *The Conservator*.

56. Goldstein, "The Anarchist Scare of 1908," 74–75.

57. On Stover's life and activities as parks commissioner, see J. K. Paulding, *Charles B. Stover: His Life and Personality* (New York: International Press, 1938); Ethan Carr, *Three Hundred Years of Parks: A Timeline of New York City Park History* (City of New York: Department of Parks and Recreation, 1988); Gregory Gilmartin, *Shaping the City. New York and the Municipal Art Society* (New York: Clarkson Potter, 1995), 241–43; Rosenzweig and Blackmar, *The Park and the People*, 412–13; and "Neighborhood Playgrounds and Parks," in *Robert Moses and the Modern City: The Transformation of New York*, ed. Hilary Ballon and Kenneth T. Jackson (New York: Norton, 2007), 174.

58. "The New Appointments," *New York Times* (January 11, 1910).

59. "Union Square Thrown Open: New Park Commissioner Promises It for Public Meetings, Sans Red Tape," *Daily People* (January 12, 1910).

60. "Union Square Thrown Open," *Daily People*.

61. "More Children of Strikers Arrive Impressive March to Union Square: Stirring Mottoes on Banners," *Daily People* (February 18, 1912); "Rowdy Protests at Union Square Socialist Labor Party Meeting a Success: Ringing Resolutions Adopted Denouncing Judge Hanford for Revoking Citizenship Papers of Socialists," *Daily People* (June 30, 1912).

62. "Thousands Protest at Union Square Monster Gathering Denounces Conduct of Paterson Authorities: Meeting Held By IWW," *Daily People* (June 8, 1912).

63. "Big Strike Parade a Model of Order; Police Praise Discipline of the Thousands Who Marched in Garment Trade Demonstration," *New York Times* (January 14, 1913); "35,000 More Women Will Strike To-Day: International Union to Call Out All Those Employed as Waist and Dress Makers," *New York Times* (January 15, 1913); "Red-Sashed Girls

in Labor Parades: Two Big Processions of Unions and Socialists to March Today," *New York Times* (May 1, 1913); "May Day Parades by 5,000 Workers," *New York Times* (May 2, 1913).

64. "Anarchists Spread Alarm in Fifth Avenue," *New York Times* (March 22, 1914); "Plan to Organize the Unemployed," *New York Times* (March 23, 1914); Alexander Berkman, "The Movement of the Unemployed," *Mother Earth* 9, no. 2 (April 1914); Avrich, *Sasha and Emma*, 217–21.

65. "Police Use Force on IWW Rioters," *New York Times* (April 5, 1914).

66. "Mob Law and the Police," *New York Times* (April 6, 1914).

67. Avrich, *Sasha and Emma*, 223.

68. "Mitchel Watching the Rioters' Trials: His Secretary Takes Notes of Police Testimony against Arthur Caron," *New York Times* (April 8, 1914).

69. "The New Police Commissioner," *World* (April 8, 1914); "The New Police Commissioner," *New York Tribune* (April 8, 1914); "Mayor Mitchel's Recent Appointments," *Irish American Weekly* (April 18, 1914); "Arthur Woods—and the Police Commissioner of New York—A National Job," *The World's Work* 28 (May–October 1914): 149–50. On Woods, see Arthur Woods, *Crime Prevention* (London: Oxford University Press, 1918); Marilynn S. Johnson, "Arthur Woods and Modern Police Reform," in *Street Justice: A History of Police Violence in New York City* (New York: Beacon, 2003), 107–13; and Thai Jones, *More Powerful than Dynamite: Radicals, Plutocrats, Progressives and New York's Year of Anarchy* (New York: Bloomsbury, 2012), 125–43.

70. *Industrial Relations. Final Report and Testimony Submitted to the Congress by the Commission of Industrial Relations Created by the Act of August 23, 1912*, vol. 11 (Washington, DC: Government Printing Office, 1916), 10550. Woods later addressed the American Sociological Society on the same subject: Arthur Woods, "Reasonable Restrictions Upon Freedom of Assemblage," *American Sociological Society: Papers and Proceedings*, no. 29 (1915), 29–35.

71. *Industrial Relations: Final Report and Testimony*, 10551.

72. *Industrial Relations: Final Report and Testimony*, 10551.

73. Johnson, *Street Justice*, 111. Following the assassination of President McKinley in 1901, Robert A. Pinkerton of the Pinkerton National Detective Agency had suggested the use of "inside men" or undercover operatives to infiltrate anarchist groups; Robert A. Pinkerton, "Detective Surveillance of Anarchists," *North American Review* 173, no. 540 (November 1901): 609–17. On police and private surveillance of radical groups during this era, see Julian F. Jaffe, *Crusade against Radicalism: New York During the Red Scare, 1914–1924* (Port Washington, NY: Kennikat Press, 1972); Thomas A. Reppetto, *Battleground New York City: Countering Spies, Saboteurs and Terrorists since 1861* (New York: Potomac Books, 2012), 9–88; and Jennifer Fronc, *New York Undercover: Private Surveillance in the Progressive Era* (Chicago: University of Chicago Press, 2009).

74. Department of Parks, *Annual Report 1913* (City of New York, 1913); Department of Parks, *Annual Report 1914* (City of New York, 1914).

75. Jaffe, *New York at War*, 201–3.

76. President Woodrow Wilson, State of the Union Address, December 7, 1915.

77. Joel Schwarz, *The New York Approach: Robert Moses, Urban Liberals and Redevelopment of the Inner City* (Columbus: Ohio State University Press, 1993), 14–16; Gabrielle Esperdy, "Defying the Grid: A Retroactive Manifesto for the Culture of Congestion," *Perspecta*, no. 30 (1999): 10–33.

78. "Tiny Farm at Union Square Dies as New Subway Comes," *New York Times* (August 12, 1928), 4.

79. *Annual Report of the Department of Parks, Borough of Manhattan for the Year 1927* (New York: I. Smigel, 1928), 91–92.

80. On antiwar activities in New York City during the World War I period, see Jaffe, *New York at War*, 177–215.

81. "Mayor's Committee for Conscription: Defense Organization Will Back President's Plan for Selective Draft. Arrange for Navy Week Replica of Battleship in Union Square Will Be Headquarters of Recruiting Committee," *New York Times* (April 27, 1917).

82. "Mayor's Wife Names Land Battleship; Big Crowd in Union Square Sees Recruiting Headquarters Dedicated," *New York Times* (May 31, 1917), 3.

83. "Mayor to 'Launch' Land Battleship," *New York Times* (April 27, 1917).

84. "Landship Recruit Sails. Ceremonies Mark Beginning of Union Square Coney Island Cruise," *New York Times* (March 17, 1920).

Chapter Six

1. Robert Ezra Park, *The Crowd and the Public and Other Essays*, ed. Henry Elsner (Chicago: University of Chicago Press, 1972). On turn-of-the-twentieth-century views of the urban crowd in the United States, see Gregory W. Bush, *Lord of Attention: Gerald Stanley Lee and the Crowd Metaphor in Industrializing America* (Amherst: University of Massachusetts Press, 1991); Clark McPhail, *The Myth of the Madding Crowd* (Chicago: University of Chicago Press, 1991); and Shelton Stromquist, *Reinventing The People: The Progressive Movement, the Class Problem, and the Origins of Modern Liberalism* (Urbana: University of Illinois Press, 2006).

2. On European writing on the urban crowd, see Robert A. Nye, *The Origins of Crowd Psychology: Gustave Le Bon and the Crisis of Mass Democracy in the Third Republic* (London: Sage, 1975); and Susanna Barrows, *Distorting Mirrors: Visions of the Crowd in Late Nineteenth Century France* (New Haven, CT: Yale University Press, 1981).

3. On the use of urban design to reinforce ideas of civic community in late nineteenth-century American cities see Mel Scott, "The Spirit of Reform," in *American City Planning Since 1890* (Berkeley: University of California Press, 1969), 6–17; Jon A. Peterson, "City Beautiful Movement: Forgotten Origins and Lost Meanings," *Journal of Urban History* (August 1976): 109–28; Paul S. Boyer, *Urban Masses and Moral Order in America 1820–1920* (Cambridge, MA: Harvard University Press, 1978), 252–60, 261–76; M. Christine Boyer, "Would America Produce a Civilization of Cities? 1890–1909," in *Dreaming the Rational City* (Cambridge, MA: MIT Press, 1983), 1–57; David Schuyler, "Transformation: The Neoclassical Cityscape," in *The New Urban Landscape: The Redefinition of City Form in Nineteenth-Century America* (Baltimore, MD: Johns Hopkins University Press, 1986), 180–95; and William H. Wilson, *The City Beautiful Movement* (Baltimore, MD: Johns Hopkins University Press, 1989).

4. Charles Mulford Robinson, "The Administrative Center," in *Modern Civic Art, or the City Made Beautiful* (New York: Putnam, 1918), 84.

5. Daniel Bluestone, "Detroit's City Beautiful and the Problem of Commerce," *Journal of the Society of Architectural Historians* 47, no. 3 (1988): 245–62; Carl Smith, *The Plan of Chicago* (Chicago: University of Chicago Press, 2009).

6. On urban planning initiatives in New York City during these years, see Boyer, *Dreaming the Rational City*; Jackson, "The Capital of Capitalism," 319–53; David Ward and Oliver Zunz, eds., "Introduction," *The Landscape of Modernity: New York City 1900–1940* (Baltimore, MD: Johns Hopkins University Press, 1992), 3–18; and Keith D. Revell, *Building*

Gotham: Civic Culture and Public Policy in New York City, 1898–1938 (Baltimore, MD: Johns Hopkins University Press, 2003).

7. Several of these projects are described in Harvey A. Kantor, "The City Beautiful in New York," *The New-York Historical Society Quarterly* 57 (1973): 149–71; and Boyer, *Manhattan Manners*, 22–23.

8. On Flagg, see Mardges Bacon, *Ernest Flagg, Beaux-Arts Architect and Urban Reformer* (Cambridge, MA: MIT Press, 1986).

9. Royal Cortissoz, "Landmarks of Manhattan," *Scribner's Magazine* 18, no. 5 (November 1895): 531–33. See also George B. Ford, "City-Planning in New York City: How All Can Cooperate," *Proceedings of the Academy of Political Science in the City of New York* 2, no. 4 (July 1912): 183. On the transformation of City Hall Park into a historic monument, see Max Page, *The Creative Destruction of Manhattan 1900–1940* (Chicago: University of Chicago Press, 1999), 111–43.

10. "Memorial of the Municipal Art Society Relative to Proposed Changes in and about City Hall Square, New York City," *Municipal Art Society of New York Bulletin* (September 1, 1902), 3–7. On the Municipal Art Society, see Gregory Gilmartin, *Shaping the City: New York and the Municipal Art Society* (New York: Clarkson Potter, 1995).

11. Herbert Croly, "What Is Civic Art?" *Architectural Record* 16, no. 1 (July 1904): 47–52.

12. Julius F. Harder, "The City's Plan," *Municipal Affairs* 2 (1898): 24–25.

13. The implementation of the New York City subway system is described in James Blaine Walker, *Fifty Years of Rapid Transit, 1864–1917* (New York: Law Print Co., 1918); Clifton Hood, *722 Miles: The Building of the Subways and How They Transformed New York* (Baltimore, MD: Johns Hopkins University Press, 1993); and Peter Derrick, *Tunneling to the Future: The Story of the Great Subway Expansion that Saved New York* (New York: New York University Press, 2001).

14. Marguerite Holloway, *The Measure of Manhattan: The Tumultuous Career and Surprising Legacy of John Randel Jr., Cartographer, Surveyor, Inventor* (New York: Norton, 2013), 281–88.

15. *New York City Central Underground Railway Company Engineer's Report, October 19, 1869* (New York: John W. Amerman, 1869); *First Report of the New York City Central Underground Railway Company, New York, December 1, 1871* (New York: Isaac Titus, 1871), 7.

16. "New Cross-Town Railroad. Tardy Remonstrance. Mutilation of Union Square," *Commercial Advertiser* (August 5, 1874); "The Union-Square Plaza to be Traversed by Railroad Tracks," *New York Tribune* (August 6, 1874); "The Row over the Railroad Track in Union Square," *Morning Telegraph* (November 26, 1876).

17. "Cab and Cable Cars in Collision: A Horse Caught between Two Cars on the Curve in Union Square," *New York Herald* (November 5, 1893); "Felled by a Cable Car," *New York Herald* (January 12, 1894); "Crash at Union Square Curve," *New York Tribune* (April 23, 1896).

18. "A Union Square Tunnel," *New York Tribune* (July 17, 1896); "Union Square to Be Preserved," *New York Tribune* (July 18, 1896); "That Union Square Tunnel Job," *New York Tribune* (January 20, 1897); "The 'Dead Man's Curve' Problem: President McMillan Would Run the Tracks through Union Square Park," *New York Tribune* (February 20, 1897); "Union Square Will Be Preserved," *New York Tribune* (March 9, 1897).

19. *The American Architect and Building News* no. 31 (February 14, 1891), 97; "Rapid Transit in New York," *British Architect* (August 14, 1891), 129; Jackson, "The Capital of Capitalism," 334.

20. Gilmartin, *Shaping the City*, 64. See also Michele H. Bogart, *The Politics of Urban Beauty: New York and Its Art Commission* (Chicago: University of Chicago Press, 2006).

21. Marc A. Weiss, "Density and Intervention: New York's Planning Traditions," in *The Landscape of Modernity*, ed. Ward and Zunz, 47.

22. Municipal Art Society of New York, *Bulletin* no. 2 (September 1, 1902), 10; Gilmartin, *Shaping the City*, 67–68.

23. Gilmartin, *Shaping the City*, 67.

24. Robinson, *Modern Civic Art*, 298.

25. John Taylor Boyd, "A Gathering Place in Town Plans," *Architectural Record* 47 (Jan–June 1920): 288.

26. Boyd, "A Gathering Place in Town Plans," *Architectural Record*, 288.

27. Lamb's plan is mentioned briefly in *Minutes and Documents of the Board of Commissioners of the Department of Parks, Year Ending December 31st 1903* (New York, 1904), 301.

28. Samuel Parsons Jr., "The Evolution of a City Square," *Scribner's Magazine* 12, no. 1 (July 1892): 107–16; Samuel Parsons Jr., "Bedding Plants," *Scribner's Magazine* 17, no. 3 (March 1895): 329–37.

29. "Some Friction over Samuel Parsons: He Does Not Favor the Ideas of Some Park Heads about 'Popularizing' the Parks," *New York Times* (April 2, 1911), 16.

30. "Union Square Court House: Eisberg's Bill Seems to Make its Erection Possible," *New York Times* (February 3, 1905), 3.

31. "Union Square Favored for Great Court House," *New York Times* (January 12, 1907), 6.

32. "The Union Square Court House Site," *New York Times* (February 6, 1907), 8.

33. Federal Writers Project, *New York City: Volume 1, New York City Guide* (New York: Random House, 1939), 201.

34. On the Lincoln Building, see Montgomery Schuyler, "The Romanesque Revival in New York," *Architectural Record* 1, no. 1 (July 1891): 26; and Montgomery Schuyler, "The Works of R. H. Robertson," *Architectural Record* 6 no. 2 (October–December 1896): 214.

35. *History and Commerce of New York 1891* (New York: American Publishing and Engraving Co., 1891), 105.

36. *History and Commerce of New York 1891*, 121.

37. Landmarks Preservation Commission, *The Union Building* (Former Decker Building) (1988). Designation List 206 LP-1538; Sarah Bradford Landau and Carl W. Condit, *Rise of the New York Skyscraper 1865–1913* (New Haven, CT: Yale University Press, 1996), 214; Charles E. Gregerson, *Louis Sullivan and His Mentor John Herman Edelmann, Architect* (Bloomington, IN: Author House, 2013), 59.

38. John Edelmann, "Pessimism of Modern Architecture," *Engineering Magazine* (April 1892): 44–54.

39. Goldman, *Living My Life*, 110.

40. "In the Real Estate Field," *New York Times* (May 3, 1903).

41. "Building of the Bank of the Metropolis, Union Square, New York," *Architectural Record* 12, no.2 (June 1902): 235; "Metropolitan Bank Building," *Real Estate Record and Guide* (June 11, 1904), 1407; "New Union Square Bank," *Real Estate Record and Guide* (October 7, 1905), 938; Robert A. M. Stern, Gregory Gilmartin, and John Massengale, *New York 1900: Metropolitan Architecture and Urbanism 1890–1915* (New York: Rizzoli, 1995), 177–78; Landmarks Preservation Commission, "Bank of the Metropolis," Designation List 206 LP-1537 (1988); Landmarks Preservation Commission, "Union Square Savings Bank," Designation List 271 LP-1945 (1996).

42. Henry W. Frohne, "A Distinctive Type of Business Building," *American Architect* 98, no. 1825 (December 14, 1910): 193–96.

43. "Plans for Everett House Site Improvement," *Real Estate Record and Guide* 81, no. 2101 (June 1908): 1178; "Architect for Everett House Site Improvement," *Real Estate Record and Guide* 82, no. 2187 (August 1908): 245; "The Everett Building, Union Square, New York. Goldwin, Starrett and Van Vleck, Architects," *Architecture and Building* 41 (1908–9): 299–303.

44. "Big Mercantile Building on Everett House Site; Seventeen Story Office and Loft Building for Union Square Corner," *New York Times* (August 30, 1908).

45. A. C. David, "The New Architecture: The First American Type of Real Value," *Architectural Record* 28, no. 6 (December 1910): 388–403.

46. "Plate L: Germania Life Insurance Building," *Architecture* (May 1911); "New Germania Life Building," *The Independent* 70, no. 3262 (June 8, 1911): 1287; Stern et al, *New York 1900*, 158; Landmarks Preservation Commission, *Germania Life Insurance Company Building* (1988).

47. "Union Square Loses Its Old Residences," *New York Times* (June 18, 1916).

48. "S. Klein Dies: Union Square Store Founder; Did $25,000,000 a Year Business without Clerks; Sold Style at Low Prices," *New York Herald Tribune* (November 16, 1942); "S. Klein Closes After 65 Years: Little Fanfare Accompanies Demise of Thrift Store," *New York Times* (August 17, 1975); Daniel Opler, "Monkey Business in Union Square: A Cultural Analysis of the Klein's-Ohrbach's strikes of 1934–35," *Journal of Social History* (Fall 2002): 149–64.

49. On Ohrbach's see Nathan Orbach, *Getting Ahead in Retailing* (New York, 1935); and "Ohrbach's," *Advertising Age* (June 4, 2004).

50. New York (City) Commission on Congestion of Population, Report of the New York City Commission on Congestion of Population (New York: Lecouver Press, 1911); "May Curtail Plots for Loft Building; Congestion Committee's Report Expected to Make Several Radical Suggestions," *New York Times* (February 26, 1911).

51. On efforts to control the growth of the city, see Carol Willis, "Zoning and 'Zeitgeist': The Skyscraper City in the 1920s," *Journal of the Society of Architectural Historians* 45, no. 1 (March 1986): 47–59; and Keith D. Revell, "Law Makes Order: The Search for the Skyscraper Ensemble, 1890–1930," in *The American Skyscraper: Cultural Histories*, ed. Roberta Moudry (Cambridge: Cambridge University Press, 2005).

52. "'City Beautiful' in Harmonized Skyscrapers: Difficulties Downtown, Where Building Lots Are Small and Irregular, Not Met by Uptown Skyscraper Builders; Lofty Buildings Soon to Appear above Fourteenth Street Will Give Architects Excellent Chances for Good Work," *New York Times* (March 1, 1908).

53. Herbert Croly, "Civic Improvements: The Case of New York City," *Architectural Record* 21, no. 5 (May 1907): 347–52.

54. Weiss, "Density and Intervention. New York's Planning Traditions," 51; Page, *Creative Destruction of Manhattan*, 53–65.

55. *Garment Manufacturer's Index* (New York: Chilton Co., 1920), 29.

56. "New Union Square Subway Station Will Be the Largest in Manhattan," *New York Times* (November 4, 1928).

57. "Building Activity in Union Square," *New York Times* (July 15, 1928).

58. On the Fourteenth Street Association, see *New York Times* (July 8, 1923), 14; and *New York Times* (January 3, 1926). The active organization of businessmen in order to revive the fortunes of downtown urban areas was a nationwide phenomenon during

the 1920s and 1930s. See Robert M. Fogelson, *Downtown: Its Rise and Fall, 1880–1950* (New Haven, CT: Yale University Press, 2001), 234–36; Alison Isenberg, *Downtown America: A History of the Place and the People Who Made It* (Chicago: University of Chicago Press, 2004), 124–65; and Jerry Mitchell, *Business Improvement Districts and the Shape of American Cities* (Albany: State University of New York Press, 2008), 28–29.

59. Ellen Wiley Todd, *The "New Woman" Revised: Painting and Gender Politics on Fourteenth Street* (Berkeley: University of California Press, 1993), 86–87, 105.

60. "Union Square Park to be Raised 3 Feet; Plans for Improvement Call for Boundary Wall and Complete Relandscaping," *New York Times* (June 6, 1929), 7. On the Art Commission of the City of New York's involvement with the 1920s era re-landscaping of Union Square Park, see Bogart, *Politics of Urban Beauty*, 162–66.

61. "The Wars of Union Square," *New York Herald Tribune* (July 28, 1931).

62. "Alas, Poor Union Square," *New York Herald Tribune* (July 18, 1931).

63. Meyers gained several other civic commissions, including the Department of Health and the Criminal Courts Building in the downtown Foley Square complex. Tammany Hall occupied the Union Square building until 1943 when it was sold to the International Ladies' Garment Workers Union.

64. "Tammany Drops Murphy Tribute in Flagpole Plan," *New York Herald Tribune* (March 28, 1930).

65. On the design of the Liberty Flagpole, see "Commemorative Flag Staff in Union Square Park, New York City and Detail of Bronze Relief Sculpture about the Base," *Metal Arts* 3 (July 1930): 49.

66. On the history of the Communist Party of the United States, see Harvey Klehr, *The Heyday of American Communism: The Depression Years* (New York: Basic Books, 1984); Harvey Klehr and John Earl Haynes, *The American Communist Movement: Storming Heaven Itself* (New York: Twayne Publishers, 1992); and Michael Brown, *New Studies in the Politics and Culture of U.S. Communism* (New York: Monthly Review Press, 1993).

67. The confluence of political and artistic life in Union Square in the 1930s is described in Albert Halper, *Union Square* (New York: Viking Press, 1933); Albert Halper, *Good-bye Union Square: A Writer's Memoirs of the 30s* (New York: Quadrangle, 1970); James M. Dennis, ed., *Between Heaven and Hell: Union Square in the 1930s* (Wilkes-Barre, PA: Sordoni Art Gallery, 1996); Todd, *The "New Woman" Revised*; Rebecca Zurier, Robert W. Snyder, and Virginia McCord Mecklenburg, eds., *Metropolitan Lives: The Ashcan Artists and Their New York* (Washington, DC: National Museum of American Art, 1996); and Andrew Hemingway, *Artists on the Left: American Artists and the Communist Movement* (New Haven, CT: Yale University Press, 2002).

68. "Whalen Bars Parade Today at Red Rally," *New York Herald Tribune* (March 6, 1930).

69. "City Will Not Tolerate the Use of Its Streets to Exploit Jobless, Mayor Declares," *New York Times* (March 4, 1930), 1; "Whalen Puts Strict Limits on Red Rally," *New York Herald Tribune* (March 5, 1930).

70. "35,000 Jammed in Square; Views of the Red Rioting in Union Square Yesterday," *New York Times* (March 7, 1930), 1; "Reds Battle Police in Union Square," *New York Times* (March 7, 1930), 1; "110,000 Demonstrate in New York for Jobless Demands; Defy Police," *Daily Worker* (March 7, 1930).

71. "Police Crush 2,000 Rioting Reds in Jam of 40,000," *New York Herald Tribune* (March 7, 1930).

72. "Business Men Begin Fight to Curb Reds," *New York Times* (March 10, 1930), 14.

73. "Ban on Union Square Meetings Asked by Merchants' Group," *New York Times* (March 23, 1932).

74. "Union Square," *New York Times* (March 25, 1932).

75. "Plans Are Revised for Union Square," *New York Times* (May 4, 1930); *Annual Report of the Department of Parks Borough of Manhattan for the Year 1929* (New York, 1930), 6; *Department of Parks Borough of Manhattan Annual Report 1931* (New York, 1932), 5, 21, 42.

76. "Shovels Rooting in Union Square for 'Last Time,'" *New York Herald Tribune* (July 25, 1931); "Completing Work on Union Square," *New York Times* (August 23, 1931).

77. Drawing no. M-T-89-100A, New York City Department of Parks and Recreation Archive, New York.

78. "Union Square Centennial Planned to Stir Patriotism," *New York Herald Tribune* (March 17, 1932); "Historic Union Square Marks Its 100th Year," *New York Herald Tribune* (March 27, 1932).

79. "Union Square in Centennial Parade Today," *New York Herald Tribune* (April 23, 1932).

80. "Union Square Centennial Proclaimed by Mayor," *New York Herald Tribune* (April 4, 1932).

81. "Union Square Marks Its Centenary Gayly," *New York Times* (April 24, 1932).

82. "Union Square's Lawns a Paean to Concrete Era," *New York Herald Tribune* (November 27, 1931).

Chapter Seven

1. Jackson, "The Capital of Capitalism, 328–30.

2. Works Projects Administration, *New York: A Guide to the Empire State* (New York: Oxford University Press, 1940), 259.

3. Richard Plunz, "The Tenement as Built Form," in *From Urban Village to East Village: The Battle for New York's Lower East Side*, ed. Janet Abu-Lughod (New York: Wiley-Blackwell, 1994), 74.

4. On Moses achievements in urban planning, see Robert Caro, *The Powerbroker: Robert Moses and the Fall of New York* (New York: Knof, 1974); Christian Zapatka, "In Progress' Own Image: The New York that Robert Moses Built," *Lotus International*, no. 89 (1996), 122–31; Ballon and Jackson, eds., *Robert Moses and the Modern City*; Schwarz, *The New York Approach*. See also Thomas Kessner, "Fiorello LaGuardia and the Challenge of Democratic Planning," in *The Landscape of Modernity: New York City 1900–1940*, ed. Ward and Zunz, 315–30.

5. Anthony Flint, "The Battle of Washington Square Park," in *Wrestling with Moses: How Jane Jacobs Took on New York's Master Builder and Transformed the American City* (New York: Random House, 2009), 61–94. On Moses's larger plans for Greenwich Village, and local opposition to them, see Robert A. M. Stern, Thomas Mellins, and David Fishman, *New York 1960: Architecture and Urbanism between the Second World War and the Bicentennial* (New York: Monacelli, 1997), 245–47; and Jennifer Hock, "Jane Jacobs and the West Village: The Neighborhood against Urban Renewal," *Journal of the Society of Architectural Historians* 66, no. 1 (March 2007): 16–19.

6. "Moses Scores Foes on Washington Square," *New York Times* (June 11, 1940).

7. Department of Parks, *Press Release 1934 Part 2* (City of New York, 1934); "Memorial Shaft Unveiled," *New York Herald Tribune* (November 13, 1934); "Opening of New Playgrounds and Parks," 30–31; "Memorial to War Dead Unveiled in Union Square: V. F. W. Dedicates Shaft to East Side Soldiers," *New York Herald Tribune* (May 23, 1936).

8. Department of Parks, *Press Release 1941 Part 2* (City of New York, 1941), 57–61.

9. "Moses Explains Union Square Rally Permits," *New York Herald Tribune* (November 17, 1941).

10. *Hague v. Committee for Industrial Organization* 307 U.S. 496 (1939).

11. "'Peace Rally' Planned: Group Here Seeks to Hold Union Square Meeting Wednesday," *New York Times* (July 30, 1950); Department of Parks, *Press Release 1950* (City of New York, 1950), 137–39; "Police Break Up 'Peace' Rioting at Union Square," *New York Herald Tribune* (August 3, 1950).

12. "Proposed New Parking Area in Union Square," *New York Times* (March 20, 1942).

13. "Busy Parking Space Used for Abandoned Vehicles," *New York Times* (February 12, 1949); Morton B. Metcalf Jr., "Union Square," *New York Herald Tribune* (July 9, 1949).

14. Work Projects Administration of the State of New York, *New York: A Guide to the Empire State* (1940), 259.

15. Kazin and Ross, "America's Labor Day," 1321.

16. "'Left' to Sponsor Today's Parade: 100,000 Expected to Take Part in May Day March," *New York Times* (May 1, 1947).

17. "Committee Formed for May Day March," *New York Amsterdam News* (March 11, 1950); "May Day Rally in City Orderly; Fewer March," *New York Herald Tribune* (May 2, 1950).

18. Isidore Wisotsky, "Echoes of the Union Square that Was," *New York Times* (October 12, 1958). See also Isidore Wisotsky, "Such a Life" (1978), unpublished manuscript, Tamiment Library and Robert F. Wagner Labor Archives, New York University.

19. "The City Under the Bomb," *Time* 56, no.14 (October 2, 1950): 14–19.

20. On the Office of Civil Defense, see Patrick S. Roberts, *Disasters and the American State: How Politicians, Bureaucrats and the Public Prepare for the Unexpected* (New York: Cambridge University Press, 2013), 44–45; and Michael J. Hogan, *A Cross of Iron: Harry S. Truman and the Origins of the National Security State 1945–54* (New York: Cambridge University Press, 1998), 65–66, 210–20.

21. "Union Square 'Bombed': Eight Control Centers Activated in Civil Defense Drill," *New York Times* (January 28, 1953).

22. Thomas Adams, ed. *The Regional Plan for New York City and its Environs* (New York: The Regional Plan, 1929). See also Carl Sussman, ed. *Planning the Fourth Migration: The Neglected Vision of the Regional Planning Association of America* (Cambridge, MA: MIT Press, 1976), 224–59; and David A. Johnson, "Regional Planning for the Great American Metropolis: New York between the World Wars," in *Planning the Great Metropolis: The 1929 Regional Plan of New York and its Environs* (New York: Taylor and Francis, 1995).

23. Thomas Adams, *The Building of the City: Regional Plan; Vol. 2* (New York: Regional Plan Association, 1931), 398–406.

24. Richard Plunz, *A History of Housing Types in New York City: Dwelling Type and Social Change in the American Metropolis* (New York: Columbia University Press, 1990), 240–79; Samuel Zipp, *Manhattan Projects: The Rise and Fall of Urban Renewal in Cold War New York* (New York: Oxford University Press, 2012), 253–98.

25. On the history of mid-twentieth-century American downtowns, see Fogelson, *Downtown*; and Isenberg, *Downtown America*.

26. On Gruen, see Victor Gruen and Larry Smith, *Shopping Town USA: The Planning of Shopping Centers* (New York: Reinhold, 1960); and M. Jeffrey Hardwick, *Mall Maker: Victor Gruen, Architect of an American Dream* (Philadelphia: University of Pennsylvania Press, 2003). On shopping malls as agents of modern architecture, see David J. Smiley, *Pedes-*

trian Modern: Architecture and Shopping, 1925–1956 (Minneapolis: University of Minnesota Press, 2013).

27. *New York City Guide and Almanac 1957–58* (New York: New York University Press, 1958), 96.

28. Isenberg, *Downtown America*, 168. See also Mitchell, *Business Improvement Districts*, 15–38.

29. As Gabrielle Esperdy describes, this process began during the 1930s under the influence of the New Deal; *Modernizing Main Street: Architecture and Consumer Culture in the New Deal* (Chicago: University of Chicago Press, 2008).

30. Isenberg, *Downtown America*, 175.

31. On the postwar equation between citizenship and consumption, see Lizabeth Cohen, *A Consumer's Republic: The Politics of Mass Consumption in Postwar America* (New York: Random House, 2003).

32. "Americanization League Holds Union Square Rally," *New York Herald Tribune* (May 3, 1936); "Boy Scouts in Annual Pilgrimage to Lincoln Statue," *New York Herald* (February 13, 1945).

33. David Wise, "May Day March Banned, Union Square Rally Stands," *New York Herald Tribune* (April 29, 1953).

34. "Only 5,000 Show Up for May Day Rally," *New York Times* (May 2, 1953).

35. "Battle of Union Square: Flag Day March Tomorrow Will Open Campaign against Reds," *New York Times* (June 3, 1953).

36. "Flag Day Opens Campaign 'to Reclaim Union Square,'" *New York Times* (June 15, 1953).

37. "5,000 Rally at Union Square for Spies," *New York Herald Tribune* (June 20, 1953).

38. "May 1 Loyalty Fete Set in Union Square," *New York Times* (March 14, 1954); "250,000 Expected in Loyalty March: Parade Down Fifth Avenue to Start at 1pm," *New York Times* (May 1, 1954).

39. Haverty-Stacke, *America's Forgotten Holiday*, 197.

40. "Loyalty Day Proclaimed: Brooklyn Observance Set for May 3 by Borough Head," *New York Times* (April 23, 1952).

41. Jan Mitchell, *Lüchow's German Cookbook* (New York: Doubleday and Co., 1986); "Jan Mitchell, Who Put the 'ü' Back in Lüchow's, Dies at 96," *New York Times* (November 30, 2009).

42. "Left-Wingers Get Union Square for 90 Minutes on May Day, Civic Group Has It for 8 Hours," *New York Times* (April 16, 1954).

43. "Loyalty Day Irks Reds at Union Square: But They Have 2-Hour Rally After," *New York Times* (May 2, 1954).

44. "Two Parades Here Mark Loyalty Day," *New York Herald Tribune* (May 1, 1955).

45. "'Union Square, U. S. A.' to Mark May Day: Seventeenth Street Sign Is Changed," *New York Times* (April 29, 1954); "250,000 Expected in Loyalty March: Parade Down Fifth Avenue to Start at 1pm," *New York Times* (May 1, 1954).

46. "Mayor Proclaims 'Union Square Day' for May Day Fete," *New York Times* (April 30, 1959); "Anti-Red Rally in Union Square Is Salute to Alaska and Hawaii," *New York Times* (May 2, 1959).

47. Robert Mayer, "The Vanished Sound and Fury of Union Square," *Newsday* (May 1, 1961).

48. "Organization Set Up to Aid Union Square," *New York Times* (April 29, 1955).

49. "Ohrbach's," *Advertising Age* (June 4, 2004).

50. "'Fair on Union Square' to Sell Wares of 200 Merchants," *New York Herald Tribune* (March 3,1955); "Union Square to Get a Vertical 'Fair,'" *New York Times* (March 3, 1955); "Fair Has Spot for Mussel, Strudel, Other Specialists," *Wall Street Journal* (March 29, 1955).

51. "Cooperative N.Y. Department Store Will Open Soon," *Washington Post and Times Herald* (September 30, 1955); "Weather No Bar at Fair's Opening," *New York Times* (October 7, 1955); *New Yorker* (November 5, 1955).

52. Murray Illson, "Veterans Solicit Memorial Funds," *New York Times* (June 21, 1962); "Vets to Build in Union Square," *New York Herald Tribune* (June 24, 1962).

53. Stern, *New York 1960*, 245–47.

54. "Atrocity at Union Square," *New York Times* (June 29, 1962).

55. "Missiles at Union Square Mark Armed Forces Week," *New York Times* (May 14, 1963).

56. Stephen Golden, "Child-Care Area Dedicated in Park," *New York Times* (May 2, 1967); "Check-a-Child Opens in Union Square Park," *New York Times* (June 21, 1967); Department of Parks, "New Playground in Union Square Park" and "Check-a-Child at Union Square Park," Press Release 1967 Part 2 (City of New York, 1967), 61, 64–67; Department of Parks, "Check-a-Child Opens June 20," Press Release 1967 Part 1 (City of New York, 1967), 80.

57. Dattner explained his theory of urban playground design in Richard Dattner, *Design for Play* (New York: Van Nostrand Reinhold Co., 1969).

58. "Check-a-Child Opens for Second Season at Union Square Park," Department of Parks, Press Release 1968, Part 2 (City of New York, 1968), 218.

59. Department of Parks, Press Release 1968, Part 2 (City of New York, 1968), 140–42.

60. Douglas Robinson, "Four Planning to Burn Draft Cards Here Tomorrow," *New York Times* (November 5, 1965); Douglas Robinson, "Five Draft Card Burners Doused at Rally," *New York Times* (November 7, 1965); Ronald Howorth, "They Brave a Shower to Defy Draft," *Newsday* (November 8, 1965); "F.B.I. Queries Five in Draft Protest: But Pacifists Who Burned Cards Are Not Arrested," *New York Times* (November 9, 1965).

61. Enabled by electronic communication, radical urban decentralization was the basis of Wright's 1935 utopian design proposal, Broadacre City, created for an exhibition at the Museum of Modern Art. Frank Lloyd Wright, "Broadacre City: A New Community Plan," *Architectural Record* 77 (April 1935), 243–54.

Chapter Eight

1. *New York Daily News* (October 30, 1975).

2. Junius Ellis, "Union Square a Hard Test for City's Recycling Efforts: Union Square a Test for Recycling," *New York Times* (May 16, 1976).

3. Charles Brecher, Raymond C. Horton, Robert A. Cropf, and Dean Michael Mead, "The Department of Parks and Recreation," *Power Failure: New York City Politics and Policy Since 1960* (New York: Oxford University Press, 1993), 304.

4. Robert Tomasson, "Major Redesign Urged for Union Square and Park," *New York Times* (May 30, 1973).

5. Alan Oser, "About Real Estate: Klein's Plan Gives Union Square a Prophet," *New York Times* (March 3, 1976).

6. *Union Square Street Revitalization* (New York City Department of Planning, 1976); "Plan to Remodel Union Square Is Urged by Community Groups," *New York Times* (March 22, 1976).

7. *Union Square Street Revitalization*, 28.

8. *Union Square Street Revitalization*, 3, 20.

9. This concept is explained by William C. Baer in "On the Death of Cities," *Public Interest* 45, no. 3 (Fall 1976). The consequences are explored in David Harvey, "From Managerial to Entrepreneurialism: The Transformation of Urban Governance in Late Capitalism," *Geografiska Annaler* (1989), 3–17; and Julian Brash, "Downtown as Brand, Downtown as Land: Urban Elites and Neoliberal Development in Contemporary New York City," in *Global Downtowns*, ed. Marina Peterson and Gary McDonogh (Philadelphia: University of Pennsylvania Press, 2011), 253–72.

10. *Union Square Street Revitalization*, 3.

11. The central tenants of this theory are summarized in Nan Ellin, *Postmodern Urbanism* (New York: Princeton Architectural Press, 1996), 60–92.

12. On the success and failure of the first generation of urban renewal, see Herbert Gans, "The Failure of Urban Renewal" (1965) in *American Urban History*, ed. Alexander B. Callow (New York: Oxford University Press, 1969), 567–81; Marc A. Weiss, "The Origins and Legacy of Urban Renewal," in *Urban and Regional Planning in an Age of Austerity*, ed. Pierre Clavel, John Forester, and William Goldsmith (New York: Pergamon Press, 1980), 53–80; Robert Beauregard, *Voices of Decline: The Postwar Fate of United States Cities* (London: Blackwell, 1993), 109–275; and Christopher Klemek, *The Transatlantic Collapse of Urban Renewal: Postwar Urbanism from New York to Berlin* (Chicago: University of Chicago Press, 2011).

13. On Lindsay's urban strategy, see Jon C. Teaford, *The Rough Road to Renaissance: Urban Revitalization in America, 1940–1985* (Baltimore, MD: Johns Hopkins University Press, 1990), 170–90; and Larry Bennett, "The Mayor among His Peers," in *The City Revisited: Urban Theory from Chicago, Los Angeles, New York*, ed. Dennis R. Judd and Dick Simpson (Minneapolis: University of Minnesota Press, 2011), 246–47. See also Roberta Brandes Gratz, *The Battle for Gotham: New York in the Shadow of Robert Moses and Jane Jacobs* (New York: Nation Books, 2010), 19–20.

14. Ellin, *Postmodern Urbanism*, 61–65.

15. *Union Square Street Revitalization*, 2.

16. Emanuel Perlmutter, "Uplift Ahead for Fourteenth Street-Union Square Area," *New York Times* (November 16, 1976). See also Robert W. Walsh, "Union Square Park: From Blight to Bloom," *Economic Development Journal* (Spring 2006), 38–46; and Sharon Zukin, "Union Square and the Paradox of Public Space," in *Naked City: The Death and Life of Authentic Urban Places* (London: Oxford University Press, 2010), 125–58.

17. Eleanor Blau, "Project Aimed at Sprucing Union Square," *New York Times* (May 19, 1977); Pamela Hollie, "Neighborhood Acts to Revitalize Union Square," *New York Times* (May 11, 1978).

18. Brecher et al., *Power Failure*, 304. On the use of cultural programming to counter the negative effects of urban decline on parks, see Cranz, *Politics of Park Design*, 137.

19. Department of Parks, Press Release 1968 Part 3 (City of New York, 1968).

20. Department of Parks, Press Release 1970 Part 3 (City of New York, 1970).

21. *Union Square Street Revitalization*, 3.

22. Ellin, *Postmodern Urbanism*, 16–18. On this process at work in the context of American cities, see Bernard J. Frieden and Lynne B. Sagalyn, *Downtown, Inc: How America Rebuilds Cities* (Cambridge, MA: MIT Press, 1989). On New York City's urban policies from the mid-1970s to the turn of the twenty-first century, see Alessandro Busà, *The Creative Destruction of New York City: Engineering the City for the Elite* (New York: Oxford University Press, 2017), 47–57.

23. On architectural tactics to counter the modernist obsession with urban obsolescence, see Daniel M. Abramson, "Reversing Obsolescence," in *Obsolescence: An Architectural History* (Chicago: University of Chicago Press, 2016), 107–34.

24. Jane Jacobs, *The Death and Life of Great American Cities* (New York: Random House, 1961); William H. Whyte, *City: Rediscovering the Center* (Philadelphia: University of Pennsylvania Press, 1988).

25. See, for example, Jim Stratton, *Pioneering in the Urban Wilderness: All about Lofts* (New York: Urizen Books, 1977); Sharon Zukin, *Loft Living: Capital and Culture in Urban Change* (Baltimore, MD: Johns Hopkins University Press, 1982); James R. Hudson, *The Unanticipated City: Loft Conversions in Lower Manhattan* (Amherst: University of Massachusetts Press, 1987); Stephen Petrus, "From Gritty to Chic: The Transformation of New York City's SoHo, 1962–1976," *New York History* 84, no. 1 (Winter 2003): 50–87; and Aaron Shkuda, *The Lofts of SoHo: Gentrification, Art, and Industry in New York, 1950–1980* (Chicago: Chicago University Press, 2016).

26. Dorothy Seiberling, "SoHo," *New York* (May 20, 1974).

27. On the J-51 program and its consequences, see Michael Stern, "City Offers Ambitious Plan for an Economic Revival," *New York Times* (February 16, 1975); "2 Tax Bills Signed by Beame," *New York Times* (December 31, 1975); Charles Kaiser, "'J-51' a Way to Save Failing Properties," *New York Times* (February 1, 1976); Kristina Ford, *Housing Policy and the Urban Middle Class* (New Brunswick, NJ: Center for Urban Policy Research, 1978), 151–53; Department of City Planning, *Residential Re-Use of Non-Residential Buildings in Manhattan* (New York, 1977), 1–12, 22–27, 39–40; and Debra S. Vorsanger, "New York City's J-51 Program: Controversy and Revision," *Fordham Urban Law Journal* 12, no. 1 (1983).

28. Ellis, "Union Square a Hard Test for City's Recycling Efforts."

29. On the rise of a new generation of office workers in the 1970s and 1980s, see Richard L. Florida, *The Rise of the Creative Class and How It's Transforming Work, Leisure, Community and Everyday Life* (New York: Basic Books, 2002); and Nikil Saval, *Cubed: A Secret History of the Workplace* (New York: Doubleday, 2014), 221–55.

30. *Proposed Union Square Special Zoning District Final Environmental Impact Statement* (New York: The City of New York Department of City Planning, November 1984), pt. 2, p. 22.

31. Whyte, *City: Rediscovering the Center*, 141. See also Project for Public Spaces, Inc., *Managing Downtown Public Spaces* (Washington, DC: Planners Press, American Planning Association, 1984).

32. Zukin, *Naked City*, 29. Neil Smith discusses the parallel role of the art world in gentrification in *The New Urban Frontier: Gentrification and the Revanchist City* (New York: Routledge, 1996).

33. "City's Greenmarkets Go into Sixth Season: Manhattan Brooklyn Queens Bronx," *New York Times* (June 3, 1981).

34. Alison Pearlman, *Smart Casual: The Transformation of Gourmet Restaurant Style in America* (Chicago: University of Chicago Press, 2013), 26–29. See also William Grimes, *Appetite City: A Culinary History of New York* (New York: Farrar, Straus and Giroux, 2009), 298.

35. On the festival marketplace as an agent of urban renewal, see Frieden and Sagalyn, *Downtown, Inc.*, 107–32; M. Christine Boyer, "Cities for Sale: Merchandising History at South Street Seaport," in *Variations on a Theme Park: The New American City and the End of Public Space*, ed. Michael Sorkin (New York: Hill and Wang, 1992), 181–204; John T. Metzger, "The Failed Promise of a Festival Marketplace: South Street Seaport in

Lower Manhattan," *Planning Perspectives* 16 no. 1 (January 2001): 25–46; Alison Isenberg, "Animated by Nostalgia: Preservation and Vacancy Since the 1960s," *Downtown America: A History of the Place and the People Who Made It* (Chicago: University of Chicago Press, 2004), 255–317; and Nicholas Dagen Bloom, "American Midas: Rouse and the Festival Marketplace," in *Merchant of Illusion: James Rouse: America's Salesman of the Businessman's Utopia* (Columbus: Ohio State University Press, 2004), 150–79.

36. Gratz, *Cities Back from the Edge*, 209–34.

37. Whyte, *City: Rediscovering the Center*, 156.

38. "Union Square Plan: A Fresh Image for a Soapbox: Removal of Barriers," *New York Times* (March 8, 1979).

39. "Union Square Plan," *New York Times*.

40. Whyte, *City: Rediscovering the Center*, 236–41; and Busà, *Creative Destruction of New York*, 48–49, 93–103.

41. Jonathan Soffer, *Ed Koch and the Rebuilding of New York City* (New York: Columbia University Press, 2010). For a description of the role of the media and advertising agencies in efforts to change the image of New York City in the 1970s, see Miriam Greenberg, *Branding New York: How a City in Crisis Was Sold to the World* (New York: Routledge, 2008).

42. Frieden and Sagalyn, *Downtown, Inc.*, 239–58; Soffer, "A New Spatial Order: Gentrification, the Parks, Times Square," in *Ed Koch and the Rebuilding of New York City*, 255–75.

43. On this period of zoning in New York City, when the practice was modified to fit unique circumstances, see Norman Marcus, "New York City Zoning 1961–1991: Turning Back the Clock; But with an Up-to-the-minute Social Agenda," *Fordham Urban Law Journal* 19, no. 3 (1991): Article 11.

44. Fourteenth Street Local Development Corporation, *Union Square Zoning Study* (1980).

45. *Proposed Union Square Special Zoning District Final Environmental Impact Statement*, pt. 2, pp. 27–28.

46. On the origins of the plaza bonus, see Jerold S. Kayden, *Privately Owned Public Space: The New York City Experience* (New York: Wiley, 2000), 1–15.

47. Marc A. Weiss, "Density and Intervention: New York's Planning Traditions," in *Landscape of Modernity*, ed. Ward and Zunz, 46–75.

48. *Proposed Union Square Special Zoning District Final Environmental Impact Statement*, pt. 2, p. 29.

49. "Speaking Up for Union Square," *New York Times* (August 16, 1984).

50. See, for example Landmarks Preservation Commission, "The Lincoln Building," Designation List 206 LP-1536 (July 12, 1988).

51. *Proposed Union Square Special Zoning District Final Environmental Impact Statement*, pt. 2, pp. 13–14.

52. On Zeckendorf Sr., see Sara Stevens, "William Zeckendorf: Entrepreneurial Capitalism," in *Developing Expertise: Architecture and Real Estate on Metropolitan America* (New Haven, CT: Yale University Press, 2016), 187–234.

53. Carter Horsley, "A Union Square Revival? Plans Stir Hope," *New York Times* (June 29, 1980); Christopher Wellisz, "Klein Site's Option Seen as a Catalyst: Union Square Poised on the Verge of Redevelopment," *New York Times* (August 14, 1983).

54. Damon Rich, "A Palladian Demise," *ANY: Architecture New York* no. 22, New York Stories (1998), 42–44.

55. Soffer, *Ed Koch*, 263–70.

56. Elizabeth Blackmar, "Appropriating 'the Commons': The Tragedy of Property Rights Discourse," in *The Politics of Public Space*, ed. Setha Low and Neil Smith (New York: Routledge, 2006), 49–77.

57. *Proposed Union Square Special Zoning District Final Environmental Impact Statement*, pt. 2, p. 15.

58. Deirdre Carmody, "Union Square Park to Undergo Overhaul," *New York Times* (November 29, 1982).

59. Smith, *New Urban Frontier*, 26.

60. Deidre Carmody, "New Day Is Celebrated for Union Square Park," *New York Times* (April 20, 1984). For a broader discussion of the rhetoric of "law and order" in American urban politics, see Michael W. Flamm, *Law and Order: Street Crime, Civil Unrest and the Crisis of Liberalism in the 1960s* (New York: Columbia University Press, 2005).

61. Oscar Newman, *Defensible Space: Crime Prevention through Urban Design* (New York: MacMillan, 1972).

62. On the relationship between ideas of defensible space and the control of urban public housing in the 1960s and 1970s, see Joy Knoblauch, "The Economy of Fear: Oscar Newman Launches Crime Prevention through Urban Design (1969–197x)," *Architectural Theory Review* 19, no. 3 (September 2015): 336–54.

63. Don Mitchell and Lynn Staeheli, *The People's Property? Power, Politics, and the Public* (New York: Routledge, 2007), 117.

64. Whyte, *City: Rediscovering the Center*, 193–94.

65. On similar efforts in Bryant Park, see David J. Madden, "Revisiting the End of Public Space: Assembling the Public in an Urban Park," *City and Community* 9, no. 2 (June 2010): 197–98.

66. Deidre Carmody, "Union Square Park Opens with Renewed Grandeur," *New York Times* (May 23, 1985).

67. The designation of publicly owned scenic landmarks was permitted under a 1973 amendment to the 1965 Landmarks Preservation law.

68. Rosalyn Deutsche, "Krzysztof Wodiczko's 'Homeless Projection' and the Site of Urban 'Revitalization,'" *October* 38 (Autumn 1986): 63–98. Reprinted as "Krzysztof Wodiczko's Homeless Projection and the Site of Urban 'Revitalization': Uneven Development: Public Art in New York City," in *Evictions: Art and Spatial Politics*, ed. Rosalyn Deutsche (Cambridge, MA: MIT Press, 1998).

69. "Goodbye to Union Square?" *Village Views* 1 no. 2 (September 1984): 2–43.

70. Iver Peterson, "Union Square: Gritty Past, Bright Future," *New York Times* (November 26, 1989).

71. *Proposed Union Square Special Zoning District Final Environmental Impact Statement*, pt. 2, p. 2; Deirdre Carmody, "Union Square Park Opens with Renewed Grandeur."

72. See, for example, Paul R. Levy, *Paying for Public Life* (New York: International Downtown Association, 1998); Lawrence Houston, *Business Improvement Districts* (Washington, DC: International Downtown Association, 1999); and Seth A. Grossman, "The Case of Business Improvement Districts: Special District Public-Private Cooperation in Community Revitalization," *Public Performance and Management Review* 32, no. 2 (December 2008): 290–308.

73. Mitchell, *Business Improvement Districts*, 17.

74. William J. Mallett, "Managing the Post-Industrial City: Business Improvement Districts in the United States," *Royal Geographical Society* 26, no. 3 (September 1994): 276–87; and Martin Symes and Mark Steel, "Lessons from America: The Role of Business

Improvement Districts as an Agent of Urban Regeneration," *Town Planning Review* 74, no. 3 (July 2003): 301–13.

75. This argument is laid out in Madden, "Revisiting the End of Public Space," 187–206.

76. David W. Dunlap, "Plan Gains for Outdoor Cafe at Site in Union Square Park," *New York Times* (June 15, 1992).

77. Isenberg, "Animated by Nostalgia," *Downtown America*, 315–17; Charles Rice, *Interior Urbanism: Architecture, John Portman and Downtown America* (London: Bloomsbury, 2016), 2–7.

78. Kevin Gray, "The Micro Economy of Union Square," *New York* (October 5, 2009).

79. Douglas Martin, "A Growth Spurt for Union Square Park: Union Square Is to Grow Under a Plan by the City," *New York Times* (September 12, 1998).

80. City of New York—Parks and Recreation, "Mayor Michael R. Bloomberg, Parks and Recreation Commissioner Adrian Benepe and Union Square Partnership Announce $14 Million Reconstruction of Union Square Park," City Press Release, October 25, 2004. See also, City of New York—Parks and Recreation, "A New Plan for Union Square Park," City Press Release, January 2006.

Conclusion

1. Reinhold Martin, *Utopia's Ghost: Architecture and Postmodernism, Again* (Minneapolis: University of Minnesota Press, 2010), xiv.

2. John D. Fairfield, *The Public and Its Possibilities: Triumphs and Tragedies in the American City* (Philadelphia: Temple University Press, 2010).

Index

Note: Italicized refer to illustrations.